"*Without a doubt, this g**ble i* *th**e best resour**ce I've found on technical hiring, by a substantial margin."*
— Kellan Elliott-McCrea, Dropbox, former CTO, Etsy

"*I want every employee at my company and every company I've ever invested in or advised to read this guide. It'll make every one of them better interviewers, better recruiters, better co-workers, and better members of our startup ecosystem. I've never seen a guide on technical recruiting that is as comprehensive or practical as this one."*
— Ankit Jain, CEO, Infinitus Systems, former Founding Partner, Google's Gradient Ventures

"*The Holloway Guide to Technical Recruiting and Hiring is invaluable—it gives you the kind of insight and wisdom that is usually only found through hard earned experience, right at your fingertips."*
— Adam Jacob, co-founder and former CTO, Chef

"*People are the lifeblood of your company, because without them, there is no company. This guide is mandatory reading for anyone who is in a hiring manager or interviewing role and wants a practical, step-by-step playbook to set up technical recruiting and hiring processes for success."*
— Tammy Han, Head of Talent, Emergence Capital

"*Talented people are your strongest asset and your biggest constraint for developing great products and solving challenging problems. This guide covers everything from understanding the many possible motivations of candidates, to designing interview questions, to helping managers find the best possible fit and ensuring they develop positive, long-term relationships with all the candidates they meet."*
— Aditya Agarwal, former CTO, Dropbox

Other Guides Available at Holloway.com

The Holloway Guide to Equity Compensation
Joshua Levy, Joe Wallin et al.

Stock options, RSUs, job offers, and taxes—a detailed reference, explained from the ground up.

The Holloway Guide to Raising Venture Capital
Andy Sparks et al.

A current and comprehensive resource for entrepreneurs, with technical detail, practical knowledge, real-world scenarios, and pitfalls to avoid.

The Holloway Guide to Using Twitter
Fadeke Adegbuyi et al.

A resource to help professionals in all fields use Twitter to find collaborators, generate ideas, build a brand, and more.

THE HOLLOWAY GUIDE TO
Technical Recruiting and Hiring

THE HOLLOWAY GUIDE TO

Technical Recruiting and Hiring

A practical, expert-reviewed guide to growing software engineering teams effectively, written by and for hiring managers, recruiters, interviewers, and candidates.

Osman (Ozzie) Osman et al.

Copyright © 2020 Holloway
All rights reserved.

No part of this publication may be reproduced or transmitted in any form or by any means, electronic or mechanical, including photocopying, recording, or any other information storage or retrieval system, without prior permission in writing from the publisher.

This work and all associated content, such as online comments and discussion, do not constitute legal or tax advice in any respect. No reader should act or refrain from acting on the basis of any information presented here without seeking the advice of counsel in the relevant jurisdiction. This work is a compilation and the contributors to this work may not be licensed in your jurisdiction. They and Holloway, Inc. expressly disclaim all warranties or liability in respect of any actions taken or not taken based on any contents or associated content.

Published in the United States by Holloway, San Francisco
Holloway.com

Typefaces: Tiempos Text and National 2, designed by Kris Sowersby of Klim Type Foundry

ISBN: 978-1-952120-08-4

Print version 1.0 (from digital e1.0.5)

A Note from the Publisher

This book is a snapshot of a digital version that continues to improve. As a reader of this limited print edition, you are granted full access to the paid digital edition. It contains hundreds of web resources, updates and corrections, and additional material. A Holloway account also gives access to search, definitions of key terms, and commenting features.

Claim your account by visiting: **holloway.com/trh2020**

Holloway Guides provide practical guidance for navigating the complexities of modern work. They are the result of extensive expert contribution, research, interviews, and editorial efforts. This resource wouldn't be possible without the support of readers like you who pay for the digital edition.

We welcome your suggestions for improvements. If you have any, please consider adding them to the digital guide so others can benefit. Or say hello@holloway.com. Thank you for reading.

The Holloway team

LEGEND

Some elements in the text are marked for special significance:

◇ IMPORTANT	Important or often overlooked tip
⚠ DANGER	Serious warning or pitfall where risks or costs are significant
◇ CAUTION	Caution, limitation, or problem
⚑ CONTROVERSY	Controversial topic where informed opinion varies significantly
☒ CONFUSION	Common confusion or misunderstanding, such as confusing terminology
🗐 CANDIDATE	Discussion from the candidate's perspective
⚙ STARTUP	Startup-specific discussion
💬 STORY	A personal anecdote or story

Web links appear as numbered footnotes in print.

References to other related sections are indicated by superscript section numbers, prefixed with §.

CONTRIBUTORS

Original Author

OSMAN (OZZIE) OSMAN (Monarch Money, formerly Quora and Google)

Contributing Authors

ADITYA AGARWAL (formerly CTO, Dropbox)
ALEX ALLAIN (Dropbox)
JOSE GUARDADO (Alpha Talent)
JENNIFER KIM (Inclusion at Work, formerly Lever)
ALINE LERNER (Interviewing.io)
JOSHUA LEVY (Holloway)
VIRAJ MODY (Convoy)
KEVIN MORRILL (formerly Mattermark)
JASON WONG (JWong Works)
SCOTT WOODY (formerly Dropbox)

Contribution and Review

LAURIE BARTH (Gatsby)
JUAN PABLO BURITICÁ (Splice)
JOE CHEUNG (Craft Ventures)
DAVID CONNORS (Sequoia Capital)
RYN DANIELS (HashiCorp)
TAMMY HAN (Emergence Capital)
ROBERT HATTA (Drive Capital)
ZACK ISAACSON (Sweat Equity Ventures)
KELLAN ELLIOTT-MCCREA (Dropbox)
PRADEEP MUTHUKRISHNAN (TrustedFor)
BENJAMIN REITZAMMER (Freelance CTO)
AARON SARAY (More Better Faster)
DAVE STORY (Next Level Leadership)
JAMES TURNBULL (Glitch)
JON VOLK (Unusual VC)
SAM WHOLLEY (Riviera Partners)

Review

DAN ABEL (Tes)
BERNARD LIANG (Door Dash)
DOBROMIR MONTAUK (Doxel.ai)
GREG MORRIS
COSMIN NICOLAESCU (Brex)
DARSHISH PATEL (Shopify)
ASHISH RAINA (Optimize Talent)
DAN RUMMEL (One Medical)
JOHN SCHMOCKER (Soma Talent)
HARJ TAGGAR (Triplebyte)
SHERWIN WU (Opendoor)

Production

HALEY ANDERSON — Research, definitions
JENNIFER DURRANT — Design
RACHEL JEPSEN — Editor
JOSHUA LEVY — Editor, design
SAKHI MACMILLAN — Proofreader
COURTNEY NASH — Editor
J. MARLOW SCHMAUDER — Copyeditor
NICK STOVER — Graphics
TITUS WORMER — Print engineering

OVERVIEW

INTRODUCTION   1
About this guide.

PART I: FOUNDATIONS   9
Hiring principles, who's involved, and the motivations of companies and candidates.

PART II: DIVERSITY AND INCLUSION   51
Building a diverse and inclusive culture and hiring process, avoiding common pitfalls, and communicating with your team.

PART III: INTERNAL ALIGNMENT   115
What's needed before sourcing begins. Aligning on roles and qualifications. Job descriptions, titles, and compensation.

PART IV: CONNECTING WITH CANDIDATES   179
Finding the right candidates. Managing the hiring funnel, selling candidates on the opportunity, and filtering for fit.

PART V: INTERVIEWING   245
Interview formats and when to use each. Best practices for conducting and evaluating technical and nontechnical interviews.

PART VI: AFTER THE INTERVIEWS   343
Checking references, reviewing evaluations, and extending offers.

APPENDICES   391
Additional resources and background readings.

TABLE OF CONTENTS

INTRODUCTION   1
- 1   The Challenge of Hiring Well   2
- 2   What Is Covered   4
- 3   Who May Find This Useful   5
- 4   What Makes This Guide Different   6

PART I: FOUNDATIONS   9
- 5   Candidate-Company Fit   9
  - 5.1   Candidate Motivators   10
  - 5.2   Company Motivators   15
  - 5.3   Values Alignment   16
  - 5.4   How Strong a Fit?   17
  - 5.5   On Hiring "The Best"   20
- 6   Do You Need to Hire?   21
  - 6.1   Hiring to Overcome Risks   24
  - 6.2   Hiring Opportunistically   25
- 7   Principles   26
  - 7.1   The Candidate Focus Principle   26
  - 7.2   The Effectiveness Principle   28
  - 7.3   The Fairness Principle   29
  - 7.4   The Efficiency Principle   29
  - 7.5   The Improvement Principle   31
- 8   Cast of Characters   33
  - 8.1   Who's Involved in Hiring?   33
  - 8.2   The Hiring Manager-Recruiter Partnership   35
- 9   Overview of the Hiring Funnel   42
  - 9.1   Stages of the Funnel   43
  - 9.2   Data and Metrics   46

PART II: DIVERSITY AND INCLUSION   51
- 10   The Tech Industry: By the Numbers   51
  - 10.1   The Role of Bias   52
  - 10.2   The Consequences   53
  - 10.3   Benefits and Opportunities   55

11	What Is D&I?	57
12	D&I in Hiring	60
	12.1 It's Not Just a Pipeline Problem	61
	12.2 Avoiding Diversity Debt	67
	12.3 Privilege and Allyship	68
13	D&I Myths and Pitfalls	72
	13.1 "We don't want to lower the hiring bar."	73
	13.2 "We believe people should be hired on their merits."	76
	13.3 "What about ideological diversity?"	79
	13.4 "Is it legal to consider race and gender in hiring?"	80
	13.5 "Our next hire must be diverse."	82
	13.6 "Let's focus on hiring women first."	83
	13.7 "We don't have the time or resources to prioritize D&I."	85
14	Improving D&I in the Hiring Process	87
	14.1 Setting Goals	87
	14.2 Write Better Job Descriptions	90
	14.3 Diversify Your Candidate Pool	96
	14.4 Evaluating and Interviewing	100
	14.5 Compensate Fairly	107
	14.6 Continued Learning	110
PART III: INTERNAL ALIGNMENT		**115**
15	How Roles, Levels, and Titles Fit Together	115
16	Defining Roles	117
	16.1 Outcomes and Responsibilities	118
	16.2 Desired Skills and Characteristics	119
	16.3 Desired Technical Skills	119
	16.4 Desired Nontechnical Skills	122
	16.5 Desired Traits and Values	123
	16.6 Desired Experience	126
	16.7 Aligning on the Role	127
17	Setting Levels and Titles	132
	17.1 Formalizing Levels	134
	17.2 Ladders	135
	17.3 Job Titles	142
18	Compensation	144
	18.1 Elements of Compensation	146
	18.2 Cash vs. Equity	147

18.3	Mapping Compensation to Job Levels	148
18.4	Salary Transparency	152
18.5	Making Exceptions	154
18.6	When to Bring up Compensation	156

19 Hiring Plans — 157
- 19.1 Budgeting — 158
- 19.2 Equity — 159
- 19.3 Job Requisition Forms — 160

20 Job Descriptions — 160
- 20.1 Crafting the Job Description — 161
- 20.2 Creating Narratives — 168
- 20.3 Where to Post Job Descriptions — 175
- 20.4 Job Description Examples and Resources — 176

PART IV: CONNECTING WITH CANDIDATES — 179

21 Early Signals — 179
- 21.1 The Trouble with Resumes — 179
- 21.2 Online Challenges — 182
- 21.3 LinkedIn, GitHub, and Personal Websites — 185
- 21.4 Cover Letters — 186
- 21.5 Selling vs. Gate-Keeping — 187

22 How To Read a Resume — 189
- 22.1 Filtering on Essential Role Requirements — 190
- 22.2 Resume Presentation — 192
- 22.3 Education and Awards — 193
- 22.4 Employment History and Achievements — 195
- 22.5 Personal History and Trajectory — 198
- 22.6 Strength in Other Domains — 200
- 22.7 Likelihood of Joining — 202

23 Candidate Sources — 202
- 23.1 Referrals — 203
- 23.2 Inbound Applicants — 211
- 23.3 Outbound Sourcing — 213
- 23.4 Agencies — 219
- 23.5 University Recruiting — 222
- 23.6 Marketplaces and Platforms — 224
- 23.7 Alternative Education Programs — 225
- 23.8 Internal Pipelines — 226

24	First Conversations	230
	24.1 Goals and Pitfalls	231
	24.2 Getting Into the Right Mindset	233
	24.3 Building Rapport and Trust	234
	24.4 Getting to Know the Candidate	234
	24.5 Your Pitch	238
	24.6 Evaluation and Next Steps	240
	24.7 Maintaining Contact	241

PART V: INTERVIEWING   **245**

25	Conducting Interviews	245
	25.1 Why Interviews?	245
	25.2 The Interview Loop	248
	25.3 Preparing Candidates	251
26	Preparing Interviewers	251
	26.1 Assembling the Interview Panel	251
	26.2 Training Interviewers	257
	26.3 Structured Interviewing	264
	26.4 Mitigating Bias	266
	26.5 Coordinating Interviewers	271
27	Technical Interview Formats	272
	27.1 Selecting Interview Formats	272
	27.2 Technical Phone Screens	276
	27.3 Onsite vs. Remote	278
	27.4 Onsite Interviews	280
	27.5 Whiteboard Interviews	288
	27.6 Hands-on Coding Interviews	289
	27.7 Take-homes	295
	27.8 Prior Work Assessment	299
28	Technical Interview Questions	300
	28.1 Coding Questions	301
	28.2 Non-coding Questions	304
	28.3 Technical Question Pitfalls	308
29	Nontechnical Interviewing	310
	29.1 Types of Nontechnical Questions	311
	29.2 Sample Nontechnical Questions	315
	29.3 Further Reading on Nontechnical Interview Questions	322

30	Best Practices for Interviewers	323
	30.1 Staying Engaged	323
	30.2 Note-Taking During Interviews	324
	30.3 Keeping the Interview on Schedule	324
	30.4 Seeking Clarity in Questions and Answers	325
	30.5 Hinting and Helping Candidates Shine	327
	30.6 Collecting Candidate Feedback	329
31	Evaluating Interviews	329
	31.1 Building Rubrics	330
	31.2 Collecting Interviewer Feedback	334
32	Legal Considerations for Interviewers	340

PART VI: AFTER THE INTERVIEWS — 343

33	Checking References	343
	33.1 Talking to References	347
	33.2 Designing Reference Questions	349
	33.3 Soliciting Back-Channel References	353
	33.4 Interpreting Reference Feedback	354
34	Making a Decision	356
	34.1 Decision-Making Archetypes	356
	34.2 Decision-Making Techniques	360
	34.3 Choosing a Decision-Making Strategy	364
	34.4 Decision-Making Tips and Pitfalls	367
	34.5 Rejections	368
35	Extending an Offer	371
	35.1 Timing Your Offer Delivery	371
	35.2 Offer Deadlines	372
	35.3 How to Extend an Offer	374
	35.4 Explaining Equity	378
	35.5 Negotiation	379
	35.6 Closing	386

APPENDICES — 391

36	Appendix A: Decision-Making	391
37	Appendix B: Communicating Your Brand	393
38	Appendix C: D&I Reading List	393
39	Appendix D: Tools and Products	393

INTRODUCTION

Software engineering has a unique place in the economy. Directly or indirectly, software touches almost every aspect of modern life. Most of the world's largest public companies are in the software industry, which far outpaces broader economic growth.[1,2] In the United States, seven out of the ten largest STEM[3] occupations relate to computers or information systems; software developers are the largest group.[4] Job growth in that sector is projected at a remarkable 21% between 2019 and 2028.[5]

Behind each software product or service is a team. Software development is a technical and creative process that relies on varied roles and rare combinations of soft and hard skills that develop with years of education and experience. The fluidity of software allows a single talented engineer, with the right support from their team and company, to have unprecedented impact. On the other hand, poorly functioning teams frequently lead to expensive and ineffective engineering efforts, flawed products, and lost opportunities, sometimes with dire consequences. The choice of *who* is in each role on a software team is arguably the most essential factor for its success.

However, hiring engineering talent is a struggle for most companies. Since the 1990s, the ever-growing need for engineers has consistently outstripped supply.[6] As software grows in economic importance, more companies with more money compete for a pool of talent that is still scarce, shifting the balance of power in favor of candidates. The software industry has the highest turnover rate of any industry in the U.S., due in large part

---

1. https://en.wikipedia.org/wiki/List_of_public_corporations_by_market_capitalization#2018
2. https://software.org/press-release/software-industry-growth-far-outpaces-us-economy-hits-1-14-trillion/
3. https://en.wikipedia.org/wiki/Science,_technology,_engineering,_and_mathematics
4. https://www.bls.gov/spotlight/2017/science-technology-engineering-and-mathematics-stem-occupations-past-present-and-future/pdf/science-technology-engineering-and-mathematics-stem-occupations-past-present-and-future.pdf
5. https://www.bls.gov/ooh/computer-and-information-technology/software-developers.htm
6. https://www.siia.net/Admin/FileManagement.aspx/LinkClick.aspx?fileticket=ffCbUo5PyEM%3D&portalid=0

to the competitive hiring market.[7,8] These factors can make the hiring process a demanding and intensive search for the right matches. A 2018 poll of thousands of C-level executives revealed access to developer talent as one of the top obstacles to growth.[10]

Candidates, too, face challenges. Job-seeking is a high-stakes process, both materially and emotionally. Frustrating interactions with recruiters and hiring managers are a common complaint among candidates, and tight competition exacerbates sloppy or aggressive behavior by some companies. A long-standing absence of diversity leaves many potential candidates neglected or feeling out of place, or subject to hiring practices that exclude—or fail to retain—underrepresented groups. In some cases, the search for a job can become a stressful or soul-crushing experience that even motivate some to opt out of the process altogether, depriving themselves and potential employers of opportunity.

1 The Challenge of Hiring Well

Every professional software engineer or manager has seen a hiring process at some point in their career. If you've worked on a software development team, you've been interviewed, interviewed others, and maybe hired team members.

Hiring creative, specialized, and skilled workers like software engineers is an inherently challenging matching process, where the variables and possible combinations are numerous. Companies and teams consistently struggle with goals that are often in tension:

- To find the right quality, quantity, and diversity of candidates.
- To make hiring decisions fairly and effectively.
- To do all this efficiently, at reasonable cost in time and money.

---

7. https://business.linkedin.com/talent-solutions/blog/trends-and-research/2018/the-3-industries-with-the-highest-turnover-rates
8. A LinkedIn study[9] found that 77% of engineers who moved to different companies received an increase in pay.
9. https://business.linkedin.com/talent-solutions/blog/trends-and-research/2018/7-linkedin-data-points-that-will-help-you-recruit-software-engineers-in-the-us
10. https://stripe.com/reports/developer-coefficient-2018

Flaws in hiring processes—including inadequate assessment, slowness in hiring, and noise and bias in evaluation—incur a major cost to companies and can have a significant toll on job-seekers and employees.

Three common pitfalls make software engineering hiring a unique challenge:

- **The difficulty of assessing skills and fit.** The factors that make a software engineer effective in their role are complex. Engineering requires significant skill and years of training, but (perhaps unlike in some fields like medicine or law) ability and fit for a role is usually not indicated by specific certifications or academic degrees. Great teams routinely include PhDs, college dropouts, and those who've learned to code mid-career. Resumes, phone screens, and interviews do measure skill, but are all highly imperfect. Interviewers often have strong opinions about candidates, for example, but evidence generally show these assessments are not reliable indicators of job performance, and most experts believe that structure, calibration, and a combination of signals is the best mitigation for noise and bias. As we will discuss, fit depends on alignment on both sides.
- **Ineffective and unfair processes.** Hiring requires making crucial decisions in the face of ambiguity. The goal is a fair, efficient, and effective process for decision making that's right for one team or company. But few people understand the technical hiring process deeply enough to design these processes well. Multi-stage hiring processes, from resume filtering to complex technical interviews, can go wrong in surprising ways. Interviewers and hiring managers may not be properly trained, or may not appreciate the importance of time spent on recruiting. This can lead to spending too much—or too little—on hiring, and ineffective or unfair hiring decisions. The fact that typical tech teams do not reflect the diversity of the population is also indicative of an uneven playing field for job seekers. Much of the "wisdom" around hiring amounts to replicating things that have become customary at other companies, but may not apply to your stage or needs.
- **Poor candidate experiences.** Companies very often underestimate the importance of the candidate experience (due to a perceived asymmetry of power) or don't even realize that their candidate experience is poor. While it's easy for a company to feel like it holds all the cards when hiring, the most desirable candidates often have many options

and will self-select out of that company's process if it doesn't take their needs and values into consideration. In fact, if your company is holding a high bar for hires—as it should—it's safe to assume that any candidate you'd want to hire has multiple options.

⚠ DANGER When thinking about recruiting, both startups and larger companies often look to other, often famous, companies for inspiration. But you are (probably) not Google, and "hire like Google" can be dangerous advice. The kinds of people you want to hire may not be the same. Each company is in a unique position—its size, growth, philosophies, and financial outlook may be very different from companies you compare against. Finally, well-known companies often have different kinds of leverage, such as a prestigious employer brand, which means that some of their practices may simply be things they can (seemingly) get away with due to their desirability. We can learn a lot from large, successful companies, but we shouldn't blindly copy them.

2 What Is Covered

This Guide covers all stages of the hiring and recruiting process for software engineering and software engineering management roles.

Hiring is the process of finding and building alignment between the needs and values of professionals and organizations. **Recruiting** is the process of attracting professionals that an organization might consider hiring.

This Guide covers the end-to-end hiring process of **full-time software engineers** including everything from sourcing candidates to interviewing to extending and closing offers.

We do not cover post-hire tasks, such as on-boarding or general engineering management. We do not offer technical preparation guidance for candidates wishing to prepare for the interviews. A few other topics we have not covered yet, but may cover in future updates include:

- Hiring hardware engineers, product managers, project managers, and other technical roles that are not software engineering roles. That said, many of the principles and ideas will apply to these roles.
- Contract roles and engineering contracting firms.

- Guidance related to hiring remote or distributed teams.
- Direction on talent acquisitions, or "acqui-hires," where a company is bought by another primarily for the purpose of acquiring its staff.

3 Who May Find This Useful

This Guide includes material of interest to anyone involved in the hiring process, including **hiring managers**, **founders**, **interviewers**, **engineers**, **recruiters**, and **candidates**. As a hiring manager, you might find this Guide useful if:

- **You work at a startup.** You might be a founder or one of the earlier engineers or engineering leaders. You may have been a part of the recruiting process at other companies, but have never had to design and build out a process yourself and are not sure where to start.
- **You work at a larger company.** You likely have a more developed recruiting process, and want to understand how to best be effective within that process and how to improve that process—why your company recruits the way it does.

Recruiting processes might look very different at small startups and large companies, but the principles we present can apply at any stage of company or team. We believe it is valuable for small, growing companies to understand the structure and processes of larger companies, and that it is equally valuable for large companies to learn from the resourcefulness and lean practices of startups. Practical advice may differ depending on the size and stage of the company as well as the needs of the team.

🌱 STARTUP Startup-specific strategies and concerns are marked with this icon.

- **Engineers** usually want to understand how their role fits in with the broader technical recruiting and hiring process. Most likely, engineers will act as interviewers or otherwise be involved in the interviewing process. We cover interviewing and interview training at length, helping engineers be more effective and engaged at this important part of their job.

- **Recruiters and other non-engineers** involved in the hiring of technical positions also care about hiring process. Pitfalls often stem from lack of a shared understanding of best practices or clear communication between recruiters, hiring managers, and candidates.
- **Candidates seeking a new role** can read this Guide to understand the systems they will be navigating and how companies make decisions. We consider candidates full participants in the hiring process, not as passive receivers of the systems of companies.

🔖 CANDIDATE Areas that are specifically important for candidates are marked with this icon.

4 What Makes This Guide Different

Much hiring and recruiting advice is anecdotal or specific to a particular type of company. It can be contradictory, even when coming from experts. It's also spread about on blogs and articles that focus on specific aspects, such as building a brand, interviewing, or closing a candidate. We believe there is a need for a consolidated and shared resource, written by and for people on different sides of hiring decisions, including hiring managers, founders, recruiters, and candidates. This reference exists to answer the needs of beginners and the more experienced.

This Guide is not perfect, but aims to be the most inclusive and practical Guide available to the subject. Every candidate and every company is unique. Whether you're a hiring manager or anyone else who's involved with the hiring process, we want to supply you with both the principles and the tools to empower you to build great teams.

Our approach to building this Guide has been to:

- **Draw knowledge from multiple experts.** We are not replicating any one company's practices or one person's perspective. Our authors and editors have drawn on the input of dozens of experts and practicing hiring managers.
- **Start with first principles.** To begin, we give a framework for thinking about the challenges of hiring, candidate-company fit, and describe a set of principles for designing a hiring process. Even experienced hiring managers can find it useful to remind themselves of the goals

and first principles of hiring, and then how those principles should be applied in the specific situation.
- **Give practical guidance on each part of the hiring process.** We've covered background knowledge and practical, in-depth guidance for every step of the hiring process. Our goal is to encourage a candidate-focused, fair and inclusive, and effective hiring process that fits a companies' needs.

We've been involved in recruiting on both sides of the table. We've been at sprawling, successful companies and tiny, unproven startups. We've seen success stories and the impact and sense of fulfillment that comes with finding good fits between candidates and companies—and we've been humbled and frustrated when things haven't worked out as well. We've had interesting and tough conversations, reviewed what's been written before, and done our best to reconcile and present the most helpful expert advice and experience.

PART I: FOUNDATIONS

5 Candidate-Company Fit

> Aditya Agarwal provided framing for this section.

Candidates and hiring managers might imagine the recruiting and hiring process fairly simply: a company describes the desired role, somehow sources people or solicits applications, filters and interviews these candidates for the role—and then picks the best. Rinse and repeat, right?

This way of thinking is dangerously oversimplified: it describes a process, but not the goals. A company or hiring team has needs. And candidates have needs. The goal of a good hiring process is to find common purpose between the candidate and the company.

Candidate-company fit is a hiring goal and philosophy that emphasizes the importance of alignment between companies and candidates. The primary factors considered in candidate-company fit are company needs, candidate motivations, and the values each party holds.

Rather than a template process or a copy of what "successful" companies do, hiring well is a matching problem, which means the process must be unique for each company and role.

◇ IMPORTANT The manager and the role are what connect the candidate and the company. Unless the manager and role are right for the candidate, the fit will be poor; one or both will have to change, or the candidate won't work out. That's true almost everywhere. But what determines that fit varies a lot. The ways these needs connect depends on the company, situation, and role.

5.0.1 FIGURE: CANDIDATE-COMPANY FIT

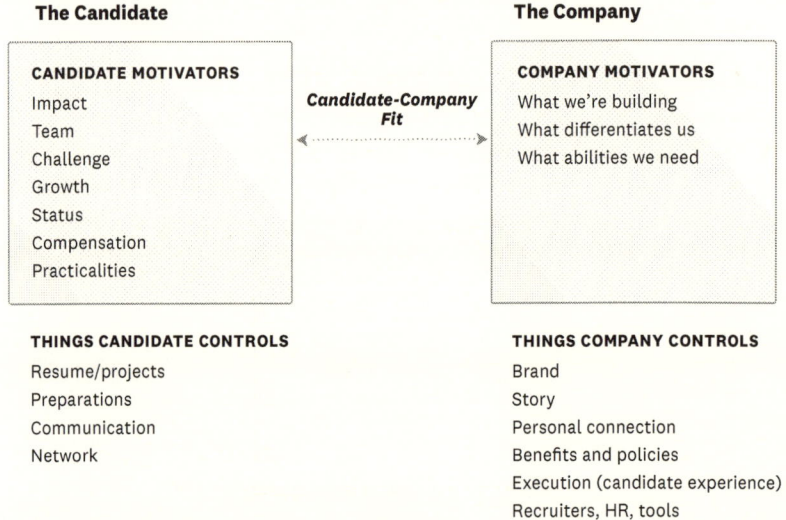

Source: Holloway

5.1 Candidate Motivators

> "I think a key to a happy and successful career might be simply working somewhere you're wanted. It's easy to talk about working somewhere with great perks and strong culture, et cetera. But if your abilities are underutilized you'll just burn out doing things nobody appreciates."
>
> — Tanner Christensen, co-founder, HelloShape[11]

When it comes to whether a candidate will accept an offer from a company, or even pursue a particular role, consider the candidate perspective—what motivates them? Motivators, which you can also think of as candidate needs or deciding factors, can be extrinsic or intrinsic.

Extrinsic motivators include title and compensation, and practical necessities like location. **Intrinsic motivators** include a sense of purpose, satisfaction from working toward a mission they believe in, feeling valued, working with a team they respect and that inspires them, and the way the work challenges them to improve.

---

11. https://twitter.com/tannerc/status/1113871004999139329

Breaking down candidate needs into internal and external motivators is inspired in part by the work of business psychology author Daniel Pink.[12] In his book *Drive*,[13] Pink breaks down[14] what motivates our work into these two categories. Pink's thesis is that for nonroutine, creative work (like software engineering), intrinsic motivators are much more powerful.[15] In fact, over-relying on extrinsic incentives like money to motivate people in those roles can be counterproductive.

How do candidates decide to join a company? Most people take on a new role because the role meets all or most of their needs. Before joining a company, a candidate may have discussions with friends and family and even do some spreadsheet math to determine what these needs are and whether they are being or would be met.

🔖 CANDIDATE In his thorough post "Visualizing a Job Search,"[16] San Francisco-based engineer Kelly Sutton maps out the process he followed to eventually land an engineering role at Gusto. For anyone looking to organize their job search, it's incredibly helpful—he even provides a template for the worksheet[17] he used to develop and track his hit list of companies.

After talking with numerous engineers, hiring managers, and recruiters, we've found these deciding factors are deeply personal but also shared among many. In practice, it seems decisions rest on one or more of seven factors; for most people, two or three of these factors will guide their decision.

- **Extrinsic.** Compensation, status, and practicalities (location, benefits, vacation policies, perks)
- **Intrinsic.** Impact, challenge, personal growth, and the team

---

12. https://www.danpink.com/about/
13. https://www.amazon.com/Drive-Surprising-Truth-About-Motivates/dp/1594484805
14. https://slooowdown.wordpress.com/2012/02/05/summary-of-drive-by-dan-pink-summarised-by-paul-arnold-trainer-facilitator-paul_arnoldme-com/
15. According to Pink, intrinsic motivation can be broken down into three components: *autonomy* (the desire to direct our own lives), *mastery* (the urge to get better and better at something that matters), and *purpose* (the yearning to do what we do in the service of something larger than ourselves). These are table-stakes—any role should provide a mix of autonomy, mastery, and purpose if you want it to be attractive to candidates.
16. https://kellysutton.com/2016/10/20/visualizing-a-job-search-or-how-to-find-a-job-as-a-software-engineer.html
17. https://docs.google.com/spreadsheets/d/1R64rVjUi5v0kaIiJMCYAXzL4Yua4ssNp11zht7pY3d4/edit?usp=sharing

It is very common for these deciding factors to change over a person's career. In fact, it's often shifts in these deciding factors that *determine* job and career changes. People's needs change when their lives change: marriage, children, and new caretaking responsibilities, for example.

In a 2019 survey,[18] Glassdoor found that mission and culture matter more to most candidates than outright compensation. Christian Sutherland-Wong, Glassdoor President and COO noted that "Job seekers want to be paid fairly but they too want to work for a company whose values align with their own and whose mission they can fully get behind."

◊ IMPORTANT Hiring managers need to understand these motivators as potential deciding factors for candidates, and which of these are considered essential motivators for new team members. For example, many executives believe in hiring only people who have strong mission alignment, meaning that they are highly motivated by the impact of the company. If the role requires learning a lot of new skills quickly, it's wise to hire someone excited not just by challenge, but by personal growth.

5.1.1 EXTRINSIC MOTIVATORS

- **Compensation.** Compensation is primarily cash (salary and bonus) and equity (some form of ownership in the company, such as stock, stock options, or RSUs). The balance someone will prefer between cash and equity depends on practicalities and risk tolerance. Practicalities like family needs are particularly important and often overlooked. Does the candidate have children in childcare, do they have caretaking responsibilities for parents or spouses? They may require cash over equity. Risk tolerance in candidates is related to whether they are willing to trade some cash for equity, with the chance to have a more lucrative outcome later. Companies that communicate with a candidate about their risk tolerance and practicalities like their family situation can tailor a compensation package to the candidate that will make them feel heard. Note that compensation also includes benefits like healthcare for the employee and their family.
- **Status.** The status of working for a well-known or well-respected company is a deciding factor for a lot of people. Impressive job titles also confer status to friends and connections. Status might give a candidate

---

18. https://www.glassdoor.com/employers/blog/mission-culture-survey

a sense of personal achievement; or it may satisfy family or impress friends. Even if people are sometimes not comfortable talking about it, status can be a very powerful consideration. For this reason, job titles can be a key concern for many people eager to see their career grow quickly. Often, people may switch companies (or teams) if they don't see a path for growth ahead. (Companies should be mindful of the fact that titles, while free, aren't cheap. Giving away senior-sounding titles arbitrarily to appease status-motivated candidates (so-called "title inflation") can lead to challenges down the road.)

- **Practicalities.** Practical aspects of a job include things like commute time, work-from-home policy, parental leave policies, time-off policies, geographic location, and schedule. Some people are also influenced by other perks, like free meals, a stylish office space, or on-site gyms or childcare.

5.1.2 INTRINSIC MOTIVATORS

- **Impact.** Does your work *matter* to the broader world? This includes both *company impact* (what effect on the world the company has) and *personal impact* (what your own impact on the company and the world is). Candidates who care about impact ask themselves, "Do I care about this company? Do I believe that what the company and I am doing is worthwhile? What is the outcome for others if I do my job well? What is the mission of the company and does it resonate with me?" Especially for senior or uniquely skilled candidates, personal impact can be a key factor: In terms of overall results, is this role the best use of the candidate's time and talent, compared to other roles they might take on elsewhere?
- **Challenge.** Technical or product challenges that are intellectually engaging can be a very strong motivator for talented, driven candidates. They might be looking for the kind of work that puts them in a state of flow, where the goals they need to meet are not daunting, but motivate them to improve. They feel a high sense of reward at accomplishing something and learning new skills in order to do so. Challenge-motivated candidates are usually also looking for hard-working teams.
- **Personal growth.** People focused on personal growth care most about gaining new skills and knowledge and experience. While this is closely related to challenge, it's not the same. Some like to repeatedly solve

hard challenges within a single domain (such as a brilliant problem-solver who tends to focus exclusively on difficult algorithmic problems). Others prefer learning entirely new skills (such as an engineer who wants to understand how her work on product development relates sales).

- **Team.** Most people want to know that the team they'll be working with won't bring them down. But how people are or are not motivated by others can be very different. Some engineers will work best when they feel needed and appreciated, while others are looking for colleagues that keep their heads down and stay out of each other's way. Some people want to learn from others, some people want to be mentors. In addition to work styles, candidates may consider what talents are strongest on the team, whether they know anyone they'd be working with, or what opportunities are offered by working with these particular people.

🗎 CANDIDATE Think about what motivates you when you're contemplating a new job. It's common for engineers to decide between jobs without sufficient reflection on what their own wants and needs are. Not doing so can pretty much guarantee dissatisfaction in a new role. It can be helpful to reflect on past experiences, good and bad, when trying to determine which factors motivate you now. At what point have you worked on something exciting? What was personally rewarding about that work? Which of these attributes made the difference? Tammy Han lays out a decision matrix for candidates in her excellent primer for startups and candidates.[19]

---

19. https://firstround.com/review/a-primer-for-startups-and-job-seekers-to-both-win-the-talent-war/

5.2 *Company Motivators*

The hiring team is wise to have a few careful conversations to be sure what they're looking for truly aligns with the company's goals, and that they can articulate this clearly to candidates. Knowing what differentiates your company is the inner work you need to do as a company and team, even before you decide what abilities are needed. Both selling and knowing your needs depend on knowing who you are. Three questions can help with this:

- **What are we building?** Every hiring manager or leader should be able to describe what their team is building and why it matters. When you're hiring, you and your team are going to have to explain this over and over to candidates.
- **What differentiates us?** What makes your company or team unique or different? Talented people do not accept jobs lightly or quickly—they need to know why they're joining your company over others. This could be what you're building, the impact, the approach, the team, the growth or traction, or even just the compensation. But you need to know what sets this team apart from others.
- **What abilities are needed on the team?** The first part of this is fundamental: Do you even need to hire?[§6] Hiring excessively is just as dangerous, if not more so, than hiring too slowly. Assuming you do need to hire, what unique abilities of employees are needed to achieve the team's goals?

It's worth taking a systematic inventory, or at least a discussion with senior staff, to be sure you're in agreement on *why* you're hiring in the first place. Reasons to hire can include:

- There is a specific job needed right now, such as an IC or a manager. This is most common.
- To prepare for a new job needed soon, due to new needs or team changes.
- To access previous knowledge or experience that fits exactly what is needed now. On a team that is building a mapping application, an engineer who has worked extensively with geospatial data has unique value.
- To lead building a team or attracting talent.

- To connect externally, via network or relationships that person has, or building trust or credibility with customers, investors, or other stakeholders.

For a big company, some of these questions would be for your organization or group, as well. For an early startup, answering these questions is one of the jobs of the founders.

5.3 Values Alignment

The terms *company values* and *culture* are often used interchangeably to refer to a company's beliefs about the world and their "way of doing things." But they are not the same. Mixing up values and culture can lead to inefficient and unfair hiring practices. When your goal is candidate-company fit, it's essential to focus on values alignment rather than "cultural fit."[§26.4.3]

Company values (or company core values) are the foundational beliefs that are meant to guide a company's behaviors and decisions. They often reflect a view of how the world is or should be.

Having a clear set of company values is tremendously important to the success of a business. These values guide decision-making in all parts of the company, whether high-stakes strategic or ethical decisions or smaller day-to-day decisions (which, in aggregate, are just as important). Clearly stated values also provide a structured way to resolve disagreements.

Company culture is a description of the traits and behaviors of people at an organization; it is defined by the set of behaviors that are tolerated, encouraged, or discouraged. Culture may or may not be founded on a set of company values, and company culture and an individual team's culture may differ.

Values alignment, an essential element of candidate-company fit, arises when the candidate and the company have compatible perspectives with regard to work styles and mission. When faced with difficult decisions, would the candidate's values help them make decisions that promote company goals? Does the candidate feel comfortable with or inspired by the way the company conducts itself, and vice versa?

Culture without values puts you in the dangerous position of repeating patterns and behaviors that do not line up with how the company wants to see itself or what the company wants to accomplish. It's worth noting that a company without explicitly defined values will *still* have a culture—just one that stems from the personalities and behaviors of its leaders and early employees, rather than one having any careful thought, design, or purpose.

Values and culture, within and outside of a company setting, usually stem from things like tradition, background, and comfort. As with any criteria that places constraints on who you hire, there's a risk that, if taken to an extreme, values and culture as hiring criteria can result in homogeneity—similarity of thought, behavior, and demographic makeup, none of which are good for business nor employee retention.

Values can be a key selling-point to potential hires—candidates want to know that what motivates them will be valued by the company and team. The product Key Values[20] lets companies share their values with candidates, who can browse and search by the values they care about to find suitable companies.

If your company values are not well-defined, it will be difficult to assess candidate-company fit properly. At larger companies, some form of written values may already exist; if you're the founder or hiring manager at a startup, or you'd like your team to reflect on its values, we cover defining company values in Appendix B.[§37]

5.4 How Strong a Fit?

Joining a company full time is a big decision. Even in an age when engineers switch jobs frequently, a successful hire will be spending years of their life, at 40 or perhaps 60 hours a week, working and thinking about their work. It usually takes months or even years to ramp up and learn the context and technical details to be successful.

Technical software hires can also be in high demand, especially for the most talented engineers. The best candidates may have many options. They are not just deciding what company to work for; they are deciding what *other opportunities they are giving up*. If it's not a good fit in terms of the work, the manager, the role, the mission, or values of the team, people are likely to move on quickly.

These considerations show how important it can be to focus on finding a strong fit for both sides.

---

20. https://www.keyvalues.com/

A **strong fit** in hiring occurs where the candidate feels fulfilled with the job and role, and the company is deriving significant value from the candidate's performance.

On the other hand, there is rarely anything like a "perfect" match. With enough shared purpose, the best candidates grow into roles and become a better fit over time. The real goal is to find a match good enough for the company and the candidate, and to subsequently invest in strengthening that relationship. From a company's perspective, how strong a fit to seek when hiring is dependent on two key concerns:

Demand and scarcity for this role. Are engineers for this role hard to hire? This could be because the demand is high (think of fullstack engineers, who are in high demand at numerous companies), or because the skill set is scarce. Scarce skills usually mean highly specialized experience and could be anything highly specific—like genomic data, high-frequency trading, geospatial systems, specific hardware, or PhD-level academic training in specific machine learning problems. What are the opportunity costs for these candidates in joining your company—that is, what are they giving up by joining? In a lot of geographies and for certain kinds of engineers (such as Stanford-educated machine learning and full-stack engineers in San Francisco or New York), demand and opportunity costs are extremely high. In a tight market, without strong candidate-company fit, this hire may move on soon.

How mission-critical the role is. Will the performance of the person filling this role make or break the team or the company? If a role is going to be part of your company's critical path or key competency, you might need a candidate who is "best in industry." The importance of software engineering as a function can vary from company to company. And the importance of roles *within* engineering teams may also vary. For example, in "deep tech"[21] industries, a company's success may hinge on its ability to deliver the most superior technology. An autonomous vehicles startup may need "best in industry" computer vision engineers, but be more comfortable taking a risk on the software engineers building its website.

Of course, how strong a fit needs to be is also related to stage and depth of skills needed for the role. In early-stage startups, or for highly specialized positions that require exceptional talent, the fit is all the more impor-

---

21. https://en.wikipedia.org/wiki/Deep_tech

tant. For larger companies, or any company that can invest more time and capital in training, finding a fit that's "good enough" may be easier.

5.4.1 COSTS OF HIRING POORLY OR TOO FAST

Almost every leader in a company will say they care about hiring the right people. A poor fit can be very costly to your company[22] and team. For instance, an employee who lacks the technical skills needed to meet expected outcomes for the role could slow down and frustrate your team, or introduce bad code into your codebase. A "toxic" employee[23] could damage your team's culture in ways that are really hard to reverse. You can work to minimize the cost of a poor fit by ensuring that you detect and rectify those situations quickly, but if you find that you are hiring poor fits repeatedly, it may be a sign that you need to slow down and iterate on your process.

No hiring process is perfect, and the costs of making the wrong hire do vary. In an early-stage company, a hire that doesn't work out can be much more costly than at a later-stage company that has a bigger team and processes to deal with inadequate performance. Similarly, for key or senior hires, the cost of poor hiring decisions can be very large, with impact on an entire team.

5.4.2 COSTS OF HIRING TOO SLOWLY

Almost every company thinks of their hiring needs as urgent, but how quickly does the company need to move to meet those needs? While the repercussions of a poor fit can be very painful, it's important to think about the opportunity cost of *not* hiring quickly enough. Part of this cost might be visible in the form of work that isn't getting done due to lack of resources. But part of that opportunity cost might be less detectable. While it's usually pretty obvious when you've made a bad hire, it's not always clear when you've missed out on a candidate that could have fundamentally altered the trajectory of your company. In a hyper-growth startup, not hiring quickly could mean failure of the whole company, so riskier hires or more aggressive processes may make sense. In an earlier-stage startup, where exceptional hires are critical, or at an established

---

22. https://www.shrm.org/resourcesandtools/hr-topics/employee-relations/pages/cost-of-bad-hires.aspx
23. https://hbr.org/2015/12/its-better-to-avoid-a-toxic-employee-than-hire-a-superstar

company where people can transition roles internally, it is often wise to prioritize care and a high bar over speed.

5.5 On Hiring "The Best"

Much conventional wisdom around recruiting centers on only hiring "the best" (or the "rockstars" or "A players" or "10x engineers"[24]—terms many engineers dislike!). Under that model, companies should hold a high bar and reject candidates whenever they are in doubt.

In reality, this advice oversimplifies the complexity of hiring well. "The best" is hardly as precise a concept as we'd like to think it is. Technical software roles can be highly specialized in both hard and soft skills, and teams vary widely in values, expectations, and style of work. In spite of technology stacks and qualifications being listed succinctly as if they are menu items—"3+ years of Python" and "GraphQL and Node experience a plus"—an engineer with those specific skills might excel at a large enterprise company, but struggle to meet expectations at a small startup in a role that has a seemingly similar job description. Or they might excel at the startup but find the lower cash pay or the stress of uncertainty incompatible with their life—someone with "the best" experience may not be the best fit for your company.

There are recruiting advantages to specificity around what makes a great engineer. If you define "the best" the same way many other companies do (by traditional pedigrees like a four-year degree from a top school and time at a FAANG company), you'll end up competing with a large number of companies[25] for a small pool of mostly homogenous candidates. Will you be able to win those candidates over? Can you pay the top-of-market compensation that those candidates expect? Are they actually the candidates most likely to help your company succeed and to succeed in the role? What qualifications are actually essential for success?

Rather than battling the forces of supply and demand, you could rethink what attributes$^{\S16.5}$ you really value. You might also explore other, creative ways of hiring great candidates that are underappreciated in the

---

24. https://redmonk.com/fryan/2016/12/12/on-the-myth-of-the-10x-engineer-and-the-reality-of-the-distinguished-engineer/
25. https://danluu.com/programmer-moneyball/

market, like candidates that other companies might frequently overlook,[26] or looking in adjacent markets. For example, when Lyft was building its self-driving car team, technical talent with familiarity in that space was in short supply (the self-driving industry is young) and high demand (due to competition from both larger companies and up-and-coming startups in the self-driving space). Rather than just compete for the same candidates as everyone else, Lyft realized that the much more established gaming industry employed many people with similar skills and interests, and tapped into that much larger and less-competitive pool of candidates.

6 Do You Need to Hire?

> *"The most important thing you can do is to figure out a way to have as few people on your team as possible. The fewer the people, the less you need to recruit. Recruiting is really hard and it takes a really long time. Recruiting one hire can take up to 100 hours of your team's collective time. That's time that is not spent making the product better or getting customers."*
>
> — Auren Hoffman, CEO, SafeGraph[27]

One of the biggest mistakes companies can make is hiring for the wrong reasons or at the wrong time. Whether you're a founder at a two-person operation or a hiring manager at a larger company, the first question you need to ask yourself when creating a hiring plan is this: do you *really* need to hire? Recruiting is an immensely time-intensive task. Just because you might have the money or budget to hire and some work you think needs to get done, that doesn't always mean you necessarily *should* hire someone new. Given the financial costs and risks to teams and infrastructure, hiring should not be taken on just because you think it's time to scale up.

---

26. https://www.quora.com/Startups-How-can-I-learn-how-to-hire-people/answer/Auren-Hoffman?ch=99&share=6a665550&srid=OYIQ

27. https://www.quora.com/What-is-the-best-way-to-recruit-engineers-in-Silicon-Valley

So before you define specific roles and start writing job openings, it's a good idea to work back from what your team or company needs to build or deliver, and then ask:

1. What is holding (or could hold) your team back from accomplishing those goals?
2. What do you believe your team should be doing that it isn't doing already, and why not?
3. Is it simply execution bandwidth, or is your team lacking certain skills and abilities needed to accomplish your goals? If your team's technical infrastructure is flakey, is that because the team lacks knowledge in that area, or because the culture or process is pushing them to undervalue work on infrastructure? Depending on the team, either of those issues could be solved with or without hiring more people.
4. What is the anatomy of your team now, and what elements do you need to add to it?

The elements your team needs can take many different forms. For instance, they might be concrete technical skills, like frontend engineering or building machine learning infrastructure. On the other hand, they might be traits that are harder to define and assess, like the ability to prioritize tasks and iterate quickly in product development without incurring technical debt. They might be skills or proclivities to meet challenges your team expects to face in the future.

> "My first piece of advice about hiring is don't do it. The most successful companies we've worked with at YC have waited a relatively long time to start hiring employees. Employees are expensive. Employees add organizational complexity and communication overhead. There are things you can say to your co-founders that you cannot say with employees in the room. Employees also add inertia—it gets exponentially harder to change direction with more people on the team. Resist the urge to derive your self-worth from your number of employees."
> — Sam Altman, chairman, Y Combinator[28]

---

28. https://playbook.samaltman.com/

⚠ DANGER Some common patterns we've seen that lead companies to hire prematurely:

- **Vanity hiring.** Founders may fall victim to vanity hiring, bringing on new employees just to signal success—we have enough money to hire, and growth is good. Hiring managers at larger companies can also be susceptible to trying to grow their team when they don't need to because it'll get them a promotion or more influence within the company.
- **Because you can.** Large companies might be inclined to hire because there's "room in the budget." Startups can also find themselves in similar situations immediately after a fundraising event, when there's suddenly money in the bank.
- **Mythical man-month hiring.** A team that is behind schedule on delivery may believe that hiring will accelerate their progress. In reality, there are short-term costs of hiring (the time spent on hiring and onboarding new engineers) and long-term costs of growing your team (increased complexity and overhead). The underlying idea of the "mythical man-month,"[29] which many managers hold dear, is that they can speed up their team by hiring more people. But, as award-winning computer scientist Fred Brooks put it (in what is commonly known as Brooks' law[30]): "adding human resources to a late software project makes it later."
- **Project-based hiring.** When teams are contemplating a new project they want to pursue, they might think that hiring someone new is the best option. But how long will this project last, and what will the new hire be expected to do once the project is complete? Instead of hiring someone new, consider hiring a contractor for a short, scoped project, or purchasing a product or service that does some of the work. Team leaders must also be certain that a new project is worth pursuing. Or perhaps there's a project already in play that can be aborted, freeing up team members to work on something more worthwhile.
- **Not looking inward.** Whether there's a specific project that needs to be completed or a new role that needs to be filled, there may be a team member ready for a promotion, or someone in a different department looking to transition. Perhaps they are capable of doing the work

---

29. https://en.wikipedia.org/wiki/The_Mythical_Man-Month
30. https://en.wikipedia.org/wiki/Brooks%27s_law

required, but they just need a bit more training. Current employees may already have the necessary skills, or be interested in a new role as a growth opportunity—does your company have the ability to help someone already on the team develop new skills, through mentorship or external training (hiring a consultant to deliver expertise to an existing team member might be possible)? Since they are already a known quantity at your company, understand its mission and values, and likely have some context on the project or new initiative you're hiring for, evaluating a current employee's fit for a new role should be easier than doing so for a completely new candidate.

6.1 Hiring to Overcome Risks

> "You want to identify the key risks in what you're trying to do, then you hire for those risks."
> — Vinod Khosla, founder, Khosla Ventures[31]

In standard approaches to hiring, teams focus on what it will take to accomplish their goals and be successful. However, in situations that require high innovation, these goals might need to change very quickly over time. In his essay "Gene Pool Engineering,"[32] Vinod Khosla writes "It is easy to hire to boost a team's strengths without addressing a team's weaknesses. Fundamentally we believe that a team can be 'precisely engineered'... to manage the risks *and* to take advantage of opportunities to create disruption without running afoul of key requirements of the industry." Khosla argues that in these situations, a team should hire based on both opportunities *and* risks. The steps he recommends (which we reproduce here) are:

1. Identifying the five biggest risks a team is facing.
2. Defining the skill-sets necessary to address those risks.
3. Locating the "centers of excellence" where those skill-sets might exist.
4. Finding and hiring the top experts in those "centers of excellence."

---

[31]. https://youtu.be/alqHBCkSN8I?list=PLoROMvodv4rNpMrTeeh-627Lajh6uSUgY&t=611
[32]. https://www.khoslaventures.com/gene-pool-engineering-for-entrepreneurs

6.2 Hiring Opportunistically

> *"I always have a role for talented people."*
> — Mark Suster, Managing Partner, Upfront Ventures[33]

Say you come across a fantastic candidate, but they just don't fit into any of the open roles you have right now. Should you try to hire them? Exceptional talent is rare; exceptional talent that is attracted to your company is even scarcer; exceptional talent that is attracted to your company *and* at a serendipitous moment where they would make a move requires the stars to all align. Can you miss that opportunity?

Stripe CTO Greg Brockman had a philosophy of hiring for people, not roles. He suggests that "If you can think of one thing this person can do, then there's probably ten more you're not thinking of that he/she can do two months from now."[34]

> *"I encourage entrepreneurs and CEOs to create positions for strong candidates—even if that position doesn't exist."*
> — Vinod Khosla, founder, Khosla Ventures[35]

On the other hand, adding people to a team has immediate cost and overhead. Hiring someone talented and driven without a clear role can result in a frustrating experience for you and for them if things don't work out. For instance, they might feel underutilized and underchallenged. In an interview with *forEntrepreneurs*,[36] Jordan Burton notes that turnover increases when companies try too hard to fit a role to a candidate, especially if that means they end up joining without a specific mandate.

---

33. https://bothsidesofthetable.com/whom-should-you-hire-at-a-startup-attitude-over-aptitude-b19ebb7f0357
34. https://firstround.com/review/How-Stripe-built-one-of-Silicon-Valleys-best-engineering-teams/
35. https://www.khoslaventures.com/the-art-science-and-labor-of-recruiting
36. https://www.forentrepreneurs.com/interviewing/

7 Principles

The overall goal of your recruiting activities is to hire the right candidates for your company's objectives now, in a way that's as efficient, timely, and fair as possible.

In this section, we've distilled the most effective and practical hiring advice from dozens of highly experienced managers to create a list of principles that will guide your hiring process toward candidate-company fit, regardless of your company's stage or specific needs.

7.1 *The Candidate Focus Principle*

Think about the way each candidate experiences your hiring process. Everything you do gives information to the candidate: the speed and level of professionalism of your process, the attitude and background of your interviewers, the types of questions they are asked, and anything else they are exposed to. A positive, professional experience for candidates is much more likely to lead to an accepted offer. It will reap benefits in the future through referrals and good word-of-mouth. A negative experience, on the other hand, will repel the very candidates you might want to hire, leaving you with just the ones willing to tolerate your process. In addition, putting your candidates under stress or adverse conditions will probably affect your ability to accurately assess them. A candidate-centric approach is crucial in all stages of your funnel.

- **Consider every interaction with a candidate to be a two-sided evaluation.** You will be assessing the candidate, but they will also be assessing you. It's a common mistake to think that some touchpoints are purely for you to evaluate the candidate (like interviews), and others are solely to sell them on your company (such as at the offer stage). But in reality, every step and every interaction should serve both purposes.
- **Start selling or advocating early.** Don't wait until you're extending an offer to convince a candidate that your company is worth joining. Candidates may drop out of your process if they're given no compelling reason to join, especially if other companies have won their interest and respect much earlier. Both the company and the role must offer something valuable for candidates: make sure you know what it is and

communicate it early. Remember that each individual candidate may have different motivations and find different parts of your value proposition compelling.
- **Set expectations up front and meet them.** Let candidates know early on what your process entails, in terms of speed, steps, and expectations. Try not to deviate from that, but if you have to, inform candidates about the deviation and the reason behind it.
- **Communicate regularly and transparently.** Maintain regular contact with candidates. Avoid bursty communication. Be responsive to candidate questions.
- **Respect all candidates.** Most of the candidates who go through your process will not receive offers or join the company, but they could be advocates for you. If they loved your process, they may send referrals your way. Or you may decide to hire them in the future. Conversely, candidates who have a bad experience will tell others to avoid you. Respect all your candidates—including the ones who weren't a strong fit or who decided to go elsewhere.

> STORY "A candidate came into my team who we really wanted to work with. We spent a lot of time trying to convince him to join us, and he loved us. But ultimately he got a chance to work on his dream job, so he passed. However, because he loved us and our process so much, he pushed several of his friends our way—and we ultimately ended up hiring one of them." —Scott Woody, former Director of Engineering, Dropbox

One example of a diligent candidate experience philosophy is Root Insurance, which has organized their people team around a product development focus on recruiting candidates. In the video "How Root Insurance Treats Recruiting Like a Product,"[37] Robert Hatta of Drive Capital interviews Root's VP of People Clara Kridler, who established their candidate-focused hiring processes, and refers to their recruiters as "candidate experience managers."

We looked at a sample of Glassdoor interview reviews, where candidates self-report their interview experience and whether they accepted or declined an offer. Out of our sample of ~500 reviews at large software com-

---

37. https://www.linkedin.com/pulse/how-root-insurance-treats-recruiting-like-product-robert-hatta/

panies, we found that candidates who reported a "positive experience" with a company were ~85% likely to accept an offer, while candidates who reported a "negative experience" with a company were only ~25% likely to accept an offer. Of course, this doesn't capture candidates who may have dropped out even earlier in the process, before they reached the offer stage.

7.2 The Effectiveness Principle

Urgency around a hiring decision shouldn't diminish the team's focus on finding candidate-company fit:

- **Define what you're looking for and decide how you will evaluate for fit before you begin recruiting.** You can iterate on your criteria and assessment methods over time, but don't bend them inconsistently on a candidate-by-candidate basis. This includes what you're willing to compromise on (nice-to-haves) and what you're not (must-haves).
- **Assess candidates in a way that's as predictive as possible of on-the-job performance.** There are many ways to assess candidates; choose the methods that will demonstrate how a candidate will perform in your role and at your company.
- **Align your assessment methods with your company's processes.** Recruiting methods should be consistent with onboarding processes and the expectations of the people you hire. For instance, if you attempt to hire for certain skills, but then judge performance based on a completely different set of skills, you are setting yourself and your hires up for failure. This also applies within the various stages of recruiting. If you screen applicants looking for certain qualities, but then interview for completely different qualities, you'll be wasting your and candidates' time.
- **Use structure and calibration when assessing candidates.** Use structured interviews and assessments during the interview process, with clearly-defined areas of evaluation. All interviewers should be calibrated.
- **Use rigor to improve your decision-making.** A large part of recruiting is an exercise in combating our own cognitive biases (especially unconscious bias), which can impact the effectiveness and fairness of

your decision-making. Any recruiting process is noisy, and predicting the success of a candidate from a few touchpoints can be very difficult. At some point, someone will have to make a call about whether to hire a candidate or not, so structure and rigor can help combat biases. At a minimum, it's helpful to be aware of the potential pitfalls that can affect decision-making, and find pragmatic ways of avoiding the risks.

7.3 The Fairness Principle

Design a recruiting process that is fair. In reality, a lot of the techniques that result in an effective process can improve fairness as well (like using structure, defining what you're looking for ahead of time, assessing candidates in a way that's predictive of job performance, and being mindful of bias), but fairness requires even more diligence.

- **Be aware of unconscious bias.** We mentioned bias above, but we mention it again here because it can impact both effectiveness and fairness. Everyone on your team who is interacting with candidates or assessing them should be aware of and undergo some unconscious bias training.
- **Compensate fairly.** Differences in compensation among engineers at the same level can be driven by unconscious bias and conscious discrimination. Having some structure and discipline around how you determine compensation can help prevent unfairness to creep in and build over time. Be careful about sources of pay disparity.
- **Hire with diversity and inclusion in mind.** We discuss many practices for building a fairer hiring process—and the benefits of doing so—in Diversity & Inclusion.[§9]

7.4 The Efficiency Principle

Keep your recruiting pipeline efficient. While recruiting is an extremely high-leverage activity, an inefficient process will waste resources and create a frustrating experience for your team and your candidates.

- **Move quickly and carefully.** Testing the efficiency of your process will protect you from losing out[38] on the most desirable candidates to companies that move faster.[39] The primary goal of efficiency should not simply be speed, however. An efficient process creates a better candidate experience, and minimizes the number of candidates that your team has to juggle at any point in time. Don't cut any corners, but ruthlessly identify and weed out any sources of delay like poor communication between recruiters and hiring managers, slow scheduling, or a lack of internal alignment.
- **Have clear cut-offs in the hiring funnel.** Knowing when to let candidates out of the pipeline will help minimize the cost and effort spent on candidates who are unlikely to make it through to the end of the hiring funnel. This is also mindful of candidates' time, since you won't be dragging candidates through the funnel when they're clearly not a fit and will inevitably be rejected. We'll discuss throughout this Guide how to fairly evaluate candidates at different stages of the funnel.
- **Ramp up.** Use low-effort methods earlier in the funnel, and only increase investment and effort (from both sides) as you both gain more confidence. Many hiring funnels are designed for quick screens at the beginning, then larger investments culminating in a full day or a few days of onsite interviews.
- **Give recruiting the time it deserves.** If you're sure that you need to grow your team, make sure you're spending enough time on recruiting. Depending on your hiring needs, some managers spend as much as 50-80% of their time on recruiting activities. Most hiring managers and founders agree that recruiting should be their top priority, but when we ask them if they think they are spending enough time on it, most of them say they aren't. That's because recruiting is hard, with delayed feedback loops, rejections, and what may seem like wasted effort. It takes grit and discipline. You might need to block off time for it on your calendar, and set expectations with your team about how much of your (and their) time will be spent on it. Throughout this Guide, we'll also highlight ways to make recruiting more fulfilling and enjoyable and less of a chore or burden.

---

38. https://www.linkedin.com/pulse/why-speed-matters-recruiting-kosar-jaff
39. https://onlinelibrary.wiley.com/doi/abs/10.1111/j.1744-6570.2009.01167.x

7.5 The Improvement Principle

◇ **IMPORTANT** Underlying each of these principles is a commitment to measure the success of your hiring process on an ongoing basis and over time, and make adjustments and improvements where necessary. As companies grow, measuring and improving the process can become a major area of focus. The sooner you can start understanding why, when, and how you hire, the more likely you'll be to build an unstoppable team.

- **Focus on both the process and the end results.** Recruiting is a complex activity, and most hiring managers are strapped for time. It might take time for changes in your process to yield results. A lot of time spent on recruiting might be repetitive, and it might be frustrating as you realize that most candidates don't end up being a fit and joining your team. Paying attention to the trees instead of just the forest can actually help.
- **Break your process down into day-to-day activities.** Each activity should be clear and concrete. Most of these activities will involve moving candidates from one stage to the next. It should be clear who is responsible for each activity.
- **Keep an eye on metrics.** Metrics help ensure that the entire pipeline is healthy. You should be able to tell whether each stage of the pipeline is functioning. Otherwise, it's easy to fall victim to the "activity trap" (where you view activity and time spent as your primary performance metric, even if that time is not fruitful).
- **Have clear areas of ownership and accountability for your hiring process.** At any point in the process, those involved within the company should know who can give them a clear answer to highly specific questions like, "Where is Candidate X in the process? What is the next step? Has that been scheduled? Where do we stand on Candidate X, and them on us?" In many cases, having *one* person own the entire process will increase efficiency, consistency, and timeliness, and ensure rigor in the overall hiring program.
- **Continuously improve your process.** There are tensions between these principles, and tradeoffs that have to be made—every company has shortcomings on some of these dimensions. Tensions and tradeoffs are OK and inevitable, but where you compromise should be aligned with the company's principles and the team's needs. As you

talk to candidates, define processes, and work with a team to scale, check whether you are meeting the demands of these principles, or having to sacrificing one for another. They will help you understand where you can improve, what you value most, and where you and your team are strongest. Even an effective process can rot over time as your company grows, as people join and leave your team, or as you get complacent.

> *"Hiring isn't the kind of work that provides you constant dopamine hits. It involves a lot of dead ends and frustration."*
> — Harj Taggar, CEO, TripleByte[40]

Given all of the interrelated elements at play, it can be helpful to think of recruiting as a product. Many readers of this Guide may be familiar with product development processes. We think treating your recruiting process as a product, with both candidates and the company as your customer, can be a powerful analogy, and can help you arrive at most of the principles we've defined. For instance, if you treat recruiting as a product, you would search for product-market fit[41] by trying to match your offering (company and role) to your customer (candidates you're trying to hire). You would focus on quantitative metrics, but also have ways to track your quality, and you would be relentlessly focused on your customers. You would be rigorous and structured, but you would experiment and use feedback loops to monitor and improve your process.

Medium's hiring process[42] (originally developed by Dan Pupius[43]) treats hiring like a product, which they've found also helps reduce bias in their hiring.

---

40. https://blog.ycombinator.com/how-to-hire-your-first-engineer/
41. https://www.holloway.com/s/rvc-fundamentals-of-product-market-fit
42. https://firstround.com/review/develop-your-hiring-system-like-a-product-to-eliminate-bias-and-boost-retention/
43. https://www.linkedin.com/in/danpupius/

8 Cast of Characters

In most companies, many people in various roles are involved in the recruiting and hiring process. You may work with a few or all of these roles depending on the size and stage of your company—if you're a founder or early-stage hiring manager, you'll likely be establishing most of these roles. Learning more about the roles will help you determine whether it is time to establish a recruiting function, and how best to establish and maintain a partnership between the hiring manager and recruiter.

CANDIDATE If you are a candidate, understanding these roles will help you better manage your own progress through the process.

8.1 Who's Involved in Hiring?

The **candidate** is the person being considered for employment at the company. Some companies refer to candidates as *applicants*, but we use the more expansive term *candidate*, since not all candidates apply directly. At the top of the hiring funnel, candidates can be either inbound or outbound.

The **hiring manager** is an employee, typically a manager with an open position on their team. The hiring manager is also usually a key interviewer, and they will be a crucial voice, if not the sole decision maker, in determining whether to extend an offer. They may become the candidate's manager if the candidate joins the company.

Some companies employ a "bootcamp" or "team-matching process" that allows for some flexibility in final team placement after the candidate joins, and in these cases the term *hiring manager* is used more loosely to refer to the primary decision maker.

The **recruiter** is a specialist in the hiring process who partners closely with the hiring manager to find and attract candidates. A recruiter contributes to crafting a job description, sourcing and screening candidates, conducting informational chats, delivering offers and rejections, and negotiating compensation packages, among other activities. Companies split responsibilities between hiring managers and recruiters in different ways, and as a company grows, recruiters may become increasingly specialized. **Internal recruiters (or in-house recruiters)** and **external recruiters** differ in their relationship to the hiring company. An internal or in-house recruiter is a full-time employee at the company, an arrangement which is common at companies that are growing quickly or have achieved a certain size.[44] An external recruiter is a contractor, typically has more limited duties, and may work with many companies.

Technical recruiters are subspecialists in hiring for engineering roles, particularly those requiring full-time, more experienced candidates. This requires enough familiarity with the technical space for which they are recruiting to enable them to effectively screen candidates and converse with them about their technical experience.

Executive recruiters (or leadership recruiters) are subspecialists in hiring for senior roles. Their work often requires extensive network-building and a high-touch approach to candidate engagement.

University recruiters are subspecialists in hiring full-time employees and interns directly from colleges and universities. This can involve building a relationship with certain universities, attending and sponsoring career fairs, organizing social gatherings or technical talks, and so on.

CONFUSION *Recruiter* is a job title that may apply to generalists and any of the above subspecialists, but it is sometimes used expansively to refer to anyone engaged in the project of recruiting.

Companies sometimes break out the tasks associated with searching for and identifying potential candidates into a specialized **sourcer** role. Sourcers may also conduct the initial outreach to a candidate.

When a sourcer reaches out to a candidate, they may do so under their own name or, less frequently, under the hiring manager's name. In the latter case, sourcers and hiring managers may agree on a template for the sourcer to use. A sourcer handling the initial outreach typically is not involved past a successful phone screen of the candidate. At this point, a recruiter takes over.

Recruiting coordinators manage the logistics of the recruiting process, including scheduling interviews and arranging candidates' travel and accommodations. The contributions of recruiting coordinators are more important than may be apparent; for a busy team that is hiring quickly, scheduling is a demanding, critical job.

---

44. https://www.shrm.org/resourcesandtools/hr-topics/talent-acquisition/pages/organizations-in-house-recruiters.aspx

Interviewers are the people selected to meet formally with candidates to assess their suitability for the company and role (and hopefully to help convince them to join the company if given an offer). After conducting an interview, the interviewer usually provides their assessment to the hiring manager in the form of a rating and written feedback, and may attend candidate debriefs to provide feedback in person. When multiple people are assigned to interview a candidate, this group is often referred to as the **interview panel** (not to be confused with a *panel interview*).

🌱 STARTUP   Early-stage startups may have a network of investors, advisors, mentors, or even clients and customers that can help out with recruiting efforts for a small team. These **advisors** or **advocates** might refer candidates to you, talk to candidates about your company's potential, or even step in to help assess candidates for skill sets that you are not equipped to test for yet.

8.2 *The Hiring Manager-Recruiter Partnership*

An effective recruiting process requires the entire cast of characters working together toward a common goal: successful hiring. A crucial part of this process is the relationship between hiring managers and recruiters. Hiring managers (and their teams) are the ultimate beneficiaries of successful hiring, so they're particularly motivated to take the process seriously every step of the way. They also know the team's needs, values, and expectations better than anyone. On the other hand, it is a recruiter's job to recruit. In addition to (theoretically) being able to devote more time to the process than a busy manager or founder, recruiters often bring insights and skills to the process based on their role-specific experience and qualifications. This may include natural talent or personality; your recruiter will likely be extroverted and describe themselves as a "people person." Additional practical knowledge may be accumulated through years of experience spent figuring out what people need and want, what attitudes or motivations they respond to, and what they will or will not compromise on, because a recruiter may see more candidates and hires in one year than a hiring manager might in their entire career. The relationship between both parties can make or break the entire recruiting process.[45]

🌱 STARTUP   A great recruiter is an invaluable partner to many hiring managers and teams, though not every company needs or wants to employ an outside party in their hiring. For most early-stage startups, having a full-blown in-house recruiting team may be unnecessary and too costly. Initially, hiring managers (or, very early on, the founding team) might take on most or all recruiting activities, simply out of necessity. Other functions may pitch in; for instance, company admins may also serve as recruiting coordinators. As many companies grow, however, they begin shifting recruiting activities onto a specialized team.[47]

> *"Never forget that hiring is the most important thing you do. Lots of people say this, but then they delegate hiring to recruiters. Everyone—EVERYONE—should invest time in hiring."*
> — Eric Schmidt, executive chairman, Alphabet[48]

🤔 CONFUSION   When should you hire in-house recruiters, and when should you outsource? *How* should you outsource? This article from First Round[49] discusses the different types of recruiting support you can get and provides a few frameworks for deciding when, what, and how to outsource.

◇ IMPORTANT   Regardless of whether you choose to employ recruiters at this time, the risks and benefits associated with the hiring manager–recruiter relationship can apply to all relationships with the people at your company involved in hiring. Fostering trust and aligning goals and priorities will allow you to avoid communication pitfalls team-wide.

---

45. Recruiters need to be candidate-first: This recruiter "horror story,"[46] centered around one engineer's experience in the hiring funnel at a FAANG company, is an unfortunate example of just how wrong things can go when the hiring manager and recruiter are not aligned on this principle.
46. https://www.igorkromin.net/index.php/2018/11/04/my-amazon-interview-horror-story/
47. http://growth.eladgil.com/book/recruiting/scaling-a-recruiting-organization/
48. https://www.slideshare.net/ericschmidt/how-google-works-final-1#35
49. https://firstround.com/review/Ive-Worked-with-Hundreds-of-Recruiters-Heres-What-I-Learned/

8.2.1 TABLE: HIRING VOLUME BY URGENCY

	LOW URGENCY	HIGH URGENCY
Low total hiring volume	In-house recruiter/contingency (maybe a combination of both until your full-time staffer has filled their pipeline).	Contingency/retained search/consulting recruiter to build candidate volume and move them through a process fast.
High total hiring volume	In-house recruiter, with the license to build out a team over time.	RPO/in-house, maybe with some contingency to supplement where necessary.

Source: First Round[50]

8.2.2 BUILDING TRUST BETWEEN RECRUITERS AND HIRING MANAGERS

At some companies, the relationship between recruiters and hiring managers is akin to a vendor–client relationship. Teams have hiring needs and make requests, and recruiters take the order and deliver the candidates. This works some of the time, but it takes a *partnership* between recruiters and hiring managers to be truly successful. The goal is for both parties to be aligned around a common goal, to agree on priorities and expectations, and to be comfortable working together and giving each other feedback. This allows a recruiter to truly understand a hiring manager's needs; and a hiring manager to understand the complexity and commitment required to successfully hire.

First, it's crucial to ensure that both parties are aligned on the same common goal: the right hiring outcomes. In particular, recruiters who are evaluated based on the number of roles they fill and who work under a short-term agreement with the company (typically contract recruiters), have a propensity to ignore the long-term implications of hiring decisions. Pushy hiring managers with urgent demands can exacerbate this. But the best hiring managers and recruiters think about both the short-term and long-term implications of their decisions.

Second, it's important to ensure everyone agrees on priorities. If a recruiter is servicing several teams or clients, how will they split and prioritize their time? What level of support can they give each team or manager? In return, what should managers be doing to help support the process as effectively as possible?

---

50. https://firstround.com/review/Ive-Worked-with-Hundreds-of-Recruiters-Heres-What-I-Learned/

Finally, both parties will benefit from working to build trust and empathy for each other, to cultivate a relationship that is collaborative instead of adversarial, and to foster comfort in giving and receiving feedback from one another. How this healthy dynamic occurs will probably depend on your company's size and culture. Netflix, for instance, prefers a "partnership model" to a "service model," granting more autonomy to both hiring managers and recruiters, which leads to better communication and a shared appreciation of each other's successes.[51]

8.2.3 FRICTION BETWEEN RECRUITERS AND HIRING MANAGERS

⚠ CAUTION Friction between recruiters and hiring managers is common. When the partnership *doesn't* work, a breakdown between recruiters and managers can lead to poor outcomes and frustrating experiences both for those parties *and* for candidates. Examples include:

- **Poor communication around hiring needs.** It's helpful for hiring managers to be able to articulate what they're looking for. This can be supported by having recruiters spend time with managers, asking questions and double-checking their own understanding. They might send hiring managers sample candidate profiles to make sure they're on the same page.
- **Unrealistic expectations.** Hiring managers may have unattainable expectations about what sort of candidate the company can succeed in hiring, or the time it might take to make a hire. For instance, the company's value proposition to candidates may not be strong enough to attract them. Recruiters may be better attuned to pick up these types of problems.
- **A mismatch in hiring priority or urgency.** Hiring managers may have sudden high urgency to fill a role, without understanding the realities of the time and effort it takes to set up a recruiting pipeline. Also, recruiters typically work with more than one hiring manager, and each hiring manager is likely to feel their role should be the top priority. Finally, a hiring manager may request that recruiters fill a role with a high degree of urgency, while not responding with the same degree of urgency themselves. For example, they might be slow to respond to requests to review resumes or meet with candidates or recruiters. Even

---

51. https://business.linkedin.com/talent-solutions/blog/hiring-managers/2017/how-netflix-recruiter-and-hiring-manager-relationship

with a recruiter involved, hiring managers still need to be appropriately present in the process.
- **Unclear expectations of responsibilities.** Either the manager or the recruiter can own different parts of the process, and that split often changes over time. It's very important that communication channels be clear, and that everyone knows how they fit in and for what they are (and are not!) responsible.
- **Mismatched incentives.** The number of roles many recruiters—and sometimes even managers—fill can influence their evaluation and compensation. This can lead to short-term thinking, where the recruiter tries to fill roles and move on to other client companies as quickly as possible, without ensuring fit or moving through a proper hiring plan. The risk of such a mismatch is greater when working with external or contract recruiters. Hiring managers are not exempt from this phenomenon, however; they may be desperate to fill a role directly, perhaps because they are compensated for doing so, or their team is in need, or they just want to get back to working on the product. Whatever the reason, mismatched incentives result in poor candidate experience and a rushed, messy process that will have to be repeated again if the hire doesn't work out.
- **Trust breakdowns.** In some extreme cases, the relationship between hiring manager and recruiter can become so strained that the hiring manager projects their negative feelings toward the recruiter onto the candidates the recruiter brings in, and vice versa.

Taken together, these problems can account for a big chunk of why recruiting can sometimes feel so broken—and it's highly likely everyone who has built or participated in a hiring process has experienced one or all of these pitfalls, either directly or with a recruiter, a boss, or a teammate.

8.2.4 RESPONSIBILITIES OF RECRUITERS AND HIRING MANAGERS

Which part or parts of the recruiting process should be conducted by recruiters, and which by hiring managers and their teams? Though each role represents a different skill set and knowledge base (managers know more about the company; recruiters may know more about the market), the beauty of the partnership model—where trust is built and expectations align—is that roles tend not to matter as much. Both sides should feel equal ownership over the outcome, but responsibilities can be handled more flexibly. If one side carries out a particular activity, the other side provides advice and feedback.

Consider application screening, for example. A recruiter might be more experienced at overall application heuristics, like detecting "job-hoppers" or other unusual patterns on a resume. But a hiring manager will have a better understanding of the technical domain. In the partnership model, either party can screen applications, with support and coaching from the other. The same applies for most parts of the recruiting process.

But there are a couple areas where one side might have a distinct advantage and should be assigned to that task or activity. Naturally, hiring managers and their teams will conduct interviews, since they are better suited to assess a candidate's fitness for the role and fit with the team. On the other hand, a recruiter can serve as a confidant and advocate for a candidate who may feel awkward discussing issues like offer negotiations or other concerns with their potential future manager. Process-oriented tasks like scheduling also will usually be handled by the recruiter.

Meetings along the way help keep both sides aligned and in sync, although at smaller companies, not all the meetings described below may be necessary (or even recommended). When possible, it's best that these meetings be held in person or via video conference, rather than over email. Live meetings allow for deep dives and debates that may uncover subtle insights.

Role intake meetings, which take place between the hiring manager and recruiter when a role is being opened, help establish high-level alignment. Often, these meetings involve a candidate profile calibration.

In a **candidate profile calibration**, the hiring manager and recruiter discuss whether sample candidates might fit the role and why. After this initial calibration, adjustments can be made periodically, including as part of the regular status meeting.

Role intake meetings may also include the following:

- Reaching a shared understanding of the role, the needs behind it, and the value proposition the company plans to extend to candidates. Candidate personas can be helpful here, and this is the point at which having a job description becomes essential.
- Setting expectations on timeline and priority of filling this role (taking into account other open roles the recruiter might be working to fill, at the same company and/or at other companies).

- Agreeing on the overall hiring process for this role. What sourcing strategy is best? What are the different stages? What kinds of interviews will the process use, and who will conduct them?
- Agreeing on who does what. How will the recruiter and the hiring manager and their team split the responsibilities?? What commitments do they make to each other and to the process? For instance, how quickly should candidates move through the process? If a recruiter sends a candidate to a hiring manager, within what timeframe should the manager respond?
- Reviewing any hiring process the company or team already has in place, including any relevant documentation, like a flowchart. If documentation doesn't exist or is out of date, consider sitting down and collaboratively creating it or updating it. This leaves a written record that clarifies the process and can allow both parties to more deeply understand it going forward.

A regular (usually weekly) **status meeting** between the hiring manager and recruiter offers the opportunity to review and reflect on the current state of the pipeline; to update the status of key candidates, especially those at later stages; and to discuss potential improvements to the process, strategy, or role.

In addition to the intake and status meetings, it's often helpful for the hiring project lead (whether the recruiter, the hiring manager, or another role) to send out periodic **status reports** with key hiring metrics to monitor progress and detect changes in the hiring funnel.

Inspired by software postmortems, a **postmortem meeting** between hiring managers, recruiters, and—as appropriate—key interviewers, provides a chance to discuss with the benefit of hindsight what happened in a given process. The primary goal of a postmortem meeting is to elicit feedback that can be used to improve future recruiting and hiring efforts. In cases where no candidate was hired, this is an opportunity to understand what went wrong. These meetings can also be useful for improving team communication and providing closure.

8.2.5 FURTHER READING ON HIRING YOUR FIRST RECRUITER

- "A founder's guide to making your first recruiting hire"[52] (Aline Lerner, interviewing.io)

---

52. http://blog.alinelerner.com/a-founders-guide-to-making-your-first-recruiting-hire/

- "How to Interview a Recruiter"[53] (Jose Guardado, veteran recruiter)
- "I've Worked With Hundreds of Recruiters—Here's What I Learned"[54] (Peter Kazanjy, co-founder of TalentBin)
- "Turbocharge Your Recruiting Machine—Here's How"[55] (Flo Thinh, VP of Talent at NerdWallet)

9 Overview of the Hiring Funnel

Between posting a job ad and onboarding a new employee, it takes many steps to help a company gain confidence that a candidate is a good fit and for the candidate to decide the company is right for them. This fundamental part of the recruiting process is called the hiring funnel.

The **hiring funnel (or funnel)** is the series of stages through which a candidate's consideration for employment progresses. It's called a "funnel" because of the shape and by analogy with the traditional purchase funnel:[56] many candidates enter the funnel, but few proceed through all the stages and are hired. Candidates enter at the top of the funnel through multiple sources. At the bottom, they accept an offer you have extended for them to join your company. A candidate's exit from the funnel at any stage can be prompted by the candidate themself or by the company. Moving forward at each stage occurs by mutual agreement.

For each role, a company will typically have multiple candidates in the funnel at different stages. And many of these candidates are likely to be exploring and interviewing with several companies at the same time.

---

53. https://medium.com/@jay_likewise/how-to-interview-a-recruiter-40e0f3e43dfd
54. https://firstround.com/review/Ive-Worked-with-Hundreds-of-Recruiters-Heres-What-I-Learned/
55. https://firstround.com/review/turbocharge-your-recruiting-machine-heres-how/
56. https://www.mckinsey.com/business-functions/marketing-and-sales/our-insights/the-consumer-decision-journey

9.0.1 **FIGURE: AN EXAMPLE HIRING FUNNEL**

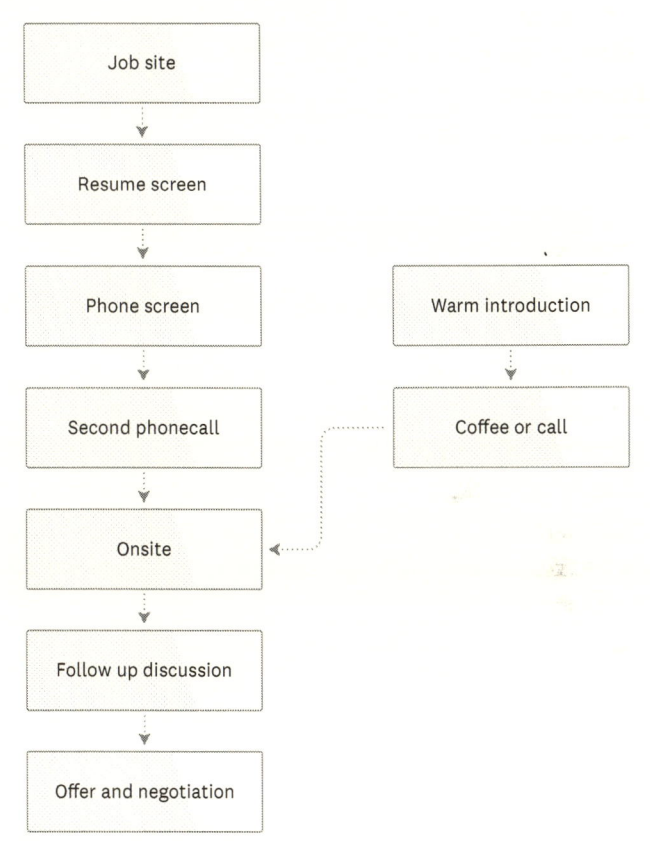

```
Job site
   ↓
Resume screen
   ↓
Phone screen          Warm introduction
   ↓                         ↓
Second phonecall      Coffee or call
   ↓                  ↙
Onsite ←·······
   ↓
Follow up discussion
   ↓
Offer and negotiation
```

Source: Holloway

9.1 *Stages of the Funnel*

The funnel might look different from company to company and even candidate to candidate. For instance, at a small startup, a founder or CTO might simply reach out to someone they have worked with closely before and convince them to join the company. The entire process may be a few meetings and a lunch with the team.[57] At a large, mature company, the process will likely be more formal and involve the following:

- **Sourcing and selecting.** You source candidates who might be a good fit for your company, and/or select from a pool of applicants.

---

57. In most situations, a more thorough process is highly advisable!

- **Screening.** A quick assessment (for instance, a quick call with a recruiter or hiring manager) that can help rule out cases where there is an obvious lack of fit.
- **Interviewing.** A deeper assessment of the candidate's skills, experience, traits, and values.
- **Making an offer decision.** The company has gathered all the information they need to decide whether to extend a job offer and what that offer will look like.
- **Extending an offer.** When the company has decided it wants to make a hire, it extends a formal job offer to the candidate.
- **Negotiating and closing.** After receiving the offer, there might be negotiations between the candidate and the company before the candidate decides whether to join the company.

◇ CAUTION At larger companies, the recruiting process can get complicated. There might be multiple people accountable for different stages of the funnel. There might also be different paths a candidate can take through the funnel (for instance, maybe candidates who don't do well enough on a technical phone screen to warrant an on-site interview and not poorly enough to be rejected are invited to take a coding challenge).

A **recruiting process flowchart** maps out the different points and paths between a candidate entering the funnel and being hired. Along the way, decision points are clearly mapped out with the corresponding paths for a candidate's progression. Anyone on your team looking at this flowchart should understand how your recruiting process works.

Whether you're designing a new process or documenting an existing one, flowcharts provide a visual way to align your team on the hiring process. In fact, when teams try to put together a flowchart of their established (and, they believe, clearly understood) process, they are often surprised to discover that not everyone expects the same things ("I thought everyone gets a HackerRank challenge?"... "No, we skip those if the candidate is a referral"). Many teams are also surprised at how complex their process has become over time, and the flowchart is a great way to identify areas that might be simplified or improved.

9.1.1 FIGURE: RECRUITING PROCESS FLOWCHART FROM GOOGLE

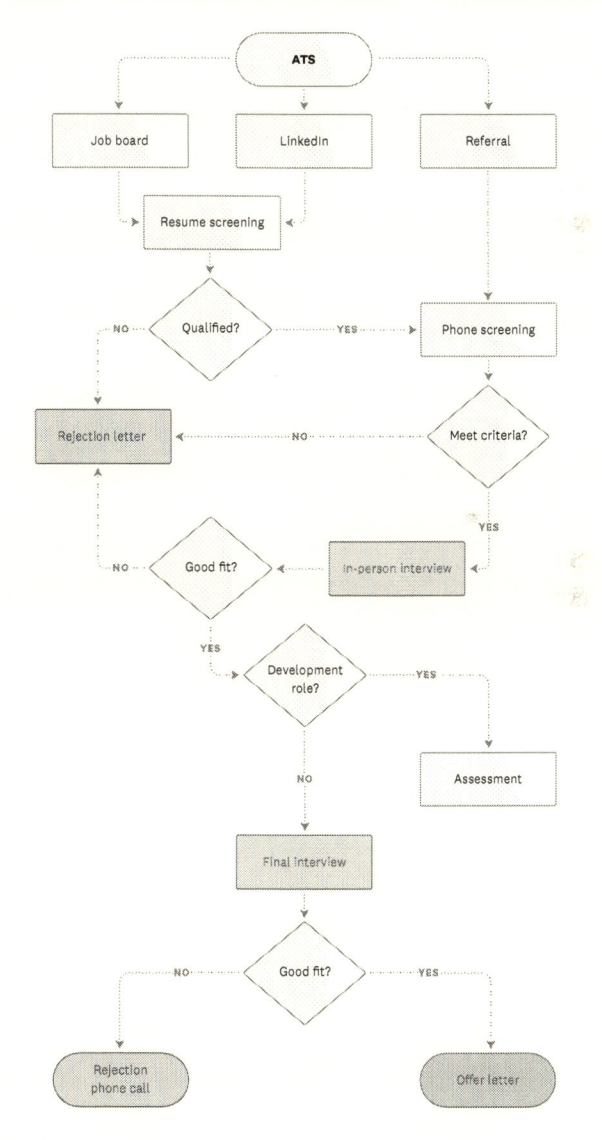

Source: Google[58]

This Hire by Google flowchart is a good overview; we'd recommend taking it a step further by indicating *who* is responsible for each stage or decision, and agree on timing around how long each stage should take.

---

58. https://hire.google.com/articles/recruitment-process-flowchart/

9.2 Data and Metrics

It's important to have a set of metrics that you can use to evaluate, diagnose, and improve your hiring funnel. Metrics can also help you predict whether your activities are putting you on track to hit your hiring goals. There is no single metric that encompasses the health of the funnel. We present several commonly used metrics that, combined, can help you understand how your recruiting process is functioning.

9.2.1 GENERAL METRICS

Reviewing the number of candidates, or **volume of candidates**, at each stage gives a broad sense of your hiring funnel. Because this metric is easy to calculate, and it's hard to have any insight without it, most companies will review their volume regularly.

Conversion rates (pass-through rates or yields) measure the percentage of candidates who move from one stage to the next—for example, the percentage of candidates who make it to an onsite interview after a phone interview.

The **offer acceptance rate** measures the percentage of candidates who accept an offer of employment from the company, whether before or after negotiating the offer's terms, and is a particularly commonly used conversion rate.

Conversion rates give you a breakdown of where you lose candidates in your funnel. A low conversion rate at one stage might indicate that you are judging candidates too harshly (or incorrectly) at that stage, but it could also indicate that you are being too lenient in preceding stages. It's also important to break down the loss at each stage by the major force behind it: whether it was company-driven (you decided not to move forward with a candidate) or candidate-driven (candidates could be pulling out of your process due to a poor experience).

9.2.2 **FIGURE: STARTUP PASS-THROUGH RATES**

HIRING PASS-THROUGH RATES

Startups that successfully hit their hiring goals were more efficient across their entire pipeline. Analyze pass-through rates regularly and address any stages that dip below benchmarks.

PASS-THROUGH RATES	OVERALL			ENGINEERING		
	EARLY	EXPANSION	LATE	EARLY	EXPANSION	LATE
Email Outreach	34%	28%	27%	28%	23%	19%
Recruiter Screen	53%	56%	53%	58%	59%	56%
Phone Interview	45%	46%	56%	44%	38%	42%
Onsite Interview	36%	39%	32%	36%	31%	31%
Offer	70%	75%	81%	67%	69%	65%
HIRED						

Lightspeed

Source: Lightspeed Venture's Startup Hiring Trends report[59] (2017-2018)

9.2.3 **EFFICIENCY METRICS**

Efficiency metrics in hiring and recruiting measure the rate and cost of candidate progression through a hiring funnel. These metrics can be used for planning (knowing how long, on average, it takes to fill a position) and budgeting (deciding how much to budget for recruiting in the future).

Time-based metrics, such as time-to-fill or time-to-hire,[60] are an efficiency metric that measures how quickly candidates move through a hiring funnel. Time end-to-end can be measured, or, for more fine-tuned diagnostics, the time between any two stages can be measured (for instance, maybe the team takes too long to schedule interviews).

Cost per hire is an efficiency metric that measures the financial expenditure required to fill an open position. Standardized ways of calculating cost-per-hire[61] divide total expenditures by the number of hires, but any meaningful method can be used. For instance, Aline Lerner encour-

---

59. http://startuphiringtrends.com/
60. https://resources.workable.com/tutorial/faq-time-to-fill-hire
61. https://www.shrm.org/ResourcesAndTools/business-solutions/Documents/shrm_ansi_cph_standard.pdf

ages engineering functions to calculate the cost of engineering time[62] (interviewing, writing feedback, debriefing) per hire because this makes up a bulk of hiring costs. Many components of cost-per-hire are tightly coupled to conversion rates—in general, the earlier you can weed out candidates who wouldn't have been a fit, the less time and money you will spend on them.

◇ CAUTION Some companies use efficiency metrics to judge how their recruiting function is performing—but they don't capture the actual *value* your process is producing. You could be hiring candidates quickly and cheaply, only to later realize that they aren't a fit for your company, and be forced to start again.

9.2.4 EFFECTIVENESS METRICS

Effectiveness metrics measure how well a company's goals in hiring and recruiting are met. Effectiveness metrics can also challenge a company to review its goals when ostensible success still leaves something lacking. In these ways, they capture important information that efficiency metrics can overlook.

Quality of hire is an effectiveness metric that attempts to provide a more holistic metric[63] by looking at the value created by new employees. There's no single, standard way of measuring this, but most variations[64] look at how an employee is faring some time after being hired by considering data like performance reviews, employee engagement surveys, or retention. Downsides of the quality-of-hire metric are that it takes a long time to measure and may conflate candidates' quality with factors outside their control, such as on-boarding and new-hire management.

Candidate-driven metrics are an effectiveness metric gathered through surveys, which can help measure the candidate experience and provide further insight into possible improvements in your process. These metrics can be as simple as calculating a Net Promoter Score[65] (NPS) or include more in-depth questions about a candidate's experience. Larger

---

62. http://blog.interviewing.io/you-probably-dont-factor-in-engineering-time-when-calculating-cost-per-hire-heres-why-you-really-should/
63. https://www.shrm.org/resourcesandtools/hr-topics/talent-acquisition/pages/how-to-measure-quality-of-hire.aspx
64. https://resources.workable.com/blog/quality-of-hire
65. https://marketinglowcost.typepad.com/files/the-one-number-you-need-to-grow-1.pdf

companies might administer these surveys formally,[66] but sometimes a simple, informal debrief with a subset of your candidates will help surface issues.

Smaller companies might opt to look at just a subset of these metrics. For instance, some startups might just look at funnel volume and offer acceptance rates on a regular basis, and only calculate other metrics should the need arise.

Larger companies may calculate many more metrics, and might even segment them in different ways:

- Segmenting conversion rates by candidate source[§23] (referrals, applicants, sourced candidates) can help assess how different sources are performing.
- Splitting out metrics along diversity axes can help uncover where in the process candidates that could add to your team's diversity are dropping out or being rejected.
- Calculating metrics like per-interviewer conversion rates can help identify opportunities for giving feedback to particular interviewers.

Metrics are only as valuable as they are useful in helping you improve your processes. "A Modern Take on Data-Driven Recruiting from a Google Recruiting Lead"[67] debunks a few myths about some of the more commonly used metrics and goes into detail about how to use past data to improve your future hiring performance.

---

66. https://rework.withgoogle.com/guides/hiring-shape-the-candidate-experience/steps/measure-candidate-experience/
67. https://hire.google.com/articles/a-modern-take-on-data-driven-recruiting/

PART II: DIVERSITY AND INCLUSION

> This section was written by Jennifer Kim, with Jason Wong.

10 The Tech Industry: By the Numbers

The tech industry is increasingly powering businesses around the globe, and creating products that dramatically impact people's lives. And yet, it is an industry that does not reflect the broader population. Women make up 57% of the U.S. workforce as a whole but only 26% of the technical workforce. Black, Latina, and Native American women make up 16% of the U.S. workforce and hold only 4% of tech jobs.[68] Pay gaps by gender and race persist. While 83% of tech executives are white, only 10% are women.[69,70] Asian and Asian American men make up 32% of the tech workforce, but only 20% hold executive positions; while Asian and Asian American women make up 15% of the workforce, they hold only 5% of executive roles in tech.

The problem, however, goes beyond race and gender, and is more pervasive than the statistics presented by Information is Beautiful.[71] Data on race and gender are the easiest to collect, but harassment and discrimination affect workers based on their caregiver status, immigration status, gender identity, sexual orientation, and disability status.

In a 2017 study, 43% of people in tech worried about losing their jobs due to their age;[72] in a more recent 2019 study, 80% did.[73]

---

68. https://sdtimes.com/softwaredev/theres-a-diversity-problem-in-the-tech-industry-and-its-not-getting-any-better/
69. https://www.eeoc.gov/eeoc/statistics/reports/hightech/
70. https://ratedly.com/women-in-tech-report/
71. https://informationisbeautiful.net/visualizations/diversity-in-tech/
72. http://blog.indeed.com/2017/10/19/tech-ageism-report/

10.1 The Role of Bias

The above statistics speak to a much deeper history of systemic bias and discrimination toward people from all these underrepresented groups.

A **bias** is an inclination in favor of or against a particular person or group based on factors such as race, ethnicity, age, educational prestige, appearance, and so on. As a type of observational error, bias leads to unfair and ineffective outcomes when it affects decision-making. Bias can operate systematically where an individual's decision-making is persistently affected or on a systemic basis where a process or group dynamic produces biased decisions. **Explicit biases (or conscious biases)** are inclinations about particular people or groups that an individual has and is aware of. **Implicit biases (or unconscious biases)** are inclinations based on subconscious associations that influence our decisions without us being aware of them.[74]

Biases are a kind of mental shortcut; rather than treating everyone as a complex individual, we pick factors by which to group them and assign that group certain expectations, with no evidence that those expectations are borne out in individual behavior. Implicit or unconscious biases are especially difficult to deal with because we don't *know* that we have them, and they may even contradict the views we consciously hold. For example, a group of physicians may not consciously believe that Black patients feel less pain than white patients, but nevertheless recommend less pain medication for their Black patients experiencing the same injury as their white patients.[75]

There are many types of unconscious bias[76] that affect people in general, and thus also affect hiring processes. Harvard developed a free online tool called the Implicit Association Test (IAT)[77] to help people become more aware of their unconscious biases.

But there are plenty of conscious biases as well. For example, an over-reliance on traditional academic pedigrees when screening for candidates vastly favors people who could afford a costly education and had access to resources and networks as a young person. We cover more biases through-

---

73. https://insights.dice.com/2019/06/24/ageism-tech-professional-earnings/
74. https://nccc.georgetown.edu/bias/module-3/1.php
75. https://www.scientificamerican.com/article/how-to-think-about-implicit-bias/
76. https://www.socialtalent.com/blog/recruitment/how-badly-is-your-unconscious-bias-affecting-your-recruiting-skills
77. https://implicit.harvard.edu/implicit/takeatest.html

out this section to help raise awareness and to provide practical suggestions on how to discuss and combat them in your organization.

10.2 The Consequences

Systemic bias and discrimination are a broad problem that affects not just recruiting and hiring, but also people's willingness to remain in a given industry that does not represent them or treat them fairly. The Kapor Center's landmark Tech Leavers Study[78] reported in 2017 that nearly 40% of people who left the tech industry cited "unfairness or mistreatment" as the major reason they left, with men of color the most likely to leave due to mistreatment; 78% reported having experienced unfair treatment. In 2016, the departure rate for women was 41%—more than twice that of men, which was 17%.[79]

Underrepresented men and women of color experience stereotyping at twice the rate of their white and Asian peers, while LGBTQ+ tech leavers report bullying and public humiliation at significantly higher rates than other underrepresented groups. However, 62% of tech leavers said they would have stayed had their employer made efforts to create a more inclusive work environment.

Along with the negative consequences for candidates and employees, homogeneous and inequitable, unfair work environments also pose significant risks to organizations.[80] The Tech Leavers Study concluded that the industry stands to lose more than $16B per year in employee replacement costs.[81] Companies also may face backlash and negative brand associations for not dealing with potentially harmful features and unforeseen consequences of their products.[82,83,84] For example, Facebook's "real name" policy—which failed to realize the importance of privacy concerns

---

78. https://www.kaporcenter.org/tech-leavers/
79. https://www.ncwit.org/sites/default/files/resources/womenintech_facts_fullreport_05132016.pdf
80. https://www.theatlantic.com/technology/archive/2019/06/tech-computers-are-bigger-problem-diversity/592456/
81. https://www.kaporcenter.org/tech-leavers/
82. https://www.theverge.com/2014/9/25/6844021/apple-promised-an-expansive-health-app-so-why-cant-i-track
83. https://www.theguardian.com/technology/2016/aug/10/snapchat-racist-asian-filter-yellowface
84. https://gizmodo.com/why-cant-this-soap-dispenser-identify-dark-skin-1797931773

of people from marginalized groups—was so controversial there's an extensive Wikipedia page[85] about it. When Twitter was in the running for acquisition, a number of potential buyers apparently balked at the company's inability to deal with the harassment issues[86] on its platform.

> "I observed a company of mostly white, affluent iPhone users delay shipping on Android because Android users reportedly earn less money, and later regretting the choice after discovering their Android users are more engaged. I've watched helplessly as another company used the data they collected on users in discriminatory ways, which not only erodes users' trust but also the trust of the employees who have been subject to discrimination in their lives. If these teams were more diverse, especially among the leadership, I doubt the same choices would have been made."
> — Leighton Wallace, engineering manager, Lever[87]

A dearth of diversity doesn't just limit the number of innovative products companies can produce and the markets they can reach—it also poses serious risks to underrepresented populations. In 2015, Google was called out for racist image search results, a problem it has not solved.[88] A recent study from the University of Georgia found that the technology used by self-driving cars may detect dark-skinned pedestrians less effectively than light-skinned ones. As Vox reports,[89] this kind of "algorithmic bias" results from many factors, including sources of training data and homogenous technical research and product development teams. This has implications both for the kinds of tools and products we use as consumers and for the work environment of the people at those companies, as much as it impacts those companies' ability to innovate and drive change.

---

85. https://en.wikipedia.org/wiki/Facebook_real-name_policy_controversy
86. https://www.linkedin.com/pulse/twitters-evan-williams-says-trolling-could-have-been-curbed-chang
87. https://inside.lever.co/a-black-engineers-take-on-why-diversity-matters-at-startups-89ade12ab204
88. https://www.theverge.com/2018/1/12/16882408/google-racist-gorillas-photo-recognition-algorithm-ai
89. https://www.vox.com/future-perfect/2019/3/5/18251924/self-driving-car-racial-bias-study-autonomous-vehicle-dark-skin

10.3 Benefits and Opportunities

Anyone who owns a company or runs a hiring process has the power to help bridge the opportunity gap that has been created through years of institutional discrimination of marginalized groups. There are also countless advantages—to your company, to candidates, to your industry, and to your customers—to embracing and supporting diversity. The rules of business-building have changed. Building a technical product today requires enormous adaptability, creativity, and global reach—all of which improves with diversity.

Research extensively and consistently bears out that diversity positively correlates to better financial performance.[90] McKinsey has conducted some of the most robust, oft-cited studies[91] on a direct correlation of diversity and better business outcomes. Among their findings: "Gender-diverse companies are 21% more likely to have better financial performance. Ethnically diverse companies are 33% more likely to financially outperform their counterparts." A 2013 report by *Harvard Business Review* found that companies that had more diverse workforces were "45% likelier to report a growth in market share over the previous year and 70% likelier to report that the firm captured a new market."[92] Researchers also found that more diverse companies announced, on average, two more products a year.[93,94]

---

90. https://hbr.org/2018/01/how-and-where-diversity-drives-financial-performance
91. https://www.mckinsey.com/business-functions/organization/our-insights/delivering-through-diversity
92. https://hbr.org/2013/12/how-diversity-can-drive-innovation
93. https://www.fastcompany.com/40515712/want-a-more-innovative-company-simple-hire-a-more-diverse-workforce
94. Diversity among companies' founders and investors improves performance as well. A study by First Round Capital[95] found their investments in companies with at least one woman founder outperformed their investments in all-male teams by 63%. A Harvard Business Review study[96] found that venture capital firms that increased their proportion of women partners by 10% saw, on average, a 1.5% spike in overall fund returns each year; those companies had 9.7% more profitable exits. More and more, we are beginning to understand that building a diverse workforce is not only the right thing to do, but also a powerful accelerant to business success.
95. https://www.forbes.com/sites/alexkonrad/2015/07/29/first-round-female-founders-outperform-the-men/#3b32f5c622f2
96. https://hbr.org/2018/07/the-other-diversity-dividend

In addition to correlational studies, diversity seems to have a causal relationship with innovation. Numerous psychology studies have shown that diverse teams shine a light on organizational blindspots, solve problems faster, and are more creative.[97,98] Diverse teams have the ability to see and solve problems that might otherwise be missed or mysterious, and increase returns for the business by doing so. In early 2019, Pinterest released a widely applauded inclusive search[99] feature. Development was driven in large part by feedback from employees and diverse members of their customer base who were looking for beauty tips for a wide range of skin tones. When it comes to the business argument, the research is conclusive: diverse teams are more productive and effective at making decisions,[100] and diversity is markedly better for a company's bottom line.

Finally, as a recruiter or hiring manager, expanding your hiring pool gives you an advantage in an increasingly competitive market. When you're no longer competing with Google and Facebook for the same set of people, you have the opportunity to find more candidates in general, adding volume along with diversity to the top of your hiring funnel.

Whatever your role in recruiting and hiring, diversity and inclusion present a complex, multifaceted challenge. The goal of this section is to provide enough background and perspective that you understand the issues, can have thoughtful conversations with anyone else involved, and can make an impact on your company's hiring processes. This is a difficult and nuanced subject to tackle, so we'll start with the basics (what *is* D&I?), and then move on to cover many of the myths and pitfalls you may encounter along the way. Finally, we provide practical tactics you can implement at your organization to improve the hiring process for everyone involved.

---

97. https://hbr.org/2016/11/why-diverse-teams-are-smarter
98. https://www.nytimes.com/2015/12/09/opinion/diversity-makes-you-brighter.html
99. https://www.yahoo.com/gma/pinterest-launches-inclusive-search-tool-beauty-enthusiasts-love-222806293--abc-news-fashion-and-beauty.html
100. https://sites.lsa.umich.edu/scottepage/wp-content/uploads/sites/344/2015/11/pnas.pdf

11 What Is D&I?

> *"Diversity is being invited to the party; inclusion is being asked to dance."*
> — Vernā Myers, VP Inclusion Strategy, Netflix[101]

Diversity and Inclusion (or D&I) is an approach taken by organizations to building diverse teams and promoting an inclusive workplace, in order to set underrepresented groups up for success. **Diversity, Equity, and Inclusion (DEI)**, **Diversity & Belonging**, and other variations are also common.

Understanding the differences between diversity and inclusion is essential, because both are necessary to building and fostering a workplace where all employees can thrive. As noted earlier, diverse teams perform better and contribute to longer-lasting, more successful companies. But having a demographically diverse team does not automatically lead to these benefits. It's not possible to reap the benefits of diversity without inclusive practices.

Diversity is a condition of reflecting demographic differences in a group of people. Elements of diversity include age, caregiver status, disability, ethnicity, gender, gender identity, immigration status, race, sexual orientation, and socioeconomic background.

◇ IMPORTANT In the U.S., *diversity* is often a shorthand for "women and people of color," as these are two of the most visible dimensions of diversity. But it actually includes all of the factors listed above, and more.

⚑ CONFUSION The term *diverse* describes differences present in a group; therefore individuals cannot be diverse. Referring to an individual as diverse (as in, "a diverse candidate") can put people from underrepresented backgrounds in a disempowering, "other" position. It can lead team members to think of certain candidates as "diversity candidates," and certain new team members as "diversity hires." It also is often used as a synonym for person of color (POC), centering "the social construct of whiteness as the normal, the axis we all move around."[102]

---

101. https://www.refinery29.com/en-us/2017/05/156009/harvard-business-school-diversity-issue-essay
102. https://twitter.com/nataliemself/status/1167962155485843457

Inclusion is the process of creating an environment that supports and encourages all employees, giving particular attention to and elevating the voices of those from underrepresented backgrounds. Inclusive processes and policies, such as eliminating vague "culture fit" interview questions and offering parental leave, address structural barriers to employees' success.

> "*Diversity means increasing the representation of people from marginalized backgrounds at all levels and across all functional areas of the company. Inclusion means building policies, procedures, communication channels, and compensation policies where everyone is a full participant in the structure of your company. Not enough of one or the other, and the true benefit of a diverse workforce will never be reached.*"
> — Nicole Sanchez, D&I strategy consultant[103]

Underrepresented groups (or URGs) are groups of people who make up a smaller percentage in an organization than they do in the overall population. The term can be used to refer either to the groups themselves or to individuals who belong to those groups.

⚠ CONFUSION As with much of the language on this topic, the language for describing underrepresented groups is shifting in real time. You may also see the term *underrepresented minorities (URMs)* used elsewhere, but this Guide will use *underrepresented groups (URGs)* throughout because we think it is the most accurate and up-to-date description available.[104]

---

103. https://medium.com/@nmsanchez/the-big-takeaway-from-atlassians-diversity-report-6d22d86325b7
104. Many of the terms you see here may be different than what you're familiar with. The past few years have seen an accelerated pace of activity in the diversity and inclusion space. In that time we have begun prioritizing the voices of underrepresented groups and the vocabulary they use to describe concepts of diversity and inclusion. We have also seen language co-opted and misused, often with harmful intent. As a result, the language we use as diversity and inclusion practitioners changes rapidly. For this section, we have made every effort to use up-to-date terminology. However, if, in the course of your efforts, you find differences in preferred language, use the terminology that will create a greater sense of inclusion for your organization.

There's plenty of research[105] that shows that diversity without inclusion doesn't work. In 2015, Rachel Thomas wrote a post[106] summarizing the available research and discussing many of the same problems we explore here. Thomas emphasizes that progress toward equity is possible when diversity and inclusion issues are both addressed, and that progress requires the involvement of everyone, especially white men and those in leadership roles. Notable among her examples were efforts at both Harvey Mudd College[107] and Harvard Business School[108] that increased the percentages of women in their programs after making a number of comprehensive, structural changes, focusing not just on recruiting but on making the student environment more welcoming and inclusive for everyone.

A few other key concepts round out the general understanding of diversity and inclusion.

Intersectionality is a prism through which to understand the interconnectedness of social categorizations, which creates overlapping and compounding systems of oppression in society. Kimberlé Crenshaw coined the term in a 1989 article[109] discussing the particular challenges faced by Black women in the workplace.[110]

As Crenshaw described in a 2016 TED talk,[111] she was inspired to give intersectionality a name by the case of a Black woman who was turned down for a job at a manufacturing plant. When she brought a lawsuit against the plant, her case was dismissed. The judge pointed to the fact that the employer hired both Black people and women. However, the Black people the plant hired were all men, and the women it hired were all white. Moreover, both groups were hired for work associated with racial and gendered stereotypes: the Black men were hired for industrial work and the white women were hired for secretarial work. Crenshaw concluded, "Only if the court was able to see how these policies came together

---

105. https://science.sciencemag.org/content/357/6356/1101
106. https://medium.com/tech-diversity-files/if-you-think-women-in-tech-is-just-a-pipeline-problem-you-haven-t-been-paying-attention-cb7a2073b996
107. http://www.npr.org/sections/alltechconsidered/2013/05/01/178810710/How-One-College-Is-Closing-The-Tech-Gender-Gap
108. http://www.nytimes.com/2013/09/08/education/harvard-case-study-gender-equity.html
109. https://chicagounbound.uchicago.edu/cgi/viewcontent.cgi?referer=&httpsredir=1&article=1052&context=uclf
110. https://www.vox.com/the-highlight/2019/5/20/18542843/intersectionality-conservatism-law-race-gender-discrimination
111. https://www.ted.com/talks/kimberle_crenshaw_the_urgency_of_intersectionality?language=en

would he be able to see the double discrimination that [the Black woman] was facing."

Tokenism is the practice of hiring or appointing a small number of people from underrepresented groups to deflect criticism that a team lacks diversity. Efforts to fill roles in this way are perfunctory and symbolic.

Tokenism is a harmful practice that creates further barriers to the success of individuals from underrepresented groups, distorts the aims and intentions of D&I efforts, and perpetuates the notion that promoting diversity means lowering the hiring bar.§13.1

12 D&I in Hiring

Whether you work at a large company with a robust hiring processes already in place or you're a startup founder figuring out how to make your first technical hires, it's never too early to start thinking critically about diversity in hiring. You may be approaching this feeling out of depth and anxious—"I know it's a problem, but who am I to help solve it?" Or maybe you're thinking, "It seems like someone else's job." Or maybe you've seen past efforts to incorporate diversity and inclusion into hiring practices fail.

◇ IMPORTANT The principles behind effective recruiting with diversity in mind are the same as great recruiting, period. Lack of diversity in an organization signals a need for better recruiting practices. Hiring with diversity in mind is the most effective way to find and recruit talent to your team, because it will help you build a process that's better for everyone, while building toward a workplace that makes employees want to *stay*.

> ⊛ STORY "In 2015, the engineers of the still small, 25-person Lever team voiced their gripe about the hiring process. As was the norm at the time, our interviews were primarily focused on evaluating technical skills. Some of the veteran engineers started saying, 'If I were a candidate now, I don't know if I could pass our technical screens.' Hearing this from some of my most tenured, productive colleagues worried me. Behind their concern about the difficulty of the technical screen, I could hear their thinking: 'Am I valued here? Do I get con-

sidered as a full person, or just a code monkey?' If it were true that these employees couldn't pass our screen, what other great candidates might we be missing out on, and how would we even know it? We gradually improved our process, moving away from a sole focus on technical skills. We added an interview that focuses on communication, collaboration, and personal motivations. We doubled-down on interviewer training. We aimed to deliver a great experience for every single candidate, so that even rejected candidates ended up referring us to their friends.[112] A couple of years later, these changes to our process resulted in gender parity across the company of 100+ people, 42% in technical roles, and significant representation of Black, Latinx, and LGBTQ+ employees, as well as parents and caregivers, and a more supportive environment for everyone. The motivation wasn't, 'Let's build a diverse team'; it was 'Let's improve our process, because something's broken here.'" —Jennifer Kim, startup advisor and inclusion advocate

D&I is not like a new feature you can simply add to your existing platform. It will most likely require re-architecturing your system. Increasing focus on D&I is more akin to going from a monolith to microservices than adding a new text box to a user profile page. But there *are* strategies to get you started.

12.1 *It's Not Just a Pipeline Problem*

Every part of the tech ecosystem, from education through the hiring processes and the culture of companies, affects overall representation in the industry. And yet, tech companies often mark the "pipeline" as the biggest impediment to increasing diversity. This often manifests in a few different concerns:

- Not enough underrepresented candidates apply for tech jobs.
- Not enough underrepresented people graduate with STEM degrees.
- Underrepresented people are not interested in STEM or in tech jobs.

---

112. https://inside.lever.co/the-craziest-hiring-stories-part-1-72ab212b78ff

There's a lot going on here. There is no evidence that certain people are simply not interested in tech. But more notably, research indicates that the *idea* that certain people aren't interested is dangerous. Stereotype threat influences performance in STEM at a young age, particularly for women.

Stereotype threat is a psychological phenomenon that affects individuals' performance when they are reminded of negative ideas about groups to which they belong or are perceived to belong.[113,114] Researchers are still discussing the exact ways that stereotype threat causes underperformance, but hypothesized causes include extra pressure to succeed in the face of negative stereotypes, negative stereotypes threatening self-integrity and belonging, and individuals subconsciously conforming to stereotypes.[115]

The seminal 1995 study[117] on the topic found that "making African American participants vulnerable to judgment by negative stereotypes about their group's intellectual ability depressed their standardized test performance relative to [white] participants." Even asking participants to record their race had this effect. However, Black participants' performance matched white participants' when the study designers removed these reminders of group identification and stereotype.[118]

In the tech industry, stereotype threat can affect individuals from underrepresented groups on the basis of negative perceptions about those groups' performance in STEM. For example, women report that the negative stereotypes about them being bad at math, not belonging on a developer team, and so on, hurt their job performance in STEM roles.[120]

---

113. https://www.aauw.org/aauw_check/pdf_download/show_pdf.php?file=why-so-few-research
114. https://diversity.nih.gov/sociocultural-factors/stereotype-threat
115. Spencer, Steven J. et al. "Stereotype Threat."[116] *Annual Review of Psychology*, vol. 67, 2016, pp. 415–37, pp. 419–22.
116. https://www.semanticscholar.org/paper/Stereotype-Threat.-Spencer-Logel/3e976529f9db4eae82d18c79f2505148d68d3a64
117. https://www.semanticscholar.org/paper/Stereotype-threat-and-the-intellectual-test-of-Steele-Aronson/9a59663d46b27dd22991852552969c8d83801e88
118. Steele, Claude M. and Joshua Aronson. "Stereotype Threat and the Intellectual Test Performance of African Americans."[119] Journal of Personality and Social Psychology, vol. 69, no. 5, 1995, pp. 797–811.
119. https://www.semanticscholar.org/paper/Stereotype-threat-and-the-intellectual-test-of-Steele-Aronson/9a59663d46b27dd22991852552969c8d83801e88
120. https://open.buffer.com/talking-about-diversity/

Among other things, this can lead women to feel isolated, suffer from imposter syndrome, and work longer hours to demonstrate their worth, which in turn can lead to burnout[121]—all of which are factors that contribute to them leaving tech in larger numbers.

Stereotype threat may hurt underrepresented groups in the recruiting process, especially when elements of the process, such as being confronted with non-diverse interview teams, draw their attention to the stereotypes against their groups.[122]

When it comes to the number of underrepresented people graduating with STEM degrees, Forbes reported[124] that access to STEM programs early in education, rather than lack of interest, affects the number of these folks who choose degrees in the field:

> *"When looking at the number of students from underrepresented backgrounds taking AP computer science courses in the state of California, Black and Hispanic students make up 60% of California's student population, yet only 16% of the population taking AP computer science courses. These underrepresented groups are also less likely to have access to and exposure to computer science at home and elsewhere. These students often do not have role models that look like them in the computer science field."*

While 53.3% of men with STEM degrees are employed in STEM within two years, 41.4% of women are.[125] However, STEM is a broad field, and it can help to look more deeply at these numbers: engineering specifically employs 14% women, up just 2% since 1990, according to Pew.[126] The same study shows that the representation of Black engineers has risen 2% since 1990, from 7% to 9%, and Hispanic representation has risen 3%, from 4% to 7%. Compared to those groups' representation in the U.S. workforce as

---

121. https://sway.office.com/ukFi83Yi6JyEdpf8
122. Ashcraft, Catherine et al. *Women in Tech: The Facts*.[123] National Center for Women & Information Technology, May 2016, pp. 23, 31.
123. https://www.ncwit.org/sites/default/files/resources/womenintech_facts_fullreport_05132016.pdf
124. https://www.forbes.com/sites/janicegassam/2018/12/18/5-reasons-why-the-pipeline-problem-is-just-a-myth/#fbf604b227ac
125. https://www.rewire.org/our-future/men-women-stem-careers/
126. https://www.pewsocialtrends.org/2018/01/09/diversity-in-the-stem-workforce-varies-widely-across-jobs/

a whole, and their graduation rates with STEM degrees, they are vastly underrepresented in tech, while whites and Asians are overrepresented.[127]

Lack of representation is a big problem for underrepresented people at every stage of their education and careers. If your company or team is homogenous, they are less likely to apply and more likely to drop out of the field due to unfairness and isolation. The "leaky pipeline"[128] is often seen as the bigger problem; the number of underrepresented people leaving tech affects representation overall.

> "*Any student of color looking at the numbers from the tech giants is going to be turned off and wary about taking a job there because it tells you something about what the climate is. They don't want to be the token.*"
> — Maya A. Beasley,[129] sociologist and author of *Opting Out: Losing the Potential of America's Young Black Elite*[130]

With more people of all backgrounds earning degrees in tech, and representation in tech jobs staying relatively stagnant, how companies design the pipeline itself is one of the biggest issues. Overreliance on requirements like four-year degrees from the same few top schools, and on referrals from current employees, limits the number and kind of people considered "qualified" for technical roles. D&I can be approved by analyzing role requirements, improving other areas of the job description,§14.2 honing your company's value proposition,§37 and changing how your company talks about and characterizes its current make-up and D&I efforts.§9

Having a narrow definition of what great technical talent looks like makes hiring needlessly difficult. If you can break out of the traditional mold of hiring—based on pedigree, network, and traditional credentialing—you dramatically expand your pool of qualified candidates. This can

---

127. See the Pew study for details.
128. https://leakytechpipeline.com/
129. https://www.nytimes.com/2016/02/26/upshot/dont-blame-recruiting-pipeline-for-lack-of-diversity-in-tech.html
130. https://www.amazon.com/Opting-Out-Losing-Potential-Americas/dp/0226040143

give your company leverage in the hiring market,[131] where there are more open positions than there are engineers to fill them.

Not only does hiring with diversity in mind allow you to escape the escalating bidding wars for the Stanford-educated engineers or Google alumni, it's also an approach that leads to a better hiring process for *all* candidates. Actively designing for fairness and mitigating biases against underrepresented people makes for a more equitable process in general.

12.1.1 TALKING ABOUT THE PIPELINE MYTH

◇ IMPORTANT   The pipeline myth often comes up because teams have talked about diversity but haven't meaningfully changed their recruiting practices or focused on *retaining* URGs. One reason people are resistant to moving beyond diversity in their hiring is that diversity is easy to measure, but assessing inclusion is much trickier.

> *"Humans fixate on the idea that diversity is mostly a hiring problem for a number of reasons. First, it's difficult to perceive the ways in which we are programmed by systemic racism and sexism—so we say it must be an issue with the pipeline instead. Second, we are each the hero in our own story, and the work it takes to de-center ourselves and understand how we are complicit in perpetuating the norm is not something we're good at. We'd rather look at the mechanics and blame the machine, without understanding who built it in the first place and who maintains it."*
>
> — Jason Wong, leadership coach

---

131. According to the Stackoverflow 2019 Developer Survey,[132] which polled 90,000 developers worldwide, 19.6% of women surveyed (11.7% of the U.S. pool) ranked diversity as a priority in whether they would accept a job offer, and 32.9% of non-binary developers did (5.6% of men responded that "diversity of the company or organization" was a priority factor in taking a job—the lowest priority for the men surveyed, though the study was not broken down by race, ethnicity, or other factors). These are global numbers; we expect them to be higher in the U.S. alone, and we can certainly expect these numbers to increase in the coming years—talented people want to be part of diverse teams that foster inclusive environments; they know those teams are more likely to succeed. Companies that begin their efforts now will be at a huge advantage as these numbers increase.

132. https://insights.stackoverflow.com/survey/2019#job-priorities

In some ways, the focus on the pipeline can distract from the larger context of D&I. Getting URGs in the door isn't effective when you're not welcoming them to an environment in which they want to stay. People in leadership positions often insist on focusing just on increasing the number of URG candidates that move through the pipeline, even though those efforts have not resulted in better hiring policies or a more equitable environment in tech.

It can be hard to convince people that there is more going on.

> 🗉 STORY "A VC recently asked me how they can help their portfolio companies 'hire more diversity.' I encouraged thinking more holistically, such as exploring how leaders can build a more inclusive organization and make thoughtful improvements to their hiring process. They got frustrated and cut me off, 'No, no, you're describing culture, which is step 2. I need step 1, hiring. Tell me what job boards to post in.' I replied, 'Given the reality of the talent market, what you think is step 2 is actually step 1. Job seekers in tech have a lot of options. You can't do the lazy thing and expect to be successful. This is the case for top talent, but especially so for people from underrepresented backgrounds.'" —Jennifer Kim, startup advisor and inclusion advocate

⚠ CAUTION Many companies mistakenly believe that they can magically hire a certain number of URGs, upon which, the work will be done, and the "problem" will have been "fixed." This is in part due to the fact that companies disproportionately expect URGs to take on the work of diversity and inclusion.

> 🗉 STORY "One of the implications of a D&I program that only focuses on hiring is 'we don't know how to fix D&I, but if we hire enough URGs, they will know,' which—either intentionally or not—places the burden of fixing a noninclusive or even hostile environment directly on the people most impacted by it." —Ryn Daniels, Senior Software Engineer, HashiCorp

In trying to shift this at your own company, when talking with people who are focused on hiring at the expense of inclusion, it's helpful to recognize that it can be daunting to feel like you're starting a step beyond where you're at. Tackling the pipeline myth requires a mindset shift—it's less

Part II: Diversity and Inclusion 67

about what the company "gets" (hiring more URGs) and more about how everyone benefits from having a more welcoming, inclusive work environment. It is best to consider this an ongoing conversation, and to explain to resistant folks that companies need to commit to changing how they source candidates *and* put effort into creating a more inclusive work environment. Once people get over this initial hurdle, further improvements are much easier to make.

This list[133] from Matt Krentz and colleagues highlights that inclusion efforts are consistently ranked more important than traditional diversity measures by both URGs and white men.

12.2 *Avoiding Diversity Debt*

STARTUP You might be familiar with the concept of technical debt, which refers to having to make imperfect decisions during a product build, a result of having to make tradeoffs between short-term, quick fixes and long-term solutions. Teams often choose to focus on the short-term, knowing they'll have to pay down the debt later as the company or project scales. Similarly, companies need to be mindful of diversity debt, especially early on when it is easier to prevent or correct.

Diversity debt is the result of expanding a team without ensuring it is diverse. The more members of majority groups on a team, the more difficult it can be to recruit members of URGs and provide an inclusive culture.

Phin Barnes refers to[134] diversity debt as "the one startup debt you can't pay back." Homebrew, an early-stage VC, strongly encourages founders to start thinking about diversity early. We suggest reading their "Diversity at Startups" guide[135] if you're currently a founder or early employee.

If your engineering team is five people, most candidates from underrepresented backgrounds won't have too many hesitations about coming in as the first woman, first Black engineer, et cetera. They might even expect it. However, if diversity debt gets racked up to the point where you have a 50-person engineering team that is entirely white and Asian men, it will be very difficult to convince talented people from underrepresented

---

133. https://www.bcg.com/publications/2019/fixing-the-flawed-approach-to-diversity.aspx
134. https://sneakerheadvc.com/the-one-startup-debt-you-cant-pay-back-64dd7be7c930
135. https://quip.com/7GSaAovqAPEh

backgrounds to even interview. And that kind of homogeneity puts the long-term performance of the entire team at risk.

12.3 *Privilege and Allyship*

Privilege in the context of diversity and inclusion is a set of unearned benefits enjoyed by people who belong to particular social groups. Privilege can be a fraught topic because no single group has a monopoly on it—whiteness conveys privilege, maleness conveys privilege, ability conveys privilege, and so on—and because many are not aware of the privilege they have.

Acknowledging privilege can be uncomfortable, especially where overlapping systems of privilege are at play. But privilege is a critical concept in D&I work because it can help identify those with the social capital to effect change. It can also help to structure allyship relationships to ensure that less privileged voices are heard.

You may hear frustration or exasperation from some people, usually from the majority group, who say things like, "What do you want from me?" or "This isn't my problem." People who are not directly affected by inequity or don't see it in their daily lives often don't understand or accept that others have to work harder while facing discrimination, harassment, threats, or worse. When this is the case, people don't always feel like doing something about a problem they don't see—one they may not even believe is real. They may think this work should be relegated to those directly affected by bias and discrimination.

On the other hand, you might hear someone say, "I'm just a white dude. How can I help?" They're saying that they really don't feel prepared to address what they understand to be a deep and major issue, and they want to know where to start.

◇ IMPORTANT When it comes to moving the needle on D&I, cisgender[136] white men have an outsized impact on bringing about change. While they may not realize it, a vote of confidence or reaffirmation of belonging from someone in this group carries more influence than from anyone else. This is true at every level of your organization, from your C-suite down to your most junior employee.

---

136. https://en.wikipedia.org/wiki/Cisgender

When someone expresses that they don't know what to do, or that they don't feel that doing anything is their responsibility, it helps to frame the situation as benefiting everyone. Even though it may not seem like it, everyone is affected by bias and discrimination. When members of a team don't feel supported or included, everyone's work suffers, and so do the people they see every day. Eventually, those people are going to leave too. If candidates you're trying to get to join the team don't feel supported or included, they're going to choose another company. By contrast, in a productive environment, everyone wants to make the team better, and that means supporting the needs of teammates *and* all of your candidates.

12.3.1 BEING AN ALLY

An **ally** is an individual who uses their privilege to advocate on behalf of someone who does not have that same privilege. Anyone can be an ally—a member of the majority group contributing to inclusion work, a white woman to women of color, a cisgender person to transgender people, an able-bodied person to people with disabilities, and so on. **Allyship** is the process of acting as an ally. Because it is a process, rather than a conclusion, allyship requires ongoing learning, development, and effort from the privileged individual.

> **CONFUSION** To highlight the importance of taking action, some prefer terms like *accomplice* to the term *ally*.[137]

Allyship is key because D&I is often misunderstood to be "a women's issue" or "just for minorities to do something about," failing to take into account the fact that D&I leads to better outcomes for everyone. One of the markers of effective D&I is when privileged allies start taking up the cause because they see themselves as part of the larger community.

> **CAUTION** Being an ally is a practice—something you do every day to support underrepresented people. Doing research and unpacking your own privilege is part of the work. It is not about getting praise for being a savior or fixing other people's problems for them. And, like any new skill, you won't get it right the first time.

---

137. https://diverseeducation.com/article/138623/

Allyship behaviors include self-education, maintaining awareness of the issues that affect the day-to-day lives of the URGs in your organization, and amplification and endorsement of the achievements and concerns brought forward by underrepresented groups in their organization. In practice, these are small everyday actions like ensuring the voices of URGs are heard in meetings, affirming the technical difficulty[138] of a completed project, or speaking up when witnessing discriminatory or exclusionary behavior. Allyship requires an ability to center the experiences of those impacted, rather than majority group experiences—including providing help and support in the ways that URGs have indicated they would like to receive it.

> **STORY** A good starting point is to find ways to listen to URGs. Allies can do this through diversifying who they follow on social media,[139] joining online groups or Slack channels where diversity and inclusion issues are discussed, or attending a D&I meetup in their local area. Learn how to participate in conversations without speaking—learn how to listen. When you hear something you disagree with, don't automatically gear up for an argument, just make a note about it and keep listening. When you hear something that you object to or that runs counter to your intuition and experiences, don't hop into the fray, don't go ask the URGs in your network to explain it. Do the work to educate yourself. Get curious and Google it.[141] The point of this is not to change your opinion or convince you of one perspective or the other. You're learning how to de-center yourself and work toward an awareness of the issues that affect URGs. The goal is to develop an ability to recognize the moments in your day when an inequity happens so that you can take action to correct it. More often than not, that action will be nothing more than a small kindness—redirecting the conversation back to someone who was cut off, ensuring work was properly attributed, providing a public endorsement, inviting someone to participate in a meeting. —Jason Wong, leadership coach

---

138. https://twitter.com/mekkaokereke/status/1027552459873378304
139. You can check the diversity of your Twitter feed using the tool #Diversifyyourfeed.[140]
140. https://www.diversifyyourfeed.org/
141. https://www.google.com/search?client=firefox-b-1-d&q=what+can+i+do+about+diversity+and+inclusion+as+a+white+dude

◇ IMPORTANT When it comes to hiring, steps you can take include listening for biased statements like, "She was too aggressive"; intervening when a hiring panel suggests adding on additional evaluation tests for URGs that no other candidate was subjected to; and trying to help candidates succeed.[§30.5]

⚠ DANGER Allyship is especially critical because research has shown that underrepresented groups are often penalized in the workplace for promoting diversity.[142] It's people from marginalized backgrounds who can see the ways the system fails them, but they often lack the power to make changes without taking on significant risk. Gaslighting,[143] retaliation, and labeling (like being called a "troublemaker") are common.

Allyship acknowledges that it is risky for URGs to help each other. In a recent academic study,[144] participants were asked to rate a fictitious manager's competence in hiring decisions after reading a description of a hiring decision and being shown a photo of the manager that revealed their race and gender. They found the following:

> "Participants rated nonwhite managers and female managers as less effective when they hired a nonwhite or female job candidate instead of a white male candidate. It didn't matter whether white male managers chose to hire a white male, white female, nonwhite male, or nonwhite female—there was no difference in how participants rated their competence and performance. Basically, all managers were judged harshly if they hired someone who looked like them, unless they were a white male."

In addition to being risky, diversity and inclusion work often falls into a category of work with no promotion track and is handed off as a set of responsibilities on top of someone's primary job. It is neither fair nor effective to ask people disadvantaged by the system—people who are historically underpaid relative to their white male peers—to be the ones charged with the bulk of the effort to fix that system.[145] Success in building a diverse team requires allies to help shoulder the burden.

---

142. https://hbr.org/2016/03/women-and-minorities-are-penalized-for-promoting-diversity
143. https://medium.com/@c0d3rgirl/gaslighting-in-the-workplace-5f44d439ca21
144. https://hbr.org/2016/03/women-and-minorities-are-penalized-for-promoting-diversity
145. https://inclusionatwork.co/obligated-to-di/

> 📖 STORY "At my last startup, some of the biggest champions of diversity were cisgender white male engineers, especially because many had been so used to homogeneity of technical teams. They said, 'It's just so much better here—there's a real culture around collaboration and thoughtful communication; I feel like we're better at supporting learning and making mistakes better here.' Having experienced the benefits of a diverse team firsthand, they said it's something they would prioritize in future job searches. In the meantime, they wanted to know how they could use their privilege to help me and the rest of the team with diversity efforts. I felt like they were really getting it, that at the end of the day, it's really about becoming better humans, not just more effective employees." —Jennifer Kim, startup advisor and inclusion advocate

12.3.2 FURTHER READING ON ALLYSHIP

- "Demystifying how to be a male ally"[146] (Better Male Allies)
- Guide to Allyship[147] (Open-source project by Amélie Lamont)
- Valerie Aurora of Frame Shift Consulting has done great work in the area; check out the Ally Skills Workshop[148]
- "Being an Effective Ally to Women and Non-Binary People"[149] (Toria Gibbs and Ian Malpass)

13 D&I Myths and Pitfalls

Given the wealth of data and well-established arguments for why D&I matters for businesses, why haven't hiring and inclusivity practices caught up? Often, hiring managers and other company leaders face multiple and sometimes conflicting priorities and constraints, and it's easy for companies that lack diversity in leadership to pay less attention to problems they don't see as impacting them directly. Even when a company of any stage or size makes the choice to improve, it is not easy to change systems that

---

146. https://medium.com/@betterallies/demystifying-how-to-be-a-male-ally-11f2eb08ee9c
147. http://www.guidetoallyship.com/
148. https://frameshiftconsulting.com/ally-skills-workshop/
149. https://codeascraft.com/2016/10/19/being-an-effective-ally-to-women-and-non-binary-people/

have been in place for so long, and it's often difficult to figure out who exactly is in charge of inventing and enforcing new policies.

Many of us understand the benefits of D&I and want to move forward, but we don't always know where to begin. Dismantling common myths and pitfalls around D&I is a good place to start.[150] (In fact, we already tackled one of the most common: "it's a pipeline problem."[§12.1]) As you seek to create a more inclusive hiring process, unpacking these myths and pitfalls can help make sure your actions are impactful and long-lasting, as opposed to performative, shallow, and misdirected. As with any organizational change, you *will* encounter pushback from many possible directions. Members of your team may take exception, your peers may question the efficacy of your new hiring proposals, you may uncover hidden racist, sexist, and ableist sentiment in your C-suite.

This is expected. Your greatest tool on this journey will be a strong sense of humility and an ability to focus on the experiences of marginalized groups.

It may be useful to refer to the following sections in the moment, when you hear one of these myths or misunderstandings in a hiring huddle. You can also share them with your team to set everyone up with the same baseline of knowledge and understanding. It is likely, too, that you'll have to have these conversations many times in different ways; it often takes people some time to unpack why they are reflexively against improving diversity and inclusion. As a hiring manager, you can help improve your retention rates and the quality of your hires by helping your team understand how they can work to foster a work environment that is welcoming and supportive of all.

13.1 *"We don't want to lower the hiring bar."*

When you hear people say this or "I know I need more diversity on my team, but I'm also supposed to hire the best person," it tells you that either they believe the hiring process would elevate unqualified candidates *just*

---

150. It may be worth mentioning that the most common myths will likely change in the coming years, as collective consciousness around D&I continues to rise. Just a few years ago, for example, a popular excuse used to pay women less was, "John has a wife and kids to support, but Joan doesn't!" You're unlikely to hear this myth today, and in a few more years, we will (hopefully) see some of today's common myths all but disappear.

because they're underrepresented, or they believe diversity efforts in general are equated with lower quality—or both.

13.1.1 THE BASICS

While the intention here may be one of concern for the quality of your organization, this statement implies[151] an underlying belief that the average performance of minorities across gender and race is less than the overall mean—that you must choose between having a high performing engineering organization and opening your doors to URGs. This belief reflects conscious or unconscious biases: the phrase reflects the thinking that "underrepresented" means "not as competent."

Laura Weidman Powers picks apart this phrase word by word in a post we highly recommend,[152] where she points out "the implication in that statement [is] that you have to defend yourself against others who want you to lower the bar." No one, least of all hiring managers, wants a process that's going to lead to a poor candidate-company fit. D&I efforts *combat* lazy hiring based on pattern-matching and kinship, which favor a limited set of experiences. D&I raises the bar.[153]

> *"We found that the engineers who are excited about the fact that we are trying to recruit women and that we have that as a value—men or women—are the people we actually want to be hiring. The men who come into our organization who are excited about the fact that we have diversity as a goal are generally the people who are better at listening, they're better at group learning, they're better at collaboration, they're better at communication. They're particularly the people you want to be your engineering managers and your technical leads."*
> — Kellan Elliott-McCrea, Dropbox[154]

---

151. https://www.kateheddleston.com/blog/improving-diversity-does-not-mean-lowering-the-bar
152. https://www.linkedin.com/pulse/what-youre-really-saying-when-you-talk-lowering-bar-weidman-powers/
153. https://medium.com/inclusion-insights/want-to-hire-more-diverse-people-raise-your-bar-b5d30f91cbd9
154. https://www.theatlantic.com/technology/archive/2013/02/etsy-cto-prioritizing-diversity-in-our-hiring-fielded-better-women-and-men/272969/

If a team member says something like, "We don't want to lower the hiring bar," here's one way to respond: "Diversity is an indicator of great hiring taking place. If our team is homogenous, it means we're over-relying on shallow signals like pedigrees. We don't want our hiring process to favor candidates that confirm our existing biases. Recruiting from more diverse pools of talent forces us as a company to make improvements at all stages of the process, from attracting candidates, to evaluations, to closing. It will help us reduce problematic biases and develop a muscle around making thoughtful hiring decisions."

> "If we juxtapose all the data we now have about the business benefits of diversity next to the demographic composition of our engineering teams, the real question we need to grapple with is whether or not we ever had a clue about what an effective engineering organization was."
>
> — Jason Wong, leadership coach

13.1.2 GOING DEEPER

◇ CAUTION Concerns about lowering the hiring bar might come up when a hiring manager or leader institutes hiring mandates, whereby a certain number of new hires must be from underrepresented groups to reach goals set by the company or team. Mandates can impact a team's sense of choice and fairness, but it's not always so simple. If your organization is falling short of its diversity hiring goals, this approach involves some sort of hard stance on who will get the spotlight in the next hiring round. Mandates might seem like the only means available at the moment, but being successful in building a diverse workforce requires a holistic approach. It can be useful to ask yourself:

- How often do you talk about the importance of a diverse workforce for the business?^{§10}
- What ways have you communicated the benefits$^{§10.3}$ of working with folks from different backgrounds?
- Have you defined what successful hiring is to your organization?
- How are you educating your team about fair and equitable interviewing and evaluation techniques?$^{§14.4}$
- What are you doing to make your organization attractive and welcoming to underrepresented groups?$^{§12.1}$

Mandates may solve your immediate goals for the next few hires, but can hurt those new employees, who may be treated as a token by their peers and potentially exposed to an unwelcoming environment once they're through the door. Ultimately, they are unlikely to stay. True success is understanding and addressing the conditions creating passivity or resistance on this issue among your employees and within yourself.

That said, it's worth noting that mandates correlate with effective change in some cases. In 2002, France enacted parity laws which mandated that each party had to field an equal number of men and women.[155] This led to the National Assembly going from 10.9% women to 39%. Title IX in the United States is another great example. Prior to 1974, fewer than 300,000 women participated in high school sports. Today, there are over 3.1 million.[156] While we can't ignore these leaps in progress, these directives were not complete solutions. Unless you're looking to create an organization that's an ever-revolving door for underrepresented people, you will need to do the hard work of changing your workplace norms in order to reap the benefits of a diverse workforce.

13.2 *"We believe people should be hired on their merits."*

Similar phrases include, "Our hiring process is fair" and "We're a meritocracy."

13.2.1 THE BASICS

While talent is evenly distributed, opportunity is not. Many URGs face barriers that people from majority groups do not. They don't receive as many referrals, they get passed over for promotions, and they get paid less, to name just a few. They often have to work twice as hard or more to get the same level of recognition, while facing continued barriers like harassment and discrimination. The merit myth is a particularly difficult one to address, because you don't want to make anyone feel that they don't deserve what they've worked for, as you work to help more privileged people recognize the barriers URGs face. But this myth can be so harmful to individuals and teams that it's critical to take steps to address it.

---

155. https://www.brookings.edu/articles/french-women-in-politics-the-long-road-to-parity/
156. https://www.womenssportsfoundation.org/education/title-ix-and-the-rise-of-female-athletes-in-america/

Part II: Diversity and Inclusion

The belief that people get where they are based on individual effort alone —hard work—rather than by a combination of hard work, talent, circumstance, support, and luck, is particularly pervasive in the U.S.[157] Faced with the kind of pressure and uncertainty that hiring presents, the idea of meritocracy has become a common mindset in tech. Believing (and being told) that those who work hard can get ahead gives us some temporary comfort that there's a sense of fairness built into the system that we all "get what we deserve."

But it isn't a benign belief. Companies that believe in the myth of meritocracy—that people who try hard and are qualified are the ones who get the job offers, the corner offices, and the big paychecks—are more likely to find themselves in trouble,[158] as they won't be as vigilant about looking out for biases and making constant process improvements as the organization grows. Studies have shown that even believing in the idea of meritocracy increases discriminatory behaviors and biased beliefs.[159]

13.2.2 GOING DEEPER

◇ IMPORTANT   The term *meritocracy* was coined by sociologist Michael Dunlop Young to warn against the privileged class justifying their success and disenfranchising others. It is satire.[160]

---

157. https://www.pewresearch.org/global/2014/10/09/emerging-and-developing-economies-much-more-optimistic-than-rich-countries-about-the-future/pg_14-09-04_usindividualism_640-px/
158. https://www.theatlantic.com/business/archive/2015/12/meritocracy/418074/
159. https://www.fastcompany.com/40510522/meritocracy-doesnt-exist-and-believing-it-does-is-bad-for-you
160. https://kottke.org/17/03/the-satirical-origins-of-the-meritocracy

> "The tech industry tends to value metrics and being 'rational' above all else, but it would also serve us well to remember that hiring is an inherently human activity. That's why it's so hard and will never be completely solved. Every individual is a rich combination of their skills, values, life experiences, and background. There is no way we can make truly objective, rational decisions without our own biases coming into play. One of the most important things you can do is to acknowledge those biases, because then (and only then) can you make meaningful, ongoing improvements to your hiring process that result in a stellar team."
>
> — Jennifer Kim, startup advisor and inclusion advocate[161]

You might notice that people saying things like "our hiring process is fair" are usually—though not always—from the majority group. People from the majority groups often benefit from biased systems, which makes them less likely to examine their own privilege and more likely to assume that the system is fair. However, people from majority groups are not the ones who can properly determine whether a system is fair or not.

Some people who hold these beliefs might say things like, "There are laws that protect people from discrimination, so it doesn't happen anymore," or "This is a legal thing, legal people will sort it out." Laws are often more punitive than preventative, and by the time a company or manager is held accountable for discrimination (if at all), the damage has been done. And it's important to note that the law does not protect against all kinds of discrimination; businesses today can still legally discriminate against transgender employees without violating federal law.[162]

13.2.3 FURTHER READING ON THE MERITOCRACY MYTH

- Is tech a meritocracy?[163]
- John Scalzi on privilege[164]

---

161. https://twitter.com/jenistyping/status/1153670803268853760?s=20
162. https://www.nytimes.com/2017/10/05/us/politics/transgender-civil-rights-act-justice-department-sessions.html
163. https://istechameritocracy.com/
164. https://whatever.scalzi.com/2012/05/15/straight-white-male-the-lowest-difficulty-setting-there-is/

13.3 *"What about ideological diversity?"*

You might also hear someone say, "What about diversity of thought, isn't that more important than what people look like?" or "Doesn't my opinion matter anymore?"

13.3.1 THE BASICS

Ideological diversity (or diversity of thought) is the presence of diverging viewpoints, especially political viewpoints, in a group of people. Measuring ideological diversity can be useful in circumstances where this heterogeneity affects behavior or outcomes.[165]

It's hard to look at a definition like that and think "diversity of thought" would be a bad thing. It's not! Inviting underrepresented people to sit at the table and giving them a microphone brings different viewpoints to an industry that has historically heard only a limited set of ideas in a feedback loop.

It's important not to conflate ideological diversity with diversity related to the immutable traits that define so much of individuals' lived experiences. It is also necessary to question the motives of the person who insists that "diversity of thought" *has nothing to do* with increasing representation in the industry.

> " *'Diversity of Thought' should be achieved as a result of diverse representation.*"
>
> — Michelle Kim, co-founder and CEO, Awaken[167]

13.3.2 GOING DEEPER

⚠ CAUTION Language doesn't exist in a vacuum. The phrase "diversity of thought" has a history, and that history is racist and misogynistic.[168] Of course not everyone who's ever asked the question is operating within

---

165. For example, a 2010 study sought to measure how elected representatives behave when they have more or less ideologically diverse constituencies. Levendusky, Matthew S. and Jeremy C. Pope. "Measuring Aggregate-Level Ideological Heterogeneity."[166] *Legislative Studies Quarterly*, vol. 35, no. 2, 2010, pp. 259–82.
166. https://cpb-us-w2.wpmucdn.com/web.sas.upenn.edu/dist/5/522/files/2016/10/lsq_heterogeneity-2ficzpv.pdf
167. https://medium.com/awaken-blog/diversity-of-thought-without-diverse-representation-is-just-status-quo-e1ae56edda74
168. https://www.theringer.com/2017/3/16/16040282/lexicon-ideological-diversity-buzzword-mark-zuckerberg-inclusivity-dbc9aff10613

those ideologies, but it may help those confused by the difference to learn a bit about how and why the phrase has been used in disingenuous ways to actively counteract D&I efforts within an organization. A notable tech industry example of the "diversity of thought" argument, in fact, comes from James Damore's infamous manifesto against diversifying Google.[169]

⚠ DANGER "Ideological diversity" and "diversity of thought" are often used as dog whistles[170] by individuals who have deliberately co-opted the language of diversity and inclusion, placing extreme conservative ideology on equal footing with systemic oppression based on race, gender, sexual orientation, and so on. They express feeling silenced and oppressed for their particular beliefs, a cousin to the idea of "reverse racism." In this case, "ideological diversity" is a cover for espousing racist or sexist beliefs.

Without assuming anything about the person using these phrases, but still being aware that they may be operating with anti-D&I sentiments, a useful question to ask is whether or not the ideological diversity argument is being used as a way to diminish or dilute the concerns of URGs.

◇ IMPORTANT But also, it is critical to be clear about where you are drawing the line. Your employees should feel free to express their views and beliefs as long as they are not harming others, and *the arbiter of harm is the people being impacted*. While this may sound unfair, it is the default for everyone who is not part of a majority group. If there were ever a time to say "when you are accustomed to privilege, equality feels like oppression,"[171] this would be it.

13.4 *"Is it legal to consider race and gender in hiring?"*

You might also hear, "Isn't this reverse sexism/racism/-ism?"

In some cases with these kinds of comments, people genuinely want to know what's allowed and what's not. But they may also be trying to get around any action the company is proposing, or they might be on the defensive. They may be afraid that their place in the company is at risk.

---

169. https://www.theroot.com/diversity-of-thought-is-just-a-euphemism-for-white-supr-18251918 39
170. https://en.wikipedia.org/wiki/Dog-whistle_politics
171. https://quoteinvestigator.com/2016/10/24/privilege/

13.4.1 THE BASICS

In the U.S., it is illegal to discriminate against an employee on account of certain immutable traits such as their race, color, religion, sex, or age.

The Equal Employment Opportunity Commission, a U.S. federal agency, encourages employers to take steps to address barriers to equality in employment. In its Compliance Manual[172] and Guidelines on Affirmative Action,[173] the EEOC specifically notes that employers may engage in efforts "to overcome the effects of past or present practices, policies, or other barriers to equal employment opportunity."[174] This may even go as far as establishing quotas for URGs, but employers should be aware that courts may see quotas as evidence of illegal discrimination in a diversity program. Other considerations include "whether the plan is flexible enough so that each candidate competes against all other qualified candidates, whether the plan unnecessarily trammels the interests of third parties, and whether the action is temporary, e.g., not designed to continue after the plan's goal has been met."[177]

For employers seeking to improve diversity, the law specifically carves out at least limited protection to correct manifest imbalances.

Manifest imbalance is a state of affairs in which a protected class[179] is drastically underrepresented in a particular workplace compared to its representation in the employable workforce.

---

172. https://www.eeoc.gov/policy/docs/race-color.pdf
173. https://www.govinfo.gov/content/pkg/CFR-2018-title29-vol4/xml/CFR-2018-title29-vol4-part1608.xml
174. *Compliance Manual.*[175] Equal Employment Opportunity Commission, April 2006, p. 15-32; *Affirmative Action Appropriate Under Title VII of the Civil Rights Act of 1964, as Amended,*[176] Equal Employment Opportunity Commission, Code of Federal Regulations, July 2018, §1608.1(c).
175. https://www.eeoc.gov/policy/docs/race-color.pdf
176. https://www.govinfo.gov/content/pkg/CFR-2018-title29-vol4/xml/CFR-2018-title29-vol4-part1608.xml
177. *Compliance Manual.*[178] Equal Employment Opportunity Commission, April 2006, p. 15-32.
178. https://www.eeoc.gov/policy/docs/race-color.pdf
179. https://content.next.westlaw.com/5-501-5857?transitionType=Default&contextData=(sc.Default)&firstPage=true&bhcp=1

⚠ DANGER Always remember to consult an attorney about these sorts of legal questions. Not only are there various restrictions—for example, efforts cannot "trammel on the rights" of members of the majority group[180]—but this is a developing area of law.[181]

13.4.2 GOING DEEPER

It's possible that this question isn't asked in earnest, but as a defense mechanism or even a mocking of D&I proposals.

It is a testament to the power of normalization that we do not question the legality of hiring another white man[184] onto an already predominantly white male team in a predominantly white male industry—we have merely accepted that what exists today is nothing out of the ordinary. However, it is not out of the ordinary to be questioned about the legality of broadening our horizons to consider hiring URGs—this is where you hear folks throw around terms like "reverse-sexism" or "reverse-racism." But if we take a step back and look at who is and who isn't on our teams, anyone would be hard pressed to conclude that it is men who are being discriminated against in our industry.

13.5 "Our next hire must be diverse."

When you hear someone say, "Our next hire must be diverse" or "We need to hire five more women and two people of color to have more diversity," it's usually said with good intentions. People are trying to be mindful of diversity debt and are determined to not make the problem worse. But this way of looking at D&I may do more harm than good.

---

180. https://www.pepperlaw.com/resource/32692/25C0
181. Some have argued that a recent U.S. Supreme Court case has undermined the foundation on which this protection for correcting manifest imbalances rests. See, for example: Clegg, Roger. "The Court after Scalia: What a conservative successor to Justice Scalia would mean for 'affirmative action.'"[182] SCOTUSblog, 31 Aug. 2016; Pandya, Sachin S. "Detecting the Stealth Erosion of Precedent: Affirmative Action After Ricci."[183] Berkeley Journal of Employment & Labor Law, vol. 31, no. 2, 2010, pp. 285–332.
182. https://www.scotusblog.com/2016/08/the-court-after-scalia-what-a-conservative-successor-to-justice-scalia-would-mean-for-affirmative-action/
183. https://scholarship.law.berkeley.edu/cgi/viewcontent.cgi?article=1424&context=bjell
184. https://chelseatroy.com/2018/04/12/why-your-efforts-to-fix-your-pipeline-arent-fixing-your-pipeline/

13.5.1 THE BASICS

Talented people of all different backgrounds want to be given a fair opportunity to succeed based on their skills and aptitude. Demanding that your next hire must be a member of one URG or another can lead them to be referred to (or thought of) as the "diversity candidate."

13.5.2 GOING DEEPER

First, let's clarify some language. Saying "our next hire must be diverse" is problematic in part because *diverse* is a quality of a group and does not describe individual people. This may sound pedantic, but misusing this term has real ramifications, including tokenism, stereotype threat, impostor syndrome,[185] and inequities that affect performance and contribute to the high leave rate among URGs in tech.

If your team has been saying "our next hire must be a woman or person of color," even if you do end up successfully hiring a stellar URG candidate, they may always wonder whether they wouldn't have gotten the job otherwise. And so may their colleagues. This may lead to resentment and defensiveness among the rest of your team, especially if you haven't yet developed a shared understanding around D&I. Likewise, if a hiring manager gets blocked from hiring someone from the majority group, they may perceive the process to be unfair, and hold a grudge against the person who does eventually get hired.

◇ CAUTION Focusing only on outwardly apparent difference limits the scope and effectiveness of any inclusivity program the company might develop, and can itself be discriminatory. Such a focus also neglects to see individuals as their fully complex selves.

13.6 *"Let's focus on hiring women first."*

You might also hear, "How do we hire women?"

A common misunderstanding is that one kind of representation equals diversity and that D&I only matters in hiring. An employee or boss who has a more PR-centric approach to D&I might think that because media attention often focuses on gender imbalance, that's where attention should be paid to avoid earning a bad reputation.

---

185. https://en.wikipedia.org/wiki/Impostor_syndrome

13.6.1 THE BASICS

This is one of the most common pitfalls for teams starting on diversity and inclusion efforts. Even when well intended, the "women-first" approach may lead to nothing getting tackled at the root cause, and surface-level solutions can actually have the opposite effect of reinforcing existing inequities. For example, the common advice for professional women to "lean in" tends to favor white women and actually punishes women of color who face additional barriers to equity, like being labeled too aggressive. "Hire more women" policies often reinforce the same inequities,[186] where white, wealthy women are the primary beneficiaries.

13.6.2 GOING DEEPER

Effective D&I is not simply about "checking the boxes" on one demographic, especially because your hiring processes could still be biased against other marginalized groups. In that case, any gains or benefits you see are not likely to be sustainable. To develop hiring policies that support *all* marginalized people, it's helpful to use intersectionality as a framework.

Programs that lack an intersectional approach can fall short of achieving the goals of D&I, instead benefitting a single group like white women at the cost of other underrepresented groups.[187] This can lead to its own diversity debt, continued poor outcomes for many groups, and frustration and fatigue with D&I efforts that are perceived as ineffective.

So when you hear this pitfall, a possible response might be, "Let's take a more intersectional approach and build a hiring process for not just women but all underrepresented people to thrive."[188]

---

186. https://medium.com/awaken-blog/intersectionality-101-why-were-focusing-on-women-does n-t-work-for-diversity-inclusion-8f591d196789
187. https://medium.com/projectinclude/true-diversity-is-intersectional-2282b8da8882
188. https://twitter.com/jenistyping/status/1085952817120960512

13.7 *"We don't have the time or resources to prioritize D&I."*

This comes up a lot, at all levels and stages of a company.

STARTUP At startups you might hear things like, "We don't have the luxury to focus on this right now" or "There will be time for this later; we have to figure out the business first." Or with even more urgency, "I'd love to think about diversity, but right now we need someone yesterday."

If you're at a larger company, you might hear something like this: "It's too late for us to build a diverse team."

13.7.1 THE BASICS

Many companies still see D&I as a nice-to-have and not an integral ingredient to success. "Diversity fatigue"[189] and the feeling of being overwhelmed are also sources here, for both small and large companies. When people don't know where to start, they might just decide to give up. Often, a fixation on diversity numbers as the end goal is the culprit.

At the same time, we are seeing how costly diversity debt can be. From founders being ousted,[190] to millions lost in employee productivity,[191] or talent drains,[192] or lost revenue and costs to the economy,[193] and even the complete collapse of companies,[194] deprioritizing D&I carries significant risk.

When someone voices this concern (or if you're feeling it yourself!), you might say, "I appreciate that this is a concern. I know how hard this can seem. But we're not going to focus on perfection here. We can change our goals and redefine success to focus on progress."

Another tactic is to say, "Let's consider the costs of inaction." You can point your employees or bosses to the data on the increased profitability and productivity of diverse teams.§10.3 But if painting a picture of D&I done

---

189. https://medium.com/smells-like-team-spirit/the-diversity-fatigue-is-real-atlassians-state-of-diversity-report-2018-2655d7eb5e2c
190. https://www.theguardian.com/technology/2017/jun/20/uber-ceo-travis-kalanick-resigns; https://bits.blogs.nytimes.com/2014/04/21/github-founder-resigns-after-investigation/
191. https://www.nytimes.com/2018/11/01/technology/google-walkout-sexual-harassment.html
192. https://www.bloomberg.com/news/articles/2018-02-12/here-s-what-happens-to-a-startup-after-a-sexual-harassment-scandal
193. https://work.qz.com/1224023/a-lack-of-diversity-isnt-just-a-social-problem-it-hurts-firms-profits/
194. https://www.bizjournals.com/sanfrancisco/news/2017/06/28/binary-capital-shutdown.html

well doesn't motivate people, it might be worth trying the opposite tactic. "We don't want to be the next Uber" can be surprisingly effective in getting different folks to pay attention. Companies have to consider not only the competitive disadvantage created by not acting, but also the higher risk of incurring an incident that will cost them something tangible—whether it be productivity,[195] shareholder value,[196] or the company itself.[197]

13.7.2 GOING DEEPER

🚀 STARTUP   If you're at a smaller or newer company, one crucial way to gain a competitive edge against other startups and larger companies is by hiring a diverse team and ensuring all of your employees are in it for the long term. The data are conclusive:[§10.3] diverse and inclusive companies have better products, more stability, and higher revenue. When someone says, "We can't afford this right now," an appropriate response is: "Can we afford not to?" Remember that the longer you put off D&I efforts, the more diversity debt you rack up, and the harder it is to get started.

Is building a diverse team harder when you're starting with a larger team? Yes. But there will never be an easier time to start than right now. There is no point of no return.[198] If your team or company has already incurred diversity debt, paying it down won't happen overnight. But the goal doesn't have to be achieving perfect parity or representation, especially for large, established teams for whom it will take many years. The goal is to make meaningful progress from wherever your starting point is today. And you can start making improvements by acknowledging blind spots and attempting to better understand the impact of your processes and decisions moving forward. You may wish to review how to set D&I goals.[§14.1] It's OK to start small if necessary.

---

195. https://www.nytimes.com/2018/11/01/technology/google-walkout-sexual-harassment.html
196. https://www.vanityfair.com/news/2017/06/travis-kalanick-resignation-from-uber
197. https://www.forbes.com/sites/nathanvardi/2019/02/28/founders-of-silicon-valley-firm-that-imploded-amid-sex-harassment-allegations-are-now-fighting-each-other
198. https://inclusionatwork.co/the-point-of-no-return/

14 Improving D&I in the Hiring Process

Jennifer Kim compares[199] underrepresented talent to the canaries in the coalmine— whatever biases exist in your hiring process, certain groups will feel them before others do. But just because they're the first to notice (and potentially the first to be harmed), doesn't mean they'll be the last. Hiring with diversity in mind isn't just about whom you let in at the top of the funnel—there are many pitfalls throughout the hiring process that can create an unfair or hostile environment. There are also many opportunities in that process for improving diversity and inclusion at your company, for current *and* future employees. There are a number of straightforward strategies and tactics you can employ as a hiring manager to make sure your team is hiring the best people out there and creating the kind of environment that will make them want to stay.

An important part of hiring with diversity and inclusion in mind is planning ahead. Many companies have an unstructured default where lack of foresight routinely catches them scrambling to fill one-off roles, and recruiting remains a stop-and-go effort.

When faced with constant firefighting, hiring becomes about "Who is available now? Who can we hire easily and quickly?" This is not a favorable environment for an underrepresented candidate. And while there's nothing wrong with scrambling once in a while to fill an unforeseen business-critical opening, if this is your group's default strategy, you'll end up with a team built of those who were easiest for you to hire—those you already know, who were available. To raise the hiring bar, you'll need to plan your hiring processes in advance. This section will help you do so with a focus on making that process more effective, and more inclusive for everyone.

14.1 *Setting Goals*

When Google released its diversity data in 2014, it led to a flurry of more big tech companies releasing theirs and promising to do better with bold targets—like reaching certain demographic percentages. Companies

---

199. https://twitter.com/jenistyping/status/1130661935387729921

largely missed these goals,[200, 201] because it is incredibly difficult to change the demographics of organizations that are already in the many thousands.[202] While the data helped to raise awareness, releasing it wasn't a solution.[204] Companies that initially championed diversity reports have since delayed releasing these reports on schedule, or stopped altogether.[206, 207]

◇ CAUTION Looking only at how many URGs are hired can lead to misaligned incentives, where recruiters and teams think they need to beef up their numbers just to look good. Facebook, for example, instituted a policy by which recruiters were given "diversity points" when they brought in "someone who was a woman, or who was not white or Asian."[209] This initiative failed, in large part because those charged with making hiring decisions felt that the company had done enough by offloading responsibilities to recruiters and asking them to broaden the pipeline. Even if Facebook had hired a significant number of underrepresented engineers, having "good" diversity numbers does not mean those numbers will last, particularly if there are no efforts at improving inclusion at the company.

---

200. https://www.wsj.com/articles/facebook-blames-lack-of-available-talent-for-diversity-problem-1468526303
201. https://www.wsj.com/articles/google-makes-slow-progress-in-diversifying-its-workforce-1467330849?mod=article_inline
202. Success can be found at the team level in larger companies. Mekka Okereke, an Engineering Director at Google, has built an engineering team that, in 2019, is 10% Black; women make up 50% of his tech leads 40% of his managers, and 40% of all engineers on his team. He's done this by following the principle of creating an organization where, "hard working, talented, collaborative people from any background can succeed and thrive."[203]
203. https://www.recallact.com/presentation/building-inclusive-engineering-teams
204. A 2018 study conducted by Atlassian[205] found that while 80% of respondents agree that D&I is important, the number of companies implementing initiatives remained flat year over year, and individual participation in those initiatives fell by as much as 50%.
205. https://www.atlassian.com/diversity/survey/2018
206. https://www.wsj.com/articles/tech-companies-delay-diversity-reports-to-rethink-goals-1480933984
207. Other companies, like Slack, continue to release these reports, and are doing well. Slack's 2019 diversity report,[208] women make up 34.6% of their technical team with 14.2% of their technical workforce coming from non-white or Asian ethnicities.
208. https://slackhq.com/diversity-at-slack-2019
209. https://www.bloomberg.com/news/articles/2017-01-09/facebook-s-hiring-process-hinders-its-effort-to-create-a-diverse-workforce

> 🗩 **STORY** "In the vast majority of cases, it is incredibly obvious to candidates when a recruiter or hiring manager is targeting them for whatever group they think they're part of. When you get some random person reaching out with a position that seems like a poor fit, it's a waste of time, and being known for doing that sort of thing is going to hurt the reputation of that company even further." —Ryn Daniels, Senior Software Engineer, HashiCorp

There is certainly disagreement among experts on whether specific number-driven goals[210] are the right approach to D&I. But it's also true that for a business initiative to be taken seriously, goals of some kind need to be set. What gets measured gets managed.

Companies may make ambitious, realistic goals more achievable by moving away from a single focus on demographic stats, and instead doing more to improve the overall hiring process. Set process goals, not outcome goals, and focus on what you can control.

Investment in an inclusive hiring *process* rather than a dedication to meeting specific demographic goals will better serve your team and future employees, for a number of reasons. First, hiring a diverse workforce is not the whole deal—an inclusive work environment[§11] must be fostered to help those individuals thrive. Second, if you are leading a reasonably sized team—say, an organization of 50+ engineers—significant demographic shifts may take something on the order of years rather months, and a focus on day-to-day processes will help ensure that your team doesn't get burnt out trying to reach only far-off goals. Finally, building a great candidate experience that's sensitive to the needs of underrepresented groups will be the biggest signal of a valuable employee experience, and will make the team that much more attractive across the board.

Making adjustments to your hiring process with a D&I lens will not only mitigate biases and allow underrepresented candidates to shine, but will make the hiring process better for *all*. So look at the process recommendations we include here and set goals to improve where you can. Don't let big goals distract you from the human beings in front of you today.

---

210. https://www.gendereconomy.org/the-debate-about-quotas/

14.1.1 REMEMBER THE BIG PICTURE

While focusing on number-driven goals may not be the best approach, it is important to remember why you're making these changes, and to make sure your team does too. Because implementing inclusive hiring practices is similar to implementing complex software systems—you can ensure that every software component is functioning as intended and still end up with a nonfunctional system. In our engineering world, this is a use case for integration tests.

When implementing changes to your recruiting and hiring process, it's easy to get too focused on the functioning of each step and lose sight of the larger *intent* of your changes. If making a particular change to your process ends up taking you further from your goals, lean toward system function over component function. At the end of the day, success is measured in how people feel about coming in again tomorrow.

14.2 Write Better Job Descriptions

At many companies, writing the job description is a perfunctory task, something to just get through *so we can hire someone right now*. But taking a thoughtful approach and investing in a good process for writing job descriptions with a D&I lens can have a significant positive effect on the rest of your hiring process. How you advertise your jobs has a proven impact on who applies.

> "*The patterns that show up across your company's jobs show what you truly value.*"
>
> — Kieran Snyder, co-founder and CEO, Textio[211]

---

211. https://textio.ai/1000-different-people-the-same-words-6149b5a1f351

14.2.1 IMPROVING THE JOB DESCRIPTION FORMAT

Because every hiring manager tends to write job descriptions differently, setting some standards and guidelines can help. One guideline might be to limit bullet points to just five, each no longer than an old-school tweet (140 characters). This is to encourage hiring managers to focus on what's essential and avoid prescribing or overdetermining potential candidate profiles too much, as that's where biases can creep in. There are a few essential guidelines for writing inclusive JDs:

- **Describe outcomes.** Describe the job that needs to be done or the problem that needs to be solved. Outcomes[§16.1] will get a candidate who's a good fit excited about the job; a job description that lists only requirements just describes what you think a candidate should look like.
- **Describe the problem.** Unhelpful job descriptions often try to appeal to the broadest applicant pool possible, which creates a high volume of applicants, most of whom can't tell if the role is right for them; and this in turn means that none of them may be the right person for the role. Instead, the best job descriptions are specific about problems the person in the role will be expected to solve. This lets the right person see themselves in the role.
- **Focus on real requirements.** Separate out and prioritize the requirements checklist into what's really needed vs. what the person might learn more about on the job. Rattling off a long list of requirements often inadvertently results in describing a candidate who doesn't exist or whom the company could not realistically recruit. By listing what's actually the core function of the job versus what can be taught, like certain tools or languages, you open the candidate pool to more nontraditional talent who may be self-taught or otherwise lack prior exposure to specific skill sets, but who have the potential to learn quickly.

14.2.2 IMPROVING JOB DESCRIPTION LANGUAGE

◇ IMPORTANT   The language you use matters.[212] Textio compared the language[213] used by ten top tech companies in their job descriptions, strikingly documenting one source of tech's homogeneity problem. Describing

---

212. http://www.fortefoundation.org/site/DocServer/gendered_wording_JPSP.pdf?docID=16121
213. https://textio.ai/1000-different-people-the-same-words-6149b5a1f351

your teams and company using the same typical language other companies use signals to candidates that your company is no different. In modeling yourself after your favorite Valley tech company, you may not realize that that company represents the exact thing that certain groups are eager to escape.

In 2015, Buffer realized their job postings were only getting 2% female applicants. They figured out this was due in part to one word they kept using: *hacker*. Buffer posted about what happened when[214] they used different language in their job descriptions, and how that changed who applied. Nvidia saw 2.5 times more applicants from female developers after they removed "weird" language from their job titles (as described in a very helpful post[215] by FastCompany)—titles like "guru," "ninja," "rockstar," or "genius," to which older candidates, women, and other underrepresented people are unlikely to respond, let alone search for.

Slate reported[216] that controlled academic studies and a ZipRecruiter analysis of millions of ads on its platform have shown the same effects of gendered and exclusionary language in job descriptions. Such language keeps candidates from applying or even seeing the job in the first place.

A great tool for discovering gendered and exclusionary language in job descriptions is Textio.[217]

14.2.3 IMPROVE YOUR VALUE PROPOSITION

Numerous studies have shown that there's a "confidence gap"[218] across genders that leads to unequal rates of access to opportunities. In your job description, it's important to focus on selling, not gate-keeping.[219] Why should these candidates join your company?

- **Mission and vision.** What are your mission and vision for the future? What impact will this role have in the company, and what impact will the company have on the world? If you work at a small company that

---

214. https://www.fastcompany.com/3044094/how-changing-one-word-in-job-descriptions-can-lead-to-more-diverse-candid
215. https://www.fastcompany.com/40514090/your-weird-job-titles-are-making-you-miss-the-best-candidates
216. https://slate.com/human-interest/2016/09/way-fewer-people-apply-when-job-descriptions-contain-gendered-words.html
217. https://textio.com/
218. https://www.theatlantic.com/magazine/archive/2014/05/the-confidence-gap/359815/
219. https://en.wikipedia.org/wiki/Gatekeeper

hasn't yet developed its value proposition or branding, visit Appendix B[§37] and our section on crafting company narratives.[§20.2]

- **Benefits.** Beyond the company's mission and vision, other ways to add to your value proposition are by honing your benefits and perks.

⚠ CAUTION Many companies proudly list their offerings without realizing that those very offerings are biased toward certain groups. A single, childless 23-year-old male candidate has different priorities than an experienced candidate with parent and elder caretaking duties. The latter is less likely to get excited about "weekly happy hours, beers on tap, and ping-pong tournaments," and much more likely to be drawn to clear parental leave policies, 401k matching, and flexible work schedules.

> *"I've seen companies whose job descriptions and careers pages mention hot-tub hangouts and regular alcohol-centered team activities be confused about why they struggle attracting a qualified, diverse pool of applicants."*
> — Jennifer Kim, startup advisor and inclusion advocate

There's no one-size-fits-all when it comes to benefits packages, so it'll take time and experimenting to figure out what works for you. It helps to keep in mind that the focus of the company, team, or role will make certain benefits more attractive to relevant candidates (for example, privacy protection may be a bigger concern for certain security roles.) Does your company offer childcare assistance, flexible hours, ability to work remotely, or student loan assistance? Have you considered covering physical safety costs in the case of harassment, including security details, anti-doxxing measures, or funding for emergency temporary relocation? Does your medical insurance policy include pregnancy and transgender health benefits? A candidate-focused job description comes from recruiting with D&I in mind.

- **Think about the visuals.** What kind of information does your jobs page communicate about the team and environment? Who is featured in the photos and what are they doing? What would candidates from underrepresented groups say about what they see?

It is critical to directly ask a variety of people if they are willing to give you feedback, instead of assuming what you think their perception will be. You might find that the casual language and photos that you thought were conveying a "relaxed, chill" vibe might be a signal for "unprofessionalism" to an engineer who was burned at her previous startup. A showcase of photos from your company's exotic retreat, the whole engineering team in their bathing suits, can be a big turnoff to URGs; this is the last thing some will be looking for.

This doesn't mean URGs are wet blankets on your cozy team bonding; it means you need to balance what you view as a "fun" workplace environment with a value proposition that reaches people with broader lives and concerns, such as family, health, personal safety, and so on. This is an exercise in considering how you might be limiting your talent pool because of the ways in which you present (and sometimes misrepresent!) your company's values.

14.2.4 PRESENT EXISTING D&I EFFORTS WITH HONESTY

Checking the About page on a company's website is an important part of the job search process for many candidates from underrepresented groups. While all candidates want to learn about the people they'll be working with, URGs tend to pay special attention to existing diversity, to figure out whether that particular environment is one where they could be set up for success, both as a candidate and as a potential employee.

◇ IMPORTANT The number-one most effective way to attract underrepresented talent is to have a proven, demonstrated record of URGs thriving at your company. That not only means effective hiring, but also retaining and promoting people from underrepresented backgrounds into leadership positions. Your company's reputation as an inclusive space amongst URG engineering networks will precede you. While changing jobs is always risky, URGs tend to be especially conservative when it comes to risk tolerance. Pay inequity, career stagnation,[220] harassment,[221] and assault[222] are just a handful of the additional concerns that URGs have to weigh when deciding on a new career opportunity. If your candidates can see that others like them have been successful at your company, they can put a lot of those concerns to rest. On the flip side, lack of these indicators makes it too easy for candidates to screen you out and move on to another

---

220. https://hbr.org/2018/02/why-arent-black-employees-getting-more-white-collar-jobs
221. https://nyti.ms/2E3kKAd
222. https://jamanetwork.com/journals/jamapediatrics/fullarticle/2375127

company. Increasingly, more candidates from all backgrounds are operating this way.

> 💬 STORY "When people interview with me, they see a signal that they can bring themselves to work. I can be a living, breathing 'Black people are welcome here' sign." —Bukky Adebayo, Product Manager, Microsoft[223]

Chances are, your organization does not currently have the halo effects of an excellent record and reputation when it comes to diversity—few companies do. Being honest about your D&I efforts likely requires changing your recruiting pitch.

⚠ DANGER Photographing the one Black employee and two women on the team and plastering their faces around your site is not a good idea. You don't want to "fake it." Never lie to candidates—it won't end well. And do not lie to your employees either. Get consent from anyone whose photo or bio you want to use in marketing material, and tell them what you will be using it for. Give them the option to opt out without professional consequences (don't tell them they're "not a team player"). In addition to privacy and safety concerns, individuals may not want to be the face of D&I at your company, especially if the company is still struggling.

But if you truly are making an effort in diversity, what *can* you show, if the numbers aren't there yet? Embrace this opportunity to engage in real talk with candidates. Acknowledge deficiencies and your growing awareness, and explain the journey behind the learning process. More and more employees are expecting this level of honesty from their leaders.

Questions to reflect on:

- How do the team or company leaders currently talk about D&I?
- Is D&I being discussed as an important part of overall business strategy, beyond hiring numbers?
- What concrete steps has the team taken or will take to expand understanding of the issues that affect underrepresented talent in tech?
- What are some recent actions you or your team have taken to create a more fair and equitable organization?

---

223. https://inclusionatwork.co/obligated-to-di/

This will allow you to point to specific examples—along with upcoming initiatives.[224]

◇ IMPORTANT You don't need to have a perfect answer. In fact, you may be the only company a candidate is talking to that has anything like a thoughtful response to their questions or concerns about D&I. They will likely find your willingness to talk refreshing. Just be honest. You'll find that candidates are much more open to the truth that you're working on it, than to a charade that you've somehow mastered D&I—they will definitely see through that.

14.3 Diversify Your Candidate Pool

In technical hiring, especially at startups, this is a common practice: "I just reached out to all the guys I know and hired who was available." In fact, your most effective recruiting channel is probably internal referrals—even for later-stage companies—and referrals typically share the demographic characteristics of your existing team. Expanding the pool and being intentional about who you are inviting to interview gives a chance to those who may otherwise have been overlooked. Luckily, there are many ways to diversify your initial candidate pool and expand your pool of qualified candidates.

14.3.1 SOURCING

If your organization already has a university recruiting program, consider expanding your efforts to include schools with more diverse populations than Stanford, MIT, and Harvard, whether that's HBCUs[225] (historically Black colleges and universities), women's colleges, or state universities and community colleges. You can choose to recruit from colleges where the student populations are closer to the audience for your product. You can look at the schools that belong to BRAID[226] or other schools that have made effective strides in diversifying their engineering programs.

---

224. https://medium.com/@jenniferkim/50-ideas-for-cultivating-diversity-and-inclusion-in-the-workplace-you-can-start-today-fd390683bc73
225. http://www.thehundred-seven.org/stem.html
226. https://anitab.org/braid-building-recruiting-and-inclusion-for-diversity/

Partnering with bootcamps that have a commitment to diversity is another great way to source candidates. Recurse Center, C4Q, and Fullstack Academy are just a few examples. Online programs like Massive Open Online Courses (MOOCs) also graduate more diverse classes of engineers than do traditional four-year schools.

One of the big pushes of the past five years of D&I efforts in tech has been the formation of self-identifying talent pools and affinity groups from which companies can hire—Code2040,[227] Hire Tech Ladies,[228] Lesbians Who Tech,[229] to name some. Name any given demographic, and there is a high chance you can find an organization looking to connect you to that group. But these groups are not all the same. It's wise not to put too much faith in an external organization, especially if you are expecting—and they are promising—an easy solution to such a complex issue.

14.3.2 SCREENING

How you screen candidates at the top of the funnel presents one of the biggest opportunities to improve your hiring process.

Decades of studies with resumes have shown that just changing the name on a resume–from traditionally white-sounding names to traditionally Black-sounding names—results in fewer callbacks, even though the qualifications are exactly the same. According to a two-year academic study from 2016, changing Black-sounding names to white-sounding names and otherwise "whitening" resumes resulted in *over twice* the number of callbacks to Black applicants, while whitening the resumes of Asian applicants resulted in about twice the number of callbacks.[230]

CONTROVERSY Taking a cue from the results of blind auditions in the music world,[231] many organizations have implemented identity scrubbing from their applications (also known as blind reviews), with promising results. The practice of removing names from resumes and coding submissions can have many positive effects. However, with identity removed from the equation, hiring teams default to evaluating based on the majority identity.

---

227. http://www.code2040.org/
228. https://www.hiretechladies.com/
229. https://lesbianswhotech.org
230. https://hbswk.hbs.edu/item/minorities-who-whiten-job-resumes-get-more-interviews
231. http://gap.hks.harvard.edu/orchestrating-impartiality-impact-%E2%80%9Cblind%E2%80%9D-auditions-female-musicians

Rather than erasing identity, consider acknowledging the social barriers your candidates have had to overcome.[232]

> "Consider two runners, one who races against a headwind, while the other runs in calm weather. They both average the same mile time, though the first is actively pushing against battering winds. Who's better?"
> — Gregory Walton, Department of Psychology, Stanford[233]

Considering social barriers means you may need to reexamine your stance on job hopping, alma maters, nontraditional educations or paths to tech, contributions to open source, GitHub activity, and awarding points for side hustles and passion projects. For many URGs, the lack (or presence) of these things in their resumes are due to the systemic challenges they face in their day-to-day lives.

"This is lowering the bar!" you might say. But evidence indicates that things traditionally lauded in resumes, like educational pedigree, have no bearing on job performance.[§21.1] Additionally, it's all too common for companies to test URGs in ways that other candidates are not. Interview panels and hiring teams are typically unwilling to take systemic challenge into account when it comes to URG candidates—interviewers often require that they have 110% of qualifications to make it through.

The truth is, however, that hiring teams compromise in hiring all the time anyway. Think about your last desperate hire and all the rules you relaxed when you were trying to find that one available person with that specific skill set that was vital to company success: when you hired that SQL expert, did you compromise on some of the other technical skills you'd otherwise require? When you hired that Android engineer, did you compromise on your "everyone is a fullstack developer" credo? When you hired the security expert, did you compromise on how well you might get along with them?

URGs add unique value, and allowances may be made accordingly, *especially* when it comes to requirements that are far more difficult for URGs to achieve because of systemic racism, like graduating with a four-year degree from a top school; or due to systemic sexism, like having expe-

---

232. Some refer to this practice as "affirmative meritocracy"; in the section of this Guide devoted to reading resumes, we refer to "grit" and "distance traveled."
233. https://gregorywalton-stanford.weebly.com/uploads/4/9/4/4/49448111/waltonspencererman2013.pdf

rience in management at a top company. Given that such requirements do not predict job performance, should they be requirements anyhow? Are there things you consider requirements that are actually better learned on the job? This is not about lowering the bar —it's about expanding your understanding of what makes a candidate a good fit and raising the bar accordingly.

14.3.3 HIRE IN COHORTS

Careful planning may allow you to hire in *cohorts*[234] or batches ("we're expecting four Data Engineer openings next quarter"). Many talented professionals from nontraditional backgrounds have stories of being given a chance that they feel they would not have otherwise received, had it not been for the opportunities provided by batch-hiring.

14.3.4 THE ROONEY RULE

One more concrete tactic you can try is the Rooney Rule.[235] It's an approach borrowed from the NFL, an organization that has faced criticism for lack of diversity in its coaching and senior staff (in marked contrast to its players). There's some variety in implementation, but the rule requires at least one underrepresented person to be interviewed before a hire can be made.

◇ **CAUTION** This approach has other effects that may not be immediately obvious: underrepresented candidates might feel like they're just being asked to interview to check off a box and that you are wasting their time. Untrained interviewers and inexperienced hiring managers may see it as a burden and may even display hostility toward the candidates ("Oh, you're not a real candidate, I'm being forced to talk to you."), causing more harm to URGs, rather than the opposite. Therefore, *how* the Rooney Rule is designed and communicated matters a lot.

◇ **IMPORTANT** Studies have shown that having only one URG in your interview process gives that person essentially no chance of being hired; and having more than one underrepresented candidate dramatically increases the chances of a URG being hired[236]—something to keep in mind if you're

---

234. http://www.nea.org/home/68489.htm
235. https://en.wikipedia.org/wiki/Rooney_Rule
236. https://hbr.org/2016/04/if-theres-only-one-woman-in-your-candidate-pool-theres-statistica lly-no-chance-shell-be-hired

thinking of implementing the Rooney Rule in your organization. Be sure to think through the first principles, potential implications, and ways to get the team on board, to make sure your efforts are successful.

As we've discussed, URGs leave tech at an alarming rate.[§10.2] Microinequities, stereotype threat, tokenism, and lack of acknowledgement of URG identities lead to career stagnation and dissatisfaction with growth opportunities.[237] Unless URGs are entering an inclusive environment—one where they're welcomed and set up for success—they are most likely to leave. In other words, improvements that focus on the top-of-funnel numbers are important, but are only a small part of the overall solution to improve D&I.

14.4 *Evaluating and Interviewing*

Evaluating other people based on the scant data we gather from a few hours of interviewing is a lofty challenge. Recruiting with diversity in mind can help you get better signal from the noise—from interpreting a nontraditional career path, to being able to take into account a candidate's obstacles that are unfamiliar to you—and account for the conscious and unconscious biases of the interviewers. There are a few strategies that we describe here, but cover in more detail in Part V.[§24]

14.4.1 BUILD A STRUCTURED INTERVIEW PROCESS

Structured interviewing has several benefits. By emphasizing the training of interviewers and the implementation of rubrics and feedback forms, structured interviewing allows for methodical evaluation for the skills required for the job. These strategies go a long way in minimizing bias and evaluative confusion in the hiring process.

- **Calibrate interviewers.** A structured interview process involves calibrating interviewers so they all come into the process with the same baseline knowledge and expectations. This is hugely important for mitigating bias in the interview process. It is important to spark a dia-

---

237. https://www.ncwit.org/sites/default/files/resources/womenintech_facts_fullreport_05132016.pdf

logue[238] with your team about bias so they feel welcome to ask questions and bring up concerns. Helpful steps in that discussion include:

- Acknowledging a candidate's identity to prime interviewers to listen for specific types of responses and feedback that might be associated with stereotypes for a particular demographic. When reviewing interviewer feedback, interviewers should be on the lookout for how bias might show up in notes and discussions.
- Reminding interviewers of common stereotypes and biases before they interview.[239] For example, someone interviewing a woman may say something like, "they're too pushy" or "she was abrasive."[240] These are signs of bias that you can counteract.

- **Evaluate fairly.** URGs generally get vague feedback[242] or feedback that is personal rather than results based.[243] A structured interview process can minimize bias by ensuring each interview question is evaluated in the same way, and that all interviewers are trained in recognizing biased language.

Sometimes, hiring managers perceive that it is more "risky" to advocate for underrepresented candidates. This bias, whether unconscious or conscious, has little to do with whether the candidate is actually qualified. Rubrics and structured feedback make it a lot easier for managers and other advocates to feel confident bringing an underrepresented candidate to the table.

> "Interviewers look at the resume as they walk into the room. Instead, train them to read the job description."
> — Nicole Sanchez, D&I strategy consultant[244]

---

238. https://medium.com/@jenniferkim/reducing-hiring-bias-a-step-by-step-guide-to-cultivating-diversity-and-inclusion-part-4-54df04223972
239. https://medium.com/inclusion-insights/raising-the-bar-how-to-be-a-less-biased-interviewer-ecda0892f8f5
240. For more on the prevalence of this issue and how it manifests, see Harvard Business Review's "Recorded VCs' Conversations and Analyzed How Differently They Talk About Female Entrepreneurs"[241]
241. https://hbr.org/2017/05/we-recorded-vcs-conversations-and-analyzed-how-differently-they-talk-about-female-entrepreneurs
242. https://hbr.org/2016/04/research-vague-feedback-is-holding-women-back
243. https://www.fastcompany.com/3034895/the-one-word-men-never-see-in-their-performance-reviews

14.4.2 FURTHER READING ON STRUCTURED INTERVIEWING

- "Real talk: the technical interview is broken"[246] (Karla Monterroso, Code2040)
- "How to Make Tech Interviews a Little Less Awful"[247] (Rachel Thomas)
- Google's guide on Structured Interviewing[248] (re:Work)

14.4.3 DIVERSE INTERVIEW PANELS

CONTROVERSY While having URG employees sitting on interview panels may increase the chance of getting more URG candidates through the pipeline, this can come at a cost. Consider the potential unintended consequences *on interviewers* from underrepresented backgrounds. Because URG employees are, by definition, underrepresented at companies, implementing a policy where URGs are required on interview panels results in a disproportionate burden on these employees. This is not only tiring; it constitutes an additional tax borne by URGs, as employees generally are required to serve as interviewers in addition to their normal job responsibilities, without extra compensation.

CAUTION Some companies deliberately staff their interview panels with URGs or default to having URGs conduct behavioral interviews to suss out noninclusive or marginalizing behaviors from potentially problematic candidates. This means companies deliberately expose URG employees to possible harmful behavior.

From the candidate perspective, candidates who interview with employees from underrepresented groups may walk away with certain assumptions about the diversity of the rest of the company, not realizing that their panel was not representative of the company or team as a whole. If an employee were to join the company and ends up feeling fooled, it doesn't bode well for performance and retention. It is better to be honest

---

244. This was heard by the author[245] at a conference and cannot be independently verified.
245. https://twitter.com/jenistyping/status/1055589014927945728
246. https://medium.com/@Code2040/real-talk-the-technical-interview-is-broken-b84b8375dccb
247. https://medium.com/@racheltho/how-to-make-tech-interviews-a-little-less-awful-c29f35431987
248. https://rework.withgoogle.com/guides/hiring-use-structured-interviewing/steps/introduction/

about your company's makeup—and deliberate about sharing details of your D&I efforts—rather than to "trick" URGs into joining.

14.4.4 INTERVIEWING FOR INCLUSION

> *"Ultimately, I had to recognize that my job here wasn't to save people. As a person who is passionate about learning and developing talent, I understood that where these candidates ended up next could mean the difference between them learning how to become allies or perpetuating the status quo. I knew that if they joined our organization, I could provide some of that guidance, but I had to ask myself whether our organization could underwrite more inclusion debt; and if we did, who would most likely be servicing it. The answers were that we could not, and of course the [URGs] in my organization would be the ones having to bear the bulk of the burden, if we tried. For those reasons, we had to favor folks who had already proven themselves as strong advocates for inclusion."*
>
> — Jason Wong, leadership coach[249]

Can you interview for inclusion? That is, is there a way to evaluate how *inclusive* an individual candidate is, or to assess their feelings about diversity and inclusion?

🚩 CONTROVERSY Interviewing explicitly for inclusion is thorny at best. The goal of doing so would be to ensure that no one joins your team who won't be on board with the company's D&I efforts, or to avoid hiring someone who would actively try to work against those efforts. You don't want to bring people onto the team who are going to be an undue burden on your URGs; but attempting to glean a candidate's feelings or current skills when it comes to D&I is fraught.

Candidates are often caught off guard by questions about inclusion, which can cause interviewers to feel like they are on moral high ground, preventing them from being able to assess the candidate accurately or fairly. When questioned about inclusion, some candidates will just say what they think the interviewer wants to hear.

---

249. https://jwongworks.com/blog/2018/07/02/inclusion-interviewing

> **STORY** "In my experience, candidates trying to show how woke they are often end up being the most difficult to work with, whereas people who honestly admit to not being comfortable and knowledgeable enough on D&I can be the most open-minded." —Jennifer Kim, startup advisor and inclusion advocate

> **STORY** "There will always be people willing to say whatever it takes to get the job, whether it's trying to display how woke they are or trying to get you to believe they are passionate about your product or culture. A significant amount of interviewing is a game of impression management." —Jason Wong, leadership coach

CAUTION Avoid judging a candidate based on how much they already know about D&I. Unless a candidate has been trained in D&I at another company or has taken it upon themselves to learn all the ever-changing lingo and best practices, it's unlikely that they'll be able to give a satisfying answer to an interviewer who's looking for these signals. It can be particularly unfair when interviewing international candidates who may have not had the opportunity to learn the complicated jargon of D&I or who are coming to the table with different cultural expectations and practices.

Rather than looking for whether a candidate can tell you the definition of "intersectionality," you can do two things to help bring values-aligned people to your team:

1. Ask behavioral questions related to how the candidate interacts with others.
2. Tell them a lot about your company's values.

> **STORY** "When you try to actively test for this specific thing, you could introduce more bias, and you would exclude more than you would actually want to. I still think you can test for that, but not in a super straightforward manner. Don't test for 'does this person have inclusive, diversity-oriented views?' Rather, you want to see how open to other points of view people are—do they treat other people like humans? Or do they go for this whole 'meritocracy' thinking? One non-obvious question you can ask to get there is, 'How have you convinced someone of something they didn't agree with at first?' Alternatively, 'How have you been convinced by someone else?' Did

they do it respectfully, do they have respect for the other person or do they demean others? When discussing these kinds of behaviors, they don't have to explicitly say anything about diversity and inclusion out loud, but they are telling you how they treat other people. Even if they don't know the lingo or even the strategies for building diverse teams and so on, they probably have a deeply ingrained thing—do I treat people like people or do I make distinctions based on arbitrary qualities or appearances?" —Benjamin Reitzammer, freelance CTO

One of the goals of asking behavioral questions is to communicate your company's values to candidates. If you say to a candidate, "Tell me about a time when you helped someone who was being excluded," they're going to have a pretty good sense that inclusiveness is important to you. (It's also helpful to look for other opportunities in your interview process to communicate your company's values.) If the candidate does not share those values, they might end up deciding to work somewhere else. This indicates that it wasn't a good candidate-company fit.

Chelsea Troy provides great questions and a rubric[250] for evaluating inclusive behaviors.

> 📖 STORY "It's impossible to build a foolproof process to weed out the people you wouldn't want on your team, because there are so many kinds of things you'd have to test against or be able to read in the right way—jerks can come in different flavors: manipulative, aggressive, charming, sociopathic, et cetera. The best strategy is preventative. Instead of trying to ID or weed out bad apples in the interview process, I think it's more effective to make your workplace/culture/external brand one where certain people wouldn't want to work! For example, making very clear signals and stances around harassment will make your company less attractive to abusers." —Jennifer Kim, startup advisor and inclusion advocate

14.4.5 LET CANDIDATES INTERVIEW YOU

It's easy to get caught up in the need to evaluate candidates while managing a high-volume pipeline. But a crucial part of the hiring process is the candidate experience; everything from your value proposition and pitch

---

250. https://chelseatroy.com/2018/05/24/why-your-efforts-to-make-your-company-inclusive-arent-working/

to the interview experience and compensation package will sell the candidates on the role, team, and company. They need to choose you, and in this hiring market, they are likely to have multiple offers on the table.

A big part of this is giving candidates the opportunity—even encouraging them—to interview you about the company, the role, the team, and anything else. This is especially important for URGs.

◊ IMPORTANT Different groups evaluate opportunities differently. Asking a lot of questions—even when they seem "picky" or "difficult"—isn't necessarily an indicator of that candidate being a bad potential employee. The history and current state of diversity and inclusion in tech means that a lot of talented people have been burned for years; URGs are more likely to have low trust in employers. They usually need to evaluate companies at a higher standard because past environments have failed them. This is true of all kinds of questions, too, certainly not just questions about your company's D&I efforts or the makeup of the team.

> STORY "When it comes to compensation, URGs are often judged in interviews or salary negotiations as being 'too focused on money.' Wanting to be compensated fairly is not a bad thing. As an interviewer, make sure that you are not judging URGs for taking their own compensation considerations seriously." —Ryn Daniels, Senior Software Engineer, HashiCorp

What talented people want at the end of the day is a great working environment so they can do their best work. Don't punish people, especially URGs, for asking a lot of questions. They are acting rationally.

> *"Candidates from underrepresented backgrounds are more likely to have been burned by previous companies due to bias, harassment, and toxicity. They have to ask a lot of questions to determine whether a startup will be a safe, supportive environment or yet another dumpster fire."*
> — Jennifer Kim, startup advisor and inclusion advocate[251]

It can definitely be difficult to be interviewed by a candidate when you're not 100% confident in your answers. One example of a common question you can expect from women candidates might be: "What is the

---

251. https://inclusionatwork.co/the-hidden-meaning/

percentage of women and nonbinary people on the existing team?" Assuming you're not proud of the percentage, don't go on the defensive. Be honest about it, but also use the opportunity to open up a conversation. From there, you can show empathy and honestly discuss that while your numbers aren't ideal today, the team is working to improve; and you can explain what approaches the team is trying.

This kind of empathy is essential to close all kinds of candidates. In this market, engineers are going to be considering choosing you from among a number of options. Being empathetic, even anticipatory, of their concerns; curious about their questions and answers; and willing to dig deep into what really matters to a candidate will give you a much better chance at bringing the best people on board.

14.5 Compensate Fairly

Compensation disparity between URGs and their white male colleagues is a particularly prevalent issue.[252, 253]

---

252. http://www.equalpaytoday.org/equalpaydays
253. https://www.forbes.com/sites/tanyatarr/2018/04/04/by-the-numbers-what-pay-inequality-looks-like-for-women-in-tech/#4579b22a60b1

14.5.1 **FIGURE: PAY DISPARITIES**

Source: Equal Payback Project[254]

Pew determined that across STEM fields, women make 79% of what men make. Blacks in STEM make 73% of what whites earn, Hispanics make 85%, and Asians make 125% more than whites.[255] Men are offered more money than women for the same role 60% of the time.[256] These disparities add up over time, as compensation adjustments are often calculated on a percentage basis from base salaries. Evidence suggests that the equity gap[257] between men and women is even higher than the pay gap. The good news is that you have control over getting pay right at the hiring stage.

◇ CAUTION The first step to compensating fairly is understanding that URGs are often under-leveled not only at their current job, but also when they change jobs. Hiring a URG at a lower level than their previous job is a red flag. It means you are very likely already starting them off in a lower salary band than they deserve.

Second, at the offer stage,[§35] it's critical to do a check to make sure the offer you're putting out is at least equal to the last offer you gave to a white male at that level. If you need help tracking that data, you can use a compensation calibration worksheet.[258]

---

254. https://nwlc.org/equal-payback-project/
255. https://www.pewsocialtrends.org/2018/01/09/diversity-in-the-stem-workforce-varies-widely-across-jobs/
256. https://hired.com/wage-inequality-report
257. https://tablestakes.com/study/
258. https://docs.google.com/spreadsheets/d/1y2MAqK8XRUboycqcjqWYQZZmtirkxHE6kP_rsmDg-kM/edit#gid=1880426148

Finally, compensation encompasses more than just salary. I's important to remember that benefits are not just something to mention in job descriptions,[20] but are also part of the compensation package. Getting them right is a crucial step in building effective D&I efforts. As Project Include writes:[259]

> "*Many benefits in the industry tend to appeal to young, single men, and feel exclusionary when they are not offered in balance with a rich mix of other benefits options (e.g., foosball but no childcare). Companies can improve this by supporting employees when they need to take leave, rearrange their schedules, or take other measures to manage their work-life balance successfully.*"

Understanding ways in which your company can close the benefits gap can give you a strong competitive edge.

14.5.2 FURTHER READING ON FAIR COMPENSATION

- A Counterintuitive System for Startup Compensation[260] (Molly Graham, First Round Review)
- Committing to Fair Compensation[261] (Sarah Nahm / Lever)
- Is Salary Transparency More Than a Trend?[262] (Glassdoor report)
  - Thompson Reuters 2018 D&I Index[263] (largely very big companies, mix of tech and other industries)
  - Forbes 2019 list[264]

Where success does happen, you'll find a deep, ongoing commitment to creating inclusive environments and a mapping of diversity and inclusion to the organization's values or business strategy.

---

259. https://projectinclude.org/compensating_fairly
260. http://firstround.com/review/A-Counterintuitive-System-for-Startup-Compensation/
261. https://www.lever.co/blog/a-step-by-step-guide-to-cultivating-diversity-and-inclusion-committing-to-fair-compensation
262. https://glassdoor.app.box.com/s/j0ntaw9w0hib3mrcvxky5xjwzvgfb16y
263. https://www.thomsonreuters.com/en/press-releases/2018/september/thomson-reuters-di-index-ranks-the-2018-top-100-most-diverse-and-inclusive-organizations-globally.html
264. https://www.forbes.com/lists/best-employers-diversity/#1df880716468

14.6 Continued Learning

In 2010, Etsy[265] was in the midst of an engineering team overhaul. They had decided they needed a fresh team to take on the challenges the company was facing, and in building this incoming team, hiring women engineers was to be a priority. Yet in the year that followed, they experienced an 86% growth in the engineering team and a 35% decline in gender diversity[266]—they had hired 38 new engineers, of which only two were women. In examining what happened during that year, they found three major contributing factors to their failure:

1. Talking about diversity on its own was not an effective strategy.
2. To change outcomes, they needed to make significant changes to their interview process.
3. Because there was no proof of their commitment to diversity, candidates from underrepresented groups were not confident in working for them.

These reflections informed a new approach that not only overhauled their recruiting efforts, but also incorporated new initiatives to create a work environment that resulted in more fair and equitable outcomes for all employees.

With this information, within a year Etsy grew their representation of women in engineering from 4.7% to 18%. Today, according to their most recent diversity report, that number stands at 29.3%. While recruiting with diversity in mind is important, it is just one part of an effective diversity and inclusion program. Enduring diversity requires a sustained commitment to inclusion—an evergreen readiness to change and adapt your organization's policies, procedures, and behaviors to create a place where every employee can thrive.

While examples from companies like Etsy can help us stay motivated, it can be misleading to look only at the percentages and demographics at other companies. People often look for these numbers elsewhere because they want to follow someone else's model and because they want or need to prove that success is possible. But "success," when it comes to D&I, is

---

265. Jason Wong, a lead author of this section, is a former Etsy Senior Director of Engineering.
266. https://firstround.com/review/How-Etsy-Grew-their-Number-of-Female-Engineers-by-500-in-One-Year/

completely dependent on your team and the company you work for. It's perfectly fair to take some tips, advice, and ideas[267] from those who have been through this before, and to take note of what the research tells us about where to look to see what's working. But your goals should be your own; and focusing on numbers can be a distraction from the deeper work of building inclusive practices and policies.

In a summary of several studies[268] into how to assess and improve inclusion, Laura Sherbin and Ripa Rashid lay out four areas for organizations to focus on, beyond the numbers:

1. **Inclusive leaders.** A collection of six behaviors, including making it safe to propose novel ideas and empowering team members to make decisions, define leaders who create more inclusive environments. According to Sherbin and Rashid, of employees who report that their team leader has at least three of these traits, "87% say they feel welcome and included in their team, 87% say they feel free to express their views and opinions, and 74% say they feel that their ideas are heard and recognized."
2. **Authenticity.** Their research also found that 37% of Black and Hispanic respondents and 45% of Asians say they "need to compromise their authenticity" in order to meet their company's standards of demeanor or style.
3. **Networking and visibility.** Sponsorship is critical for career advancement for members of URGs. "A sponsor is a senior-level leader who elevates their protégé's visibility within the corridors of power, advocates for key assignments and promotions for them, and puts their reputation on the line for the protégé's advancement." A sponsor also improves a URG's satisfaction with their rate of career advancement and reduces the likelihood of that person quitting.
4. **Clear career paths.** Sherbin and Rashid found that, among women, "29% say their career isn't satisfying, and 23% feel stalled in their careers." Other URGs feel similarly stymied, often without a clear course for how to improve their situation. In the sections on levels and compensation,§14 we strongly advocate for having clearly defined lad-

---

267. https://medium.com/@jenniferkim/50-ideas-for-cultivating-diversity-and-inclusion-in-the-workplace-you-can-start-today-fd390683bc73
268. https://hbr.org/2017/02/diversity-doesnt-stick-without-inclusion

ders for career progression, which are transparently mapped to salary and other compensation.

Beyond the advice above, three additional strategies can help you iterate and improve your hiring process.

14.6.1 SOLICIT AND EVALUATE CANDIDATE FEEDBACK

Setting up a basic feedback process is low-hanging fruit that all hiring teams can grab, and it's especially helpful in the context of D&I. Anonymous feedback can show you a lot that's going on in your process that you wouldn't catch otherwise. But do this only if you plan to listen closely to the feedback, even when it hurts.

Send a survey to candidates with both quantitative questions (such as, "How likely are you to reapply for one of our positions in the future?") and qualitative questions (like, "What was the highlight of your interview experience? What about a low point?").

Have every single response read by a human. You never know how much impact one comment from an underrepresented candidate could have in making you aware of your blind spots. And if you end up hearing about an inappropriate joke from an interviewer or a hiring manager who was passive-aggressive, treat the feedback as a gift to help you improve in a way that you would not have known about otherwise. By ensuring the same mistake doesn't get repeated, you're getting better at your game and will be less likely to lose top candidates in the future.

14.6.2 LOOK AT CONVERSION RATES WITH D&I IN MIND

Take your conversion rates (for example, what percentage of resumes submitted are moved to phone screen?) and intersect them with demographic data collected by Equal Employment Opportunity, an optional set of questions that can be enabled in your ATS, like Lever.[269]

For example, you might find that underrepresented candidates are passing phone screens but falling off after onsite panels at a disproportionately high rate. This tells you there is likely some sort of bias in a particular stage. With this information, you can identify the problem like a

---

[269]. This content was adapted from Jennifer Kim's post "Inclusive Hiring: Why it's hard, why it's important, and how you can start making a difference."[270]

[270]. https://medium.com/@jenniferkim/reducing-hiring-bias-a-step-by-step-guide-to-cultivating-diversity-and-inclusion-part-4-54df04223972

detective: maybe it's an untrained interviewer turning people off. Maybe the type of questions asked are unfair to a certain group.

In addition to conversion rates, you can run the same analysis with interview scores. If underrepresented groups are consistently ranking lower in certain stages and questions, maybe there's underlying bias at play. More opportunities for detective work! (If you aren't yet confident about how to employ recruiting metrics, Jennifer Kim wrote a beginner's guide, "Recruiting Analytics Made Simple."[271])

14.6.3 FURTHER READING ON D&I

We've compiled all the links and resources from this section, plus many more that we didn't include, into Appendix C[§38] for easy reference.

How does a senior director of engineering end up working to help companies improve their D&I efforts? Read Jason Wong's story, "My Journey in Diversity and Inclusion,"[272] on the Holloway blog.

---

271. https://www.linkedin.com/pulse/recruiting-analytics-made-simple-5-useful-reports-you-jennifer-kim/
272. https://www.holloway.com/s/trh-jason-wong-diversityandinclusion-story

PART III: INTERNAL ALIGNMENT

15 How Roles, Levels, and Titles Fit Together

Hiring succeeds best when the hiring team clarifies both their needs and the parameters of the role required to meet those needs. Parameters may include the scope and impact of the role, the job level and title, day-to-day expectations, and what qualities and skills will help a candidate succeed in the role. Thinking seriously about roles will make every stage of hiring easier and less prone to bias—from job descriptions, sourcing, and interviews, to making an offer and onboarding.

A **role (or position)** is the part an employee plays within a team and company, including the set of formal and informal expectations that define the employee's responsibilities. A role also situates an employee within an organization, and it may correspond to the job level into which they fall.

Every role has certain responsibilities and authority. But more specifically, a person's impact arises from outcomes—the tangible value to the company, such as revenue, technology, product, or customers, that is uniquely attributable to that person's work. In practice, a role requires a combination of:

- **Ability.** What skills, knowledge, and past experience are required?
- **Autonomy.** To what degree will the person operate on their own? How much leadership, decision-making authority, and handling of ambiguity is required?
- **Influence.** Will this person have softer ability or less formal agency to positively affect key decisions or people internally at the company?
- **Accountability.** How well does the person carry responsibility? Do they have a reputation for owning responsibility for the outcomes of their work?

The better you can translate your company's needs into a role, the better you'll be able to refine the role's appropriate level, title, and compensation, which inform a job description that will attract the right candidates.

🄲 CONFUSION Roles are often conflated with titles, but they are not the same thing.

A **job title** is the name assigned to a particular position at a company. Job titles provide a brief description of the position, and can vary in that descriptiveness, ranging from the general—Software Engineer or Web Developer—to the specific—Senior Staff ML Engineer. Job titles are usually public facing and may only loosely reflect the true scope and impact of a job, which is conveyed more formally and internally by the job level.

🄲 CONFUSION Informally, people often talk about the **seniority** of a role. Seniority can mean one of three things: Responsibility and authority of the role they hold (a "senior manager"), total experience in their past career (a "senior candidate"), or actual time with the company (an employee "with seniority").

Is an individual contributor with the title Senior Software Engineer who has been with the company for ten years "more senior" than a recently hired Director of Engineering? To avoid confusion, it's usually best to talk about job *levels* when discussing roles.

Job levels (levels or job grades) are formal categories of increasing responsibility and authority in a company. In general, the higher level the role, the more autonomy and the greater skill, independence, accountability, and leadership the company expects. Companies can also draw on job levels for such classification tasks as determining compensation, codifying role-appropriate expectations for employees, or supporting internal lateral movement.

Levels often have variations in nomenclature and associated scope and responsibilities, but nonetheless tend to align to fairly standard designations set by compensation survey companies like Radford,[273] Connery,[274] and RHR.[275] As companies grow, their incentive systems often become more complex and granular. Established, mature companies have well-

---

273. https://radford.aon.com/
274. https://www.conneryconsulting.com/
275. https://www.rhrinternational.com/

codified levels, though they still vary to some degree. For instance, Google has eight levels in its standard engineering track, and Microsoft has thirteen. Levels and titles often (but not always) interact here, applying additional details to titles like "I, II, III," and moving up to more detailed seniority classifications like *Staff*, *Principal*, *Distinguished*, and *Fellow*.

Ultimately, levels reflect the employee's value to the company based on the impact they're expected to deliver. For this reason, compensation is typically tied directly to clearly established, standardized levels. This helps demonstrate career progression for candidates and employees, and reduces bias in setting pay levels and determining promotion and other performance rewards.

CANDIDATE It's rare to be able to negotiate on your level, title, *and* compensation. As a candidate, reflect on what motivates you; if you're asking for a better title, an upleveled position, or more cash or equity, it's critical to have a clear personal rationale for why. Determining your must-haves and your nice-to-haves will better prepare you for negotiation.

Industry tactics for establishing roles, titles, levels, and compensation can be helpful, and can also serve as a basis for creating effective hiring plans and writing compelling job descriptions.

16 Defining Roles

Understanding the role you need to fill is one of the most challenging parts of the hiring process. It is a bit of an art, but it will be a lot easier if you've seriously considered your company motivators[§5.2] and the potential needs of your candidates.[§5.1]

When defining the role you'll be hiring for, it's best to begin by identifying what you would consider to be successful outcomes for that role. The next step is to determine what strengths and competencies will predict a candidate's success in the role. This will likely encompass some mix of technical skills, nontechnical skills, and a certain set of traits and values.

16.1 Outcomes and Responsibilities

It's tempting to want to jump into specifying concrete things about the *person* you want to hire by describing their skills or experience. However, because you want someone who will succeed in the role, it's helpful to specify the outcomes you want *before* attempting to describe candidates. Starting with individual requirements might cause you to lose perspective of what you actually want to accomplish later in the hiring process.

Answering the following questions will help determine successful outcomes for this role:

- What will occur if you hire someone who is successful in this role?
- What would be the impact on the team, the business, or the product?

Next, you can pick a time period—a year, five years, ten?—and then break that down into what would need to be accomplished in shorter periods to meet those outcomes:

> "[What would] a typical day or quarter [look like] for a person in this job? If someone executed perfectly in this day or quarter you designed, would it meaningfully and reliably drive impact for the company and business? Will executing at that level even be feasible and fulfilling for a single person?"
> — AnnE Deimer, Inclusion and Diversity Program Specialist, Stripe[276]

You'll begin to see what responsibilities the role should entail to reach these desired outcomes. Note that responsibilities are *activity-based* (like "design, implement, and maintain software") and outcomes are *results-based* (like "help rewrite our feed service to improve the experience of over 100M monthly users"). When aligning with your team, it is best to focus on outcomes. The responsibilities of the role may make more sense for a manager to determine.

◇ CAUTION One pitfall to avoid when thinking about outcomes is making them too temporal or short-term focused. If the immediate need is for a specific project, what will the role look like beyond that? If you can't artic-

---

276. https://stripe.com/atlas/guides/recruiting#step-1-determine-what-roles-you-want-to-hire-for-and-their-core-responsibilities

ulate how the role will evolve over time, you may not need to hire a new full-time employee.

16.2 Desired Skills and Characteristics

Once you have clarity on what success looks like for the role, the next step is to come up with a set of competencies and characteristics that will make that success likely, including specific technical skills, nontechnical skills, and traits and values.

While seriously considering each of these buckets is important, it's wise to be careful not to end up with a list of rigid (and uninspiring) check-the-box criteria. If your criteria are too rigid, you might overlook some of the most promising candidates, especially if the role itself is a little ambiguous or is expected to evolve in the future.

16.3 Desired Technical Skills

When compiling a list of competencies needed for an open role, an obvious starting point is to define what **technical skills** are needed for the job. Technical skills relevant to software engineering positions most commonly include familiarity with or mastery of a software-related domain (like machine learning or cloud infrastructure), a coding language (like C++), or a tool or framework (like Apache Kafka). Technical skills more broadly involve actionable knowledge related to math, science, finance, and project management, technical writing, and many other fields.[277]

A list of desired technical skills also flows from the outcomes and responsibilities you determined for the role. What technical skills are necessary for success?

These skills may not be strict requirements, but the more concrete they are, the better you or your team can judge them from a candidate's profile (for instance, when screening resumes) and assess them in interviews or work samples. A good list of skills will also help candidates better understand the role and whether they should apply.

It's important to think about which technical skills are strict requirements and which are skills that can be easily picked up on the job. For instance, for an entry-level engineering role, you might expect a candidate

---
277. https://www.thebalancecareers.com/technical-skills-list-2063775

to have good working knowledge of at least one programming language, and will likely want to assure yourself that they'll be able to learn other programming languages on the job. It might be worth splitting out which skills the candidate must have to succeed in the role, and which skills would be nice to have—preferred, but not required. Google calls these minimum vs. preferred qualifications[278] and uses them pretty consistently in its job descriptions. It's tempting to think that *all* the skills you think you need are must-haves, so it's helpful to list out all the skills and push yourself to prioritize them.

> "I believe that you should always hire people who are looking to 'punch above their weight class,' which means to hire people who want to be one league above where they are today."
> — Mark Suster, Managing Partner, Upfront Ventures[279]

16.3.1 GENERALIST VS. SPECIALIST CANDIDATES

> "You need a balance between hiring an expert in the area and a great athlete who is flexible and can adapt to your domain."
> — Vinod Khosla, founder, Khosla Ventures[280]

Typical wisdom says that earlier-stage startups (where teams are small and the nature of the work is ambiguous and variable) tend to hire generalists, while larger companies tend to need specialists. But there's more to it than that. A small startup in a heavily technical space (like autonomous vehicles) may need specialists from the outset. Some large companies, like Google, try to hire as many smart generalists as possible because they're better suited to handle the dynamic, changing conditions of the tech industry. Jonathan Rosenberg, former SVP of products at Google, refers to them as "learning animals."[281]

Of course, it's not an either-or choice for each role. Indeed, the ideal skill set for many roles is a T-shaped skill set,[282] with both depth in one area and a degree of breadth. For example, a backend engineer working on

---

278. https://rework.withgoogle.com/guides/hiring-review-resumes/steps/review-for-qualifications/
279. https://bothsidesofthetable.com/whom-should-you-hire-at-a-startup-bc47cac70e49
280. https://www.khoslaventures.com/the-art-science-and-labor-of-recruiting
281. https://whenihavetime.com/2014/10/22/how-google-manages-talent-generalists-vs-specialists/
282. https://en.wikipedia.org/wiki/T-shaped_skills

a critical analytics system may need depth in databases and quantitative skills as well as some basic proficiency in fullstack web engineering.

It's useful to think about what level of flexibility and specialization your team and company need. Will your team's needs—and the role—evolve over time? Do you value the ability to move people between roles and teams over time? Depending on your answers and your current needs, you might value generalists or specialists, but ultimately any company ends up with a mix of both.

🌱 STARTUP In addition to preferring to hire generalists at early-stage startups, Dharmesh Shah, founder and CTO at HubSpot, advocates for hiring for talent versus specific skills: "The best people are problem solvers and like to build elegant solutions and are not hung up on specific languages or technologies."[283]

16.3.2 CONSIDERING "STEP-UP" CANDIDATES

If you directly map a role's required responsibilities into skills, you might end up trying to hire people who have performed that exact same role before. That might make sense since they've proven they can succeed in that role, and assessing their skills might be easier and more direct. In fact, they may have learned vital lessons doing this task before and may be able to perform even better the second (or third) time around. It sounds like a safe bet, but it might not always be the best approach.

> "When hiring it is tempting to employ someone who has done it before. You actually don't want that person. You want someone who is about to do it. After all, if they've done it before, why would they do it again? Either they're not ambitious, not growth-oriented, or weren't that good in their previous role. No matter which it is, you don't want 'em."
>
> — Andy Dunn, co-founder, Bonobos[284]

No one wants to hire someone who's clearly under-qualified. But the up-and-comer who wants a "stretch challenge" has something to prove. And in some cases, they might be ready for the role but just haven't been promoted into it for various reasons—for instance, maybe their old

---

283. http://www.onstartups.com/tabid/3339/bid/1278/5-Quick-Pointers-On-Startup-Hiring.aspx
284. https://medium.com/@dunn/creating-culture-21a117803f80

employer doesn't have room to promote them as long as their boss is around.

You should still be aware that this is a risky strategy. Make sure your stance on taking such risks with external candidates is consistent with your internal processes. If your internal promotion strategy is to only promote people to a new role after they have shown that they can perform it, but you're taking risks on outsiders, your team will likely feel frustrated.

16.3.3 COMMON ENGINEERING ROLES BY SKILL

Which of the needs you and your team identified can be grouped together into a set of tasks and attributes that can be accomplished by a single person while keeping that person excited and fulfilled by their work? For example, can you actually make do with one fullstack engineer, or will you need both a frontend and a backend engineer? While the role you ultimately describe may not fit neatly into one of these categories—and the ideal person may not have a rigid or even focused area of expertise or experience—it's helpful to know what are considered common engineering roles.

16.4 Desired Nontechnical Skills

Nontechnical skills (or soft skills) are cognitive, social, and personal abilities that contribute to an effective work environment but are not always easy to measure. They include communication, situational awareness, emotional intelligence and self-awareness, creativity, persistence, adaptability, teamwork, leadership, and time management.

◇ CAUTION It's easy to focus primarily on technical skills, especially when engineers are hiring other engineers. In reality, it takes a lot more than technical skills alone to succeed in the modern workplace.

Here are some examples of nontechnical skills to consider when defining roles:

- Internal communication skills, in meetings or calls, in written form, or as technical documentation. This can include both clarity and timeliness of communication.

- External communication skills, such as for sales or support, including the ability to be professional with external parties and balance internal and customer needs. This is often essential for sales positions or solutions engineers.
- Emotional intelligence (also known as EQ[285]), which is largely a person's ability to identify and manage their own emotions and empathize with others.
- Teamwork and collaborative skills.
- Creativity and product skills, such as the ability to reason about product priorities or make specific product choices.
- Management of multiple responsibilities. Includes managing time well, project management, and structuring of tasks.
- Persistence, including the discipline to tackle and solve large or complex problems over weeks or months.
- Ability to learn quickly in an unstructured environment.
- Ability and interest in mentoring others.

Well-defined nontechnical skills for a role will be:

- **Relevant to the role.** To achieve the outcomes you listed for the role, would a new hire need to collaborate a lot with colleagues? Will they be expected to give presentations to the team or to other departments?
- **Compatible with your company's stage and work style.** Is this a high-growth startup that requires employees to be self-motivated? Do people need to learn new things quickly, and hopefully enjoy doing so?
- **Compatible with your company's values.** Do you expect this person to be empathetic to those around them? What does effective communication mean at your company—are directness and decisive action valued? Transparency and consensus?

16.5 Desired Traits and Values

In addition to skills, it helps to consider what traits and values could help a candidate succeed in their role. In a startup, you might need people who are highly adaptable to changing circumstances and are able to weather the volatility and ambiguity that come with building an early-stage com-

---

285. https://en.wikipedia.org/wiki/Emotional_intelligence

pany; or you might be looking for highly mission-aligned candidates who share your company's vision.

> *"I always made it a habit of talking to people that I knew de facto were world class, and then asking them specifically: 'What are the key traits or characteristics that you look for? What are the questions that you ask, and how do you find them? And if you're looking for the next person that's as good as you, where is that person working right now?'"*
> — Ben Silbermann, co-founder and CEO, Pinterest[286]

Traits are characteristics of a person that describe how they tend to feel, think, and behave, such as patience, adaptability, and being detail-oriented.

Values are fundamental ideas and beliefs that guide a person or organization's motivations and decisions, such as honesty, transparency, and being helpful.

If your company does not yet have a clear set of values that will help you assess candidates on that dimension, visit Appendix B.[§37]

Many engineering leaders have very specific traits and values that they viewed as highly predictive of on-the-job success:[287]

- Dave Story, who has built teams at Intuit, Adobe, and Tableau, always tests for "self-motivation," or the desire and ability to perform well and work hard even without oversight or encouragement.
- Jean-Denis Greze, head of engineering at Plaid, looks for a focus on impact—the desire and ability to perform even without oversight or encouragement—as a highly prized personality trait.
- Ozzie Osman, Monarch co-founder and former Head of Product Engineering at Quora,[288] advocates for finding people who value conscientiousness.

Thoughtful leaders all have something they look for in hires—and it takes experience to know out how to find it. Ozzie Osman shares why he prizes one trait above all others, in "Hiring for Conscientiousness: Why

---

286. https://genius.com/4359175
287. Quotes are from selected engineering leaders interviewed for this Guide.
288. And lead author of this Guide.

startups should hire conscientiousness people—and how to find them,"[289] on the Holloway blog.

🔶 CAUTION Traits and values can be viewed as an extension of nontechnical skills, and many companies combine them into one bucket called "culture fit."[§26.4.3] This can introduce dangerous biases that hinder diversity and downgrade your hiring standards.

Instead, we advocate splitting nontechnical skills—which are often more learnable (like communication skills)—from personality traits (like low ego and adaptability) and values (like honesty and transparency), and being very structured about what each quality is and why it matters. That said, the line between nontechnical skills and traits or values is not always clear. Other ways of considering these qualities include the following:

- Marco Rogers recommends asking questions about the candidate's ego, adaptability, technical communication skills, and cross-functional collaboration.[290]
- This hiring checklist[291] from Drift covers a mix of soft skills and traits that the company looks for before they hire a candidate.
- Kristen Hamilton[292] describes measuring candidates' "characteristics": grit, rigor, impact, teamwork, ownership, curiosity, and polish.[293]
- Recruiting startup TripleByte breaks apart[294] soft skills like communication, positivity, and ownership, from personality traits like friendliness or honesty—and separates them further from the "friend test."
- In the book *Who: The A Method for Hiring*, author Geoff Smart separates behavioral competencies[295] like efficiency, integrity, planning, and so on, from cultural competencies that focus more on organizational fit.

---

289. https://www.holloway.com/s/trh-hiring-for-conscientiousness
290. https://firstround.com/review/my-lessons-from-interviewing-400-engineers-over-three-startups/
291. https://docs.google.com/document/d/1v3kWRKwz05PHyFsn-sDPDBOxIGpokCaK2zYICrZtkMA/edit
292. https://www.linkedin.com/in/kristenm/
293. https://firstround.com/review/the-best-interview-questions-weve-ever-published/
294. https://triplebyte.com/blog/what-companies-mean-by-culture-fit
295. https://www.thedynamicsale.com/wp-content/uploads/2014/06/Who-Geoff-Smart-Executive-Book-Summary.pdf

16.5.1 MISSION-DRIVEN CANDIDATES

"Hiring: values first, aptitude second, specific skills third."
— Sam Altman, chairman, Y Combinator[296]

Veteran venture capitalist John Doerr once said that he prefers to invest in entrepreneurs who are missionaries, not mercenaries.[297] The same can be said for hiring, especially if your company has a strong mission.

Hiring for mission means that you seek out and hire candidates who resonate with and are motivated by the impact your company is working to have. When hiring for mission, you might seek a candidate with passion accompanied by qualities like intrinsic drive and raw intellectual power, and weight skills and experience much less critically. Note that this is stronger than just considering passion for the mission as one hiring criteria—it entails viewing passion for mission as *the* main hiring criteria. The underlying belief is that if you find someone who is motivated by your mission, is intelligent, and is highly motivated, these things will be better indicators of success in the role than previous experience or meeting a laundry list of hard skills. As Mark Suster suggests, "Choose attitude over aptitude."[298]

16.6 *Desired Experience*

When defining a role, it's crucial to consider its level—that is, what degree of experience and impact you need and expect from a candidate. Are you hiring a junior engineer,[299] where they may require a significant amount of time to ramp up, or should they have enough experience to be able to hit the ground running? How independently can they operate? Are they going to be given well-defined tasks to execute, or will they have to proactively identify problems and break them down into solutions? How much of their role is individual work versus influencing and leading others?

In general, for higher job levels, less guidance is needed to achieve an outcome, and greater impact is expected of candidates. In a more senior candidate, this represents a mix of technical skills, soft skills, and expe-

---

296. https://twitter.com/sama/status/981690839280771073?lang=en
297. http://knowledge.wharton.upenn.edu/article/mercenaries-vs-missionaries-john-doerr-sees-two-kinds-of-internet-entrepreneurs/
298. https://techcrunch.com/2011/03/17/whom-to-hire-at-a-startup-attitude-over-aptitude/
299. https://www.kartar.net/2015/09/so-what-exactly-is-a-junior-software-engineer/

rience or talent in technical leadership or management. Such candidates typically have more overall experience than junior employees, or have been at the company longer. A senior employee may be more involved in high-level planning and directing junior employees in the day-to-day work needed to meet an outcome, deadline, or goal.

GitLab distinguishes between increasing degrees of values alignment, technical competencies, and leadership competencies across their seniority levels, which they present in a career matrix.[300] As an engineer progresses through levels of experience, they are expected to take on more capacity in each of those three domains. In particular, as the engineer's level of seniority increases, they must handle a higher degree of ambiguity along with a greater scope of responsibility (The discussion on levels in the next section goes into further detail). GitLab captures this succinctly: "The most senior engineers may even be in a position where they know that something is wrong, but they are not exactly sure what it is—and they work to define the problem."

When writing a role or job description, some translate skills or seniority into strict **experience requirements**, designating minimum amounts of time that candidates must have spent working on particular types of problems. For example, the requirement could be that a candidate should have "at least five years of experience developing Android applications." After all, if someone has spent five years developing Android applications, a company can have *some* confidence that they have skill and interest in that area—enough confidence, at least, to interview and assess them.

⚠ CONFUSION Seniority in a candidate is difficult to specify quantitatively. Concrete durations of experience, such as "five years in a systems engineering role" may be used, but durations are widely acknowledged to be poor and highly approximate proxies for actual seniority.

16.7 *Aligning on the Role*

Your team will most likely be involved in the interview process, they may bring in referral candidates, and they will be working with the new hire day in and day out. The team is a resource for defining and refining the role, at any stage.

---

300. https://about.gitlab.com/handbook/engineering/career-development/career-matrix.html

The process of defining a role may end up being iterative. A hiring manager may have an initial set of criteria, but as you share them with your team, and as you test them out in practice, it's best to incorporate what you learn back into your criteria. For instance, maybe a certain set of skills is rare and extremely difficult to find; or maybe that set doesn't really correlate with what you discover you need to hire for. Listening to your team along the way will help you iterate.

16.7.1 CANDIDATE PERSONAS

Some teams fail to fill a role for months, only to realize they were all looking for different things or assessing candidates in different ways.

Finding agreement on certain questions at the role-defining stage will help your team avoid such situations. These may include:

- Which of these skills are must-haves, and which are nice-to-haves?
- Do candidates like this actually exist?
- If so, how do we find and identify them?
- Would they really want to join our company?
- Do they have the skills and values needed to thrive in the role?
- How do we assess each of these skills and values?

Creating candidate personas can help the team align on each of these.

> "A well-crafted candidate persona puts you in the shoes of your ideal candidate."
> — Krysta Williams, Marketing Content Specialist, ZoomInfo[301]

A **candidate persona** is a description of the ideal candidate for a role. Preparing a candidate persona can help the team agree on the types of candidates to look for and how to identify and attract them (especially at the top of the funnel[§20]).

Like marketing personas,[302] candidate personas are fictitious archetypes that represent the candidates that might go through your funnel. With a candidate persona in place, your team has a physical document that you can look at together to check for inconsistencies.

---

301. https://www.glassdoor.com/employers/blog/the-beginners-guide-to-candidate-personas/
302. https://en.wikipedia.org/wiki/Persona_(user_experience)

To create a representation of your candidate, here are a few areas to think through (if you haven't already):

- **Background.** What sort of work would an ideal candidate have done in the past and why? What kind of companies might they have worked for, and what roles would they have held?
- **Skills.** What skills and experience might they have? Which ones would they list more prominently on their resume or profile and why?
- **Employment.** Where might they work right now? An obvious place might be at your direct competitors, but you can get creative. Do you have any functional competitors (companies that employ people with transferable skills/interests)?
- **Job-search behavior.** How do they find jobs, or how do employers find them? Would they check job boards? Do they work with recruiters? Do they mainly use their network?
- **Use of time outside work.** Are they part of any groups or meetups? Do they spend time on certain sites? Do they contribute to open-source?
- **Long-term career goals.** Do they want to specialize in a particular technology? Might they aspire to start their own company?
- **What excites them.** Do they want to work on and solve hard problems? Do they want to be part of a company with a positive mission?
- **Decision-making.** How else might this candidate make decisions about where to work? What would get them excited, and what would turn them off? Who would they consult with as they were making their decision? What would they research?

It's important to involve your team, rather than doing this in a vacuum. You can interview top performers on your own team, recruiters, and other hiring managers. You can think back to other people you've worked with in your career and consider which of their attributes would make them a good (or bad) fit for your current role. If your team is small, you can use your network and talk to investors, advisors, or managers who have hired for similar roles.

Once you've answered these questions and consulted with your team, put what you've learned together into a format that is easy to read and use as a reference. You can find structured templates on the internet, but a shared document with a few sentences can be a lightweight method to achieve the same effect. Once you share that document with your team, you can incorporate their feedback to ensure you are all in agreement. If this is your first time doing this, it might be worth getting feedback from more experienced recruiters and engineering managers as well.

In addition to identifying inconsistencies, good personas will help you accomplish a number of essential recruiting tasks that we'll cover later in this Guide:

- Craft a role narrative that captures the imagination of your ideal candidate.
- Select the types of candidates to screen for at the top of the funnel.[20] Based on the personas, what attributes might a candidate exhibit in their application?
- Identify the channels and messaging to use when reaching out to candidates. Where might you find candidates who are passive, and how can you best get their attention? How might you ensure that active candidates are able to find you, especially at the opportune time?
- Be prepared to tailor your story and value proposition for each candidate, especially in the first conversation.[24]

⚠ DANGER   Personas, if taken too literally, can be overly restrictive and even lead to discriminatory hiring practices. Here are some pitfalls to avoid:

- Over-generalized assumptions. For instance, a persona for a candidate for an early-stage startup might specify that they thrive under the pressures and urgency they encounter on the job. You might not typically find such candidates at larger, slower-paced companies, but there are always exceptions that you might not want to miss out on. People are unique, complex, and constantly evolving.
- Sticking to your personas too literally. Hiring clones of your personas will create a homogenous team. Another way to avoid this is to have multiple personas per role. For example, let's say you need to hire an engineer for a data-intensive early-stage startup, and their work will require both "scrappiness" but also the ability to work with large-scale data. For that position, you could hire someone with a startup background who has an interest in working with large-scale data, or you could hire someone who has experience with large-scale data at a large company but is interested in joining a startup (and has, for example, exhibited that through side projects or attendance of meetups). Those might be two different personas for the same position.

- Discriminatory assumptions. Correlating attributes to personal details (like age, marital status, or gender) is unfair and illegal.

◇ IMPORTANT Remember that personas are simply a tool for you to use. They are representative and illustrative, rather than prescriptive.

16.7.2 FURTHER READING ON CREATING CANDIDATE PERSONAS

- "How to Create a Candidate Persona"[303] (Beamery)
- "The Beginner's Guide to Candidate Personas"[304] (Glassdoor)
- "How to Create Candidate Persona Maps (Template Included!),"[305] (Rally)
- "Know Who You're Looking for with a Candidate Persona"[306] (BuiltIn)
- "The Essential Guide to Creating Candidate Personas"[307] (Gr8 People)

16.7.3 DEFINING UNFAMILIAR ROLES

> *"There are things you may be unfamiliar with and therefore cannot appropriately judge. Not only will a knowledgeable person help you find better candidates (and maybe even candidates who can grow from the small five-person early-stage team to the very different manifestation of the same role when the team grows to fifty people…or five hundred), their knowledge may help integrate the new person more efficiently and help you better appreciate the role."*
>
> — Vinod Khosla, founder, Khosla Ventures[308]

In some cases, you might find it difficult to even begin defining a role if you or your company have never hired for it before. If you're in that situation, one solution might be finding someone outside of your company (through friends, former colleagues or classmates, or investors) that you believe—and can validate—has been really successful in that role. Assuming you can't hire *that* person, you can at least ask them what character-

---

303. https://beamery.com/blog/create-a-candidate-persona
304. https://www.glassdoor.com/employers/blog/the-beginners-guide-to-candidate-personas/
305. https://www.rallyrecruitmentmarketing.com/2018/06/how-to-create-candidate-persona-maps-template-included/
306. https://builtin.com/recruiting/candidate-persona-template
307. https://www.gr8people.com/ui/assets/uploads/files/gr8-ebook-candidate-personas.pdf
308. https://www.khoslaventures.com/the-art-science-and-labor-of-recruiting

istics they believe make someone successful in this sort of role, and how they would determine whether someone has those characteristics.

Another potential solution is for you or someone on your team to try to act out the role yourself. That is, you can pretend for a day that you're the person hired for the role in question. This will reveal any false assumptions you made about the role, specific skills needed that you overlooked, and much more. Wade Foster of Zapier suggests that by doing the role yourself, "you'll also be able to write a more compelling job description and be better able to define how the role relates to the company and its success."[309]

> "When it comes to an all-new position at the company, we like to try to do it first with the people we have so we really understand the work. If you don't understand the work, it's really hard to evaluate someone's abilities."
> — Jason Fried, co-founder and CEO, Basecamp[310]

◇ IMPORTANT Depending on the role, your background, and the amount of time you have available, testing the role yourself may not always be feasible. But if there is someone on your team who can act out the role and share their insights, the results can be tremendously illuminating. In addition to helping you get clarity on your needs, the experience will allow you to write a more accurate job description and increase your empathy with the candidates and the person who ends up joining the team.

17 Setting Levels and Titles

> "Leveling is a discussion, not a homework exercise. It is a significant change in your culture and your way of doing things."
> — Ashish Raina, compensation consultant[311]

---

309. https://zapier.com/learn/remote-work/how-to-hire-remote-team/
310. https://www.reddit.com/r/socialcitizens/comments/291zp4/hey_im_jason_fried_founder_ce o_at_basecamp_ama/cigr2qf/?utm_source=zapier.com&utm_medium=referral&utm_campaig n=zapier
311. In conversation with Holloway, October 2019.

Levels help to support meaningful growth for engineers, unify expectations across engineering, map compensation fairly, and allow for consistent and ideally unbiased evaluation of candidates. Employees at the most junior levels are typically those without much industry experience, like interns or recent graduates. At the highest levels are employees who may have broad and deep enough impact to significantly change the trajectory of your team or company.

⚡ STARTUP Smaller companies without much structure—and where engineers cover a wide variety of responsibilities—may have very simple titles without any levels, or some very simple levels (for instance, junior and senior software engineer). Hiringplan.io provides a helpful general structure to start thinking about levels.

17.0.1 TABLE: GENERAL LEVELS STRUCTURE

LEVEL	DESCRIPTION	TYPICAL EXPERIENCE
1	Developing professional and technical expertise. Able to resolve routine issues and problems.	0–2 years
2	Well developed professional and technical expertise. Affects quality and timeline of part of product or service.	2–3 years
3	Seasoned professional with competence, creativity in wide range of technical areas. Resolves most issues and problems effectively.	3–6 years
4	Extremely seasoned professional. Able to solve most issues and problems. Uses skills to drive company objectives and achieve goals.	4–7 years
5	Wide range of experience, and is looked to as a thought leader and technical guru. Affects design, quality and timeline of entire product or service.	6+ years
6	Superstar. Critically important to growth and product development. Only a handful at this level throughout the company. Develops department objectives from company strategies.	8+ years

Source: Hiringplan.io

Levels.fyi has collected data from thousands of software professionals about their level, title, and associated compensation. You can see a sample of levels for a variety of companies on their site.[312] Below are a few repre-

---

312. https://www.levels.fyi/

sentative companies plus a "Standard" set of levels that they've abstracted from all the self-reported data they've collected.

17.0.2 **FIGURE: EXAMPLE TECH COMPANY LEVELS**

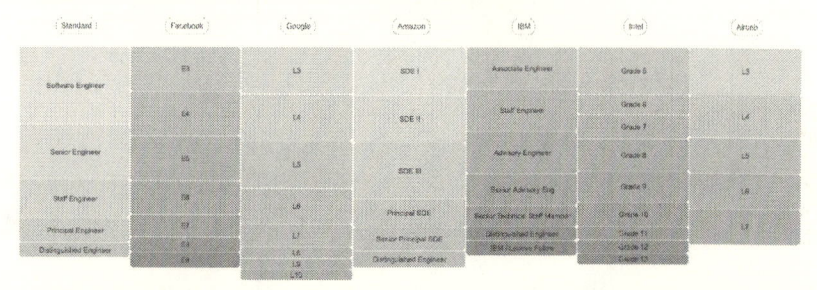

Source: Levels.fyi

17.1 *Formalizing Levels*

Recruiting veteran Jose Guardado[313] suggests that startups generally be post-product-market fit[314] with defensible revenue and enough size and complexity in their engineering organization—typically around 100 people—before they consider implementing levels. Series C funding appears to be a common inflection point for this, which also often coincides with when the startup begins considering creating an HR role. "Many companies don't really start doing this, though, until they're feeling some significant pain," he notes.

Companies wishing to establish more formal levels typically use leveling rubrics from companies like Radford,[315] Connery,[316] or RHR.[317] These companies establish a set of levels based on extensive survey data, including salary information that can be used to set compensation for each level.§18.3 (At some point, likely when you get into the high hundreds to thousands of employees, you may find that the complexity of your organization merits a little extra help. Salary survey consulting groups specialize in helping companies do just this.) Here's a sample level rubric from Radford, which specializes in technology and life science companies.

---

313. https://www.linkedin.com/in/joseguardado/
314. https://www.holloway.com/s/rvc-fundamentals-of-product-market-fit
315. https://radford.aon.com/insights/articles/2018/as-market-realities-change-radford-global-job-leveling-model-rises-to-the-challenge
316. https://www.conneryconsulting.com/
317. https://www.rhrinternational.com

17.1.1 FIGURE: RADFORD LEVELING RUBRIC

Sample Career Ladders within a Global Job Leveling System

Category	Grade	Management	Level	Professional	Level	Support
Business Leadership	Executive		7	Vice President		
	Grade 11		6	Sr. Director		
	Grade 10		5	Director	6	Principal
Management and Professional	Grade 9	Sr. Manager	4	Sr. Manager	5	Expert
	Grade 8	Manager	3	Manager	4	Advanced
	Grade 7	Sr. Supervisor	2	Sr. Supervisor	3	Career
	Grade 6	Supervisor	1	Supervisor	2	Developing
Entry Level and Support	Grade 5				1	Entry
	Grade 4					
	Grade 3					
	Grade 2					

Support: 5 Specialist, 4 Highly Skilled, 3 Senior, 2 Intermediate, 1 Entry

Source: Radford[318]

The Professional designations roughly correlate to engineering levels, and you can use this as a baseline to customize the specific impact details for each level to your needs.

17.2 Ladders

Companies often create **career ladders** or **career lattices** that illustrate the job levels at the company, explain what is expected of employees at each level, and clarify the different growth paths an employee can take. A career ladder shows only vertical progression through job levels, while a career lattice shows possible lateral movement as well. For instance, a common pattern at tech companies is to provide a **dual-ladder**[319] **approach**, in which there is a technical ladder for individual contributors and a management ladder for more senior employees.

---

318. https://radford.aon.com/insights/articles/2018/as-market-realities-change-radford-global-job-leveling-model-rises-to-the-challenge
319. https://hackernoon.com/why-all-engineers-must-understand-management-the-view-from-both-ladders-cc749ae14905

17.2.1 FIGURE: EXAMPLE DUAL-LADDER APPROACH

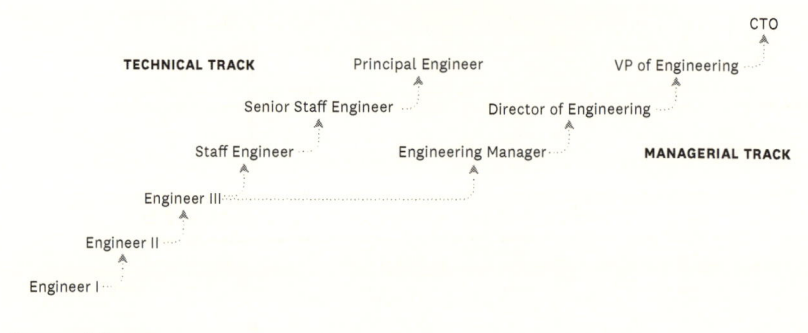

```
                                                                    CTO
                                                                     ▲
         TECHNICAL TRACK      Principal Engineer      VP of Engineering
                                     ▲                      ▲
                     Senior Staff Engineer      Director of Engineering
                              ▲                         ▲
                Staff Engineer           Engineering Manager    MANAGERIAL TRACK
                        ▲                      ▲
          Engineer III
                ▲
     Engineer II
           ▲
Engineer I
```

Source: Holloway

There are both benefits and risks to having more structure around levels. On one hand, without levels, engineers may be unsure about how to progress in their career and have more impact, and the company might end up making arbitrary decisions around promotions and performance management. Clearly delineated levels in a career ladder help mitigate bias and provide fairness and transparency. On the other hand, these systems add complexity. They also risk undermining employees' intrinsic motivations,[§5.1] and many companies find that people can become fixated on their level or title and lose a focus on teamwork and collaboration. A dual-ladder approach in particular can introduce concerns about fairness between individual contributors' and managers' career prospects.[320]

For the purposes of hiring, it's important to have some sort of structure, with the appropriate level of complexity based on your company's stage. This structure will help ensure that your hiring assessments and your expectations of future employees are aligned. It will also help you decide what role (and corresponding level, title, and compensation) a new hire should receive.

You can browse a collection of ladders and rubrics made public by their respective companies at progression.fyi.[321] It's a good exercise to read through a few of them and understand the reasoning and philosophies behind them.

---

320. https://onlinelibrary.wiley.com/doi/abs/10.1002/9781118785317.weom130022
321. https://www.progression.fyi/

Sequoia Capital shared an anonymized example leveling rubric for one of their portfolio companies; it shows how they map knowledge/skills, complexity, independence, and character (traits and values) to similar levels (across Starting, Individual Contributor, and Magagement tracks):

17.2.2 TABLE: STARTING TRACK

	SE2	SE3	SENIOR
	Entry-level	*Mid-level*	*Experienced*
Knowledge	Has engineering and programming foundation. Expected to spend majority of time learning about code and development best practices. Understands scope of small features. Has a basic understanding of what all components in their product are.	Has a basic understanding of development best practices and comfortable writing code. Uses and understands tools needed to debug and diagnose issues in a test and/or simple production environment. Understands the scope of medium features. Has a basic understanding of all their product components.	Has in-depth understanding of development best practices. Has mastered the tools needed to debug and diagnose issues in any type of environment. Understands the scope and relationships of large features and production stack for their area. Has subject matter expertise in at least one component. Has a good understanding of all components of their product.
Job Complexity	Performs basic programming tasks. Contributes to functional specifications and participates in code reviews. Writes and executes test plans.	Performs standard programming tasks. Contributes to functional specifications and participates in code reviews. Writes and executes test plans.	Performs complex programming tasks. Participates in code reviews and can sign off on small features. Writes and executes test plans. Can write functional specifications for small features.

	SE2	**SE3**	**SENIOR**
Independence	Given an introduction to a small task from a more senior engineer, can drive a task to completion independently. (Can fill in the blanks)	Given an introduction to the context in which a task fits, can design and complete a small to medium sized task independently. (Can create some blanks)	Given a medium to large understood problem, can design and implement a solution.
Professional Character	Shows initiative and is motivated to learn. Provides guidance to interns.	Shows initiative and offers assistance when needed without being asked. Provides guidance to entry-level engineers. Constructively escalates problems and issues.	Shows initiative and offers assistance when needed without being asked. Delivers feedback in a constructive manner. Provides guidance to entry-level engineers. Works well with technical leads, incorporating feedback as needed. Helps focus discussion on important aspects.

Source: Sequoia Capital[322]

---

322. Shared privately with Holloway, 2019.

17.2.3 **TABLE: INDIVIDUAL CONTRIBUTOR TRACK**

	STAFF	**SENIOR STAFF**
	Advanced	*(Advanced)^2*
Knowledge	Has mastered development best practices. Understands the limits of our tools and when a problem that exceeds those limits deserves the effort of producing a new tool. Understands the scope and relationships of large features and production stack for their area. Has subject matter expertise on multiple components. Has a strong understanding of all products relevant to own areas of expertise.	Has deep knowledge of entire system, and can jump into code in any component and fire fight and contribute. Makes decisions on product direction and internals based on deep subject matter knowledge.
Job Complexity	Performs expert programming tasks. Handles large-scale technical debt and refactoring. Shapes coding methodologies and best practices. Participates in code reviews and can sign-off on large features. Can sign off on test plans. Participates in requirements gathering with a customer.	Sets product direction and has ownership over large components. Thinks both strategically and tactically, keeping in mind both technical goals and company goals.
Independence	Given a large, poorly understood problem, can explore the solution space (possibly with numerous POCs) to determine correct course of action. Participates in and supports initiatives outside of main area of responsibility. Provides technical leadership for projects including 1-2 individuals.	Given long term strategic goals, can lay out a path across many versions. Participates in and supports initiatives outside of main area of responsibility. Provides technical leadership for projects including 3-4 individuals.
Professional Character	An approachable mentor who is viewed as an expert and acts like one. Constructively challenges assumptions. Guides more junior engineers to correct solutions while encouraging collaboration.	Builds strong relationships in their own team and across the company. Understands multiple points of view and drives a process to conclusions in a timely and respectful manner.

Source: Sequoia Capital[323]

---

323. Shared privately with Holloway, 2019.

17.2.4 TABLE: MANAGEMENT TRACK

	LEAD	**DIRECTOR**	**VP**
	Leads team and/or projects	*Manages teams*	*Product owner*
Knowledge	A senior engineer, who in addition has very broad knowledge of the entire product, and can help with any component, or type of issues. Strong awareness of the state of the product and team at all times.	A great lead engineer, who knows how to allocate resources among projects and understands how company priorities map to their tasks.	Knows the entire product, how customers use it, what they want, and where it should go.
Job Complexity	Contributes to code at a Senior engineer level (or above). Prioritizes work across projects and people. An expert firefighter who is often called in to make things right. Shows great ability to direct project and/or people.	Balances strategic and tactical goals, distributes work across team. Shapes coding methodologies and best practices. Participates in requirements gathering with a customer.	Owns a product, the team, and is responsible for both.
Independence	Leads projects and/or small teams. Participates in and supports initiatives outside of main area of responsibility.	Manages multiple teams and projects. Responsible for team retention and hiring.	Is a great leader, sets direction for product. Understands vision, drives it forward.
Professional Character	Takes responsibility for their team/project. Communicates effectively and respectfully to all members of the organization. Keeps team morale high. Supports and motivates team members.	Takes personal accountability for failure, while praising team for accomplishments. Communicates effectively and respectfully to all members of the organization. Keeps team morale high. Mentors team members.	Works exceptionally well with their own team, other engineering teams, and the company at large. Takes responsibility for their team and product.

Source: Sequoia Capital[324]

---

324. Shared privately with Holloway, 2019.

You'll notice that both the Radford and Sequoia rubrics split the levels between individual contributors (ICs) and managers. The tech industry has moved away from viewing management as the de facto progression in an engineer's career, with an increasing number of companies providing separate management and IC tracks[325] that can support both paths without forcing engineers into management. While levels alone indicate some degree of advancement and progression, most companies that have formal levels eventually establish ladders to further clarify how employees can progress up levels, either on IC or management tracks.

17.2.5 FURTHER READING ON LADDERS

Here are some additional resources and a few public examples of ladders that aren't on progression.fyi:

- Engineering director Chuck Groom highlights key differences[326] people might see between ladders, including:
  - How many individual-contributor levels should there be? (Three? Six?) What do you do with your super-senior folks?
  - How detailed should your job ladder be? (This runs the gamut of complex point systems, spreadsheet matrix, paragraphs of text, or just a few general guideline bullet points.)
  - What are the specific roles and responsibilities for a "tech lead"?
- "How to implement an engineering ladder at your organization"[327] (Lisa van Gelder)
- Axelerant[328]
- Buffer[329]
- Foursquare[330]
- Glossier[331]

---

325. https://hackernoon.com/why-all-engineers-must-understand-management-the-view-from-both-ladders-cc749ae14905
326. https://blog.usejournal.com/the-software-engineering-job-ladder-4bf70b4c24f3
327. https://dev.to/lvangelder/how-to-implement-an-engineering-ladder-at-your-organization-2pc3
328. https://www.axelerant.com/resources/articles/how-to-design-an-effective-career-ladder-for-engineers
329. https://open.buffer.com/engineering-career-framework/
330. https://docs.google.com/spreadsheets/d/1k4sO6pyCl_YYnfoPAXSBcX776rNcTjSOqDxZ5SDty-4/edit#gid=0
331. https://ladder.glossier.io/

17.3 Job Titles

Something as seemingly simple as a job title can contain and convey a complex range of information—the nature and scope of work someone is responsible for; how senior they are; and potentially whether they report to or manage other people.

Titles can be confusing. *Systems Engineer* could mean very different things to different teams or companies depending on the degree of specialization. Someone who works on applications could be an *Application Engineer* or a *Fullstack Engineer* or a *Frontend Developer*. And yes, you'll even see *Programmer* thrown around as an actual title. Any titles might also be combined with seniority designations such as Junior, Senior, Manager, Director, and more. This can make it hard to determine meaningful relative comparison across organizations—an Engineering Manager at a startup compared to one at Google likely have very different responsibilities.

Larger companies typically develop specialized titles based on the functional area, as shown in the table below.

17.3.1 TABLE: EXAMPLE TECHNICAL TITLES

GROUP OR TRACK	EXAMPLE TITLES
Generic	Developer; Software Developer; Programmer; Engineer; Software Engineer; SDE (Software Development Engineer); Software Engineer (SWE)
Systems	Systems Engineer; Systems Architect; Systems Analyst; Software Architect
Product	Product Engineer; Full Stack Engineer; Backend Engineer; Frontend Engineer; Web Developer; Application Engineer; Application Architect; Enterprise Architect; Information Architect
Data	Machine Learning Engineer; Data Scientist; Data Architect; Data Analyst; Data Engineer
Operations	DevOps Engineer; Site Reliability Engineer; System Administrator; Cloud Architect; Infrastructure Engineer
Quality Assurance (QA)	QA Engineer; SDE in test (SDET); Test Engineer; Quality Engineer; Automation Engineer
Solutions or Sales	Solutions Engineer; Customer Support Engineer; Solutions Architect; Sales Engineer; Professional Services Engineer

GROUP OR TRACK	EXAMPLE TITLES
IT	IT Administrator; System Administrator; Network Administrator; Database Administrator
Security and Compliance	Security Engineer; Security Architect; Information Security Analyst; Information Security Architect
Management	Engineering Manager; Development Manager; Software Engineering Lead; Senior Software Engineering Lead; Director of Engineering; Senior Director of Engineering; VP of Engineering; Senior VP of Engineering; CTO; CISO; CIO

Source: Holloway

Some companies take a philosophical stance against job titles. For example, Gusto had no job titles,[332] even at 800 employees and including its executives. Stripe and Cloudflare have similar approaches.[333,334] Others allow anyone to choose their own job titles.[335] But typically, smaller companies start with a simple approach, like dividing roles into really broad categories like Developer or Software Engineer, and maybe Frontend and Backend, depending on the role. For comparison, see how Basecamp (50 employees) handles their developer titles.[336]

Ideally, titles also map to levels, but this isn't always possible or necessary. The role (and its own associated level, responsibilities, and outcomes) conveys much more about what the candidate's experience will be, should they join your company.

No matter what, as you think about titles for roles you intend to fill, consider the candidate perspective. For many companies, titles are merely perfunctory words that describe a role; but the title you choose for a role is often the first thing that a candidate sees. And to candidates, titles can reflect a complex interplay[337] of self-worth, social status and influence, and potential advantages or pitfalls when they look to get promoted or find another job.

---

332. https://qz.com/work/1478072/payroll-startup-gusto-has-800-employees-and-no-job-titles/
333. https://firstround.com/review/to-grow-faster-hit-pause-and-ask-these-questions-from-stripes-coo/
334. https://www.inc.com/magazine/201310/jeff-haden/why-there-are-no-job-titles-at-my-company.html
335. https://www.fastcompany.com/3034987/the-case-for-letting-employees-choose-their-own-job-titles
336. https://github.com/basecamp/handbook/blob/master/titles-for-programmers.md
337. https://finance.yahoo.com/news/does-job-title-really-matter-090000333.html

17.3.2 TIPS FOR WRITING EFFECTIVE JOB TITLES

The most effective titles are specific, descriptive, and concise. This post[338] from Recruiting Intelligence on writing effective job titles covers a few key guidelines, including specificity and clarity about the role (details like seniority, backend vs. frontend engineer); avoiding abbreviations or acronyms and quirky descriptions (Sr. Happiness Mgr); and skipping superlative or idiomatic descriptions (because terms like "rockstar" or "guru" may deter qualified applicants from applying).

Job titles are a form of marketing. Most inbound candidates will find a job listing via some form of online search. With that in mind, it helps to consider some search engine optimization (SEO) tactics that will help your job show up and stand out. (These principles will apply to the content of your job descriptions as well.) Here are a few resources for factoring in SEO when deciding on titles:

- "How to Write SEO-Friendly Job Titles and Descriptions,"[339] (Recruiting.com)
- "Search engine optimized job descriptions: dos and don'ts"[340] (Workable)
- "8 Ways to Make Your Job Title SEO-Friendly"[341] (TMP Worldwide)
- Keyword planner[342] (Google)
- Keywordtool.io[343]

18 Compensation

> "It isn't easy to build pay systems that inspire, guide, and energize people without at the same time damaging your organization and people... Don't try to solve every problem with financial incentives."
>
> — Jeffrey Pfeffer and Robert Sutton, co-authors and professors, Stanford[344]

---

338. https://www.ere.net/5-rules-for-effective-job-titles/
339. https://www.recruiting.com/blog/how-to-write-seo-friendly-job-titles-and-descriptions/
340. https://resources.workable.com/tutorial/seo-job-descriptions
341. https://blog.tmp.com/2018/01/10/8-ways-to-make-your-job-titles-seo-friendly/
342. https://ads.google.com/home/tools/keyword-planner/
343. http://keywordtool.io/

Compensation is any remuneration to a person—including employees, contractors, advisors, founders, and board members—for services performed or rendered to a company. Compensation may be in any combination of cash (salary and any bonuses); equity in the company; and non-cash pay, such as health insurance or other benefits, family-related protections, perks, and retirement plans.

Some companies underestimate the importance of compensation, perhaps by not understanding a candidate's financial needs or by overlooking what compensation can signal. Compensation can be intertwined with other things[§5.1] candidates care about. For instance, a candidate might implicitly correlate the impact of their role with their level of compensation and thus interpret compensation as a signal for whether their company cares about them and the work they do. Candidates might consider an increase in compensation as a signifier of progression in their career. They may derive their self-esteem from that number, or compare it against what's earned by peers, friends, or family. Or, they might use compensation as a proxy to judge how "elite" a team is. These correlations may not always be valid—a company with high salaries may be packed with all-stars, or it could just be overpaying to compensate for something else, like poor work-life balance or a toxic culture.

The more you consider the candidate perspective on compensation in the early stages of your hiring process, the more capable you will be of having open and honest discussions with candidates about compensation later on. This will also give you a chance to think about how compensation fits into your company's mission and values—and the other way around. Some companies overestimate the importance of compensation, spending too much time on equity percentages and not enough on their value proposition. These companies will likely make compensation a key discussion point when communicating with candidates, which will undermine the company's ability to engage candidates with other potentially motivating factors, and will affect how closely they can get to candidate-company fit. Some companies will discuss compensation directly and negotiate it aggressively, while many companies—and candidates—might shy away from discussing compensation because it feels awkward and transactional.

---

344. https://www.amazon.com/Facts-Dangerous-Half-Truths-Total-Nonsense/dp/1591398622

18.1 Elements of Compensation

Total target compensation (TTC, total compensation, target compensation, or TC) is the value of an employee's cash and equity compensation, assuming any relevant conditions are met. This measure typically does not include benefits, which may also be part of an employee's compensation package.[345]

Depending on the company, a compensation package may be made up of some or all of the following:

Base salary is a fixed amount paid to an employee at regular intervals. Although it is often expressed as an annual number, companies generally pay it out in weekly, biweekly, or monthly installments.

A **sign-on bonus (or signing bonus)** is a one-time payment to an employee that is associated with them joining a company. Sign-on bonuses are often contingent on the candidate staying with the company for a certain period of time—usually one year. If an employee's sign-on bonus includes this contingency and they leave the company before the end of the relevant period, they may be required to repay the sign-on bonus.

A **relocation bonus** is a one-time payment made to assist candidates who might incur moving expenses as a result of their new role. Companies can offer relocation bonuses when a new employee is joining or when an existing employee is moving to a new role at the company in a different location.

An **annual bonus** is compensation issued once a year to an employee. It can come in the form of cash—a lump-sum payment on top of an employee's base salary—or equity. When companies pay annual bonuses in cash, they often quote the bonus as a target percentage of the employee's base salary. Some employers make annual bonuses contingent on employee and/or company performance.

Equity is ownership in a company, and it can be given to employees as a form of compensation. Equity may take the form of stock, stock options, restricted stock units, warrants, and so on. Many technology companies, including most startups, grant some form of equity-based compensation to employees.

---

345. https://www.lawinsider.com/clause/target-compensation

Benefits are non-cash services and advantages that a company offers to employees. Benefits may include various levels of healthcare coverage; family-related protections like childcare or health insurance for partners and dependents; perks like meals, the coverage of transportation costs, or enrichment classes; retirement plans; paid leave for vacations, parental leave, and family medical leave; and more unexpected benefits[346] that emphasize health, curiosity, and mission alignment. Benefits programs vary from company to company in their level of systematization, treatment of seniority, and rules on the inclusion or exclusion of contract workers and part-time employees.

18.2 Cash vs. Equity

It has become common practice in the tech industry, both at startups and large companies, to grant some form of equity to employees. And compared to cash, equity may much better align the interests of employees with the long-term interests of the company—or at least that is its intention. For earlier-stage employees, equity is a much riskier form of compensation because of the wide variance in eventual value—an employee's shares in the company (not to mention those of the founders and investors) could end up being worth nothing, or hundreds of millions of dollars or more. Equity compensation is a notoriously complex subject. (For a deep, practical dive into the complexities of equity compensation, see The Holloway Guide to Equity Compensation.[347])

Candidates can have very different needs and preferences when it comes to cash and equity. Cash has a guaranteed value (setting aside changes like inflation), while equity can end up being worth a lot more or less than anyone's best guess. Cash is a commodity; equity in a company is not.

A candidate's response to equity vs. cash may stem from their risk preference. But often, it comes down to practical necessities. Founders may feel that a candidate unwilling to sacrifice cash for equity doesn't believe in the company, when in fact, differing financial and familial situations may determine candidate response. For example, a candidate who has a family to provide for, or obligations like student debt to repay or mort-

---

346. https://medium.com/startup-grind/employee-benefits-that-actually-matter-99181b1d40
347. https://www.holloway.com/g/equity-compensation

gages to maintain, may be unable to sacrifice a guaranteed salary, even if they are passionate about your company's mission. Companies do well to foster sensitivity to this reality in their candidate pool.

Ideally, the candidate's position on cash vs. equity will align with what your company can offer. A candidate that really needs more take-home pay might not be a good fit for an early-stage startup that can only afford to offer—or prefers to offer—partial ownership in the company instead. If you have flexibility, one technique you can use is to offer candidates the ability to "trade cash and equity" by letting them choose between a low equity/high cash or high equity/low cash offer, depending on their cash needs and risk appetite. Matt Mochary's book, *The Great CEO Within*,[348] recommends offering the amount of cash a candidate would need to live comfortably, finding what an all-cash offer might look like at a large company, and then bridging the difference in equity.

18.3 Mapping Compensation to Job Levels

> "Where I have seen most companies get this wrong is that they do not extend their leveling system into the hiring process, or they do not have compensation tied directly to leveling. Missing either of these leaves huge loopholes in any system."
> — Marco Rogers, veteran engineering manager[349]

Compensation is a complex subject rife with potential pitfalls. It's important to develop a compensation philosophy and explore various strategies when building a compensation plan for new hires. Even if you work for a large company with an established compensation plan, you still may gain from reading through these strategies for mapping levels to compensation, as it will help you better understand your company's and candidates' perspectives, and will better prepare you to communicate with candidates about compensation.[§18.6]

> "The best use of money as a motivator is to pay people enough to take the issue of money off the table."
> — Daniel Pink, bestselling author[350]

---

348. https://docs.google.com/document/d/1ZJZbv4J6FZ8DnboJuMhJxTnwl-dwqx5xl0s65DE3w O8/edit#heading=h.w1yl31z0tqdz
349. https://twitter.com/polotek/status/1178128958178525184?s=20

When interviewing and assessing candidates, taking a candidate-company fit approach helps you map candidates to your existing structure. The goal is to be able to predictably determine their compensation based on the role and level.

18.3.1 UNDERSTAND THE MARKET

Developing an understanding of the talent market in which you're competing is the first step. For example, early-stage startups may rely more on equity than cash for compensation. Roles that are more senior or more scarce might command higher compensation. Supply and demand really do come into play here. Ultimately, for a particular role—with its associated level of seniority, geographic area, and stage of company—there will be a distribution of what companies offer to their employees (with a high end and low end, and some mix of cash, equity, bonuses, and/or benefits). You can find this type of data through specialized companies that run salary surveys (like Radford,[351] OptionImpact,[352] RHR,[353] or Connery Consulting[354]), on AngelList,[355] through your investors, or even by browsing sites like Levels.fyi,[356] Glassdoor,[357] or Paysa.[358] (The latter group of sources rely on unvalidated, self-reported data, and so may be less accurate.)

The benefit of using data from sources like Radford and Connery is that they're inherently tied to their leveling rubrics; if your levels correspond to theirs, you've got a head start on mapping your compensation to those levels. These data give you a solid indication of what market rates are. The next step is to adjust for your own hiring philosophy and practicalities, and then actually test out your numbers in the market. If you're losing a big chunk of your offers because of your compensation package, that is the market's way of telling you something is off.

---

350. https://www.amazon.com/Drive-Surprising-Truth-About-Motivates/dp/1594484805
351. https://radford.aon.com
352. https://www.optionimpact.com
353. https://www.rhrinternational.com/
354. https://www.conneryconsulting.com
355. https://angel.co/salaries
356. https://www.levels.fyi
357. https://www.glassdoor.com
358. https://www.paysa.com

⊘ CAUTION In dynamic markets, large-scale salary survey data can lag as an indicator, and tend to be weighted toward levels in larger companies in larger markets. So you'll want to factor this in as you consider your own company's size, maturity, and needs.

Levels.fyi has collected a trove of employee-submitted salary and level data, allowing you to benchmark compensation across levels for a variety of larger tech companies (bearing in mind that these are not vetted in the way that data from formal salary surveys are).

18.3.2 **FIGURE: COMPENSATION BY LEVEL**

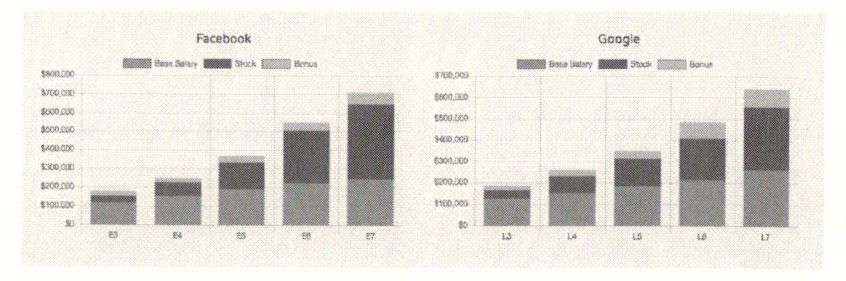

Source: Levels.fyi[359]

18.3.3 **ESTABLISH YOUR COMPENSATION PHILOSOPHY**

Once you understand the market, you will likely want to consider how or whether your compensation plan might align with your value proposition to candidates, the types of candidates you want to hire, and your company's constraints. For example, you might consider offering top-of-market compensation to all candidates (sometimes called "the Yankees approach"), in the hopes of increasing your offer acceptance rate. But keep in mind that offering high compensation won't hide a bad work environment or lack of vision from new employees.

On the other hand, you might compensate a little more conservatively, hoping to put more of your money into scaling your company. If you can offer candidates a really strong value proposition, like opportunities for growth or a mission they are passionate about, or if they have confidence in how successful your company will be, they might place less weight on cash, and you might offer more in equity.

---

359. https://www.levels.fyi/charts.html

⚠ DANGER Some companies can use this strategy exploitatively—but it's unscrupulous to over-promise on any dimension simply to convince someone to take lower pay than they should. It is likewise short-sighted to pay someone less than they deserve because they are motivated by the company's mission and might choose to work for less. Others may be motivated by mission but unable to sacrifice making a living.

Ultimately, the best strategy is to compensate as fairly and transparently as possible, and to find candidates whose needs align with what you can offer. If you overpay, you risk attracting the candidates who only respond to extrinsic motivations. If you underpay, you may not be able to hire and retain the people you need to succeed.

18.3.4 PICK A RANGE

Building a healthy compensation system requires associating a compensation band with each job level.

A **compensation band (or pay band)** is the range of compensation a company offers to all employees at a certain job level. Within a band, individual employees' compensation varies based on factors such as job function, experience, location, and performance.

Again, salary survey data offer good starting benchmarks for this. Companies typically make compensation bands wide enough to have some flexibility, and often these bands overlap. If you want to be really structured, you can peg your compensation to a percentile. For instance, you might decide your compensation will be at some percentile of the data you gathered when developing your compensation philosophy. The 75th percentile is usually a good place to aim for—it's higher than the average, but not high enough to make your offer "only about the money."

⚠ CONFUSION People often confuse percentiles and percents, with serious consequences. When someone recommends compensating at the 75th percentile,[360] they are talking about percentile rank,[361] or paying at a rate that is greater than what 75% of companies pay for a role (in a given market, stage, et cetera). This is very different from paying 75% of what a fair market salary would be.

---

360. https://en.wikipedia.org/wiki/Percentile
361. https://en.wikipedia.org/wiki/Percentile_rank

⚠ CAUTION How you fit people into roles or levels and how those levels relate to compensation is a minefield for discriminatory practices. Take great care when leveling a candidate and deciding compensation. Under-leveling may result in a weak offer that won't appeal to the candidate and is also more likely to happen to URG candidates. Former Google engineer Kelly Ellis and two colleagues filed a class-action lawsuit against Google alleging that they were consistently placed in lower levels than male colleagues, resulting in lower salaries, bonus and stock grants, and promotion opportunities.[362] Conversely, over-leveling might mean you have expectations for performance beyond what the hire can deliver.[363]

Veteran engineering manager Marco Rogers wrote a must-read Twitter thread[364] about how he approached mapping levels to compensation at Clover Health, and the pros and cons their approach had when it came to bias, discrimination, and the overall integrity of their hiring practices. (He also discusses salary transparency and non-negotiation policies, which are helpful to understand when preparing to make offers to candidates, and which we will get into next.)

18.4 Salary Transparency

> "When you start talking about pay transparency, the first thing everyone thinks is 'I'm going to know how much everybody makes.' I think a better way to frame it is 'I'm going to understand why I'm paid what I'm paid and how I can increase my comp.'"
> — bethanye McKinney Blount, founder and CEO, Compaas[365]

An important decision for leadership to make is how much transparency to offer in compensation and leveling. The social media management company Buffer holds transparency as a key value[366] and has made compensation information completely transparent, publishing not only for-

---

362. https://www.theguardian.com/technology/2018/nov/02/google-protests-gender-pay-gap-harassment-kelly-ellis
363. https://www.shrm.org/resourcesandtools/hr-topics/compensation/pages/job-leveling.aspx
364. https://twitter.com/polotek/status/1178121398763474944
365. https://firstround.com/review/opening-up-about-comp-isnt-easy-heres-how-to-get-more-transparent/
366. https://buffer.com/about

mulas[367] for how they determine compensation, but also publicly releasing[368] every employee's salary and level. That level of extreme transparency is rare, but many companies appreciate the benefits of some level of transparency around compensation.

◇ CAUTION However, there are many other companies that try to avoid any level of transparency around compensation in order to avoid negotiation with candidates. This is both unrealistic and counterproductive; and in some cases it might even be illegal (for instance, in California, employers have to provide pay scales for positions when asked, but it's complicated[369]). First, platforms like Glassdoor or Blind (or plain old gossip) usually make compensation data for most companies available to the public. Second, avoiding a conversation about a candidate's level and expected impact might only end up kicking the can down the road and creating surprises later—and these conversations are a lot more difficult to have after someone joins a company.

First Round has some additional insights[370] into why it is wise to treat compensation transparency as a spectrum, and shares some of the risks involved. It's perhaps best to consider a middle ground, which might not entail making everyone's salary and level public (though Buffer has enjoyed positive reactions[371] to their efforts), but could include letting candidates know what level they would be joining at, and then letting them access information about what you expect at different levels. This can help set expectations around their role when they join and point to future avenues for growth. You can do this directly with a candidate or by publicly sharing your rubric or ladder. You can also explain the logic behind how you determine candidate compensation. This will help force you to be fair about how you compensate, while potentially avoiding zero-sum negotiations.

---

367. https://buffer.com/transparency
368. https://open.buffer.com/salary-formula/
369. https://www.shrm.org/resourcesandtools/hr-topics/talent-acquisition/pages/california-attempts-clarify-salary-history-ban.aspx
370. https://firstround.com/review/opening-up-about-comp-isnt-easy-heres-how-to-get-more-transparent/
371. https://news.ycombinator.com/item?id=6936085

If you would be mortified to find out that all your team or company's compensation data was leaked to the public, asking yourself why can be very eye-opening. There are serious pros and cons[372] to consider on both sides of the debate, and each company has the right to decide where on the spectrum they belong; but it's wise to reflect on how you compensate your team before you post a job opening or extend an offer. If you wouldn't be comfortable explaining to a candidate how you arrived at their compensation package, you may need to take a look at your current approach and go back to the drawing board.

18.5 *Making Exceptions*

Having a clear policy around compensation, levels, and titles can help make sure you are able to attract the right talent for the right reasons. However, you will come across cases where your structure doesn't quite match candidate expectations. After all, the data you gathered about the market or about the candidate may not be perfect.

While ignoring your structure may lead to arbitrary and unfair decisions, sticking to your policy too rigidly may result in losing out on great candidates. (Some people are OK with this[373] in the long run, based on their specific values and hiring philosophy.) No incentive structure is perfect. So when and how should you make exceptions?

A balanced approach would be for every company to be highly disciplined about how they compensate employees, but allow themselves a certain degree of flexibility to exercise in certain situations. These guidelines may be useful:

- If a candidate is going to bring disproportionate value to your company, it's fair to compensate them disproportionately. This is especially true in the early stages of a company or for highly specialized roles with very scarce talent. Sometimes, a single hire can dramatically change the trajectory of a company either directly, by bringing a unique set of skills; or indirectly, by showing credibility to investors, candidates, and customers.

---

372. https://time.com/5353848/salary-pay-transparency-work/
373. https://twitter.com/polotek/status/1178131207436922880

- When compensating disproportionately, it's worth considering skewing toward equity over cash. This will help maintain long-term alignment and minimize risk.
- ⚠ DANGER Don't make exceptions for candidates who are simply good negotiators, have astronomical competing offers, or were overpaid in their last role. (Note that while this information may surface, it is illegal to ask candidates about past compensation in several states,[374] including California; the "salary history" bans are an effort to combat pay disparity and discrimination.) These types of exceptions aren't fair to your existing team. It's also important to know that some types of candidates will be less or more likely to feel empowered and entitled to negotiate. For instance, young women are a lot less likely to negotiate[375] than men of any age, because people treat them differently[376] in negotiations, not because they "lack confidence."
- If you find that you are frequently making exceptions, you might consider revising your existing structure and applying changes both to future candidates and to your existing team. If you had to rehire your existing team, what would their compensation look like?

◇ CAUTION Even though experts recommend having discipline and structure around compensation, many companies don't run their hiring this way. Certain large software companies are notorious for making notable exceptions for candidates with competing offers (especially if those offers are from competitors), and "bidding wars" can ensue. On the other hand, high-growth startups that have substantial funding and a "grow at all costs" mentality can be very undisciplined about the offers they extend. It's helpful to know that you might end up faced with these dynamics. The companies that navigate this the most successfully—both for themselves and with their candidates—have a combination of structure, awareness around unconscious bias, and integrity in their decision-making processes.

---

374. https://www.hrdive.com/news/salary-history-ban-states-list/516662/
375. https://www.washingtonpost.com/news/wonk/wp/2016/07/07/young-women-are-still-less-likely-to-negotiate-a-job-offer-but-why/?noredirect=on&utm_term=.5aeddbb78847
376. https://www.sciencedirect.com/science/article/pii/S0749597806000884

18.6 When to Bring up Compensation

Compensation can be a tricky subject. It's uncomfortable for a lot of people, and there might be laws that govern how you can have that conversation (for example, in California[377] and a number of other[378] cities and states it is illegal to ask a candidate what their current compensation is, and you are legally required to disclose a salary range for a position if they ask you). However, compensation is an important criterion for all parties, and it has to be discussed—but when?

Bringing up the issue of compensation too early can be a distraction for you and the candidate, pulling attention away from more important issues. That said, there's a risk that if you don't broach the subject early, you can both waste a lot of time working through the rest of the process only to realize later that what you can pay is incompatible with what the candidate needs. For example, if a candidate is moving from a large, well-paying company to a startup where cash compensation might be much lower, it's important to bring this up early to avoid surprises later. And of course, even if your plan is to delay that conversation, it's not uncommon for a candidate to bring it up before you'd planned to.

Furthermore, some companies run a candidate through their process, extend an offer, and have the candidate reject the offer based primarily on compensation, without either party having ever brought up the subject. Sometimes the company isn't even aware that compensation was the problem; often, this is because both parties are uncomfortable discussing it.

One way to avoid such situations is to give the salary range early and ask the candidate if there is enough overlap with that range to continue the conversation.

> **STORY** "The best way I've seen this done is giving a range for the role in the initial phone call. This way they know the lower bound and can make a determination based on that. In one situation I was told the upper bound, and they noted it was rare for that to be offered to a candidate. That upper bound was my lower bound, so I knew right away it wasn't a fit." —Laurie Barth, Staff Engineer, Gatsby

---

377. https://www.battery.com/powered/ready-californias-new-compensation-law-employers-job-seekers-need-know/
378. https://www.businessinsider.com/places-where-salary-question-banned-us-2017-10

If you are certain that your offer will be the fair market rate for a company of your stage, it's fine to ask the candidate whether being paid fair market rate works for them. (Unfortunately, some companies will claim that they are paying market rate, but aren't, either knowingly or not.)

◇ CAUTION Avoid asking specifically about a candidate's compensation needs. Whether they have financial obligations that necessitate a certain monthly income may be uncomfortable for them to discuss, and it's not fair for you to ask this of some candidates and not others—you also don't want to skirt any legal issues[§32] with your questions. However, it is appropriate to ask whether the candidate has a strong preference on cash vs. equity.

19 Hiring Plans

You've decided that it's the right time to hire and you aren't at risk of hiring for the wrong reasons. You've considered some hiring philosophies that will help guide your planning, and you've mapped out the appropriate title, level, and compensation for the role. The next step is to become aware of any constraints you might have. Time to devise a hiring plan.

A **hiring plan** is a strategic document that outlines the budget and option pool amounts available for hiring new employees into specific roles. It may take the form of a spreadsheet, formal document, or some other form of written target, typically over a one-year period.

"Hiring plan" is a frustratingly loose term—some people take it to mean the plan for your entire hiring process, while others use it to mean a very specific financially driven document that allocates dollar amounts and headcount numbers by team. What constitutes a hiring plan can also vary widely across size, stage, and maturity of a company. At a startup, the hiring plan might simply be, "We have $2M in runway and can afford two engineers this year." At a much larger, decades-old organization, there will likely be a budgeting department, layers of management, and a formal process for requesting headcount numbers for a given timeframe.

◇ IMPORTANT Hiring plans ultimately require companies to evaluate constraints: What are your goals as a company or team? What roles (and associated skills and qualities) do you need to accomplish those goals? How much will it cost to hire and employ those people? How much money can you allocate to that? In other words, what are your *goals, roles, and dollars*? Hiring managers are almost always the ones coming up with the goals and roles; depending on the organization, they may also have budgetary insight, or they have to get approval from somewhere higher up. More advanced teams might also need to factor in recruiting costs and metrics to gain a complete picture of their recruiting and hiring effort's budgetary impacts.

The folks over at Workable wrote about the process of developing a hiring plan[379] at a larger organization, and offer a sample goals, roles and dollars spreadsheet. Hiringplan.io offers a tool for startups[380] to use in modeling compensation for new hires, using market data from HR firm Connery.

19.1 *Budgeting*

The gory details of financial planning for hiring budgets are out of the scope of this Guide, but it's important to know who makes those decisions in your organization, what the process is, and what the deadline is for making sure your hiring needs are included. There is always time between when a company opens a role, and finds, hires, and onboards a candidate. Some searches, especially for rare and senior roles, can take months to complete. A proper hiring plan thus looks not just at the present moment, but where the team and company might be in the future. This is also why it's important to be proactive about things like building a network[381] and investing in your employer brand,[§37] and any other activity that can reduce the time it takes to make a hire. If you're in a position where you "need that role filled yesterday," not only will your team be lacking the people it needs for that stretch of time, but you'll also be more likely to lower your hiring bar out of desperation.

---

379. https://resources.workable.com/blog/how-to-build-a-hiring-plan
380. https://hiringplan.io/
381. https://www.holloway.com/s/excerpt-networking-for-founders

19.2 Equity

Equity is a key part of compensation and hiring plans. In larger companies, defined employee stock plans or grants of restricted stock units (RSUs) are common.

Startups grant equity as a key part of compensation, and plan its allocation. Generally before the first employees are hired, the founders will reserve a number of shares for an employee option pool[382] (or employee pool), which is part of a legal structure called an equity incentive plan. A typical size for the option pool is 20% of the stock of the company; but especially for earlier-stage companies, the option pool can be 10%, 15%, or other sizes.

Well-advised companies will reserve in the option pool only what they expect to use[383] over approximately the next 12 months, so as not to overgrant equity. Your company may never use the whole pool, but it's still wise to try not to reserve more than you plan to use. The size of the pool is determined by complex factors[384] between founders and investors. It's important for employees (and founders) to understand that a small pool can be a good thing in that it reflects the company preserving ownership in negotiations with investors. You can always increase the size of the pool later.

◊ IMPORTANT Once the pool is established, the company's board of directors[385] grants stock from the pool to employees as they join the company. Hiring managers don't typically have much say over those amounts, but you will want to be aware of the details so as to be able to discuss compensation[§18] with candidates.

CANDIDATE For more information on equity as part of the compensation package, visit The Holloway Guide to Equity Compensation.[386]

---

382. http://www.investopedia.com/terms/o/option-pool.asp
383. http://siliconhillslawyer.com/2014/05/01/option-pool-not-ocean-startups/
384. http://venturehacks.com/articles/option-pool-shuffle
385. https://www.holloway.com/definitions/board-of-directors-and-inside-directors-and-outsid e-directors-and-board-members-and-board-seat
386. http://www.holloway.com/g/equity-compensation

19.3 Job Requisition Forms

A **job requisition (or job requisition form)** is an internal company document a manager uses to formally request permission to fill a role or position. These documents are particularly useful for coordination and wider alignment at larger companies. For instance, the requisition might require approval (often from finance, HR, and upper management) to ensure sufficient space and funding are available for a new hire. Once the requisition receives the necessary approvals, it can serve as the starting point for a discussion between the hiring manager and their designated recruiter (for instance, at a role intake meeting).

Companies that use such forms will usually have a template the manager can fill out to share information the decision makers need, including:

- A title and brief description of the role
- The team or manager requesting the new hire
- Targeted start date
- Salary and other budget considerations
- Reason for the new hire (a new project, backfilling a departing employee, and so on).

20 Job Descriptions

A **job description** outlines the main features of an open position at a company, including the work the future employee will be expected to do, expectations for applicants, and ideally, a number of reasons a candidate should want to apply, including a description of the company's mission and the benefits offered. It also typically includes the position's title; it may or may not disclose its compensation. The job description may be in the form of a single-page statement, or a position may have a marketing-like web page to it. The hiring team may create a few versions of each job description, so that people can share it externally across a variety of platforms, like career sites, job boards, and the company website. A well-written job description should give an accurate picture of the role, and entice desirable candidates to apply.

◇ CAUTION Writing a job description before having had any conversation with your team or colleagues is a common pitfall; it's essential to understand the role you are hiring for and the value proposition of the company, and to be aligned internally on each. If a candidate meets with interviewers who all have different ideas of what the role is or why the person might want to join the company, this leads to confusion, a poor candidate experience. It's also inefficient. It's critical to have clarity on the position's target level and compensation before advertising for the job.

◇ IMPORTANT Many large companies offload the responsibilities of writing the job description to a recruiter. You know more about your company, the role, and your ideal candidate than the recruiter does. The most effective way to craft a great job description is for the hiring manager to work with the recruiter directly whenever possible.

20.1 Crafting the Job Description

While every job description will have its own set of unique details, there are a few basic principles that you can use repeatedly as you continue to hire. (Many of the practices in writing good job titles$^{§17.3}$ also apply to writing good job descriptions.)

20.1.1 ANATOMY OF A JOB DESCRIPTION

An informative and compelling job description may have some or all of the following elements:

- job title
- job level
- location (and/or "remote friendly")
- company name (including logo or branding, if available)
- company narrative
- role narrative
- outcomes expected for the role
- skills and/or experience required to meet expected outcomes
- skills and/or experience that is preferred but not necessary
- traits and values of the ideal candidate
- compensation, benefits, perks
- how to apply

- EEO statement.

Depending on your priorities, you may spend more space on one or another of these elements, or combine some of them. How you choose to structure these elements typically indicates a lot about the company's priorities and even their hiring philosophy: Does the job description focus on a long list of requirements first? Does it describe the ideal candidate up front? Or does it begin with a detailed description of the company's mission, or conversely, omit it?

If you've already established the outcomes of the role and the skills, characteristics, values, and experience that will make success in the role likely, listing these in the context of a job description will be relatively easy.

◇ CAUTION Be mindful of length. Candidates will often skim quickly and may not even make it to material lower on the page. Put what you most want your ideal candidate to read at the top—is it the company's mission, the candidate's traits and values, their required expertise, or something else?

Here's what that can look like in practice, from a Splice job description for a Software Engineer position:

20.1.2 FIGURE: AN ANNOTATED JOB DESCRIPTION

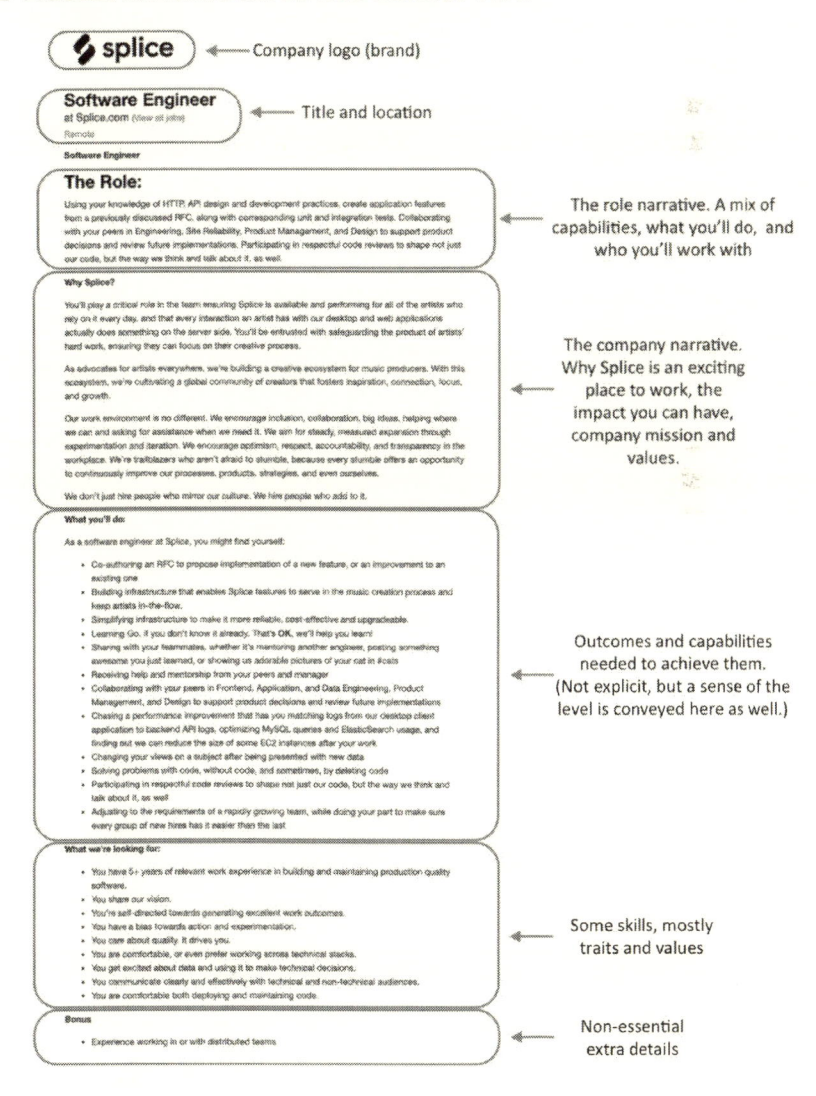

Company logo (brand) — Splice

Title and location — Software Engineer at Splice.com, Remote

The Role: The role narrative. A mix of capabilities, what you'll do, and who you'll work with

Why Splice? The company narrative. Why Splice is an exciting place to work, the impact you can have, company mission and values.

What you'll do: Outcomes and capabilities needed to achieve them. (Not explicit, but a sense of the level is conveyed here as well.)

What we're looking for: Some skills, mostly traits and values

Bonus: Non-essential extra details

Source: Splice; annotation by Holloway

20.1.3 BALANCING OUTCOMES AND REQUIREMENTS

A key goal is to find a balance between making the role description too broad (which may make it less enticing to candidates with a specific set of experiences and interests) or too narrow (which can cause candidates who may have been a good fit to self-select out).

If your job description is built around checklists of requirements, it will be a lot less compelling to candidates than if it is built around the challenges and impact of the work—the outcomes.

Experience requirements are tempting to use because they are concrete, so someone on your team can easily compare a candidate's profile to the experience required. Likewise, candidates can look at the required experience and decide whether or not to apply. But experience may not always translate to ability or even seniority, so you may wish to be more specific about the *kind* of experience you are looking for.

For example, if you're looking for someone with "5+ years of C++ experience," you might end up spending a disproportionate amount of time assessing candidates' C++ skills (and probably will struggle to attract the best candidates). But if you focus on the outcomes *for the role*, you might say something like, "successfully develop and scale microservices handling 10M requests per day." This description can help to filter out candidates who don't have enough experience to be able to accomplish that kind of work, while leaving the application open for the kind of experience that might surprise you.

◇ CAUTION There is research indicating that certain candidates may take requirements more literally than others—[387]in particular, women may be less likely to apply if they don't meet *all* the requirements listed for a job. There are plenty of anecdotes of companies themselves not taking the requirements they list literally.[388] Only use requirements if they are truly requirements; and when you do, it can be helpful to list which requirements are "minimum requirements" and which are simply "preferred." For many roles, a degree in computer science may be preferred, for example; but there might be plenty of qualified candidates who don't have one. If you don't really need it, consider not including it at all.

---

387. https://hbr.org/2014/08/why-women-dont-apply-for-jobs-unless-theyre-100-qualified
388. https://qz.com/255565/job-requirements-are-mostly-fiction-and-you-should-ignore-them/

Remember, this is all about finding candidate-company fit, not about enticing the "best"[§5.5] people to join your team.

20.1.4 FAIRNESS AND INCLUSIVITY

⚠ DANGER Wording in your job description can have unintended consequences in determining who applies. Attempts to make your roles sound more enticing can actually discourage people from applying. Researchers have found evidence that using gendered language[389] contributes to an imbalanced pipeline of candidates; certain language can also discourage older candidates or candidates from marginalized communities from applying.

To avoid this, it's critical to think carefully about your word choice and test your wording on a variety of people. There are also tools like Textio[390] that you can use to check your text for discriminatory or biased language.

◇ IMPORTANT There are a number of ways in which you can make your job descriptions and company About pages more inclusive, thereby increasing the number of qualified candidates who will be interested in working for you. These include the job description format, its language, the company's value proposition, and how the company talks about Diversity and Inclusion[§9] on its website or in the context of the job description.

20.1.5 SHOULD JOB DESCRIPTIONS INCLUDE SALARY INFORMATION?

⚐ CONTROVERSY Many companies include such compensation details as benefits, time-off policies, and perks like remote work, gyms, and free lunches; but they rarely include specific salary information.[391] While a small number of tech companies (like Glitch[393] and a handful of others[394]) and all U.S. government agencies do, most organizations prefer not to include salary data so as to allow room for negotiation. Salary trans-

---

389. https://www.ncbi.nlm.nih.gov/pubmed/21381851
390. https://textio.com/
391. A Glassdoor survey[392] found that one in ten job postings on their site included specific salary information.
392. https://www.glassdoor.com/about-us/glassdoor-survey-finds-more-employees-expected-to-quit-in-upcoming-year/
393. https://glitch.com/about/careers
394. https://www.glassdoor.com/blog/companies-salary-estimates/

parency in job postings might also reveal inequities in the pay structure for existing employees.

Many recruiting and HR experts advocate[395] for putting salary information in job descriptions, noting that this reduces the amount of time you have to spend screening early in the process, and leads to better retention rates and more productive, satisfied employees.[396]

Candidates prefer to know the salary up front,[397] or they risk wasting their time applying for a position that cannot meet their needs. In a candidate-focused hiring process, it's worth considering including the expected salary, a salary range, only the lower bound (assuming candidates will negotiate up), or only the upper band ("up to" X amount). Of these choices, a salary range is most often what specialists recommend.[398]

Sharing information about salary can be positive for companies: As reported by Dice, in an A/B test Stack Overflow found "ads that featured a salary range experienced a 75% average increase in click-through rates. Even jobs that advertised salaries below $100,000 saw a 60% increase."[399]

Another concern competitive companies express is that including high salaries will bring in a whole lot of unqualified applications. This may well be true. In the same Dice report, the company Proforma is said to have found an increase in the number of unqualified applicants when they included salary ranges. However, it also ultimately increased the efficiency of their hiring process: "My closing rate has jumped from the mid-40% range to 84%, so I've more than made up for the extra time I spend screening applicants," said Proforma's Director of Career Advancement.

⚡ STARTUP   If you're worried about not being able to offer a competitive salary, it's still not wise to avoid including it. Candidates will find out sooner or later, and keeping them in the dark will build bad will and may

---

395. https://www.forbes.com/sites/lizryan/2015/03/30/just-put-the-salary-range-in-your-job-ad-already/#196e18316d39
396. https://www.glassdoor.com/employers/blog/salary-estimates-in-jobs-what-employers-need-to-know/
397. https://www.shrm.org/resourcesandtools/hr-topics/talent-acquisition/pages/salary-most-important-part-job-ad.aspx
398. https://www.codementor.io/blog/software-engineer-job-descriptions-that-attract-the-best-developers-241lev4cs8
399. https://insights.dice.com/employer-resource-center/payoff-including-pay-information-job-postings/

cause them to withdraw from the process. Instead, it's best to include the salary or a band, and bring attention to other parts of your job description—if you're highly mission-driven, emphasize why the mission matters; state that you offer competitive equity packages and benefits; and include narratives about the team and the impact they're having or working to have. Your transparency alone may be attractive to candidates.

20.1.6 THE EEO STATEMENT

An **equal employment opportunity statement (EEO statement, equal opportunity employer statement, or diversity statement)** is an expression of a company's compliance with federal equal opportunity law, which is administered and enforced by the Equal Employment Opportunity Commission (EEOC).[400] Only federal government contractors and subcontractors are required to include EEO statements in their job descriptions,[401] but many other companies do so voluntarily.

The advantage of EEO statements is that they show the company is operating in good faith—but they're also part of how the company markets itself. Companies often opt to make the EEO statement specific to the company's values, even if their practices do not always comply.[402]

Examples of EEO statements:

- **Basic:** "Acme Corp is an equal opportunity employer."
- **Google:** "At Google, we don't just accept difference—we celebrate it, we support it, and we thrive on it for the benefit of our employees, our products, and our community. Google is proud to be an equal opportunity workplace and is an affirmative action employer."
- **Dropbox:** "Dropbox is an equal opportunity employer. We are a welcoming place for everyone, and we do our best to make sure all people feel supported and connected at work. A big part of that effort is our support for members and allies of internal groups like Asians at Dropbox, BlackDropboxers, Latinx, Pridebox (LGBTQ), Vets at Dropbox, Women at Dropbox, ATX Diversity (based in Austin, Texas) and the Dropbox Empowerment Network (based in Dublin, Ireland)."

---

400. https://www.eeoc.gov/index.cfm
401. https://www.dol.gov/ofccp/TAguides/sbguide.htm#Q9
402. https://resources.workable.com/tutorial/eeo-statement

- **Dell:** "Dell is an Equal Opportunity Employer and Prohibits Discrimination and Harassment of Any Kind: Dell is committed to the principle of equal employment opportunity for all employees and to providing employees with a work environment free of discrimination and harassment. All employment decisions at Dell are based on business needs, job requirements and individual qualifications, without regard to race, color, religion or belief, national, social or ethnic origin, sex (including pregnancy), age, physical, mental or sensory disability, HIV Status, sexual orientation, gender identity and/or expression, marital, civil union or domestic partnership status, past or present military service, family medical history or genetic information, family or parental status, or any other status protected by the laws or regulations in the locations where we operate. Dell will not tolerate discrimination or harassment based on any of these characteristics."

This is an interesting, if niche, topic. If you'd like to read more about EEO statements:

- "Why EEO statements fall short"[403] (Workable; this is a great introduction to the topic and includes analyses of EEO statements, including Dell's)
- "The Unintended Consequences of Diversity Statements"[404] (Harvard Business Review)

20.2 Creating Narratives

The job description is a tool for reaching toward candidate-company fit: it is as much about the people you hope will apply for the role as it is about the company. The job description exposes your company—possibly for the first time—to the candidate pool, so it's crucial to think about how you are representing the value proposition of your company and team through this medium. At the same time, a good job description will be designed to find and attract candidates who are both *qualified for* and *interested in* the role. The best way to do this is to build narratives—that is, telling stories—about the company and the ideal candidate.

---

403. https://resources.workable.com/tutorial/eeo-statement
404. https://hbr.org/2016/03/the-unintended-consequences-of-diversity-statements

Storytelling doesn't come naturally to everyone; it's easy to do too little, with a list of requirements awkwardly crammed into a character study, and too much, with a grandiose story that doesn't map to people's expectations about the nature of their work. After all, you're hiring people to solve engineering challenges, not fight dragons. And odds are, you don't have a writer on staff to help you craft these artifacts. For a smaller company or team, you're probably best off having everyone, even non-engineers, review the job description to make sure the mission, company narrative, and role narrative feel right. Larger organizations might already have enough experience writing these that you'll have a bank of options to choose from, but that doesn't mean what you've been working with has really been effective. It may be time to update your story for the next great candidate.

20.2.1 COMPANY NARRATIVE

> *"People want to be emotionally engaged in your story, and the journey of your company, and the arc—and to feel like it's on an upward arc."*
>
> — Aileen Lee, founder, Cowboy Ventures[405]

The **company narrative** is a concise expression of how a company wants to be perceived—that is, a distilled version of the brand it hopes to project. It typically describes the company's mission, which may be supported by an origin story and a statement of the company's vision. A company narrative may also include a brief pitch about what it's like to work there and what values the company holds.

The story you tell about your company is one of the more powerful ways to convey your values and brand to a candidate. To be effective, it needs to be concise (a paragraph or two at the most) and evoke an emotional reaction. Standard corporate boilerplate won't attract curious candidates—neither will descriptions that are heavy with company jargon. Consider this example from Jan Tegze at SourceCon:

> *"Which company would you like to join? 'We are an international company focusing on space with offices across the globe, and our goal is to send people to other planets.' Or the second company, 'Our company was founded under the belief that a future where*

---

405. https://youtu.be/vrBhB48qPUM?t=1265

humanity is out exploring the stars is fundamentally more exciting than one where we are not. Today we are actively developing the technologies to make this possible with the ultimate goal of enabling human life on Mars.'"
— Jan Tegze, author and Senior Recruiting Manager, SolarWinds[406]

Both descriptions are for SpaceX; the second is directly from the company, and the first is a version of it that Tegze wrote based on common pitfalls in how companies write about themselves. His version is a collection of facts, while SpaceX's version is an actual story, grown out of the company's origin, mission, and unique vision.

Here are a few questions to get you started building your company narrative:

- Why does the company exist? Why does it matter? What is the founding story?

  - If you're the founder of a company, think back to what you told investors or your first customers. What was the problem you saw, and why did you choose to solve it? Why are you the right person or team to solve it?

- Why will the company be successful? What unique attributes does it have, and what has it accomplished so far to prove that it can succeed in the future?
- What is *your* personal story with the company? Why did you join and why are you excited about it?
- Why do current employees choose to work for this company instead of any other?

You won't use all of this—your narrative will be shorter—but these questions can get you thinking about what your ideal candidate will most want to hear.

---

406. https://www.sourcecon.com/the-power-and-importance-of-storytelling-in-recruitment/

In "The Power of Company Narratives,"[407] management expert John Hagel provides hypothetical examples of these narratives, and identifies two key elements of great company narratives:

- They are open-ended: there is no clear resolution to the story.
- The narrative is about the intended audience (the candidate), not the organization telling the story.

Rather than being strictly about the company, a great company narrative connects the mission to the work the candidate would be doing to tackle that open-ended challenge. (For an even more in-depth look into company narrative, we recommend Hagel's post on narrative as a "powerful agent of pull."[408])

Obviously, if you are a hiring manager at a larger company, branding will already have been established and you most likely will have a lot less power to change the company story. It still might be helpful to consider whether the company story can be adapted to suit *this* role and the kinds of candidates you're hoping to bring on.

20.2.2 EXAMPLE COMPANY NARRATIVES

Many job descriptions lead with their company story first, to help get the candidate familiar with its goals and values and hopefully generate intrigue or excitement about joining the team. Here are a few examples of brief, compelling company narratives we pulled from job descriptions for engineering roles. Notably, each of these avoids company-specific jargon that can be alienating to candidates:

- **Nike.** NIKE, Inc. does more than outfit the world's best athletes. It is a place to explore potential, obliterate boundaries and push out the edges of what can be. The company looks for people who can grow, think, dream and create. Its culture thrives by embracing diversity and rewarding imagination. The brand seeks achievers, leaders and visionaries. At NIKE, Inc. it's about each person bringing skills and passion to a challenging and constantly evolving game.[409]

---

407. http://www.marketingjournal.org/the-power-of-company-narratives-john-hagel/
408. https://edgeperspectives.typepad.com/edge_perspectives/2011/05/the-pull-of-narrative-in-search-of-persistent-context.html
409. https://careers.nike.com/jobs/software-engineer-ii-nike-innovation-labs-portland-oregon-united-states

- **Splice.** We're building a creative ecosystem for music producers. With this ecosystem, we're cultivating a global community of creators that fosters inspiration, connection, focus, and growth.

    Our work environment is no different. We champion collaboration, big ideas, helping where we can and asking for assistance when we need it. We aim for steady, measured expansion through experimentation and iteration. We encourage optimism, inclusion, and transparency in the workplace. We aren't afraid to stumble, because every stumble can teach us something about our processes, strategies, and even ourselves.

    We don't just hire people who mirror our culture. We hire people who add to it.[410]

- **Nordstrom.** We're a fast-moving fashion company that empowers our people to be innovative, creative and always focused on providing the best service to our customers. The retail industry is rapidly changing, and we have interesting, complex problems to solve every day—from developing cutting-edge technology and opening new stores, to designing fresh, must-have fashion.[411]

Appendix B[§37] has more on building your company's value system and sharing it with the world.

Additionally, the Holloway Guide to Raising Venture Capital[412] offers guidance on building mission and vision statements.

20.2.3 ROLE NARRATIVE

A **role narrative** is a short story that appears in a job description and appealingly illustrates to potential candidates—especially the company's ideal candidates—what it would be like to work in the advertised role. It may describe the outcomes of the role, how the role would benefit the candidate, why the role exists, characteristics and skills that will help a candidate succeed in the role, and the role's organizational context. Role narratives are often written in the second person, addressing the candidate as "you" to allow them to envision themself in the role.

---

410. https://boards.greenhouse.io/splice/jobs/4459571002
411. https://nordstrom.wd5.myworkdayjobs.com/en-US/nordstrom_careers/job/Seattle-WA/Mgr-Engineering_R-136315
412. http://www.holloway.com/g/raising-venture-capital

In addition to a narrative for your company, it will also be helpful to develop a story for each role. The process of considering all the elements of a role, including candidate personas[§16.7.1] and whether your company is interested in certain types of candidates, should lead you to be able to answer the following:

- Why does this role exist? Why is it needed now?
  - How will the role impact the company and the wider world?
  - What challenges will this role help the team face? Why is that work exciting?
- What skills or characteristics does a candidate need in order to succeed in the role?
  - Are you looking for an up-and-comer? Someone motivated by the company's mission? Someone very self-motivated? Someone with specific experience?
- What benefits does the candidate gain in taking on this role?
  - What sorts of challenges would the candidate work on?
  - What growth and learning opportunities does this role provide?

It's easy to fall into the trap of merely describing the factual details of the role, but answering these questions in a job description helps place the candidate as the protagonist in a story. This provides imagery and concrete details that lead the person to imagine jumping into that role, tackling the challenges, and working for a company they'd be legitimately excited to join. It's motivating instead of merely intimidating.

20.2.4 EXAMPLE ROLE NARRATIVES

Here are some examples of well-crafted role narratives:

- **Culture Amp:**[413] *Senior Software Engineer (Front end), Payment Platform Web*
  We are searching for experienced frontend engineers to join our team in Melbourne, delivering new and updated product features in our JavaScript and CSS codebases.

---

413. https://boards.greenhouse.io/cultureamp/jobs/186850

Depending on which team you join, you may work with React (typed with TypeScript or Flow), Apollo GraphQL, Redux or even the newest addition to our frontend stack, Elm (no experience required!). For styles, we use CSS Modules written in Sass, which our React and Elm components are able to share. We write JavaScript tests in Jest, Elm tests with elm-test, and end-to-end feature tests with RSpec and Cucumber. We also have a suite of visual regression tests, that automatically catch CSS bugs across our entire browser support matrix. Our back end is Ruby on Rails, with a growing constellation of microservices written in Ruby and Elixir.

You should love crafting beautifully designed and intuitive user experiences, and believe that creating well-tested, clean code is just as important for the front end as the back end. You should enjoy being surrounded by talented engineers, learning from others, as well as contributing to their development. To top it off, we hope you'll share our passion for culture and changing the world of work for the better.

- **Netflix:**[414] *Engineering Director - Netflix APIs*

  Our API strategy has paid off in our consumer product offering. Signup and content discovery experiences on TV, mobile, and web rely on the API layer to provide their data and functionality. Hundreds of A/B tests are supported through this API. Millions of devices interact with it every day. We're not done yet, though; as Netflix grows the needs of the API layer continue to evolve. You would guide the team in exploring ideas like API federation, alternate protocols and query languages like GraphQL, and many more ideas for how to accelerate our API development velocity.

  This past summer we made a new strategic bet—the patterns behind our consumer product API success could similarly pay off in our studio product. Netflix's studio product is a suite of applications that enable content production, from the idea stage to a finished film or series, for 100s of Netflix originals each year. We formed a new group focused on building and scaling API layers for studio applications in addition to consumer applications. Come lead this combined group that is driving Netflix's API evolution.

- **Square:**[415] *Senior Software Engineer (Frontend), Payment Platform*

---

414. https://jobs.netflix.com/jobs/870836

415. https://www.smartrecruiters.com/Square/743999695909014

Commerce is changing, and as part of that Square is transforming from a product company to a platform company. If you join now, you will ride the massive wave of omnichannel retail combining in-store and online / in-app payments. You'll help create an "AWS of Commerce" as our developer platform exposes core primitives for other companies to build on top of. And you'll have a great experience with our motivated, friendly, and diverse team.

20.3 *Where to Post Job Descriptions*

Along with posting job descriptions on your own site (typically in a careers or "work with us" section), you may consider posting in a number of common places that candidates look when conducting a job search.

20.3.1 TABLE: WHERE TO POST JOB DESCRIPTIONS

SITE	PRICING	DETAILS
LinkedIn	Pay per views/post; extensive custom recruiting products	You can post individual jobs, or pay more for LinkedIn Recruiter, which offers advanced search tools and bulk InMail options.
Glassdoor	$199-$699/month	Companies can set up a free account to build their brand (and see what employees/candidates say about them), but have to pay to list jobs.
Lever	Custom pricing depending on company plan	If you use Lever for your ATS, you can integrate with your site to post jobs there, along with other job sites.
AngelList	Free	Typically, but not exclusively, for startup positions
A-List (from AngelList)	Custom pricing	Custom pricing
Career Builder	$375/job; $219-$499/month	Larger scale job site, better for accounting, clerical, retail, etc. Not well suited to tech hiring. Caters to a more Midwestern audience.
Indeed	Free options; pay per click; 10% of salary of hired candidates	Larger scale, lower-skilled job site. Not typically used for tech hiring.
Monster	Free options; $249-$999/month	Larger scale job site, better for accounting, clerical, retail, etc. Not well suited to tech hiring.

SITE	PRICING	DETAILS
Zip Recruiter	$249-$1,569/month	Large platform that's been around for a long time.
Remote.com	Free options; $295/ posting; 10% of project cost per hire; custom pricing	For hiring remote talent.

See Appendix B[§37] for more details about promoting jobs, which can be done more broadly via blogging, social media, at events/hackathons, and more.

◇ IMPORTANT While crafting great job descriptions for platforms like these is important, most jobs aren't advertised; an estimated 70–80% of jobs[416] (across industries) are only available through the hidden job market—networks and social media. The pitfall of relying on the hidden job market to find candidates is that that pool is small and will typically be pretty homogenous. Posting job descriptions gives great candidates the opportunity to find *you*, without having to be part of your in-crowd.

20.4 *Job Description Examples and Resources*

Here are some valuable examples of job descriptions we like and why we like them:

- The social media management company Buffer has an interesting approach to job descriptions. Even when they have no job openings, their company website maintains a full page[417] dedicated to telling the company's story in a way that anchors the reader as a potential character in that story. The page begins with a short story about Buffer, then tells the reader where they could work, what the team is like, benefits the company offers and the values it holds. By the end, someone who's really drawn to working there will already be picturing joining the team and can get on a waiting list to find out when new roles open up.

---

416. https://www.npr.org/2011/02/08/133474431/a-successful-job-search-its-all-about-networking

417. https://journey.buffer.com/

- Stripe:[418] Most of Stripe's job descriptions start with the company's mission and/or the team's goals, and then share the objectives and impact of each role. This is a lot more compelling to candidates than just listing qualifications, which are still included, but come later in the description.
- Splice:[419] These job descriptions not only help candidates concretely understand the role ("What you'll do"), but also set expectations about how the process will look ("How we'll handle your application").
- Culture Amp:[420] This company clearly put quite a bit of effort into their role narrative, and additionally links out to other things they've written on the culture at their company.
- LinkedIn's Recruiter Toolbox:[421] This resource includes tips, templates, and different examples of job descriptions.
- LinkedIn's Talent Solution Template:[422] This is another example from LinkedIn that uses the sequence of objectives, responsibilities, required qualifications, and preferred qualifications.

20.4.1 FURTHER READING ON JOB DESCRIPTIONS

Here are some additional resources for writing great job descriptions:

- "Software Engineer Job Descriptions that Attract the Best Developers"[423] (Jennifer Fu). A fantastic quick resource, covering everything from salary ranges to SEO and Google metadata.
- This 20-minute podcast[424] (Manager Tools) has a good walk-through of writing a job description.
- Buffer's rationale for removing the word *hacker* from their job descriptions[425] has excellent reasoning on why titles matter.
- More details from Slate on how gendered language in job descriptions can dramatically reduce the number of applicants you'll get.[426]

---

418. https://stripe.com/jobs/search?t=engineering
419. https://boards.greenhouse.io/splice/jobs/4200135002
420. https://boards.greenhouse.io/cultureamp/jobs/186850
421. https://business.linkedin.com/content/dam/me/business/en-us/talent-solutions/cx/2018/pdf/2019-Ultimate-Recruiting-Toolbox.pdf
422. https://business.linkedin.com/talent-solutions/job-descriptions/software-engineer?trk=lts-pros-ebook-2018-job-description-template
423. https://www.codementor.io/blog/software-engineer-job-descriptions-that-attract-the-best-developers-241lev4cs8
424. https://www.manager-tools.com/2011/02/write-a-job-advertisement-part-1
425. https://open.buffer.com/job-descriptions-diversity/

- Mitchell Pronschinske covers how to skip the buzzword soup[427] and write more helpful job descriptions.
- The 2019 Hired Global Brand Health Report[428] summarizes a number of ways companies can better appeal to candidates, which may help with how you describe your company in job descriptions.

---

426. https://slate.com/human-interest/2016/09/way-fewer-people-apply-when-job-descriptions-contain-gendered-words.html

427. https://www.linkedin.com/pulse/how-we-should-write-developer-job-postings-mitchell-pronschinske/

428. https://hired.com/brand-health-report?utm_source=twitter&utm_medium=social

PART IV: CONNECTING WITH CANDIDATES

21 Early Signals

> Aline Lerner provided major contributions to this section.

Most hiring teams make decisions about whom to advance through the top of the funnel based on candidate resumes. Especially for inbound candidates, the resume may be the primary or only source of signal. Companies with strong brands and lots of inbound applicants rely on resumes to filter large numbers of candidates very quickly. Candidates selected via outbound sourcing or referrals usually get a chance to stand out in other ways.

Companies often screen LinkedIn profiles alongside or in place of resumes. Both allow filtering based on a candidate's pedigree—where they've worked and where they've gone to school. Companies may also lean on different sources of early signal, like GitHub repositories, personal websites, and online challenges, any one of which can supplement, or in rarer cases, replace a traditional resume.

21.1 *The Trouble with Resumes*

While hiring teams often view resumes as the primary means of making top-of-funnel decisions, filtering candidates by their resumes is noisy, biased, and inefficient. Although little academic research exists on the predictive use of resumes in software engineering hiring specifically, research has been done on the function of resumes across all industries. An 85-year meta-analysis[429] found that resumes (along with other traditional assessment methods like interviews) are very poor predictors of subsequent job performance.

---

429. http://citeseerx.ist.psu.edu/viewdoc/download?doi=10.1.1.172.1733&rep=rep1&type=pdf

Engineering managers tend to harbor the suspicion that engineers are better at reading technical resumes than recruiters: "We're domain experts! We don't need to rely on proxies and can actually tell what the candidate can do!" But even the most experienced, qualified engineers aren't always on the same page when it comes to what makes a good technical hire. In fact, the more experience you gain, the higher the risk that you may be stuck in your own way of seeing things. This makes the static data of a resume a particularly poor alignment tool.

Interviewing.io recently conducted a study[430,431] in which researchers removed all personally identifying information (name, contact information, dates, et cetera) from a set of resumes, and showed them to hundreds of recruiters and engineers. For each resume, researchers asked participating recruiters and engineers just one question: "Would you interview this candidate?"

On average, participants correctly guessed which candidates were strong[432] 53% of the time, and there was no statistically significant difference between engineers and recruiters. Moreover, and even more importantly, people's errors weren't consistent. In other words, everyone disagreed about what a good candidate looked like in the first place.[433]

---

430. http://blog.alinelerner.com/resumes-suck-heres-the-data/?hn=1
431. A contributor to this section, Aline Lerner, is the co-founder founder and CEO of interviewing.io.
432. Researchers had pre-screened the resumes into two strength-based groups, but did not reveal that to participants ahead of time.
433. http://blog.interviewing.io/resumes-suck-heres-the-data/

21.1.1 FIGURE: DISTRIBUTION OF RESUME SCORES

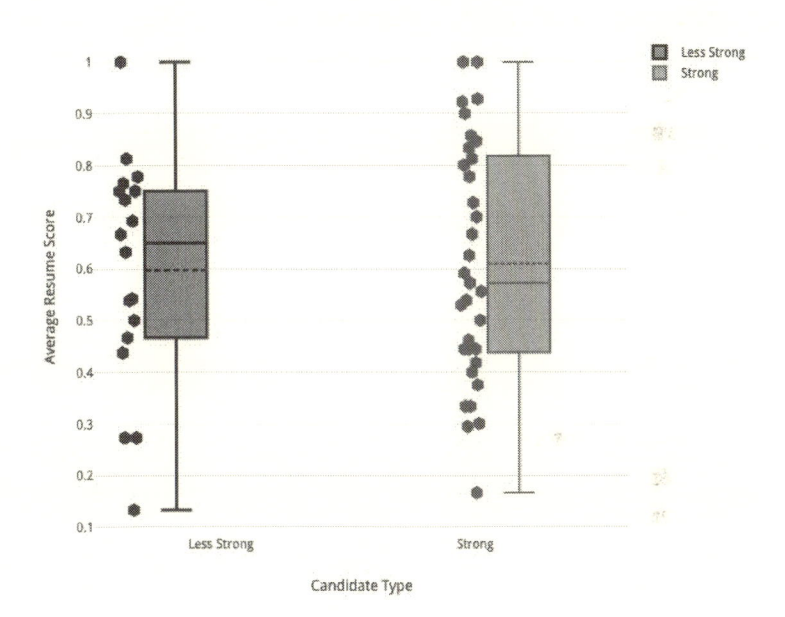

Distribution of Resume Scores for Each Group

Source: interviewing.io[434]

Academic and industry research has consistently proven that bias is a common problem in resume filtering as well. In a 2003 study[435] on resumes by the National Bureau of Economic Research, experimenters submitted identical resumes to a series of help-wanted ads in the Boston and Chicago areas where the only difference between resumes was candidate name; some names were thought of as traditionally white and others as traditionally Black. Resumes belonging to candidates with "white-sounding" names received 50% more callbacks. These results were repeated in a 2016 study[436] at Harvard Business School, targeting 16 metropolitan areas and including traditionally Asian names. Another study[437] showed bias along class and gender lines in law firms.

---

434. http://blog.interviewing.io/resumes-suck-heres-the-data/
435. https://www.nber.org/papers/w9873
436. https://hbswk.hbs.edu/item/minorities-who-whiten-job-resumes-get-more-interviews
437. https://hbr.org/2016/12/research-how-subtle-class-cues-can-backfire-on-your-resume

🛈 CANDIDATE As a candidate, you will increase your chances of being judged by your strongest attributes by doing everything in your power *not* to be filtered by your resume alone. If you have a resume with no name-brand schools or companies, the reality is that you'll face stiff odds at companies with many applicants who do. And even if you have a degree from an elite university and employment with a top company, you'll still have more luck advancing through the hiring process at any company if you can get into the funnel later, via a warm introduction, referral, or any other connection you can find. A few things to consider when building a resume:

- **Attention to detail.** Avoid typos, poor organization, or other easy-to-fix formatting problems. These can mean automatic rejection. Many people looking at a resume think, "If you can't write one page without four typos, how are you going to do other work where attention to detail matters?"
- **Provide context.** When describing work, include context on your role (and how it fit into the team) and the business impact. had so reviewers know why it was important and how you performed. An ineffective, mechanistic description would be: "Worked on Java backend of the AcmeTronix 7000." Something like this is far better: "Was main developer of backend of Acme's e-commerce platform used for $1M/month in transactions. Led team of four."
- **Look forward.** Highlight what you *want* your job to be, by writing your resume to show your aspirations, not just what you factually have done in the past.

21.2 *Online Challenges*

Online challenges (or coding challenges) are tests that a company sends to prospective candidates in order to screen them for specific criteria early in the hiring process, usually before phone screens or more in-depth interviews. Online challenges typically involve a small set of predetermined programming problems. Either the company or a third-party company will have created them, and the hiring team will expect candidates to complete them in a specified amount of time and without any assistance.

When candidate volume is high, screening mechanisms like online challenges can make sense; they are easier for companies to scale and assess than other types of evaluations, and they are less biased than traditional screening mechanisms like resumes. Hiring teams use online challenges to identify unqualified leads.

Companies can learn a lot about candidates by giving them a homework assignment in which they have to write code to solve a problem. These technical screens are almost always scored automatically—once the candidate writes and submits code, the assessment system runs it against a bunch of tests to verify that the code outputs are correct and that the code runs efficiently.

> *STORY* "At Dropbox, we would go to a campus and would get a thousand people who would apply from that school for an internship, but we'd only have five interviewers on the campus. We would have them use Hackerrank X (a code-screening software) to tackle a simple problem, because what we didn't want to do was destigmatize the really good people in the pool from doing it—it was basically, 'can you code or not?' We were trying to differentiate between classroom students and engineers." —Scott Woody, former Director of Engineering, Dropbox

Examples of widely used assessment tools[§39] include HackerRank,[438] Codility,[439] CodeSignal,[440] and Qualified.io.[441]

Because these assessments take minimal time and effort for companies to give out, they're an appealing approach to making hiring a bit more fair. The idea is that if someone can pass a coding challenge, regardless of how they look on paper, they should get to advance to an interview. In some cases, online assessments can replace reliance on traditionally poor-signal screening formats like resumes: there is less bias in testing someone's code output than in placing worth on where they went to school.

Still, there is value asymmetry in online challenges.

Value asymmetry is a state of affairs in which one party derives greater value from a transaction than the other. Value asymmetry in hiring and recruiting can arise when companies require candidates to expend significant effort in the interviewing process, such as asking a candidate to complete a lengthy coding challenge that provides little benefit

---

438. https://www.hackerrank.com/
439. https://www.codility.com/
440. https://codesignal.com/
441. https://www.qualified.io/

to them. Value asymmetry can lead to frustration, disaffection, and candidates dropping out of the hiring funnel.

If your company is a household name, you can get away with having value asymmetry in your process because candidates value the chance to work for you so highly. But there are very few companies that are household names; and until yours is one, it's wise to weigh whether it makes sense to ask candidates to do something up front without giving them anything in return.

21.2.1 FIGURE: VALUE ASYMMETRY AS A FUNCTION OF BRAND STRENGTH

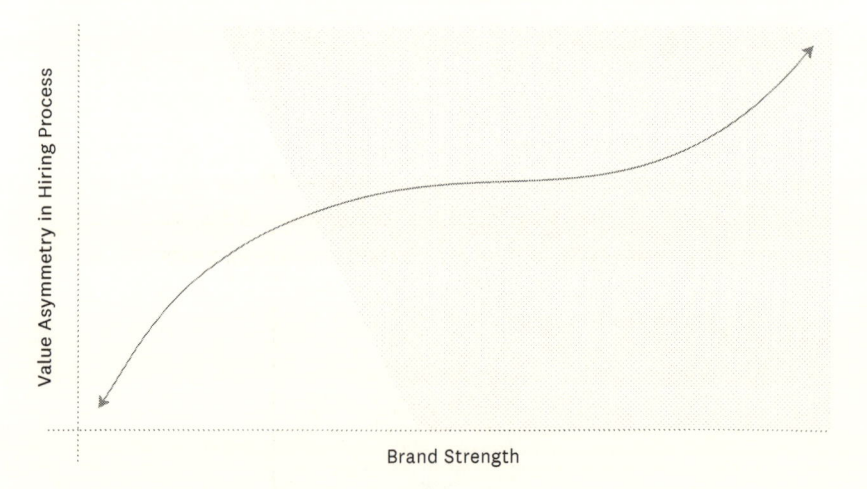

Source: Aline Lerner

To combat value asymmetry, companies often choose to send coding assessments just to candidates that they perceive as less marketable; that is, those that don't look good on paper. One pitfall is that even when those candidates do well in these assessments, they may not get to move to the next step—either because they made a mistake on the online assignment or because after they pass, a recruiter may revisit the candidate's resume and notice a practical reason that disqualifies them (like location).

◇ CAUTION It's wise not to make the common mistake of assigning the same online coding challenges for all developer roles. Typically (1) frontend or fullstack, (2) data science or machine learning, and (3) devops roles all are different enough they should be assessed with different challenges. Effective hiring teams test for and assess candidates' ability to fulfill the requirements of the *specific* role all along the funnel.

🔊 STORY "Online challenges are incredibly irritating. They're things like, 'Create a map of 8 by 14, and then write a program that navigates that in as little moves as possible.' They're asking you to build out chess boards for web developer positions. I'm a great programmer, but I'm not a computer scientist. I fail these things repeatedly. I know the people who can pass these kinds of challenges, and they're the worst programmers I've ever worked with. For every one company that uses these, there are four or five that don't—and I've worked for them instead." —Aaron Saray, engineer

Many companies with high applicant volume at the top of the funnel use some kind of online challenge. They are automated, skills-based, and less biased than using resumes. If you choose the right platform,[442] such challenges can increase hiring efficiency. But they will never give you a complete picture of a candidate's ability to do a job, and high potential for false negatives remains, especially if you make the mistake of assigning challenges that have little or nothing to do with the skills required for the role. These are screens meant to disqualify poor fits, and are not useful for qualifying further.

21.3 LinkedIn, GitHub, and Personal Websites

The same principles for collecting signal from resumes apply to LinkedIn profiles, if the profiles are sufficiently filled in.

⚠ CAUTION An incomplete or out-of-date LinkedIn profile presents a challenge. It's common for people with significant experience to have a minimalistic profile.[443] As a recruiter or hiring manager, you may want to ask a candidate if their LinkedIn is current . At the same, demanding that they update it before entering your process can create unnecessary friction. It's wise to be flexible.

With an ever-growing number of engineers contributing to open source, GitHub profiles and GitHub contributions have become a potentially powerful complement (or even a partial replacement) to LinkedIn profiles. Looking at someone's code output in the form of an open-source

---

442. https://engineering.mixmax.com/blog/recruiting-engineers-with-online-challenges
443. In fact, good engineers may have poorly filled-in LinkedIn profiles specifically to help them evade recruiters!

project or GitHub repo can work well at the top of the funnel, if the candidate has produced a large volume of code—effort on the candidate's part is small (they just have to show you where to look), and signal is high. (Later on, you may ask the candidate to dive deeper with you on one or two projects, as part of a past work sample[§27.8] interview.)

While GitHub stars and published code are powerful signals, it's worth remembering that most engineers don't have meaningful projects they can publish. A notable exception is students or other nontraditional candidates who deliberately publish projects on GitHub.

If an engineer has built a personal website or online resume it can be helpful to look at the site itself, both for links to projects and as a demonstration of frontend design or engineering, as appropriate.

21.4 Cover Letters

Cover letters (and whether to include them when you're a candidate or consider them when you're an employer) have historically been a bit of a contentious topic, mostly because of the purported time they take reviewers to read. As a recruiter or hiring manager, you'll be able to tell quickly if it's a generic, copy-pasted form letter. If it is, the letter can't tell you much. But if it's not, then it's absolutely worth reading—the candidate just gave you a huge window into who they are and how they communicate, in a way that a resume cannot. If the letter reads like a thoughtful, passionate human wrote it, then wise hiring teams will seriously consider talking to the candidate. This holds true even if you'd be on the fence just judging from their resume alone.

The converse doesn't always hold true, however. If a candidate looks competent but isn't over the moon about your company yet and hasn't gone out of their way to show their enthusiasm, that's *not* a reason to reject them. If you feel strongly that they'd be great in the position, it's best to let them know you want to talk—you'll have plenty of chances to sell them later.

21.5 Selling vs. Gate-Keeping

Despite changes to technical hiring practices, related hiring practices have been slow to catch up—especially when it comes to filtering candidates through the top of the funnel. Companies typically set up hiring processes to gate-keep rather than sell. But the demands of the market dictate that technical hiring be more about *selling* than filtering. The difficult part for companies isn't sorting through a sea of candidates to figure out who's "the best" or who's worth engaging with.[444] Rather, technical hiring is a sourcing problem. A successful effort begins with getting candidates interested enough to talk to you in the first place and remain engaged as they go through the hiring process.

At a high level, selling is no different in the context of recruiting than it is in more traditional sales of goods and services. You talk to your customer (the candidate), ask questions, listen closely, and learn about their past, what their pain points are, and their hopes and dreams—and then you weave a carefully crafted narrative about how working at your company can actually deliver on those things.

Selling starts with writing great job descriptions that focus on how the role will improve the candidate's life. This may include learning new things, gaining more responsibility, helping to fix problems in the world that matter to them, and so on. Selling ends with compelling offers tailored to the candidate's needs. And in between, a good process will treat every candidate like a unique individual, never taking for granted that they have plenty of other options.

How is this approach different from what most employers are doing?

Read a typical job description, noting the ubiquitous laundry list of sometimes literally impossible[446] requirements, and you'll see that the typical hiring process is set up to exclude rather than attract. Many people involved in technical recruiting and hiring take for granted the fact that the people whose applications cross their desk want to work at their company. The common belief is that it's not worth the time to engage with anyone who doesn't fit an "ideal" mold.

---

444. For further reading on the failures of focusing on weak, traditional top-of-funnel signal, we highly recommend Dan Luu's post, "We only hire the trendiest."[445]

445. https://danluu.com/programmer-moneyball/

446. https://www.linkedin.com/pulse/unrealistic-job-requirements-trouble-jackalopes-george-blomgren/

Given the data available on the internet, a recruiter could reach out to every engineer at Facebook or Google who went to MIT or Stanford. That data is already out there, and between LinkedIn, Clearbit, Entelo, other candidate search aggregators, with a little bit of quick scripting, doing this isn't that hard. What's hard is finding the ones who want to talk to you, and finding the right fit between candidate and company. Companies who understand this are orders of magnitude more successful than ones that don't, and the implications of a candidate-friendly market are what drive wise tactics at every stage of the modern technical hiring process.

Another important reason to develop a better top-of-funnel process is that, despite the volume of candidates out there, traditional hiring practices really only serve candidates who meet a specific small set of qualifications. Every company pushes pedigreed candidates—those with four-year degrees from top schools, who have already worked for a FAANG company—through their funnel, leaving candidates from nontraditional backgrounds feeling like they don't hold a lot of cards. This is not a failure on the part of those candidates, but rather represents maladaptive hiring processes that smaller companies copy from the bigger, more established companies.

No matter where talented engineers come from, they won't join your company unless someone sells them on the idea. This requires optimizing the time you spend on the candidates who want to talk to you. Filtering well at the top of the funnel becomes even more important, so that you do not waste time on candidates who won't engage. There are a number of things you can do[§14] to sell candidates on joining your team when you are making the effort to diversify your pipeline. Each of these methods will help all potential employees feel supported.

This represents a big departure from the more traditional filtering approach, where you would try to save time by cutting candidates who aren't skilled enough to make it through your process. Instead, this approach entails thinking about how you might gauge whether a candidate is likely to want to work for you. Maybe they feel alignment with your mission (or just the more nebulous alignment with your general approach to problems, like disrupting an antiquated, inefficient market space with new technology). Or perhaps they feel excitement about your stack, a history of thematically relevant past projects, or something else. Of course, the hiring process will always contain deal-breakers like whether or not the candidate has the appropriate level of seniority, specific skills, or location; but once those are off the table, the main question isn't "does this candidate seem likely to fail my interview process based on their qualifications?" but rather "would this candidate be excited to work on the stuff we're working on?"

A new wave of tools and credentialing approaches has arisen in recent years to help meet demand for talent in an increasingly competitive hiring market. Assessment tools like online challenges and hiring marketplaces[§23.6] can surface and filter engineers based on skill, rather than pedigree. Educational institutions like bootcamps train new engineers and connect graduates directly with employers. Companies can use these tools in conjunction with resumes, but it may be possible to effectively broaden the applicant pool by ditching the use of resumes in hiring[447] altogether.

Software engineering credentialing *is* changing, and fast. Enrollment in undergraduate computer science programs is growing linearly (and not at all quickly at the very top schools companies recruit from most). On the other hand, enrollment is growing exponentially in software engineering-focused alternative programs/bootcamps and MOOCs. Those who can find a way to surface talent using other credentialing means are going to have a serious advantage for some time.

22 How To Read a Resume

> Aline Lerner provided major contributions to this section.

Most recruiters spend 7.4 seconds[448] on a resume before deciding whether to advance a candidate. This is troubling because a resume is a collection of weak and imperfect signals—some positive, some negative, and some just informative. The purely informative signals can't wisely be used for screening, but they do provide more information about a candidate for later discussion.

> *"A well-formed resume is like a map of where someone can dig later in the interview process."*
> — Scott Woody, former Director of Engineering, Dropbox

---

447. http://blog.alinelerner.com/what-happens-when-you-stop-relying-on-resumes/
448. http://go.theladders.com/rs/539-NBG-120/images/EyeTracking-Study.pdf

Gleaning useful information from resumes requires reading them differently than many companies typically do. There are a variety of signals to look for, and interpreting them in an effective way can take practice.

⚠ **DANGER** In general, not only is the set of signals in a resume noisy, but every signal is imperfect! This means it's important not to qualify or reject any resume from just one or two signals. Taking a holistic view and noting positive and negative signals will allow you to compare them across the pool of candidates you're currently looking at.

Resumes don't provide reviewers with enough information to make thorough and truly fair decisions. The key challenge is, how well can you filter candidates within tight time constraints? How can you make the best of what you *can* learn from resumes?

Resume reviews have three goals:

- **Screening.** To filter out obviously unqualified candidates—those that are least likely to make it further in the hiring process. This can be a large fraction of candidates for roles with popular public job postings.
- **Prioritizing.** Candidates that look especially well suited may be put on the "top of the pile" for the next stage of the funnel.
- **Informing the hiring process.** For candidates you do speak with, resumes help highlight areas of interest and potential concerns to cover in future conversations.

Every signal you look at on a resume can help with one or more of these goals.

22.1 *Filtering on Essential Role Requirements*

Based on the job description and known needs, are there specific types of expertise, experience, and interests that are *essential*? These are deal-breakers—things you can't budge on. Some requirements are pragmatic; others will have been determined when you aligned on the role$^{§16.7}$ with your team.

- **Location.** Must the person work onsite? If so, and they are not local, are they willing to relocate?

Part IV: Connecting With Candidates   191

- **H1B or other visa sponsorship.** Especially if you're a smaller company, sponsoring a new visa can be logistically prohibitive because you have to wait over a year before the candidate can start. In general, H1B *transfers* are less demanding. TN and H1B1 visas are also less onerous.[449]
- **Domain expertise.** Does the candidate have the specific background needed for the role? For software engineers, this might include web or fullstack app development, mobile app development, backend engineering, or data science or machine learning. This also includes the general area of work, such as SaaS and enterprise software, healthcare or biology, finance or accounting, and so on.
- **Previous roles.** Do the nature and scope of past roles demonstrate that the candidate is prepared for or likely to succeed in this role? Has the candidate done the same type of job before? Must the person have management or product experience, or experience solving technical problems with customers? If all previous roles differ greatly from what the candidate would be responsible for in this role, it's probably not a fit.
- **Seniority.** Do the breadth and scope of experience reflect the level of seniority required for this role? Are you willing to hire someone into their first management position, or do you require that they have management experience?

    - 🔥 CONFUSION Seniority can be a hard requirement to nail down because companies often over-index on it as a proxy for ability. Some roles really do require candidates to have five or more years of experience, but if you're hiring for a generalist role that prizes execution, you may weigh the extra couple years a more senior candidate offers against the energy and potential of a gritty, hungry, more junior candidate who's been coding since before college.[450]

- **Technology experience.** If the new role requires a significant level of depth in a specific technology—be it React, AWS, Java EE, Keras and Tensorflow, Java memory management, high-performance C++, or web performance optimization—then it makes sense to filter on that.

---

449. Consult an immigration lawyer for the details on visa sponsorship.
450. It's so common for recruiters to have excessive experience requirements that developers routinely joke about impossibly many[451] years of experience.
451. https://dev.to/jsrn/you-want-how-many-years-experience-4jl4

This is more likely to apply to rarer skills that require years to develop, such as GIS systems, embedded systems, or particular hardware architectures. But if your company is willing to mentor engineers or you expect the candidate to learn on the job, specific technical skills are less relevant.

- ◇ CAUTION It's common to over-index on specific tech "keywords" when filtering resumes. Talented engineers pick up technologies quickly, especially if they're early in their career or not hyper-specialized. Passing over a talented engineer because of what language or technologies they know only makes sense if the knowledge is truly essential and you can't afford ramp-up time. More often, it will make sense to use specific technologies as a search or *prioritization* parameter, but not as a blind filter.

> "Don't ask the candidate for things you don't really need. Any friction you add at the earliest stages of the filtering process will ultimately hurt you."
> — Aline Lerner, co-founder and CEO, interviewing.io

22.2 Resume Presentation

Presentation may seem less important than content, but in fact indicates an understanding of audience (and even empathy for others), clarity in writing, and attention to detail.

A study at TrialPay[452] tried to find patterns between all candidates who had been interviewed within a year's period, and everyone who had been offered a position at the company. What mattered in a resume when it came to on-the-job performance? Which school they attended? Seniority or advanced degrees? Side projects? Number of languages they'd mastered?

Far and away, what mattered most was the number of typos and grammatical errors on someone's resume—most people who got an offer had two errors or fewer. This study also revealed that where people went to school had no effect on their performance. The only other factors that predicted on-the-job performance that could be found on a resume were the

---

452. This study was conducted by the author of this section, Aline Lerner, when she ran hiring at TrialPay.

clarity with which candidates described what they worked on at previous jobs, and whether they had worked at a top company (this mattered least).[453]

- **Language, spelling, and punctuation.** Writing a full-page resume that is cleanly formatted with no detectable errors in grammar, spelling, or punctuation always requires attention to detail. Does the resume have conspicuous errors, like multiple typos, spelling errors, or inconsistency in formatting and punctuation? If someone can't write a page of text without typos, it's not unreasonable to expect typos to appear in other material they write—like in their code.

  - ⚠ CAUTION Poor English alone isn't a strong negative signal for non-native speakers, unless strong English skills are required for the role.

- **Technical clarity and accuracy.** Clarity in role descriptions is actually quite rare on resumes. Are the descriptions of roles or projects unusually hard to follow? Most engineers aren't great writers, or are not focused on business context, so this is only a negative signal if the descriptions themselves are quite unclear or technically suspect.
- **Context and impact.** Does the description of roles include enough context to understand the role? Does it include impact in terms of product relevance or business metrics? Engineers fairly rarely describe this well, so this is mainly a positive signal for senior candidates.

22.3 Education and Awards

22.3.1 ACADEMIC BACKGROUND AND ACHIEVEMENT

Degrees from academically exclusive schools are a notable signal, because getting into and graduating from an elite institution like MIT reflects success with well-known curriculum and level of rigor. When assessing how rigorous a computer science program is, it can help to know rankings of these programs in the United States[454] as well as those in other countries;

---

453. http://blog.interviewing.io/lessons-from-a-years-worth-of-hiring-data/
454. https://www.usnews.com/best-graduate-schools/top-science-schools/computer-science-rankings

for example, the IIT[455] schools and the related JEE rankings[456] reflect competitive admissions across India.

However, it's a common pitfall to look mainly for "brand name" schools or obsess on school rankings. (For more detail on how academic background can be a source of bias, see Diversity and Inclusion.[§9]) Interviewing.io looked at whether the school that candidates attended had any bearing on interview performance. In a study of 1,000 college students, it turned out there wasn't any statistically significant difference in performance between students who went to elite universities and students who went to other schools (at least among those who had decided to sign up for an interview practice platform of their own volition).[457]

For many general programming and engineering roles, a higher degree is not required. But some roles, like machine learning or algorithmic roles, do require graduate-level knowledge.

⚠ DANGER School rankings is probably the one signal that's most overweighted. Exceptional technical talent can come out of any school, or from no school at all. In another study[458] from interviewing.io, researchers cross-referenced interview performance data from 3,000 candidates with attributes listed on their resumes. This time, what mattered most was whether a candidate had taken programming classes via MOOCs like Udacity and Coursera.

22.3.2 AWARDS OR OTHER ACHIEVEMENTS

Has the person achieved something that requires unusual talent or dedication to achieve? This may include side projects that achieved some recognition or significant use, talks, industry awards, or the like.

> *"One of the things we've seen from all our data crunching is that GPAs are worthless as a criteria for hiring, and test scores are worthless—[there is] no correlation at all except for brand-new college grads, where there's a slight correlation."*
> — Laszlo Bock, former SVP of People Operations, Google[459]

---

455. https://en.wikipedia.org/wiki/Indian_Institutes_of_Technology
456. https://en.wikipedia.org/wiki/Joint_Entrance_Examination_%E2%80%93_Advanced
457. http://blog.interviewing.io/we-looked-at-how-a-thousand-college-students-performed-in-technical-interviews-to-see-if-where-they-went-to-school-mattered-it-didnt/
458. http://blog.interviewing.io/lessons-from-3000-technical-interviews/
459. https://www.nytimes.com/2013/06/20/business/in-head-hunting-big-data-may-not-be-suc

⚑ CONTROVERSY Computer science MS degrees can be a confusing signal, especially when achieved after a non-computer science undergraduate degree. Some recruiters find that people returning to school for an MS degree in CS may signal inadequate programming experience, which could lead to poor technical interview performance. One theory as to why this occurs is that CS fundamentals instruction tends to happen in undergraduate computer science courses, and some MS programs are geared toward students who have never done any programming either—such programs serve professionals eager to return to school and learn some basic technical skills. At certain schools it is possible to get an MS in CS without ever taking an algorithms or data structures class. Another point is that MS degrees tend to increase income by about $10K per year. But someone already employed and successful as a software engineer would probably earn more by staying in their job, rather than leaving work to return to school for an MS degree.

22.4 Employment History and Achievements

Next are the signals you can collect from all of a candidate's past roles.

22.4.1 NOTABLE ROLES AND ACHIEVEMENTS

Getting an offer and holding a job at a company that has a well-known, high hiring bar is a notable positive signal. For some companies, the stage at which a person joins may indicate level of difficulty in being admitted; for example, it was probably harder to get a job at Google in 2005 than in 2015. The same caveats apply to name-brand companies as to name-brand schools. Key here are unique high-responsibility roles. Someone who is tech lead, architect, or manager of a team with significant importance to a company is a particularly strong signal.

Notable achievements can include open-source projects, businesses or products built, or patents. This includes traction. Do any businesses or projects (open-source or otherwise) have objective signs of interest and value to others? GitHub stars? Numbers of users? Revenue?

22.4.2 CAREER TRANSITIONS AND TRAJECTORY

The set of job transitions a person has had can indicate one of two patterns:

- **Job hopping.** Does the person tend to stay at some jobs for a longer period, or do they tend to move on after a year or so? How much of a signal this is depends on the length of someone's career so far. For more senior candidates, the pattern can be more obvious.
- **Very few job changes.** Has the candidate been in their most recent job 10+ years? Were there signs of career advancement? This may not be a negative signal, unless it's most of the person's career and that past work differs greatly from the new role. If the candidate has only had one role, and that was in a very different environment or domain than the new role, there may not be a fit.

🌶 CONTROVERSY How much you can infer about someone based on "job hopping" is a controversial topic. Switching jobs once or twice quickly is *not* a negative signal. If a candidate has had six positions, and never stayed at any one of them more than a year or two, that indicates a pattern worth considering carefully. This may mean that they are difficult to work with or have had poor performance in the past. That said, URG employees do leave companies at higher rates, often due to unwelcoming work environments or discrimination, and that's important to note as another plausible cause for frequent transitions. Overall, it's important to learn more and discuss with the candidate before judging.

When evaluating a candidate's career trajectory, a number of factors are worth considering. How far has someone come in their career? How have their roles evolved, and how quickly? Where have their roles shifted?

Career trajectory is one of the more powerful signals a resume carries. However, it can be difficult to tease apart real career growth from flowery embellishments, and to put growth in the context of the candidate's circumstances. One of the surest positive signals comes from consistent increase in responsibility over a number of years, both within a single company and at company transitions. In a healthy and *growing* company, such as a mid-stage startup, a strong employee will take on more responsibility every year or two.

The most immediate and obvious way to spot growing responsibility is to look at job titles, but it's not always that straightforward. Titles are typically not standardized—startups often provide much broader exposure to problems, higher levels of ownership, and more rapid growth opportunity given the distribution of problems to the people able to own them. Reading leveling documents, like Square's open-source framework,[460] might also give you a good idea of what to look for, but it's important to remember that most startups won't be at the point where they have a formalized leveling system. (See Setting Levels and Titles[§17] for more.)

Note that at more mature companies, lack of visible promotion may not be a negative signal. At large companies, it can get very difficult to get a promotion, especially when working in hyper-mature product environments. For example, when working on infrastructure at a huge search engine, the only way to get a promotion might be through squeezing nanoseconds of latency out of returned results, after hundreds of other brilliant minds have already tried. Certain types of engineers might be well-suited to this, but others may have a much more rapid trajectory in a broader, more exploratory environment.

Of course, the candidate may have moved between companies often as well, so it's worth considering if their role expanded or evolved at each transition.

22.4.3 DESCRIPTIONS OF PAST WORK AND ROLES

Candidates can also stand out in the way they describe their experience. A candidate's ability to write about their work with clarity is highly valuable, and is likely to translate to good communication skills in their work.

It's easy to forget what clear communication looks like because it's rare; when you read a bunch of bad descriptions in a row, they start to seem normal. And it's hard to deprioritize or even reject candidates who have gone to great schools or have worked at top companies just because they didn't describe what they did at their last job particularly well.

◇ IMPORTANT When looking at an actual resume, the ultimate test for whether a description of a role is well-written is to read it, and then try to explain it out loud, in your own words. If you can't do it, the description isn't effective.

---

460. https://developer.squareup.com/blog/squares-growth-framework-for-engineers-and-engineering-managers/

Especially with nontraditional candidates, good writing is everything, because the rest of their resume will likely not have as much helpful information—either they're junior or they've worked at places you haven't heard of. In these situations, how well they understand their work and how much they care about it is the best signal you have.

A well-written role description:

1. Includes quantifiable, results-driven descriptions of the impact of the candidate's work.
2. Demonstrates an understanding of the nuance really required to own a function.
3. Has simple and direct language that's not fluffy or riddled with obscure or confusing phrasing.
4. Goes beyond lists of tools to give details of the candidate's work in the larger context of their team or the company.

CANDIDATE When describing past work, focus on giving the reader as much context as they need to understand your role and its impact on the company. What were you responsible for and why did it matter? If there is a role you're particularly interested in, you may also choose to highlight experiences that represent your interest in that space, or any relevant tools or techniques that demonstrate skill and context. Visualize explaining your work to someone who is intelligent but knows nothing of what you do. Where do you start and where do you end? You probably wouldn't jump into the middle, with lots of internal jargon or specific bug fixes; you'd go "top down" and explain why your work matters and what makes it interesting or difficult, include any key results, and omit extraneous details.

Note that the same rules may not apply to LinkedIn profiles, as those are in the public sphere, whether a candidate is looking or not, and often candidates who are in high demand will purposely keep their LinkedIns sparse to discourage recruiter spam.

22.5 *Personal History and Trajectory*

Considering how a candidate got to where they are gives insight into their abilities. Some people call this "grit," or "distance traveled," or "affirmative meritocracy." Where did this person begin, and where are they now? Have they come further than one might expect? Are there signs they have overcome significant obstacles in life through hard work or creativity? Candidates with a less advantaged background may have had to work very hard to get to the same position another candidate attained more easily. A job at an elite tech company is much easier to land after a Stanford CS degree than for someone from a small community college far from any technology hubs.

> 📖 STORY Many years ago, when I was working as a software engineer at a small company, one of the existing engineers referred a close friend of his from high school. Though they had taken many of the same classes and spent a good amount of time building projects together, their paths diverged pretty wildly after graduation. The employee graduated from a top 10 computer science school. His friend, on the other hand, attended a much lower-tier college for a semester before dropping out, and at the time of the referral, he was doing data entry. When we first looked at the referral's resume, we had no idea what to do with it, and most people on the team wanted to pass on him. But, one thing on his resume stood out—he had spent several seasons teaching programming at a prestigious summer program for gifted high school students. This type of leadership and initiative were largely at odds with what we expected a candidate with his profile, and ultimately that's what tipped us into hiring him. To this day (close to a decade later), he works at the aforementioned company, and has ownership over much of the application's backend architecture. —Aline Lerner, co-founder and CEO, interviewing.io

22.5.1 HOW DID THEY LEARN TO BE A PROGRAMMER?

While rarely of use for filtering, how a candidate became a programmer can give a lot of insight into their personal journey and technical temperament. There are many ways to become a good engineer, but these backgrounds can cultivate different strengths and styles, and the story can help you get to know someone better. The most common paths to becoming a programmer are:

- Self-taught at a young age (perhaps they started with an interest in building video games or taking apart and rebuilding computers)

- Switched course mid-career to become a developer, perhaps going back to school or a coding bootcamp
- A background in business or finance that led to a focus on programming
- A role in IT or system administration that led to software engineering
- Desire to build a product or business (often a young entrepreneur)
- Formal college or graduate education (in computer science or computer engineering, math, or a field of science where computation was involved).

22.6 Strength in Other Domains

In addition to engineering skills, many other areas of drive and skill are relevant for technical roles. If an unusual combination of skills is relevant for the role, these kinds of signals are powerful and excellent for prioritizing resumes. By specifically looking for these signals, you can turn a tedious resume screening process into a huge value add by finding rare candidates with exceptional *combinations* of skills.

- **Entrepreneurial focus.** Has this person started a business before? This can often be seen by project descriptions—does the candidate focus on technical concerns only, or do they include business impact? A purely technical engineering role doesn't need a proclivity for entrepreneurship or an obsession with revenue, but senior roles or roles at smaller companies can greatly benefit from these qualities.
- **Growth or marketing focus.** Does the candidate talk a lot about moving metrics? Are they focused on quantifiable impact? Have they had marketing-affiliated roles?
- **Customer focus.** Have past roles included talking to customers or external people? Solutions engineers and sales engineers often need to do this.
- **Product focus.** Do they describe what the value of a product is to its end-users, or why they built certain pieces of software? This is great for product engineering roles.
- **Design focus.** A visually polished resume, with carefully selected typography or web design, shows the candidate probably has a focus on design. You can also see this from projects or role descriptions.

A few more technical areas to consider:

- **Data science or machine learning focus.** Is there evidence this person been excited by problems that involve data challenges, noisy data, or extracting insights from datasets using a variety of tools?
- **Mathematical or algorithmic focus.** Is the candidate focused on technical problems involving algorithmic or mathematical challenges? Have they published research papers? Typically these are people who've developed these skills in an academic setting.
- **Writing and documentation focus.** Does the candidate have experience and skill with written communication, internally or externally? Is this a skill they value? You can also tell by how they write about past work.
- **Past work environment.** This is more subjective, and usually isn't useful for filtering, but can be good to know when discussing past work.
- **Company size.** Has the person worked only at small, growth stage, or large companies? It's not unusual to see an engineer who has only worked at companies of 1,000 or more people. That can mean a big shift in working style compared to being an engineer at early or growth-stage startups. Exceptionally talented engineers can excel in one environment and flounder in the other.
- **Enterprise vs. consumer product experience.** Engineers used to enterprise products, or building purely internal tooling for use within a large company, tend to be used to different objectives than consumer-facing product engineers. Another variation is people who've worked primarily on internal tooling, which is often closer to enterprise experience.
- **Experimentation vs. focus.** Does the candidate work on side projects or seem to do a lot of different things, or stick to their one job? If the role involves a lot of novel or creative prototyping of new work, a track record of building new things could be a strong asset. But for some roles, this is not required.

◇ IMPORTANT It might be useful to have a list of things you don't screen for.[461]

---

461. https://medium.engineering/engineering-interviews-what-we-dont-screen-for-4381cfdfa703

22.7 Likelihood of Joining

Given the current hiring market for technical roles, it's essential to consider early on whether a candidate is reasonably likely to be interested in your company, and leave their current role. Switching to a selling rather than a vetting mindset might include prioritizing their interest in your space (have they blogged about something relevant, do they have relevant work on GitHub?) over their pedigree. This is also an excellent opportunity for arbitrage—if you can spot something in prospective candidates that others cannot, your odds of closing them will be much higher, because those candidates won't be bombarded by requests from the open market. In other words, if you can spot grit and passion in lieu of traditional markers like pedigree, you'll wind up making much more efficient use of your limited time.

23 Candidate Sources

Most companies hire using a mix of sources or channels, and these evolve as a company grows and matures.

In the early days of a small startup, the founders often use their personal networks to hire people they have a pre-existing relationship with. They might start to tap into some candidate flow from recruiting platforms and marketplaces. As their hiring needs grow, hiring managers might start doing outbound sourcing for really specific roles, and working with external recruiters, either on a contingency or contract basis. Eventually, as a company scales and matures, it usually makes sense to start hiring internal recruiters to take on some of the responsibility of generating candidate flow. At scale, most companies rely on a mix of employee referrals, inbound applicants, and outbound sourcing.

⚡ **STARTUP** Although data is hard to come by, Lightspeed Ventures' Startup Hiring Trends[462] report cited that startups at different stages seemed to maintain "the rule of happy thirds": relying for about a third each of their hires on sourced candidates, inbound candidates, and referrals.

---

462. http://startuphiringtrends.com/

Image and video processing startup Kapwing detailed their top-of-funnel strategy,[463] which helpfully walks readers through the channels they sourced candidates from, where job ads were posted, and ultimately what the most effective channels were.

> *"The metric you're looking to optimize is number of high quality hires—not number of candidates. Even if one channel brings in hundreds of good candidates, another channel that results in fewer hires but requires less effort will be a more efficient use of your time."*
>
> — Greg Brockman, Chairman and CTO, OpenAI[464]

23.0.1 FIGURE: HIRING SOURCES BY COMPANY STAGE AND VOLUME

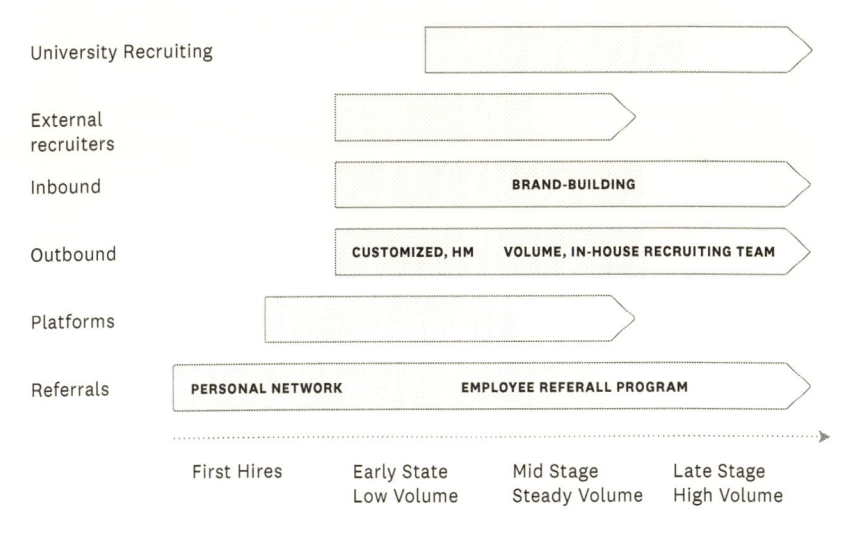

University Recruiting			
External recruiters			
Inbound		BRAND-BUILDING	
Outbound	CUSTOMIZED, HM	VOLUME, IN-HOUSE RECRUITING TEAM	
Platforms			
Referrals	PERSONAL NETWORK	EMPLOYEE REFERRAL PROGRAM	
	First Hires	Early State / Low Volume	Mid Stage / Steady Volume	Late Stage / High Volume

Source: Holloway

23.1 Referrals

A **referral candidate** is a candidate brought to a company's attention by an individual who has an existing relationship with the company. Founders, employees, investors, advisors, and even other candidates may refer candidates. Referrals, and particularly referrals from employees, are

---

463. https://www.kapwing.com/blog/what-it-takes-to-hire-10-employees-in-san-francisco/
464. https://firstround.com/review/How-Stripe-built-one-of-Silicon-Valleys-best-engineering-teams/

the most common source of hires across industries and stage of company.[465]

23.1.1 ADVANTAGES AND RISKS

Key advantages of referrals, particularly those referred by a current team member, include:

- **Knowledge of their abilities.** Years of working together are far better signal of skills than an interview process can give.
- **Knowledge of their ability to work with the existing team.** There is always risk when hiring people with no previous relationship with anyone on a team that trust is lower, or hard-to-predict interpersonal dynamics make a hire less effective. This is why it's a common pattern in startups for one senior hire to bring with them one or two people from a previous team.
- **Team coherence and commitment.** When joining a company where a person has long-term relationships, people may be more committed and unwilling to depart unexpectedly or in an unprofessional way.
- **Cost savings.** Sourcing through referrals means you don't have to hire a recruiter or spend time and money marketing your company and the position to the general public.

> "Focus on the right ways to source candidates. Basically, this boils down to 'use your personal networks more.' By at least a 10x margin, the best candidate sources I've ever seen are friends and friends of friends."
>
> — Sam Altman, chairman, Y Combinator[466]

⚠ DANGER While Altman's advice is very common in technical hiring and across fields, prioritizing hiring through referrals over all other sourcing and recruiting efforts can lead to a highly homogenous team that lacks the ability to challenge and question its decisions, directions, and tactics. Especially in early-stage companies, it can lead to diversity debt, which is difficult to remedy. Lack of diversity is an egregious problem[§9] in techni-

---

465. https://www.shrm.org/resourcesandtools/hr-topics/talent-acquisition/pages/employee-referrals-remains-top-source-hires.aspx
466. https://blog.samaltman.com/how-to-hire

cal teams; Aline Lerner talks more about the relationship between referrals and diversity in a Software Engineering Daily podcast.[467]

⚠ DANGER There are other risks from relying too heavily on referrals:

- **Lack of fairness.** Heavy use of referral recommendations can lead to lack of fair hiring decisions because they may not prioritize an equitable assessment of abilities. Especially for early-stage startups, where networks might be limited to those of two or three people, referral-dependent sourcing can lead to hiring friends and family over the most qualified candidates.
- **Poor team dynamics.** It can encourage the formation of cliques of people who know each other better than others on a team, which can lead to resentment.

These risks don't mean that you should ignore your network entirely, but that you should approach your network with an eye for its gaps and blindspots. If the majority of candidates sourced through your network look the same, have similar backgrounds, and bring similar ideas and experiences to the table, make a careful assessment of who you're asking for help and how you can widen your own network—you'll want to explore the other methods for finding candidates in this section as well. As we discuss in Diversity and Inclusion in Tech,§9 diverse teams, especially at the early stage where they set a hiring precedent, are highly influential to companies' success and ability to innovate.

23.1.2 STARTUPS: WORKING YOUR NETWORK

🌱 STARTUP Given that referrals remain the most common source of hires, it's important to put effort into expanding the candidate source that is your network. When you do so with an understanding of the risks of referral reliance, you'll have a better chance of hiring qualified people who might otherwise not have the chance to meet, rather than clones of current employees.

At some point, a purely referral-based candidate generation strategy might start hitting diminishing returns. You and your team might "max out" your networks, or your networks may not have the diversity or skill sets you need. Exactly when this happens can vary from team to team.

---

467. https://softwareengineeringdaily.com/2017/10/19/interviewing-io-with-aline-lerner/

Many teams might start maxing out their networks at or below 10 engineers, but one of this Guide's well-connected contributors was able to grow to almost 100 engineers almost solely using referrals.

As a general rule of thumb, most people end up realizing that with a little persistence they can push their network further than they initially thought. Peter Kazanjy, co-founder of TalentBin, details his process for treating recruiting like a sales pipeline[468] to maximize the potential of employee referrals. He even includes his outreach templates that you can use when you need to start sending emails to prospective candidates.

TripleByte co-founder Harj Taggar suggests asking referred candidates who they would refer as well–even if they're not interested.[469] This is a second-order option that can expand the reach of your network but still originates from closely trusted sources.

Curious about how two early engineers at Facebook had to adjust when they created their own business? Read Aditya Agarwal's story on his and Ruchi Sanghvi's experience in "Hiring at Startups Vs. Big Companies: Hiring at a startup was drastically different than at Facebook,"[470] on the Holloway blog.

> "Early on, the best approach to recruiting is to have people on your team actively refer in people from their network."
> — Elad Gil, entrepreneur, author, and investor[471]

⚡ STARTUP Founders or hiring managers at early-stage companies should allocate a chunk of time to working their network. Some approaches:

- Perform systematic scans of your network. Browse your entire list of connections on LinkedIn to jog your memory. Ask investors, advisors, friends, and former coworkers for referrals, giving them enough context to allow them to make good referrals.
- Nurture mutually trusting relationships with others who are well-connected and a good judge of talent. When the time is right, reach out to friends and explain what you're trying to hire for and why.

---

468. https://firstround.com/review/Mine-Your-Network-for-Early-Stage-Hiring-Gold/
469. https://blog.ycombinator.com/how-to-hire-your-first-engineer/
470. https://www.holloway.com/s/trh-aditya-agarwal-startup-hiring
471. http://growth.eladgil.com/book/recruiting/scaling-a-recruiting-organization/

- Whenever you can, offer to help others with referrals, too. This may not immediately solve your recruiting needs, but being helpful to others helps everyone, including yourself, in the long run.
- Identify candidates who are known by your existing connections, and ask if they're willing to make an intro, taking care to make the introduction both optional and easy.
- Ask your referrals for referrals.

People are often glad to make referrals, as a good referral is a positive thing for all three people involved.

⚠ DANGER A common pitfall for those looking to get referrals is to be too transactional or thoughtless when asking for help. Unfortunately, it is common for people to reach out wildly to hundreds of connections in a way that inconveniences or annoys. Referrals take time, thought, and social capital from the person making the referral. Don't ask for them lightly, or act like you value your time more than the person you're asking a referral from. Explain the real value of what your company does, or what's interesting about the role. Try to reciprocate with help. Don't expect to reach out to someone you've not bothered to talk to in years, only to ask them to enthusiastically introduce you to their most talented friends.

Always remember, you're asking for a favor. It's important to make it easy to say yes:[472]

- **Be specific.** Ask for what you need and explain why. Don't be vague in the hopes that the person will make an offer to help you with exactly what you're looking for. If the person you're asking for help can't figure out what their role is supposed to be, it's going to create more work for them to go back and forth with you until they can pull it out. But specificity does not mean over-explaining. You also want to keep it short. You can (and should) include a line like, "Please let me know if there's any more information I can provide."
- **Be complimentary.** It never hurts to pump the person up a little. Are they uniquely positioned to help you because they've been really successful at hiring fullstack engineers in the past? Do you completely trust their opinion and ability to judge the quality of someone's work

---

472. https://okdork.com/make-it-easy-to-say-yes/

because so-and-so in your circle speaks highly of them? Maybe you read a recent blog post of theirs that blew you out of the water. Let them know.

- **Don't be selfish.** Yes, many people in the startup community are eager to help others. But you are not entitled to other people's time or to a connection. Don't use language like "I need," or anything that sounds like "It's really important that you do this for me." Don't demand anything, and be sensitive of their time even if you're running on a deadline.
- **Encourage the double opt-in introduction.** This strategy is for the person making the connection for you, but it's good for you to know, because with a forwardable introduction email (below), you can help. The double opt-in introduction[473] is a mouthful but pretty straightforward. When you ask someone for an introduction, that person should double check that the person you want to meet is actually interested in being introduced. If they say yes, your contact is free to make the connection. People are busy and this is a gesture of respect. So in the future if someone asks you to connect them to another person, you'll want to check and see if that person is interested and if they have the time.
- **Use the forwardable introduction email.** The forwardable introduction email[474] is a way to maximize your chances of success with double opt-in introductions and make it easy for the people you're asking for help to say yes. This is a big one.

  - The problem with most double opt-in introduction requests is that they create work for the person connecting the two parties. To check whether the person you want to meet is interested, they have to write an email that lays out why you want to be connected and why they should speak with you. For most people, writing an email about someone else's company isn't the biggest priority in the work day. As a result, doing so gets deprioritized and may never happen.
  - To get around this, when you're asking for an introduction, you should write an email to the connector that they can simply forward to the person you're asking to meet. This email should contain

---

473. https://www.inc.com/jordan-harbinger/how-to-make-sure-your-email-introductions-always-succeed.html
474. https://alexiskold.net/2015/06/24/how-to-write-a-forwardable-introduction-email/

a bit about you and why you want to be introduced. This way, the connector can simply press "forward," and add a short note along the lines of, "So-and-so is terrific; I think you should meet them." It only takes a few seconds. If the person says they're interested, then all the connector has to do is add you on a new reply on the same email thread and the connection is made.

- ◇ IMPORTANT When you get this far, make sure to Bcc your connector[475] when you thank them in your reply.

- **Say thank you.** In addition to thanking the person and Bcc'ing them, it's always nice to send them a follow-up email letting them know that the connection was successful and you really appreciate their involvement. If the connection turns out to be huge for you—if you end up hiring the person—you can even send a handwritten note or a small token of appreciation. When you're the person being asked for help, what would you like to hear?

For more tips on building a great network, visit Networking for Startup Founders,[476] a free excerpt from the Holloway Guide to Raising Venture Capital,[477] from which this list was adapted.

23.1.3 LARGER COMPANY STRATEGIES

For mid-sized and large companies with multiple sources of candidates, referrals usually remain one of the most important channels. After all, every new member of the team has their own network just waiting to be tapped into. Some mid-sized or large companies invest in systemizing the referral process by:

- **Offering incentives.** Incentives for employees who successfully refer candidates can range from simple recognition to a cash bonus to stock (from 2013-2017, Uber gave out 500 shares to employees who successfully referred new hires in software engineering, even for the recruiting team).[478] At some companies, this cash bonus can be in the thousands of dollars (as high as $5K for some roles). But don't make it

---

475. https://www.theatlantic.com/entertainment/archive/2017/04/im-moving-you-to-bcc/522885/
476. https://www.holloway.com/s/excerpt-networking-for-founders
477. https://www.holloway.com/g/venture-capital/details
478. Private conversation with Ozzie Osman, San Francisco, 2019.

just about the cash.[479] Your team should be convinced that referring a friend or acquaintance is a win for both their referral and for the company; you want them to be intrinsically motivated to help make that happen. Digital Ocean overhauled their referral program[480] to include charitable donations along with cash for referrals, and saw a significant bump in the number of employee referrals.

- **Regular network reviews.** Creating a regular cadence for recruiters or hiring managers to meet with employees to scan and tap into their networks can be a great strategy. Some companies conduct "sourcing jams" where groups of employees meet to go through their networks together. These can also be one-on-one meetings between a recruiter or hiring manager and each employee.
- **Memory-jogging techniques.** Most people can't keep their entire network top of mind. Sequoia's Human Capital Team uses the memory palace to help employees dig deep into their memories for possible referrals, a technique they describe in a blog post, "3X Your Referral Rates."[481] Google found that aided recall using specific prompts helped significantly, while referral incentives did not.[482]
- **Involving the referrer.** Giving employees regular updates on the progress of candidates they referred can encourage future referrals (as opposed to letting them feel like their referrals are going into a black hole). In addition, you can use the referrer to help build the candidate's excitement throughout the process (and especially at the offer stage). Some companies give special attention to referral candidates by fast-tracking them through the process, but this can affect the fairness of your process.

CANDIDATE If you're applying to a company, a referral from an existing employee is a great way to get your foot in the door. We've seen some candidates feel uncomfortable asking their connections for a referral into a company, but you shouldn't feel like you're pulling any favors. After all, if a referral works out, it's a win for you, a win for your referrer, and a win for the company you're joining.

---

479. https://business.linkedin.com/talent-solutions/blog/2015/05/how-google-dramatically-increased-referrals-hint-more-money-didnt-work
480. https://brightfunds.blog/2017/09/06/digitalocean-case-study/
481. https://www.sequoiacap.com/article/3x-referral-rates/
482. https://qz.com/404494/the-simple-way-google-supercharged-employee-referrals-and-why-it-wasnt-enough/

23.2 Inbound Applicants

At first glance, this channel may seem low-effort because the setup is so simple: post your job descriptions to your own website and to other job sites and watch the applicants roll in. But because it's easy for people to find and apply for these positions, the bulk of applicants may not be relevant to what you're looking for. In fact, while some applicants may be really interested in your company, many others may not be and may have applied to dozens of openings without looking closely at the company or role.

The candidate flow you receive will also be a function of your employer brand. While having a strong employer brand may help attract more candidates, it can also further increase noise.

Ultimately, it's useful to think about the types of candidates that will find and apply to your job postings. Many of the best candidates may never apply to job postings because they are so actively sought after. But there might be a fantastic new up-and-comer applying for jobs who hasn't been given a shot yet or isn't connected to your networks. Inbound applicants can also give you a more diverse pool of candidates than relying solely on who-knows-who.

We do know some really great hiring managers who rarely rely on inbound applicants, but that's typically because they've been around for a while and have built strong networks. Inbound can be a good way to supplement other channels if you approach it with the right strategy:

- Try to get your job postings and company in front of a *targeted* audience. Think about where you can reach the types of candidates you want to hire: mailing lists, products, conference, or meetups. Will exposure in that channel increase your signal, or your noise?
- Have a systemized way of easily screening[§21] applicants for appropriate technical knowledge.
- Consider introducing some friction, but be careful about what this friction selects for. For example, if you're a desirable company trying to hire new grads, asking applicants to complete a coding challenge can help filter out candidates that lack a serious interest in your company or the requisite technical skills. But not all friction is good friction. Extra steps might end up deterring desirable candidates as well. After all, they might be less likely to be willing to jump through hoops before

you've even established a relationship with them. Some applicants will simply follow the path of least resistance.
- Inbound applications can also help you gauge market sentiment and brand value of your company. You can add a brief survey to job site applicants asking about how they found your company, their opinion of your company, and asking them for feedback on your process.

An Intercom guest post[483] by Oren Ellenbogen lists a few helpful suggestions for increasing your inbound leads, including:

- Engaging with people online, through social media, and answering questions on StackOverflow, Quora, and elsewhere.
- Writing about your product, team, and engineering practices—if you don't have your own blog, seek out those that you think best attract your target candidates and ask to write there.
- Hosting hackathons, giving talks, and creating public coding challenges.
- Open sourcing some of your tools.

23.2.1 FILTERING INBOUND CANDIDATES

Many companies don't give inbound candidates as much time as their other channels. Because the market is saturated with candidates, the perception is that the most talented people do not *need* to apply anywhere—the jobs will come to them. But the better you can treat your inbound channel, the more leverage you can gain over competitors who neglect this source. Along with junior candidates, like those just graduating from college, the inbound channel is typically where you'll find more nontraditional candidates who have typically been gatekept from tech. There are certainly diamonds to be found.

We cover this topic in detail in Connecting With Candidates,[§20] but while you're here, these are the two most important things to look for when filtering inbound candidates:

1. **Polish.** The number of grammatical errors and typos in a resume matters more when it comes to job performance than a candidate's pedigree.[484] Polish is one of the first things you can look for when filtering through your inbound. It's not a hard and fast rule, but the ability to

---

483. https://www.intercom.com/blog/inbound-recruiting-engineers/
484. http://blog.interviewing.io/lessons-from-a-years-worth-of-hiring-data/

communicate well, especially in a document that has had the chance to go through multiple revisions, is a strong signal that this person is conscientious and cares.
2. **How they talk about past work.** How someone talks about their past work can give you a good indication of not only what the candidate has worked on but also how much they care about the work they're doing or have done, how well they understand it, what actually matters to them, and of course, whether they can communicate complex concepts clearly to others.

23.3 Outbound Sourcing

> "The great software developers, indeed, the best people in every field, are quite simply never on the market."
> — Joel Spolsky, chairman and co-founder, Trello, Glitch, Stack Overflow[485]

Sourcing is a great way to find candidates who might not be actively looking for a job—many of the most talented engineers are rarely on the market. It can also be a good way to uncover candidates who may be overlooked by more brand-recognizable companies. But this channel does come with challenges. Many candidates may not be open to new opportunities, and so getting your timing right can be difficult. Additionally, so many companies have abused this method by spamming people that many have just learned to tune out the noise. At this point, most people you reach out to will never respond to your message, if they read it at all. And of course, the most sought-after candidates receive the most messages, and so are *less* likely to respond—that is, unless your message resonates and the timing works out.

Because of these significant challenges, outbound sourcing may seem like a numbers game: the more messages you send, the more likely you are to hit the right candidate with the right message at the right time... right? Perhaps, but getting them to then join your company is going to be an even more significant challenge—becoming a company or individual known for spamming the engineering community is not good for you. Every time you reach out to a candidate you are consuming some of your company's

---
485. https://www.joelonsoftware.com/2006/09/06/finding-great-developers-2/

brand equity. Unsolicited messaging is always a potential unwarranted interruption. But if your outbound sourcing is targeted and thoughtful, the less cost there will be to the brand, and the more likely the person will be to respond.

23.3.1 TIPS AND STRATEGIES

- **Personalize your message.** When reaching out to a candidate, it's worth telling them why you found their background interesting and why you think they might be a good fit for your company. *You-centric* language (such as "your profile really stood out because X" is often more effective than *we-centric* language ("this is how cool our team and CEO are"). If you can't do this authentically, you probably shouldn't reach out to them at all. To stay efficient, you might still have templates that you use to form your messages, but any template you use should be customized for each candidate.
- **Keep it short.** Your messages should be concise and to the point. Your message should contain enough information to help the recipient decide whether to respond, but most people process messages really quickly and will outright ignore messages that are too long or dense.
- **Tell them what they need to know.** Say hello, say thank you, and cover the following:

  1. If you have a good understanding of what the candidate you're reaching out to cares about, focus your pitch on those pieces. For instance, do they seem very mission-aligned? Have they expressed interest in this kind of role in the past, like on social media? Does it seem like they would fine the company's business potential intriguing?
  2. If you don't have concrete areas you can focus your pitch on, let them know the nature of the problems they would solve in the role, the potential financial upside of joining, and any proof that there are credible people on or behind the team.
  3. Include a call-to-action at the end, such as inviting to read more about your company or welcoming them to have a call to talk more, but without pressuring them.

- ⚠ DANGER **Don't be too pushy or salesy.** Most people have really good "bullshit detectors." Most people don't like to feel prematurely pressured to take action or invest their time, so don't do things like withhold information from them until they agree to get on a call.
- ⚠ DANGER **Don't use gimmicks.** Jokes and "catchy" subjects are not a safe way to get people's attention—you don't yet know the person's sense of humor. For some recipients, a little color can help you stand out, but to others it will come across as spammy or even offensive.
- **Follow up, politely.** Do send follow-ups, but again, don't spam people. A polite follow-up could solicit a reply from a candidate who missed your first message or saw it and forgot to respond. Keep follow-ups as short as possible, but use them as a way to check in and trickle some more information to the candidate (for instance, tell them about progress the team has made like a product launch or fundraising round). A good cadence might be a follow-up a week after the first outreach (to make sure they saw your original message), and another one a couple months later to check in (by giving an update and seeing if timing looks better on their side).
- **Timing matters.** A candidate's "recruitability" can vary over time. For instance, this study[486] was able to predict recruitability based on an individual's past job tenure and their current company and role's average tenure: "If a UX worker has been at their job at Microsoft for 2.5 years, and they've never stayed at any job for longer than three years, and the average UX job at Microsoft is two years, then that worker is probably highly recruitable." Of course, there are other factors that influence recruitability that may not be evident from a candidate's profile. Maybe they haven't found a way to move up at their company and are looking for more responsibility. Maybe they want to start working remotely, or they need a better benefits package because they've started a family, and can't get these things at their current job. You can't know this person's circumstances until you reach out; sometimes it can be just what they were waiting for.
- **Play a long game.** Do build relationships when you can. Some candidates might express some initial interest, but the timing might not work out. Keep track of those candidates and check back in with them regularly. You can use a spreadsheet, or relationship management soft-

---

486. https://blog.humanpredictions.io/turnover-in-tech/

ware like an Applicant Tracking System (ATS) or Talent Relationship Management (TRM)[487] to help manage all your follow-ups.[488] One idea is to add candidates on LinkedIn so they can see the updates you post about your company.

- **Block off time.** If you don't have a recruiter, sourcer, or agency in charge of outbound sourcing, and sourcing candidates isn't your main job responsibility, it might be worth blocking off time on your calendar. Otherwise, it's very easy to put off sourcing in lieu of your day-to-day activities.
- **Improve.** Iterate on your targeting and your message as you learn patterns and heuristics for what works and what doesn't. In fact, what you learn from your outreach can feed back into your job description and candidate personas.
- **Be careful about who's doing the outreach.** At many companies, teams delegate sourcing to specialized in-house sourcers, to recruiters, or to external agencies. After all, someone who is able to spend a lot of time performing outreach will probably learn what works and what doesn't more quickly than a hiring manager who only spends an hour (or less) on outreach each week.
- ◇ CAUTION That said, there are risks with doing so. Firstly, the more detached the person doing the outreach is from the actual work, the less likely they'll be able to effectively target or engage the right candidates. Secondly, especially with external agencies, the person doing outreach may not be as protective of your company's brand as you would be. Candidates have begun to learn this, and many have learned[490] to respond only to hiring managers, and not recruiters. Make sure you take steps to ensure that the person doing outreach understands the role and the team, and that they are being as protective of your reputation and your candidates' time as you would be.

---

487. https://thrivetrm.com/applicant-tracking-systems-vs-talent-relationship-management-tools-one/
488. If you're interested in learning more about customer relationship management and its applications in hiring, fundraising, and more, it's covered in the Holloway Guide to Raising Venture Capital.[489]
489. http://www.holloway.com/g/venture-capital/details
490. https://www.yegor256.com/2017/02/21/say-no-to-google-recruiters.html

Over time, you will learn tactical tips and tricks on outbound sourcing. Small things like how you structure your search queries on different sites, what time and day you reach out to candidates, and the ability to find a candidate's email address can all make a difference in your response rate. We don't cover these types of tips in this Guide (yet), but there are sites like Boolean Black Belt[491] dedicated to providing them. They are worth visiting if you will be spending time on outbound sourcing.

23.3.2 FURTHER READING ON OUTBOUND SOURCING

- "What I learned from reading 8,000 recruiting messages"[492] (Aline Lerner, interviewing.io)
- "Startup advice: cold recruiting"[493] (Greg Brockman, Stripe)
- "Recruiting outside your personal network"[494] (AnnE Diemer, Stripe)
- "The best recruiters—followup"[495] (Elaine Wherry)
- "Here's What Engineers Hate About Your Recruiting Emails"[496] (Kiran Dhillon, Lever)

23.3.3 FILTERING OUTBOUND CANDIDATES

When it comes to outbound sourcing, many hiring managers conduct searches for engineers who went to Stanford or MIT and have worked at a FAANG company, and then blind email every name that comes up. Startups tend to copy the hiring plans and processes of large companies, who favor these filtering mechanisms for candidates.

But traditional markers like where people went to school or where they worked are not nearly as predictive as people tend to think,[§21.1] and there is a whole world of candidates who are just as competent but who are currently being overlooked by other companies. *Not* copying big, well-branded companies can actually give you a strong competitive edge. You'll find that the perfect candidate may be someone who's mission-aligned, driven, self-motivated, and will likely stay longer at your company—which may not be the person with an MIT degree and experience at Google. Don't optimize for the candidates you've been taught are "per-

---

491. http://booleanblackbelt.com/free-sourcing-recruiting-tools-guides-resources/
492. http://blog.alinelerner.com/what-i-learned-from-reading-8000-recruiting-messages/
493. https://stripe.com/blog/startup-advice-cold-recruiting
494. https://stripe.com/atlas/guides/recruiting#cold-outreach
495. https://elainewherry.com/2012/08/07/the-best-recruiters-followup/
496. https://www.lever.co/blog/heres-what-engineers-hate-about-your-recruiting-emails

fect." Instead, optimize for candidates who satisfy your deal-breakers and are likely to be interested in *you*.

Rather than looking only for people with a traditional pedigree, consider reaching out to people who:

- Are interested in your space because they've blogged or tweeted about it or have contributed to or started open source projects related to your work.
- Are active in a nice language community that your company loves, who are excited to be able to use this language in production.
- Are existing users of your product who are engineers (here's some guidance on how to surface them[497] without a lot of manual work)
- Have previously worked at companies solving similar problems, even if those companies aren't household names.

It might not be easy when starting out to figure out which candidates are likely to be interested in you, but the more patient you are up front, the more repeatable patterns you'll surface and the more unexpected pockets of engaged candidates you'll find. Then, over time, you'll be able to take what you learned and turn it into a sourcing machine that will put you miles ahead of everyone else who's sourcing the same old candidates against the tide of market forces. There's more detail on this topic in Early Signals[§21] and How To Read a Resume.[§22] And regardless of which type of candidate you're looking for in your outbound sourcing, Aline Lerner's Sourcing for Founders[498] deck, originally presented to Y Combinator companies, will help you if you feel like you're doing fifty things every day *besides* looking for your next technical hire.

If you decide to reach out to FAANG engineers or other traditionally pedigreed engineers, or well-known people in general, less is typically more. These people are likely fielding all kinds of outreach, so make sure you follow the tips and strategies above closely; one or two really well-written emails will get you better results than hundreds of automated, impersonal spam messages.

---

497. http://blog.alinelerner.com/hire-from-your-user-base/
498. https://drive.google.com/file/d/13QyEly3iidWxRNIFUd94W7cqz-8E0BTS/view

23.4 Agencies

In theory, you can contract out almost any part of your recruiting process to an external recruiter. This particular section is about working with recruiting agencies on a contingency basis, and less about retained or contracted recruiters, which we discuss in The Hiring Manager-Recruiter Partnership.§8.2

Contingency recruiters are recruiters employed by an agency who work to place a pool of candidates in open positions at one or more companies, and they receive payment only for successful placements. Placement fees for contingency recruiters are paid by the company where the recruiter places a candidate and calculated as a percentage of the candidate's annual salary, with typical fees ranging from 15–25%.

⚠ DANGER Contingency recruiting can be fraught with mismatched incentives:

- The recruiter may be working with more than one company, and could be incentivized to push the candidate toward the company with the largest potential placement fee (not just in percentage, but also in potential volume of candidates).
- The recruiter may not properly represent your company or opportunity to the candidate. This might be due to lack of a deep understanding of your company or role. They might also oversell the fit in an attempt to win their placement fee.
- If the recruiter is *really* unskilled, they may send you candidates that are not a good fit at all, causing this channel to resemble an unfiltered inbound channel, and flooding your funnel with noise.

That said, a really good contingency recruiter will be focused on long-term relationships (with both candidates and companies) rather than chasing quick placement fees. They will have a healthy pipeline of candidates, and will put in the effort to find a match between the right candidate and the right company. Great contingency recruiters can be a valuable source of candidates. Jose Guardado has some great tips on choosing a contingency recruiter.[499]

---

499. https://medium.com/@jay_likewise/the-basics-orking-with-contingency-recruiters-8ee3c39f9242

⚠ CAUTION But in general, we recommend getting a trusted referral when selecting a contingency recruiter, and vetting both the agency and the individual recruiter (the quality of recruiters at a given agency might vary).

23.4.1 FILTERING CANDIDATES FROM AGENCIES

Candidates who come in through agencies tend to fall into two categories:

1. They look good on paper but have some tragic flaw you find later, after investing non-trivial resources to interview them.
2. Strong candidates who are much harder to close than similar candidates from other sources.

Market forces affect agencies. In this market, where strong candidates (or at least those who look strong on paper) have plenty of options, there's not much incentive for them to work with agencies.

🖼 CANDIDATE While agencies sound tempting at first—you have someone who knows more about which companies are out there than you do and can make recommendations, actually connect you to companies, and even schedule interviews—the reality is very different.

- In practice, agencies tend to add extra steps to the top of the funnel for candidates—now instead of just talking to company recruiters, they also have to have the same conversation with a slew of agency recruiters first.
- Moreover, despite positioning themselves as trusted advisors, agency recruiters typically don't have much insider knowledge about the companies they hire for, often not being able to summarize the basic value proposition, much less speak cogently about the roadmap, projects, or market positioning. (Of course, there are always exceptions, and there are truly excellent agency recruiters, but they're rare.)

Working with an agency does not add value for candidates, so when candidates choose to do it, it's often out of desperation, because of their inability to gain access to an employer through other channels.

Additionally, very few agencies have the means to vet candidates at their disposal. As a result, they tend to focus almost exclusively on candidates who look good on paper (for the reason that employers usually won't engage with them if they present nontraditional candidates), but those candidates, more often than not, tend to come with some tragic flaw. If they didn't have one, they probably wouldn't be working with agencies in the first place.

If you're fortunate enough to talk to an agency candidate who isn't flawed and does well in your process, you have one more hurdle in front of you—actually convincing the candidate to accept your offer. And you'll find that doing so will be unreasonably difficult. Agency recruiters get paid when they make hires, so it's in their interest to get their candidates to interview with as many companies as possible. As such, any candidate who is presented to you will likely be presented to as many as 10–20 other companies. You can do the math from there.

23.4.2 HOW TO EFFECTIVELY ENGAGE WITH AGENCIES

While we advise avoiding agencies when possible, if you're really struggling finding the right candidates, you may feel compelled to give agencies a chance. The most realistic (and probably ideal) setup is that they're there to get candidates in the door, not to own the process, despite how much control they might want. Here's how to find and vet decent agencies and make the relationship with them as productive as possible.

First off, ask around for recommendations from your network. Good agencies are so rare that they're often a well-kept secret.

Once you find a promising agency, do a mock call with them and have them pitch you as though you were a candidate. Ask them a lot of questions about the company and the role. The goal here is to figure out whether this agency would reply with something like, "I'm not sure, but I can find out." What you don't want to hear is the agency making something up just to seem knowledgeable, or pivoting away from the question. Another good answer would be, "You should ask the hiring manager about that, whom I'd like to put you in touch with—they'd likely have a better sense than I would, and I don't want to give you the wrong information."

If you do start working with an agency, have them Bcc you on emails for quality control. Tell them you want to be conferenced in on mute for a call or two. Are they representing your brand well?

◇ CAUTION Don't give them roles that require very high-touch time management, as the best candidates are often off the market very quickly. They're managing many clients, and unless you're their cash cow, they're probably not always going to optimize for you.

⚠ CAUTION Don't give them roles that require complex selling. They aren't embedded in a company's culture, internal communications, and knowledge base, and will lack the ambient knowledge to be effective. Train them to defer to you on hard questions.

23.5 University Recruiting

> This section was written by Viraj Mody.

Setting up a good campus recruiting program can create a pipeline of junior talent that pays dividends over several years. Interns and new grad candidates can bring energy and ideas that complement those of more experienced members of your team, and can help scale your team rapidly.

The university recruiting machinery works pretty efficiently at large companies with well-known brands. Typically, large companies have established relationships with colleges, have large college recruiting budgets, and employ teams who focus entirely on university recruiting programs.

🚀 STARTUP Getting the university recruiting flywheel going for smaller startups is an entirely different ballgame. Smaller startups don't have the budget to spend extravagantly on campus recruiting, nor do they have dedicated recruiters or established relationships with colleges to give them leverage. Lavish perks and fancy offices often aren't a tool they can use to attract interns and new grads against the bigger companies. But perhaps the biggest challenge is the lack of brand name. Undergraduate interns and recent graduates are trying to build impressive-looking resumes, and getting a job at a well-known company is the most obvious way to do so.

⚠ CAUTION For a startup, a foray into university recruiting would be a huge and speculative investment of time and money. Interviewing candidates, flying out your team to campuses, and closing candidates will take a toll on your resources. The key to success when it comes to recruiting is to maximize return on investment, and many of the tactics described below are articulated with this primary goal in mind.

So when should a startup begin investing in university recruiting? At early stages, it might be worth exploring one-offs like attending a career fair or posting to university mailing lists. At some point, when a company has achieved product-market fit, hired an experienced engineering team, and built an environment where engineers with less experience can thrive, it might be worth investing more in university recruiting.

The first step is to choose which colleges or programs to focus on. It's tempting to focus your university recruiting efforts on the most well-known or impressive-sounding schools, the same way students think it's in their best interest to shoot only for employment at Google or Facebook. But if you only look at Harvard and Stanford, it's to your detriment. You will target a group that is largely homogenous,[500] in a very expensive process.[501] Instead, we recommend that you:

- Focus on local universities with reputable engineering programs. Having easy access to campus allows for stronger, more frequent engagement without a lot of the costs. Home-field advantage matters.
- Some investors might hold career fairs to bring university students and companies together. Check if your investors have a university program you can leverage (such as Greylock's Tech Fair[502] and Sequoia Campus[503]).
- Consider the alma-maters of engineers on your team, especially those with strong connections to the university (recent graduates, honor society members, employees who have kept in touch with professors, those with connections to the Dean's office, et cetera).
- Colleges with a reputation for entrepreneur programs. You're likely to attract and close candidates who are more comfortable with the risks and challenges that joining a startup provides them.
- See Diversity and Inclusion in Tech[§9] for more on expanding the pipeline.

---

500. http://blog.interviewing.io/if-you-care-about-diversity-you-should-stop-hiring-from-the-same-five-schools/
501. https://hbr.org/2015/10/firms-are-wasting-millions-recruiting-on-only-a-few-campuses
502. https://www.greylock.com/greylock-u/techfair/
503. https://www.sequoiacap.com/campus

Finally, it's worth noting that new graduates and interns may require a different approach to attract and hire; while many of them may receive many offers, they may have limited understanding of the startup ecosystem. Here are some recommendations:

- 🟊 STARTUP Attend startup-focused recruiting fairs, rather than the standard career fair, to attract students who are specifically interested in startups.
- Reach out to reputable entrepreneurship societies or clubs at the schools you want to engage with, and work closely with them to organize events.
- If you already know some students, ask if they can help you identify the super-connectors on campus, and establish a relationship with them that you can leverage to get introductions to the most promising candidates. Previous interns can also help serve as ambassadors.
- Reach out to college's career services center and talk to them about how you can get creative together.
- Find unique, product-aligned ways to get students' attention. One idea could be to hold interview-preparation workshops for students.
- Invest time with candidates that you extend offers to, with a goal of helping them learn to navigate the startup ecosystem and learn more about your company in particular. Provide opportunities for face-to-face interaction with people on your team that the candidate is likely to work with or relate to.

You can read more about setting up a university recruiting program at this article by Viraj Mody.[504]

23.6 Marketplaces and Platforms

In the past decade or so, several companies have sprouted up with the goal of making the hiring process more efficient. Each of these platforms has different theses and selling points, but the basic idea is to go beyond traditional job boards by using technology to generate a two-sided marketplace of candidates and companies. As these platforms grow, they have also started to experiment with novel methods of matching and evaluat-

---

504. https://medium.com/convoy-tech/university-recruiting-for-your-startup-929545c0ddcd

ing candidates and companies. Some of the more well-known platforms include:

- TripleByte[505]
- interviewing.io[506]
- Hired.com[507]
- Vettery[508]
- A-List[509]
- Eightfold[510]

Platforms can be straightforward to use, even for small companies. The set-up cost is low, and you can easily ramp up or down as your hiring needs change. Most of these platforms are free to try but they charge a placement fee per candidate hired (usually a little lower than agency contingency fees). Hiring desirable candidates from these platforms can get quite competitive, as they are usually placed in front of multiple companies and may end up receiving several offers.

23.7 *Alternative Education Programs*

As demand for software engineers has skyrocketed and as traditional, 4-year university computer science programs have failed to keep up, a plethora of alternative education programs and bootcamps have sprung up to meet demand.

In some ways, the bootcamp industry, in its nascent stages, is the Wild West—program quality varies wildly, as does the hireability of graduates, but one of the biggest challenges of hiring from bootcamps is how hard it is to filter students because many of them have no previous experience and have the same collection of projects they did during their studies. If you've ever felt a bit lost when looking at a prospective internship candidate's resume, because they simply haven't done much yet, you'll find that a bootcamp grad's resume is even more sparse in most cases.

---

505. https://triplebyte.com
506. https://interviewing.io
507. https://hired.com
508. https://www.vettery.com
509. https://alist.co
510. https://eightfold.ai

◇ CAUTION Not all programs are created equal. Some are known for the stack they teach, some are known for a more in-depth theoretical CS curriculum (though, odds are, it'll still be way less computer science than you'd see at university), and some are known for not being quite good enough at anything. One of the best things you can do to vet a bootcamp is to research their placement rates and look at the employer logos on their site—is your hiring bar on par with those employers (though watch out, as you might expect, they'll feature the shiniest brands first).

Once you've chosen your pool to fish from, form a relationship with the career services team of the programs in question. Having this relationship will give you extra dimensions to choose from when deciding which grads you want to talk to. For instance, you can ask for people who studied STEM in undergrad or ask for the top X% of grads based on their performance.

Understand that any grads you hire are going to be at the junior level and will need mentorship before they can comfortably work in production. Do yourselves and them a favor and only pursue these candidates if you can honestly allocate the requisite time and patience.

23.8 *Internal Pipelines*

> This section was written by Scott Woody.

One of the bigger sourcing opportunities for technology companies lies in the nontechnical staff they already have. We have seen successful companies convert non-engineers into engineers through thoughtful application of an internal conversion process.

23.8.1 VALUE OF INTERNAL PIPELINES

- **Promotes nontraditional backgrounds.** Engineering teams tend to be a monoculture of people from the same tech companies and top CS programs. Supporting people already familiar with your organization can be a great way to bring different backgrounds and ideas to your team.
- **Cultural risk is mitigated.** Internal transfers are already employees, the cultural risk goes way down if you convert from internal employees.

- **Faster time to hire.** Gauging interests, coordinating interviews, and getting references can be much faster when the candidates are "in the building."
- **Internal mobility is a morale win.** Internal mobility is one of the best ways to ensure that top talent feels like your company will always be their home.
- **Insights and motivation.** Because they have experience outside of engineering, engineers who come through this channel have unique insights into product development. Additionally, because this process is so out of the norm, these engineers tend to push themselves to learn and grow at a faster clip than most new engineers.

23.8.2 THE PROCESS

Before the interview you want to put up some filters to ensure that the candidates who interview are likely to succeed in the process, and interested in a new role. Suggested filters include:

- **Excellent performance review.** You want this program to be a reward to high achieving employees, so insist that they are already doing well in their current job.
- **Manager recommendation.** In order to conduct an expedited interview process, you are leaning on signal from a manager in your organization who supports the transition. Keep in mind that this person likely can't comment on their technical ability, but should be able to provide signal on behavioral and company-culture dimensions.
- **Prior engineering experience.** This can be a class like Code Academy or Udacity and should include ample code samples to review. This gives you a minimal filter on their engineering ability, a sample of code to review, and direct evidence of the grit that they will need to convert to software engineering.

After filtering, you might do one of two things, or both.

1. **Run a normal interview process.** Treat the candidate like a new grad hire. Ensure that they do not have access to the questions beforehand by modifying interview questions.

- **Use trusted interviewers.** Internal candidates frequently have less CS experience (for example, they might not be super familiar with Big O notation). You want interviewers who are capable of distinguishing potential and ability to produce code from 'familiarity with CS classes.' You are likely trading off raw CS knowledge for hustle, values alignment, and raw talent to learn. These candidates start off slower than most CS new grads, but climb the learning curve much faster.
- **Use their prior managers as the ultimate reference checks.** Lean into the performance review signal from their managers to help guide your decision. As mentioned above, you are not getting a new grad CS student, you are getting a seasoned employee with enough engineering chops to do the job. This raw material is great for *creating* excellent engineers, but it requires work.

1. **Have them step into an internship.** Run it like a normal internship for a new grad. Give them a mentor, place them on a team they'd love to be on. Expect them to start off slowly but grow exponentially over a 3 month period. An internship is a great method of internal conversion: it allows you to sand down rough edges, ensure that they get the on-the-job-training to truly become a great engineer, and acknowledges the fact that this person will need a bit of time to get up to speed. The output signal is also a lot stronger: you can directly review their work and more objectively understand if they're at the bar you expect.

- **Get a senior engineer to do the final evaluation.** Internal pipelines require buy-in from senior engineers that set the bar for who is a 'good engineer.' By bringing in an independent staff engineer to do the final assessment, you are ensuring the output is objectively good enough for your organization.

23.8.3 HOW TO MAKE IT SUCCESSFUL

Ensure the candidates land in teams that can use their skills, and that can support them and help them grow. Choose a team that can leverage their prior backgrounds (for example, if they came from the sales department, place them on a team that works closely with sales). This will enable them to punch above their weight while they develop their engineering skills.

Whether you do an internship or normal interview, understand these engineers are going to start a little slower than most new grads you would hire. That is fine, because they will ultimately quickly accelerate their growth curve to match or exceed all but the best new hires. You know they are capable of being excellent employees, and you're betting they can *become* excellent engineers. Because this is their first engineering job, they will likely need close mentorship and feedback continuously over the first six months. After that they will be indistinguishable from every other engineer in your organization.

23.8.4 TIPS FOR DEVELOPING YOUR INTERNAL PIPELINE

- **Ensure equal access.** You should advertise that you're doing this program to all members of the company and approach it carefully. Engineering will be looking at these people and assessing whether they are at the right level of skill. Many people in non-engineering parts of the company will want to join. There will be a spotlight on this process, so ensure that qualifications and procedures are publicly known and equally accessible.
- **Maintain the same entry criteria.** If the candidates that come out of this process are worse engineers than the ones you hire from outside the company, the program will not survive. You need to strive for independent evaluation of candidates. The best way is to find senior engineers who will do final assessment of the signal and place their stamp of approval on each internal applicant.
- **Guide your mentors closely.** When running an internal pipeline internship, keep in mind that interns are already employees—they may have lots of pre-established relationships with the employees around them. This can lead to situations where an intern that is struggling isn't honestly assessed by their mentor; the mentor may be afraid to give hard feedback or they may sandbag their expectations. As the manager, it is your job to precisely guide the mentor's expectations and ensure they are not succumbing to social pressure to get this person though the process.
- **Limit the teams these employees can start on.** These employees usually start from a slightly lower base of CS knowledge that they would have gotten in school or previous internships. This means they will start a little slower, but ultimately accelerate very quickly. The teams they land on need to understand this deeply, or risk making the new engineer feel excluded, or worse. Explain to the team that they need to be more forgiving in the beginning, and ensure the new engineer is working on projects appropriate to their level. At the same

time, the team should hold high expectations for fast growth in this engineer's abilities over the first six months, which can help them feel motivated and supported—everyone wants to know that their team believes in them. Rather than throwing these employees on a random team that's not prepared for them, make sure they'll be working with people who will help them fulfill their potential.

24 First Conversations

While the typical interview loop begins with a screening process, a more general first conversation is usually appropriate for outbound candidates, referral candidates, high-value candidates, and when hiring for senior positions. You may have exchanged a brief amount of information over email, or they've submitted an impressive application and you want to start with something more personal or intimate than a phone screen.

For this conversation, most companies will schedule a 30–60 minute call with the hiring manager, founder, or recruiter, depending on the size and stage of the company. For high-value candidates and where time and location allow, it might be more effective to try to do this in person, and for the manager or founder to reach out rather than a recruiter.

If the candidate is a referral, is a known quantity in some other way, or has done the exact job you're looking to fill, you might have one of these calls with them to begin selling them and make a personal connection, and put them in the right pipeline. The general phone call at medium and large companies is sometimes conducted by a recruiter. The goal is simply to have a verbal touchpoint—likely the first—after some communication has taken place over email.

The purpose of this conversation is threefold:

1. Selling the candidate on the company.
2. Routing the candidate to the appropriate role or team if it's unclear where they'd make the best fit.
3. Gauging their interest in the role, team, and company.

There are no hard and fast rules for going about this, other than to think of what helps build the mutual understanding and trust that could lead to a successful hire.[511]

24.1 Goals and Pitfalls

For many busy and distracted hiring managers, a first conversation with a candidate may feel like a way to quickly determine if someone is a fit, and rule out poor fits quickly, much like a technical phone screen.

We suggest taking a more thoughtful, candidate-focused attitude.[512] Approach every first conversation with the intention, "How can I best help this person?" At its core, hiring is about building deep, trusted relationships. Directly optimizing for the candidate's outcome (how can I help them be successful?), particularly at this early stage, leads to the best long-term outcome for your company. So start by putting the candidate first. Treat them as you'd want to be treated, or how you would a future teammate. Think about the long term. At this point, some hiring managers might scoff. "This is idealistic! It's impractical! We're crazy pressed for time over here!" In reality, this candidate-centric approach is the best way to ensure strong fit, longevity of employment, and a number of other pragmatic hiring goals:

- **Maintaining the efficiency of your pipeline.** One important function of this first conversation is to prevent yourself from investing more time if there obviously isn't going to be a fit. If you're being considerate of the candidate's time, you'll find yourself more effective with your own time as well.
- **Getting the candidate more interested in your opportunity (if it makes sense).** You'll be able to build a solid rapport with the candidate, since you're looking out for their best interest. This can help now (by encouraging the candidate to explore your opportunity) and in the future (you'll more likely be able to convince them to join if you extend

---

511. There can be many ways to successfully conduct the first conversation with a candidate. Based on the experience of this Guide's contributors, we present a philosophy (and corresponding tactics) that we think is most likely to be positive and effective. But, like many parts of recruiting, this isn't a hard science. Other approaches may work.
512. Much of the material here is from private conversation with Aditya Agarwal.

an offer). If things don't end up being a good fit at the moment, you'll have built an important relationship for the longer term.
- **Determining the best fit for candidate within the company.** By really understanding the candidate, and putting them first, you might be able to better match them to a different role at your company.

A candidate-centric approach will make you more successful at reaching all of these goals. You'll engage in the conversation with a more curious mindset and avoid some of the more transactional dynamics that plague recruiting today.

⚠ CAUTION It will also help you avoid some common pitfalls:

- **Avoid hard selling.** A common mistake is to try and convince a candidate to engage in your recruiting process without really understanding what they're looking for. This can be a strong turn-off and deterrent for candidates. Even if your sales pitch works, and they continue for now, they're more likely to withdraw later.
- **Don't spend the entire time assessing the candidate.** It's easy to assume that the goal of that first conversation is to dive into immediately assessing the candidate's skills and experience, but you shouldn't do that until you and the candidate both understand each other's needs and goals. There are other opportunities before and after this touchpoint to assess the candidate's skills.
- **Don't be too scripted or transactional.** This can rightfully turn candidates off and cause you to miss opportunities for engaging them on their interests and talents. For instance, maybe the candidate would be a great fit for a different role or team at your company, but if you're too scripted, you'll never get a chance to explore that possibility.

⚠ DANGER Broadly, you want to avoid two negative outcomes:

1. **Force-feeding your pipeline.** Trying to push a candidate forward to the next stage in your process prematurely might feel like progress, but ultimately, can be inefficient both for you and for the candidate. You might not truly understand the candidate's needs and priorities only to discover them later on in a downstream stage. You might also miss opportunities to match them with a better team or role.

2. **Providing a poor candidate experience.** It is a truism that first impressions last and are hard to change. If your first interaction with a candidate feels inauthentic, transactional, or adversarial, it will be difficult to change that impression later on in the process—if your candidate makes it that far.

Recruiting can be a grueling process on both sides of the table; it can even get adversarial at certain times. We don't think it should be that way. Taking a candidate-centric approach can make the overall process both more humane and more effective. It will make the time you spend on recruiting a lot more fulfilling—which, as an added bonus, will make it easier for you to dedicate more time to it.

By putting the candidate's needs first, you might find that after one or two first conversations, you end up telling them that you don't think you can offer what they are looking for, or you may even introduce them to a different company that can be a better fit. That's OK. It's better for both you and the candidate, especially in the long-term.

24.2 Getting Into the Right Mindset

It's easy even for people with the right intentions to revert to a more transactional, "let's get down to business" attitude when they jump into a call with a candidate. To avoid that, we've found it helpful to take a few minutes before any call to get into the right mindset.

Timing can make this task easier. Try to buffer some time before every call to mentally prepare. You should also schedule calls for the time of day where you will have the most focus and energy to devote to candidates. Try to avoid times when you might be stressed, drained, or crunched for time. In particular, doing several back-to-back recruiting calls might make it more difficult to maintain focus.

⚠ CAUTION Make sure that during your call, you are solely focused on the conversation. If the hiring manager or recruiter is reading and responding to emails or checking messages during the conversation, it's disrespectful of the candidate and will reduce the value of the call.

24.3 Building Rapport and Trust

Take the time at the start of a conversation to humanize yourself to the candidate and make the process—and your company—seem less alien. Ask how the candidate is doing. Be friendly and considerate, and note whether the candidate seems nervous.

Next, introduce yourself and talk a little about your background. Briefly sharing a few personal details or stories can help put the candidate at ease. This can also be a great point to mention why you are at your company. The candidate will remember that you, too, were once just starting out in a new position.

As you begin to develop some trust and rapport with the candidate, try to form a connection. For instance, you might find some common ground, like an aquaintance you share or a favorite band. Maybe you used to travel through their hometown. Just a small connection can put the candidate at ease. Alternatively, you can try to note something unique or interesting about their background and bring it up. "So I heard you used to roadie for Black Sabbath. Did you learn to code on the tour bus?" A little prior research can help here.

After these opening lines, maybe a laugh or two, explain the purpose of your conversation. For a first conversation, you'll say something like, "Today is a chance for us both learn a bit about each other and better understand each other, and explore whether there might be a fit." This is where your candidate-centric approach can really show. If this meeting has a specific agenda, let them know what to expect.

◇ IMPORTANT This conversation may or may not be around five minutes. With a shy or nervous candidate, you might spend more time chatting and making them feel comfortable. If you've already had a chance to build rapport (over email or if you met at an event), you could spend less time in this opening conversation. The candidate may also just not be willing to get into too much small talk; you don't have to force them.

24.4 Getting to Know the Candidate

After this introduction, your next step should be discovery. Ask questions and listen carefully. If asked with genuine interest, most people will really tell you honestly what they want and are looking for, what makes them a good fit or a poor fit for a role, and their self-perceived strengths and weaknesses. If they trust your intentions, they might also go further by seeking your advice.

24.4.1 THEIR DIRECTION

It's important to understand why (and whether) they are actively looking and how serious they are. You might have some prior signal here depending on how you and the candidate connected (for instance, whether they applied to an open position or whether you reached out to them).

As a first step, try to assess their level of interest in your company and your role. BINC co-founder Boris Epstein calls this the difference between "yes, but…" and "no, unless…" Typically, candidates have made some gut call about the job, and are trying to prove or disprove whatever feeling they have. "Yes, but…" candidates are excited about the prospect of working with you, and are essentially yours to lose. But you should understand what questions or hesitations they have. "No, unless…" candidates might be open to exploring the opportunity, but are initially disinclined to take the role.

After discovering their level of eagerness, you should break down that eagerness into two components, one related to their current situation ("going-away"), and one related to your company ("going-toward"). (These are also sometimes referred to as "pushes and pulls."[513]) "Going-away" candidates have reason to leave or have already left their current job. "Going-toward" candidates are attracted to your role or company specifically. The easiest candidates to recruit will be high on both dimensions. Candidates that are mostly "going-away" candidates might seem very eager to talk, but not for the right reasons. Their eagerness can change for reasons beyond your control, for instance, if they receive a counter-offer from their current company that solves their problems, or if they receive offers from other companies. "Going-toward" candidates may be excited but not willing to move if they're happy in their current role.

24.4.2 THEIR INTERESTS

Dig into their past. What have they accomplished, and what are they most proud of? What motivates and excites them? You can often detect a noticeable shift in a candidate's tone and volume when you hit on one of these chords.

---

513. https://news.greylock.com/a-blueprint-for-executive-hiring-f5a1da18b53b

When discussing their interests, some candidates might just take what they've read online or seen on your career page about your mission or culture, and regurgitate it because they know it's what you want to hear. In some cases, this might be to purposely manipulate you and advance their prospects with you. But, of course, they're not always "lying" deliberately. In many cases, it could just be that the person doesn't really know what they want, and feel like admitting that could reflect poorly on them.

Sometimes, people aren't even honest with themselves about what they want. We often make important decisions based on instinct and subtle judgment calls, then confabulate stories that try to make sense of our actions (or are consistent with our own image of ourselves). And, many times, people start their job search with one set of priorities and, as they talk to companies and run through their process, those priorities evolve.

So it's wise to note that there can be a difference between what someone *actually* wants out of a job, what they tell *themselves* they want, and what they tell *you* they want. It's *your* job, by asking the right questions and building trust, to try and work with them to uncover the truth. Some tactics we've found to help with this include:

- If they are leaving a job, ask them what would have had to change for them to stay.
- Ask them to design a "dream job" (it doesn't have to exist). What are they emphasizing?
- Look for consistency between what they're saying and past and current behavior. In particular, if you've built up enough trust and rapport, ask them if they're OK sharing what companies they're talking to or are excited about. For example, if they say they care about autonomy and being part of a small team, but they're also interviewing at really large companies, that might be something worth digging into. If they list companies that are all over the place, that might be an indicator that they don't really know what they want yet.

It's also important to gauge interest for the *role*. For larger companies, this conversation can serve to route the person to the right team within the company, by sussing out the candidate's motivations and passions. But this only makes sense in certain situations, like if someone has applied and looks talented or is a known talent, is already mission aligned, but it isn't clear they're qualified for the specific role that was posted, or you suspect they wouldn't be happy in that particular role, or if this is an opportunistic hire.[§6.2]

24.4.3 THEIR MOTIVATIONS

You will want to explore what's important to each candidate to get a sense of how they make decisions, and what their motivations[§5.1] are.

- What is their risk profile, and why? This can be both a question of how they are compensated and how willing they are to forgo career stability. A large, mature company may offer more predictability, certainty, and structure. A smaller or unproven company might be more of a risk.
- To what extent are they motivated by a company's mission, and what types of missions excite them?
- What do they value in a company's culture or environment?
- How do they view their career development? Do they want to learn certain skills (like a particular tech stack) or achieve certain milestones in the near future (like leading a project) or far future (like starting their own company)?
- Where do they see themselves five or ten years in the future? (This is a good "discovery" question, but also shows that you care about them and not just about filling a role.)
- Are there certain types of challenges that excite them? Why do those types of challenges excite them? Most driven individuals enjoy challenges, but often for different reasons. Some people enjoy overcoming the challenges themselves, like solving a puzzle. Others might feel a sense of fulfillment from the *impact* they can achieve by solving a certain problem, or from the experience of collaborating or mentoring. Some may prefer a type of challenge because it helps them learn a skill that can further their career.
- Are there practical considerations they care about, like location, commute, work-life balance, benefits like family healthcare, or ability to work from home?

Depending on whether and to what degree a candidate is actively looking for a new position, and how structured their thinking about their career is, they may have very clear answers to these questions: "I'm looking for a fullstack role at a mid-stage consumer internet company." Other candidates, especially passive ones that you have reached out to, may have a lot less clarity.

24.4.4 DIGGING DEEPER

No matter where it seems like the candidate is coming from, you should dig in deeper to explore *why* they're saying what they're saying. This is another area where a candidate-centric approach will be helpful—it will be easier to have this conversation if the candidate feels a sense of genuine empathy from the other side.

Engineers often use the 5 Whys technique[514] to understand the root cause of a technical issue. You shouldn't interrogate your candidates, but the mental model of digging deeper by asking "why" can be helpful as you're trying to understand what drives them.

For instance, let's take a candidate who says she wants to work at a consumer internet company. Asking why helps you discover whether this work interests her because she wants to work on a product that is used by millions of people, or because she enjoys the type of technology stack and scalability problems that she would encounter. Or perhaps she wants to be employed at a company that her friends or family know and love. Depending on the answer, you can again dig deeper. At some point, you'll hit a limit of either what the candidate is comfortable sharing or their own self-awareness. But the more you understand their needs, the better.

24.4.5 PRACTICALITIES

Finally, there might be some more practical questions you should cover. Does the candidate's work-authorization situation match what your company can provide? For instance, if they need visa sponsorship, is that something your company is able to do?

What is their timeline like for making a decision? Are they close to getting offers from other companies or do they have to make a decision by a certain date?

Depending on your rapport with the candidate, this may be a good time to talk about compensation.[§18]

24.5 Your Pitch

Next, it's your chance to express your company's value proposition to the candidate and answer any questions about the company or the role that they may have. You have built a compelling narrative for the company and

---

514. https://en.wikipedia.org/wiki/5_Whys

the role, and have learned enough about the candidate to communicate the opportunity to them in terms of what they value. Without being pushy, scripted, or salesy, you have to remember that the candidate is meeting the company through you; you and the company are being interviewed too, so you want to put your best forward.

Begin by asking the candidate what they know about the company. This can serve as a good transition between getting to know them and talking about the job. It will also prevent you from repeating things they already know, or overwhelming them with detail too soon. Based on how much they already know, and what they think they know, you can begin talking about the company and the role.

While you might have a general backdrop that you use for this part of the conversation (something about the company or its history that you like to focus on, some theme or part of the mission that you personally connect to, or something else), it's helpful to customize your script based on what you now know about the candidate. Connect dots that they might find appealing (or better yet, let *them* connect the dots). This is where having more than superficial knowledge of the candidate helps.

For instance, let's use our candidate who said she wanted to work at a consumer internet company. If that's all you know, and you're recruiting for an enterprise company, you might hit a dead end. But if you know that the candidate is interested in consumer internet companies because of the scale, and your enterprise company also has interesting scalability challenges, that is something you can focus on.

Finally, it might be worth proactively volunteering any areas where the dots *don't* connect, and asking them if that might be a problem. For example, if they mentioned that they prefer technical challenges to working on user-facing products, which is important to the role you're filling, ask them how they feel about that potential alignment issue. This is another point where empathy can serve your interests in a way that might seem counterintuitive. If the candidate responds that a certain attribute of the role or company might be a deal-breaker, that's actually helpful—you've caught the deal-breaker early on in the process. If, instead, the candidate starts selling the role to themselves, that's a great sign. They might be connecting the dots in a way that you weren't able to.

24.6 Evaluation and Next Steps

If you've covered everything in the previous sections and the conversation has gone well, you may not need to ask the candidate further questions. You've already spent time understanding what the candidate values and what they have worked on in the past, so you may already be able to tell whether they would work well with the team or have the particular skill sets required by your role.

If you feel like you do have a few specific questions you need answered, now's the time to ask. But the less evaluative you can make the first conversation feel, the better. Leave the technical grilling for later, when both you and the candidate have more explicitly opted-in to continuing the process.

At this point, there is a menu of options, and you have to pick one:

Advance. If the candidate seems like a fit for the role, and has shown genuine interest, you can advance them to the next stage of your funnel.

Pass. If the candidate is *not* a fit, and would most likely be rejected further in the process, you probably shouldn't move them along. Don't waste your time *or* the candidate's. If you can still help the candidate in some way, easily, this is always a good thing to do! If you know another company where they might be a good fit, tell them.

Explore other roles. If the candidate is not a fit for the specific role, but could be a fit at your company, is there another open role at your company they might be a fit for?

Deepen the relationship. If the candidate is a fit, but you're not confident they are genuinely interested, you shouldn't move them forward yet. There are a few options here:

- If you believe you know what their reasons for lack of interest are, and that you can overcome those concerns, you can introduce them to someone else at your company. For instance, if they aren't sold on the technical challenges, you can have them talk to another engineer on the team. If you're a startup and they aren't sure about the company's potential, you could put them in touch with one of your investors.
- You can try to maintain a long-term relationship with them.

If the outcome of the decision seems obvious to both sides (for instance, you both agree there is not a fit at the moment, or you both agree to move forward), some hiring managers or recruiters will communicate that immediately at the end of the call. But this requires experience and finesse, so we usually recommend following up with the decision later.

◇ IMPORTANT You need to set expectations for the rest of the process. Most people are stressed about uncertainty[515] more than anything. While you can't guarantee the candidate that they will get an offer (or even move forward past this point), you *can* remove some uncertainty by explaining what the process looks like and what the timeline might be. In other words, while the outcome might be uncertain, you can add certainty around the process and timeline.

Even if you feel like you have made a decision, delivering that decision a little later can help in a few ways:

- You don't want to rush into a decision. You might change your mind after reviewing your notes, talking to your teammates, or just sleeping on it.
- If you are rejecting the candidate, it might be better to do it after the stress and adrenaline of the call has worn off a little bit.
- Of course, never leave a candidate hanging for more than two or three days before delivering a decision, whatever it may be.

24.7 *Maintaining Contact*

For candidates who will be moving through the process, this is a great place to establish a few elements that will help you maintain a great candidate experience and be well-situated to close a candidate should you end up extending an offer.

First, establish someone on your team to be the candidate's confidant. The candidate should have someone that they can reach out to if they have questions or concerns during the process. At larger companies, this is often a recruiter, but it may be someone else at the company. Either way, the confidant should be someone that the candidate will feel comfortable talking to without risk of hurting their future working relationship (in other words, usually not the hiring manager). The candidate should really trust that they can talk openly to the confidant, and that the confidant will

---

515. https://www.forbes.com/sites/alicegwalton/2016/03/29/uncertainty-about-the-future-is-more-stressful-than-knowing-that-the-future-is-going-to-suck/#466f1485646a

be quickly responsive, available to reply to emails or hop on the phone at short notice. The confidant is important throughout the process, but perhaps will be most critical at the offer stage.[35]

Second, make sure you (or someone on your team) maintains a regular cadence of contact with the candidate to stay top of mind, keep them engaged, and find out if there are any updates from their side. This can involve sending them updates about where they are in the process, or sometimes just sharing exciting milestones or announcements from your company. If, at any point, a candidate is confused about where they stand or is reaching out to you for updates, you've probably done something wrong; either you haven't set expectations with them about the timeline, or you've set expectations and failed to meet them. It can be a good idea to have regular pipeline review meetings with your team, to check on the status of everyone in your pipeline and make sure no one is "stuck" or hasn't been communicated with in a while.

This cadence should increase as a candidate progresses through your pipeline. For instance, initially, while the candidate is early in your process, you might be communicating with them on a weekly basis to check-in and build trust and excitement through repeated interactions. By the time you have extended (or are close to extending) an offer, you might aim to have a touchpoint every couple of days.

◇ IMPORTANT Many companies lose candidates because they aren't in close contact with them, especially if they are in the pipelines of other companies and receive competing offers.

24.7.1 NURTURING FOR THE LONG TERM

For positive candidates that you won't be putting through the process, either because you don't have a suitable role or the timing isn't right for them, it's valuable to try and maintain a long-term relationship.

For candidates who aren't fully convinced they'd take the job (or, if you've sought them out, have not formally applied), maintaining contact could help you sway their opinion of your company, or catch them at that serendipitous moment in the future when they *are* open to switching. On the other hand, maintaining a relationship with candidates who you don't have a current role for can be very valuable in the future by saving you the time and cost of having to build a pipeline of candidates from scratch whenever you open a new role. In either case, these relationships can accrue other dividends, for instance, these candidates might refer *other* candidates to you.

How you maintain these relationships will differ. It might entail a simple check-in email every few months, perhaps coupled with some updates or announcements about your team and company. Other ways to maintain contact could be giving them early access to parts of your product (if it's a product they would use) or inviting them to events (if you're hosting events at your company). You might connect with them on LinkedIn so that they can see when you post company updates. For higher-value candidates, you might take a higher-touch approach, by meeting with them every few months to get coffee and catch up. If you're really aiming to build a trustful relationship with the candidate, you might offer access to your network or an intro to another recruiter or company that might be a better fit for them right now.

> *"Whenever I meet a candidate at the top of the funnel, my only goal in that conversation is to do right by the candidate. I take this to an extreme. During our conversation, if I know that my company is not right for this candidate I let them know of another company who is [a] better fit and I make the necessary introductions. My take is that if you have discovered that with Dropbox for example, productivity software is not what the candidate really wants to work on, why would you want them in the company? Instead, do right by the candidate and pay it forward. You'll be surprised by the network you end up building. Every one of the candidates I've referred to a different company has sent me someone else in their network that is a better fit for my company."*
>
> — Aditya Agarwal, former CTO, Dropbox[516]

CAUTION If a candidate isn't interested in maintaining a relationship with you or your company, don't try to force it. Never spam candidates or overwhelm them. When in doubt, give candidates a polite "out." For instance, your emails could mention that while you're reaching out because you want to maintain a relationship, you'd be happy to just let them reach out themselves when things change on their end.

---

516. https://news.greylock.com/mastering-the-art-of-recruiting-f3660744ee20

◇ IMPORTANT   Note that nurturing for the long-term can be important for candidates all along the funnel, not just at the beginning, who enter your process and aren't suitable for the job or self-select out. Even candidates who have made it all the way through the process and ultimately don't receive a job offer from your company (or don't accept an offer) can be valuable assets in the future—and rather than pretending they never existed, continuing to stay in touch with those you respect and admire is the right thing to do.

PART V: INTERVIEWING

25 Conducting Interviews

25.1 *Why Interviews?*

The purpose of the interview process is twofold:

1. **Companies assessing candidates.** Once candidates have passed through the top of the funnel, companies need to gauge candidate-company fit based on deeper skills assessment; suitability for the role, including values alignment; and the candidate's interest in the role, team, and company. In some cases, a candidate will not be screened at the top of the funnel; this occurs most frequently with senior candidates and referrals, whom the company will get to know first through more casual interviews.
2. **Candidates assessing companies.** Interviews typically provide the best opportunity for candidates to evaluate whether the company is a good fit for them. Interviews offer the candidate's first opportunity to interact directly with people on the team and to meet a larger part of the company or team as they progress further through the pipeline. At Google, internal research showed that interactions with interviewers are the top-mentioned factor[517] in candidate feedback—more important than recruiter interactions, company benefits, or even type of work.

The interview process for technical roles typically involves some kind of technical skills assessment, including writing code and answering coding questions, as well as answering non-coding technical questions and nontechnical behavioral and situational questions. Much of the software industry emphasizes technical interviews—the portion of the interview

---

517. https://rework.withgoogle.com/guides/hiring-train-your-interviewers/steps/make-interviewing-everyones-job/

process that covers practical technical skills—as the main mechanism for candidate assessment.

A **technical interview** is a portion of the hiring process for technical roles that assesses technical skills and thinking through coding questions[§28.1] and technical non-coding questions.[§28.2] The technical interview may take any number of forms, including technical phone screens, onsite interviews, hands-on coding interviews, take-home assignments, and prior work assessments.

⚠ CONFUSION Some people use the term *technical interview* to refer to the entire interview process for technical roles, but more precise usage leads to greater clarity, especially in complex interview processes.

In the past, interviews for technical candidates rarely focused on non-technical skills like collaboration, communication, and empathy; but today more companies embrace the importance of these skills, for all roles. Academic and industry research shows that diverse teams with people who value communication, equal participation, and good EQ[518] outperform teams with only highly skilled or high-intelligence members.[519,520] Amanda Sopkin's post, "Are Technical Interviews a good measure of software engineering ability?"[521] describes the path that led the industry to focus on narrow skills assessment and the ways in which that is changing for the better. And an excerpt[522] from Laszlo Bock's *Work Rules!* explains the thinking (and data) behind Google's eventual embrace of structured behavioral and situational interviews as a means to get the full picture of a candidate's ability.

---

518. https://en.wikipedia.org/wiki/Emotional_intelligence
519. https://nytimes.com/2015/01/18/opinion/sunday/why-some-teams-are-smarter-than-others.html?%5C_r=0
520. https://rework.withgoogle.com/blog/five-keys-to-a-successful-google-team/
521. https://dev.to/amandasopkin/are-technical-interviews-a-good-measure-of-software-engineering-ability-1cp9
522. https://www.wired.com/2015/04/hire-like-google/

◊ CAUTION There's plenty of research showing that interviews are poor predictors of on-the-job performance.[523,524,525] Every interview process will filter candidates according to some criteria; a poorly designed interview process will favor candidates who are simply good at *interviewing in a particular setting* that does not assess fit for the role. Interviews that are too specific—covering one skill set, being prescriptive about languages, focusing on brain teasers, or not asking any behavioral questions—also fail to gather accurate or complete signal. In contrast, a well-designed and well-run process mirrors the actual work the person would do at the company, focuses on how they go about solving problems, and includes behavioral assessments that test for things like communication ability.

Interviews are noisy, and biases are often present and unaccounted for. No process can eliminate bias and noise completely, but adherence to principles and a commitment to structured interviewing will help reduce bias and get clearer signal out of interviews, while creating a better candidate experience.

◊ IMPORTANT There is no magic formula when it comes to interviewing for technical roles. It helps to let interview and assessment formats flow from the kind of signal a company needs to gather for the role; knowing what you're listening for can turn down the noise. The best formats for technical interviews—and the balance between technical and nontechnical interviews—also depend on candidate sourcing, what part of the funnel a candidate enters into, whether they're hiring for a senior role, the company's resources, values, and philosophies, and the availability of a given candidate. These differ from company to company, role to role, and, in some cases, candidate to candidate, and so the technical interview loop that works well for one company in one situation might not work at all for another.

---

523. http://citeseerx.ist.psu.edu/viewdoc/download?doi=10.1.1.172.1733&rep=rep1&type=pdf
524. https://medium.com/@Tomyani/a-history-of-interviews-do-job-interviews-work-9b83dff91e6c
525. http://blog.interviewing.io/technical-interview-performance-is-kind-of-arbitrary-heres-the-data

On the whole, a well-designed and well-run interview process—consistent with our hiring principles—will:

- **Be predictive.** Accurately assess the candidate's fitness for performance in a specific role.
- **Be fair.** Minimize noise and bias while not being easily faked, gamed, or manipulated.
- **Be respectful.** Make good use of the time invested by the candidate and by everyone at the company who participates.
- **Be positive.** Leave the candidate with a favorable experience regardless of whether they receive or accept an offer.

Interviews may not be a perfect tool, but with proper design and execution, the right mix of questions can fulfill most of these core principles.

25.2 The Interview Loop

The **interview loop** is the series of conversations and tests a company designs to assess a candidate's fitness for a role. Interview loops are most effective when they are standardized—to the extent possible, the process puts every candidate for a role through the same loop. This practice helps to calibrate expectations of candidates, interviewers, recruiters, and hiring managers.[526]

At the outset of an interview process, the company may change some specifics of the interview loop after the first couple of candidates to account for unforeseen gaps or to adjust expectations based on how the first round of candidates perform. When hiring for roles that no one at the company has held before—for example, hiring the company's first QA engineer—the loop may need multiple rounds of adjustments.

A company's style and priorities inform the structure of interviews. To balance candidate experience with the signal you need to gather, traditional interview loops likely include one or two phone screens and an onsite interview. Effective interview processes increase time and effort demands on the candidate as they progress[527] rather than being front-loaded with "hoop-jumping" exercises, and they also avoid any surprises

---

526. The interview "loop" is not literally a loop in a technical sense. Instead it is a series of events in which the hiring team and candidate interview and circle back to a conclusion.

527. https://hackernoon.com/beyond-the-recruiting-funnel-the-candidate-climb-d9eb79ffcf0a

for the candidate, which the hiring manager or recruiter can facilitate by telling the candidate what to expect from the process.

A sample interview loop might include:

1. **Recruiter screening call or meeting.** The recruiter screens for general role fit, and fact-finds to prepare the rest of the loop. (This could instead be done by a hiring manager, especially if the company doesn't have recruiters.)
2. **Technical phone screen.** A phone conversation tests for core skills, typically basic programming or technical concepts. (Some companies may conduct two phone screens to gather more signal, or so a second interviewer can offer perspective.)
3. **Take-home evaluation.** This is a variant of the basic skills screen that may take the form of an online challenge or simpler take-home test. (Many companies skip this.)
4. **Onsite interviews.** These typically extend half or most of a day and include three to six interviews in several formats, covering:
   a. in-person coding questions
   b. non-coding technical questions
   c. behavioral questions
   d. wrap-up conversation with the hiring manager that includes questions, concerns, or loose ends, and sets expectations on next steps
   e. some kind of social event, like lunch with the team.
5. **Interviewer feedback.** Each interviewer offers written feedback on the candidate, and/or discussion among the interviewing panel.
6. **Post-interview follow-ups.** Calls, meetings, and possibly second onsite visits allow the hiring team to assess anything not yet covered or to gather more signal on something interviewers disagree about.
7. **Reference checks.** The hiring manager or interviewers call past employers and colleagues to verify aspects of the candidate's experience.
8. **Decision and negotiation.** The company gives either a rejection or an offer. An offer leads to negotiation and acceptance or rejection by the candidate.

◇ IMPORTANT Note that this is one of many possible paths. In particular, outbound candidates or senior candidates may necessitate a more selling-focused, organic process that begins with conversations rather than skills assessments and moves more quickly to onsite interviews.

25.2.1 FIGURE: EXAMPLE INTERVIEW LOOP WITH TARGETS

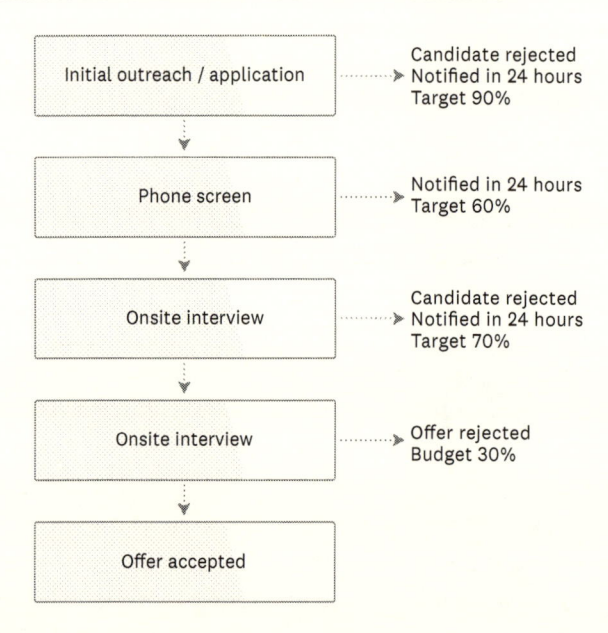

```
Initial outreach / application  ·······►  Candidate rejected
                                          Notified in 24 hours
                                          Target 90%
            ▼
      Phone screen              ·······►  Notified in 24 hours
                                          Target 60%
            ▼
    Onsite interview            ·······►  Candidate rejected
                                          Notified in 24 hours
                                          Target 70%
            ▼
    Onsite interview            ·······►  Offer rejected
                                          Budget 30%
            ▼
     Offer accepted
```

Source: Kevin Morrill

A company may offer **trial employment**, in which the candidate joins the company for a short probationary period while the employer decides whether to offer them a full-time position. During the trial employment period, the candidate may occupy an internship or contractor position, and both the candidate and the company have the opportunity to get a more complete feel for whether there's a fit. However, many candidates cannot accommodate trial employment requests, especially if they have existing jobs or other commitments.[528]

---

528. See the controversy discussed on Twitter.[529]
529. https://twitter.com/austen/status/1116801535944478720?s=12

25.3 Preparing Candidates

An interview is most effective when each party approaches it with a mutually agreed purpose: to get to know each other and to assess fit. Candidates need to know how long the interview will be, what kinds of questions to expect, and if possible, some insightful detail about the people they are going to talk to.

This typically includes sharing the general structure of the process. As the interviewer, you may let the candidate know the types of questions to expect (specific coding knowledge? or probing previous work?). Offering tips for how your company likes to get answers and a bit about what you're looking for will help them rise, not sink. This kind of transparency leads to a better overall candidate experience and can reduce stumbles due to anxiety, which can lead to false negatives.

Candidates benefit from preparation at multiple stages: before the process begins (you can tell them what to expect by email or phone); at the start of each change in interview format; and at the end, to explain what's next. Preparing candidates to do well also entails checking in along the way to confirm that they understand what to expect, asking if they have any questions, and offering encouragement.

At the outset of any of these conversations, it helps to break the ice with some small talk and compliment the candidate on specific work they've done that's gotten them this far in the process. A nervous candidate who feels unwelcome or out of place won't give an accurate signal of their abilities and capabilities.

26 Preparing Interviewers

26.1 Assembling the Interview Panel

The people included in an interview loop convey a great deal about your company to candidates. These people must successfully interview candidates while also positively representing the company. The choice of interview panel members has an outsize effect on the candidate's ultimate assessment of a company and thus plays a significant role in their final decision should you extend an offer.

26.1.1 SHOULD EVERYONE INTERVIEW?

> *"Your entire team should conduct interviews. Everybody. If you don't want some people to interview, ask yourself why. If you're worried about how they're representing the company, there's a bigger issue at hand."*
>
> — Marco Rogers, veteran engineering manager[530]

It's beneficial to have everyone involved in some way in the recruiting process. Exposure to the recruiting process provides an opportunity to familiarize the people who work at your company with the expectations you have for employees, because the interview process filters for people who would do well at your company. That said, successful interviews require that interviewer roles be determined carefully based on the skills of individual interviewers. Some people excel at evaluating a candidate's ability to demonstrate a specific skill set. Other roles are purely recruitment—social events like lunch with candidates or getting on the phone to answer their questions. Not everyone has the skills or qualifications to do both.

> 🔖 STORY "The interview process is an opportunity for everyone to better understand the company's values and how it evaluates, and it helps you wrestle with questions like, 'How do I level up and evaluate my own performance?' The interview process should map to your performance review process. What the performance review grades you on, the interview process should evaluate on. These should be aligned."
> —Scott Woody, former Director of Engineering, Dropbox

⚠ DANGER Note that forcing people to interview candidates without getting their buy-in on the importance of interviewing can be a bad experience for everyone involved. Interviewers will feel like their time is being wasted, and candidates will be exposed to people who don't want to talk to them. This thread[531] on Blind has several comments about how employees who have been forced to conduct interviews against their wishes create a bad experience for candidates: "interviewing candidates became an unpleasant burden no one really enjoys, but [everyone has] to do anyway to report

---

530. https://firstround.com/review/my-lessons-from-interviewing-400-engineers-over-three-startups/
531. https://www.teamblind.com/article/FANG-interviews-a-joke-EpMKc0e0

in the next performance cycle." Likewise, letting truly low-quality candidates progress into your funnel wastes interviewers' time and causes them to lose buy-in. Ideally, interviewers will view the process as a high-impact activity and as a privilege they have to earn and maintain.

Also note that while, ideally, everyone should be involved in the interview process to some degree, not everyone is suited to conduct interviews. If an engineer has a poor bedside manner that could sour the candidate's opinion of the company, that person should not be interviewing. Such people often self-identify as being poor interviewers or make it known that they dislike interviews strongly. Keeping these people as interviewers can be extremely costly—they might take their frustration out on the candidate. Alternately, some might not be aware that interviewing isn't their strong suit. In these cases, their interview conclusions tend to be either very positive or very negative but offer low signal about why. Internal recruiters often get to know interviewers' styles, so if you're assembling a panel, it can be helpful to talk to them about who might need to be added or removed.

◇ IMPORTANT If someone is not happy at the company or appears to be bitter about being asked to interview, they shouldn't be interviewing. Anyone who has given their notice to leave the company should never interview candidates.

> 🗩 STORY "There are certainly people who shouldn't be interviewing, and it's people who are not as self-reflective as they should be—who are not aware of their biases or are unwilling to engage in a conversation about bias. Just being aware goes a long way to reducing their effect. There are so many people who say, 'I don't believe in biases.' That person should not be charged with evaluating talent, assessing skills, or judging others in any way." —Benjamin Reitzammer, freelance CTO

Good interviewers are always communicating their excitement and passion for the company—they are excited about the company and have their own compelling reasons to work there. They likely have a captivating story about why they work there and what will excite a candidate about both the company and the role itself (if the role is on the same team as the interviewer). These personal stories help humanize the company.

⚠ DANGER It's important not to over-sell your company, however; gross misrepresentations about the day-to-day reality of the company will cause pain and trouble for everyone after a candidate joins and learns the interviewer misled them.

◇ CAUTION Ensuring that your interviewers represent the diversity of your company creates a better interview process. There is a balance here. Your intention might be to ensure that you gather a diverse set of opinions on every candidate, but it's critical to avoid overloading underrepresented folks by asking them to take on a disproportionate number of interviews (and also thus taking time away from their other day-to-day responsibilities). Creating an inaccurate representation of your company's diversity does no good; misleading candidates can result in low retention rates, not to mention resentment. See Diversity and Inclusion in Tech[§9] for more.

26.1.2 FACTORING IN SENIORITY

It's probably not reasonable to have senior engineers involved in every level of the hiring process, even if they could be calibrated to interview any level of candidate—senior time is worth a lot. Instead, hiring managers may wish to consider how to deploy levels of seniority and determine the best use of senior engineers' time in any given situation.

Having had the comparative experiences of working with hundreds of colleagues and numerous hiring decisions, senior engineers are equipped to better measure and evaluate certain signals like trustworthiness and long-term potential or talent. Senior engineers may join later in the hiring process to conduct behavioral interviews or more complex technical noncoding interviews to assess architectural questions, or to dive deep into why a candidate made certain technical decisions in the past. Engineer seniority *at the company* is particularly important because it lends the process the perspective of deeper understanding of company values.

On the other hand, many technical skills are easier to assess with less experience and only basic training, so it's acceptable for junior engineers to conduct earlier screens. That said, technical assessments can go wrong: junior engineers may not have sufficient experience to lend awareness of where they can make high-confidence assessments, where they may have inadvertent bias, or where they may be prone to proceed with overgeneralizations. The best interviewers are able to put their egos aside and ask questions of the candidate—but not all junior engineers are willing to appear as if there is something they don't understand.

⚑ CONTROVERSY   Should junior candidates ever interview senior candidates? Asking a junior engineer to evaluate a senior engineer's merit can be fraught. Even if the interviewer has been properly trained, they might misunderstand the abilities necessary to do a job they're unfamiliar with, especially if they are separated from the candidate by fifteen years of experience. Having a junior engineer involved may also hurt both the candidate experience and the candidate's perception of the company—for example, the more senior person might encounter ill-formed questions from a more junior interviewer and make a reverse judgment, like "this person doesn't value me."

◇ CAUTION   A common pitfall for junior interviewers is to grade candidates' answers based on how they *themselves* would solve the problem; they may be very literal in interpreting right and wrong responses based on a rubric. Senior and out-of-the-box-thinking candidates often do go "off book" on interview questions, and this can signal serious creativity. However, interviewers should be able to distinguish brilliant out-of-box thinking from unwillingness to do necessary laborious or technical work. This isn't always easy and usually requires follow-up questions. Experienced interviewers tend to find these interviews less stressful to conduct than more junior people do, and they are more likely to be able to dig deep enough to get the right signal.

Creating established rubrics for each interview format and making interviewers aware of potential biases will help protect against these pitfalls.

26.1.3   WHO SHOULD INTERVIEW?

Better candidate experiences result from having some interviewers be individuals the candidate would work with directly if hired. This can give the candidate a sense of the team environment and also what their day-to-day will be like. Interviewers who know that they might work with a given candidate tend to be more invested and engaged.

Some companies compose the interview panel entirely of the team the candidate would be working with. Others include a mix of those who will work closely with the new employee and trusted individuals from other areas of the company. Having more people from the team increases buy-in and incentive alignment—the team is part of the process and will have to work with the candidate. The team will best know what the candidate needs to be capable of to succeed. On the other hand, this can lead to situations where separate teams within a company develop different hiring philosophies. It can also make it harder to schedule candidates because it reduces the pool of available interviewers.

The balance between local empowerment of individual teams and global company standards will vary from company to company based on size and culture.

◇ IMPORTANT If you are hiring for a senior role with direct reports, it is wise to include one or more of the people who will work *for* the candidate.

> "In every interview I've ever had with another company, I've met my potential boss and several peers. But rarely have I met anyone who would be working for me. Google turns this approach upside down. You'll probably meet your prospective manager (where possible—for some large job groups like 'software engineer' or 'account strategist' there is no single hiring manager) and a peer, but more important is meeting one or two of the people who will work for you. In a way, their assessments are more important than anyone else's—after all, they're going to have to live with you. This sends a strong signal to candidates about Google being nonhierarchical, and it also helps prevent cronyism, where managers hire their old buddies for their new teams. We find that the best candidates leave subordinates feeling inspired or excited to learn from them."
> — Laszlo Bock, Senior VP of People Operations, Google[532]

> STORY "If being able to guide or mentor others is something you expect of senior engineers, having more junior people interview them can be a good way to figure out how well they can explain things and how they treat people who are junior to them, which can be useful signal." —Ryn Daniels, Senior Software Engineer, HashiCorp

---

532. https://www.wired.com/2015/04/hire-like-google/

If you decide that it's important to the team or company that everyone be involved in the interview process, keep in mind that everyone needs to be trained. Interviewer training and calibration are necessary for juniors *and* seniors on a per-role basis.

26.2 *Training Interviewers*

> 📖 STORY "It's ridiculous to expect engineers to be competent interviewers with little to no training. To the extent you can be good at interviewing, it comes from repetition, learning the failure modes and bolstering against those. Experience just makes you much better at navigating the myriad situations. If this is your first remote interview, you're not going to be able to tell if it's bad because of the candidate or because it's remote. Training often doesn't exist, or it's done really poorly. If you can't invest in training engineers to interview, you can't expect to get any real signal on candidates." —Scott Woody, former Director of Engineering, Dropbox

Effective interviewing is a learned skill. It requires a mix of technical knowledge, emotional intelligence, and thinking on your feet, while being fair and rational. None of this comes easily, and doing it all at once is *really* difficult. Having experienced employees who have done interviews elsewhere go through your organization's interviewer training will help ensure alignment.

Calibration is the process of developing the ability to accurately assess whether a candidate will succeed in a role. A calibrated interviewer will not only be able to assess a candidate's interview performance but draw an informed conclusion about whether the candidate should be hired for a given role.

> ⚠ DANGER Candidates may have poor experiences if they are exposed to anyone involved in the interview process who is interviewing for the first time or who is not prepared to assess with respect to the specific role. Whether it's an interviewer, hiring manager, or hiring committee member, without calibration, they will be unable to make a data-based recommendation.

> 🗎 STORY "*Uncalibrated* people are not aware of common biases. It's as much about self-awareness as it is about training. Broadly, engineers are pretty good at sussing out whether a person is like them, even if they're not particularly trained. Engineers can be trained to be more flexible in who they can evaluate. Backend engineers self-identify as being unable to evaluate frontend. That's common. So how are they going to bridge that gap? If they're trained, they can." —Scott Woody, former Director of Engineering, Dropbox

Calibration occurs through a mix of:

- Interview training and shadow interviewing.
- Question banks and structured rubrics that specify what level of performance is expected on different questions. Good rubrics draw on the collective experience of seasoned interviewers and recruiters.
- Mock internal interviews. You can train new interviewers and test new questions by mock interviewing candidates who are already on your team.
- Giving data and feedback to interviewers, like how their ratings for candidates compare to other interviewers' ratings and how predictive their ratings are. This can help interviewers detect things like whether they are too lenient or too strict or are otherwise highly inconsistent with other interviewers.

> "We don't just look at the candidate side of hiring. Interviewers also receive feedback on their own personal ability to predict whether someone should be hired. Every interviewer sees a record of the interview scores they have given in the past and whether those people were hired or not."
> — Laszlo Bock, former SVP of People Operations, Google[533]

Interviewers and decision-makers perpetually improve their calibration as they gain more experience and interview more candidates, so no one is ever "fully calibrated." But setting *some* minimum level of calibration helps any person be equipped to draw effective conclusions as they assess a candidate. For example, it helps to know whether the hiring team considers a particular question easy or hard, or whether a particular type of mistake should disqualify a candidate or not.

---

533. Bock, Laszlo. *Work Rules!*, Twelve, 2015, p 103.

⚠ DANGER If your only source of calibration is the candidates you've seen, you could be at risk of incorrect calibration. This is especially likely to happen with new roles or new interview questions, where your company lacks a baseline. It is also likely if you are letting weak candidates into your funnel, because interviewers might find their perceptions shifting over time. They might then be overly impressed by a candidate who is "above average" (without realizing that the "average" is really poor for this particular search). This is sometimes referred to as "hiring the tallest of the bunch."

One step to help counter this is to incorporate recordings of real-life interviews into your calibration process; interviewing.io published a few mock interviews[534] on their platform.

26.2.1 ALIGN ON THE PROCESS AND ROLE

It's helpful to provide a general presentation or discussion of interviewing to everyone who will be involved. This briefing can be delivered by a hiring manager, an experienced interviewer, or a recruiter and can include:

- Why hiring (and interviewing in particular) is so crucial. Your team may be spending valuable time on interviewing candidates, and it's important that they view it as an important responsibility (and not a chore or a waste of time).
- The existence and risks of unconscious bias and how it can affect judgments, as well as strategies for mitigating bias.
- The benefits of structured interviewing.
- What their role is as interviewers, and how that fits into the hiring process at large.
- What the interview process will look like.
- The fact that interviewers function as team ambassadors, and that in addition to assessing candidates, their actions may encourage or discourage candidates from joining the company.
- How to write effective interview feedback.§31.2
- What the interviewers' role will be in the hiring decision. For instance, will they need to participate in debrief or huddle sessions after an interview? This information sets the right expectations about how hiring decisions will be made.

---

534. https://interviewing.io/recordings/

- The legal considerations for interviewers,[32] including what questions the law restricts interviewers from asking.

Chuck Groom, Director of Engineering at Truva, provides a useful overview of the interview process[535] that provides additional perspective.

An important part of interview training is ensuring interviewers understand the importance of their role in building a team. Keith Adams, Chief Architect at Slack, once interviewed a candidate who greatly impressed him: "I rated him a strong hire." But during the interview debrief, it turned out that the candidate hadn't impressed the rest of the interviewers. Keith made a passionate case anyway, and Facebook hired the candidate, who went on to have massive impact at the company. "To any engineer, interviewing can feel like a 45-minute interruption to your immediate work. But the people you help hire are a huge part of your legacy. Hiring that candidate was the most important thing I did that year," Keith said. (Keith's bar for impactful work is pretty high.[536])

Next, interviewers benefit from having information specific to each role or type of interview. What are the roles they might help interview for? What types of interviews will they conduct, and what primary competencies will they be assessing? Are there secondary things they may be looking for as well (maybe they are assessing technical skills, but should still note arrogance in a candidate)? Are there predetermined, structural interview questions to follow?

Occasional uncomfortable interactions may help make an interview more functional. We are taught to never interrupt, yet it's not productive to let a candidate go down the wrong conversational rabbit hole; it's appropriate instead to intervene and steer the discussion in a more helpful direction. This can be even harder to do with behavioral interviews. Most people are very good at talking at a high level about their experience but don't go into any significant depth. It's the interviewer's job to help the candidate tell their story, which might mean cutting them off when they go off course and knowing when to steer more and when to steer less, which comes with time and experience.

---

535. https://blog.usejournal.com/the-software-engineers-guide-to-interviewing-software-engineers-980bbfdb4006
536. https://www.wired.com/2013/06/facebook-hhvm-saga/

> 📖 STORY "When I start an interview, I often tell the candidate I want to get certain kinds of signals. This means I might cut off certain directions of discussions or lines of thought to help with that. It's not me being rude; it's just me trying to make the best use of our time."
> —Scott Woody, former Director of Engineering, Dropbox

A typical interview process may include four to eight interviews, where each interview is between 45 and 60 minutes. That means there's never enough time to get every data point you'd like, and because interviews provide noisy signal, you can only have so much confidence in the information you collect. Therefore, it's important to prioritize both for what really matters to you and what you can reasonably assess.

⚠ CAUTION An interviewer may not like the style or "attitude" of a candidate's response to a question. The candidate may deflect, go on a tangent, or even refuse to answer. This definitely means something is awry, but the cause may not be what you expect. On the interviewer or company side, an excessively junior interviewer may ask a question in a way that doesn't suit a senior candidate; it could be a poorly designed question; or possibly the hiring team failed to convey to the candidate accurate expectations for the interview. On the candidate side, personality style or inadequate technical ability may result in an unwillingness to dive into technical material, even in response to a well-phrased question. The best solution is for interviewers to ask themselves, "What is the signal we want to get here?" and to focus on that. As an interviewer, you help avoid generating such candidate responses by knowing your role in the interviewing process, what signal you want to get, and why you're asking these specific questions.

A good alignment process will usefully communicate to interviewers the scope and nature of the role:

The **scope of the role** is a reflection of how a role fits into an organization. Scope often aligns to a particular rung of a career ladder and conveys how much responsibility the candidate will be trusted to handle. Senior members of an organization can best discern whether a candidate is well suited to the scope of the role, especially in interviews designed to assess technical skills beyond coding and nontechnical skills.

The **nature of the role** is a reflection of the specific technical skills that the role requires. Individuals directly familiar with the work and the challenges facing the team can best discern whether a candidate is well suited to the nature of the role.

By way of reducing noise, Ammon Bartram at TripleByte suggests looking for signal on max skill,[537] not average or minimal skill (or on where a candidate may make mistakes). This approach focuses on "looking for strong reasons to say yes and not worrying so much about technical areas where the candidate was weak."

For an in-depth look at collecting signal, David Anderson's thoughts on hiring for leadership roles at Amazon[538] include a host of specific questions that build on each other, a practice that TripleByte also encourages.

26.2.2 MOCK INTERVIEWS

Mock interviews are educational simulations in which individuals act out the roles of interviewer and candidate. Successful mock interviews resemble real interviews as closely as possible. Either potential candidates or potential interviewers can use them to prepare for the real thing. Companies may film mock interviews for the benefit of other trainees when preparing potential interviewers. Best practice includes following an observed mock interview session—whether live or filmed—with a debrief with senior interviewers who discuss what was successful and unsuccessful in the exercise.

Within a technical organization, mock interviews help junior engineers practice their interviewing skills and start to recognize what makes an interview successful or unsuccessful, focusing both on interviewer behavior and on how candidates navigate questions. This means that the person playing the candidate ideally will embody typical responses to the question, both successful and unsuccessful. Debriefs then focus on any pitfalls, patterns, or typical responses, and highlight what success looks like.

Behavioral interviewer training can be more difficult, and practicing with co-workers can be extremely helpful. Trainees practice how to probe into answers deeply, helping to build confidence around steering the candidate. The art is in knowing when to steer, and when you're steering so

---

537. https://triplebyte.com/blog/how-to-interview-engineers
538. https://www.linkedin.com/pulse/how-interview-amazon-leadership-david-anderson/

much that you're making the interview too easy—this comes with time and experience, and mock interviews simulate that.

26.2.3 SHADOW INTERVIEWS

Shadow interviews are the next step. They provide crucial preparation for less experienced interviewers.

A **shadow interview** is an opportunity for a new interviewer (the shadow) to observe a more experienced interviewer (the lead) working with a candidate. Later, a trainee may lead an interview with a more experienced interviewer shadowing them in a **reverse shadow interview.**

In effective training, the shadow takes full part in the non-evaluative parts of the interview, including introductions, selling the candidate on the company, and answering the candidate's questions, and remains attentive during the remainder.

◇ IMPORTANT Having two interviewers present might seem awkward or intimidating to candidates. Just as with pair interviewing, it's important to prepare the candidate by letting them know there will be a shadow present, and that the purpose is to help train interviewers and provide a consistent experience for interviewees. Both interviewers can introduce themselves, and then the lead can clarify that one interviewer will conduct the interview and the other will mostly observe. Explaining that the shadow interviewer isn't expected to say much (if anything) will help make sure the candidate doesn't misinterpret their behavior as silent judgment.

After the shadow, the lead and shadow debrief by talking through what they saw, having the trainee share their thoughts about the candidate, and discussing the nuances of the question flow. A trainee might do this five or ten times and then be ready for the reverse shadow interview, with the more experienced interviewer providing one-on-one feedback afterward. Successfully completing the shadow interviewing process will prepare a new interviewer to go solo.

Many companies use similar processes, but Google has published their own shadowing process[539] as part of an extensive online resource[540] for training interviewers, with the caveat that it is designed in line with their

---

539. https://rework.withgoogle.com/guides/hiring-train-your-interviewers/steps/giving-interviewers-practice/
540. https://rework.withgoogle.com/guides/hiring-train-your-interviewers/steps/introduction/

own, atypical interviewing philosophy and infrastructure (for example, they use independent hiring committees,[541] which may not be practical for other organizations).

If you're interested in improving as an interviewer, read Alex Allain's work on the Holloway blog.[542]

26.3 Structured Interviewing

Good interview questions help sell the specific technical challenges of your team and ensure that you are looking at the right things in hiring. How do you get the signal you need and help to sell candidates on the priorities and competencies of the company?

Structured interviewing is the practice of applying the same assessment methods to review the competencies and traits of every candidate for a given role. This requires a calibrated set of interview questions that reviewers pose with consistency to candidates, as well as clear criteria for assessing candidates' responses. In addition, interviewers must have familiarity with the question set and any associated expectations. Studies have shown that structured interviewing more effectively predicts job performance and is less prone to bias than letting interviewers casually decide what questions to ask.[543]

The purpose of structured interviewing is to improve the signal-to-noise ratio.

Noise is an incidental error that can distract from substantively useful information. Factors that can produce noise in an interview process include an interview starting off on the wrong foot, the candidate having seen a similar problem before, the interviewer's mood, and so on. Any particular candidate's performance assessment can vary from interview to interview, as demonstrated in a 2016 study by interviewing.io,[544] and noise can account for many of those fluctuations.

---

541. https://rework.withgoogle.com/guides/hiring-hire-by-committe/steps/introduction/
542. https://www.holloway.com/s/trh-what-i-learned-from-conducting-500-technical-interviews-part-1
543. https://rework.withgoogle.com/guides/hiring-use-structured-interviewing/steps/learn-the-external-research/
544. http://blog.interviewing.io/after-a-lot-more-data-technical-interview-performance-really-is-kind-of-arbitrary/

Conducting multiple structured interviews can minimize noise. Google found that in their process,[545] conducting up to four interviews increased their hiring accuracy—after four, accuracy increased, but only marginally.

Structured interviews often pull from question banks to ensure that all candidates are interviewed the same way.

A **question bank** is a collection of scripted interview topics and problems. An effective question bank also includes examples of expected answers and a rubric by which to assess candidates' actual answers. Question banks will be tailored to reflect the nature of a company's technical challenges and needs, and they take time to build.

◇ CAUTION Structured interviewing has a few downsides. If your questions are too rigid, you might not be able to effectively assess candidates with unique or uncommon skill sets. You can also acclimatize to your own questions, not realizing you have made them too difficult for most candidates. Lastly, every time a candidate performs better on an interview question than anyone you've ever seen, there's a risk of letting that set a new standard that everyone else is judged against. Here, as always, rubrics help.

26.3.1 LEAKED QUESTIONS

It is wise to be aware of the possibility that candidates or even teammates may leak the interview questions.

A **leaked question** is an interview topic or problem that is made available to a candidate before their interview. A candidate may have heard about the question online or from previous candidates. Leaked questions affect a company's ability to fairly and effectively assess all candidates.

Repeatedly using the same questions increases the chance of leaks. There is a delicate balance between worrying about leaked questions too much and worrying about them too little. Most people won't leak your questions, and if they do, it'll likely be to a very narrow audience. You're probably at higher risk of mis-signal in situations where a candidate has interviewed at a lot of companies at once, excels at whiteboard coding and storytelling, and maybe encountered similar questions elsewhere. That said, people who are good at spotting patterns and adapting like this are probably not the worst people to hire! Being good at ramping up on some-

---

545. https://rework.withgoogle.com/blog/google-rule-of-four/

thing is a useful skill for your employees. Nonetheless, with a little work, you can make your questions comparatively leak resistant.

First, rotate your questions. You can do this in a rolling fashion—that is, add a new question, test it for a while, remove the oldest question from the rotation, and repeat. This gives time to calibrate the rubric for the new question.

Second, leaks are less likely when you have questions with depth and nuance, rather than relying on questions that can be unlocked with a single trick; people who may be inclined to leak your questions likely can't also leak every detail of the hardest parts. You can increase the depth your questions have by asking candidates to go beyond mechanical answers, with follow-up questions that require an understanding of underlying principles. Answers to the most subtle and nuanced questions can't be faked—if the interviewee can navigate them, it means they really do have command of the material.

26.3.2 FURTHER READING ON STRUCTURED INTERVIEWING

- Google's guide to structured interviewing[546]
- U.S. Office of Personnel Management overview of structured interviewing and structured interviewing guide[547]
- "12 Tactics to Perfect your Interviewing Process"[548] (*forEntrepreneurs*)

26.4 *Mitigating Bias*

Bias is an observational error[549] that tends to over-favor or under-favor certain types of candidates. As a systematic error, it is a common source of noise. For example, likability bias might cause an interviewer to view a friendly candidate as being more competent.

Bias constitutes a fundamental problem in hiring, and one key goal of interviewer training is to reduce the impact of interviewer biases on the final outcome. Bias detracts from interviewers' ability to accurately assess candidates' ability or fitness and thus increases the odds that you

---

546. https://rework.withgoogle.com/guides/hiring-use-structured-interviewing/steps/introduction/
547. https://www.opm.gov/policy-data-oversight/assessment-and-selection/structured-interviews/
548. https://www.forentrepreneurs.com/interviewing/
549. https://en.wikipedia.org/wiki/Observational_error

will hire the wrong people and create homogeneous teams.[550] Structured interviewing helps mitigate bias in interviews by using rubrics and requiring written justifications for decisions. Good training prepares interviewers to expect and detect the presence of bias in their own evaluations.

26.4.1 EVALUATING OBJECTIVELY

Even with standardization, interviews progress fluidly and thus can provide the greatest challenge in collecting signal in a way that mitigates bias. Good training and practice will help interviewers be aware of their biases and the ways their evaluations may fall prey to those biases.

The halo/horn effect[552] suggests that candidate performance on one part of a question will influence how the interviewer evaluates the rest of the candidate's performance. To counter this, the interviewer can use the success criteria from the rubric to evaluate each part of a question separately. Only when a candidate has met the rubric's requirements on the key elements of a question can the effective interviewer cut the questioning short and shift to selling.

Consistent questioning across candidates also plays a role in reducing bias, with specific structure and key points not changing from interview to interview. (Small conversational changes are fine.) It's helpful to provide interviewers with clear, consistent triggers for when and why to provide hints[§30.5] to avoid the temptation to tip off candidates the interviewer likes. On the flip side, if a candidate says things that don't seem correct, the interviewer may reasonably give them a chance to correct themselves by probing more deeply in an ad-hoc way. It's important to be consistent in doing this for all candidates.

It's very easy for new interviewers to get attached to a likeable candidate and round up on their evaluation. This form of bias is particularly tricky because some candidates *are* likeable or have a story that makes people want to hire them. There have also been studies that show that first impressions[553] (even in the first few moments of meeting) can stick with an interviewer for the rest of the interview. It's critical to never let these

---

550. We cover the issues of homogeneity in Diversity and Inclusion,[§9] and you can read more about it from MIT Sloan.[551]
551. https://sloanreview.mit.edu/article/the-trouble-with-homogeneous-teams/
552. https://en.wikipedia.org/wiki/Horn_effect
553. https://www.researchgate.net/publication/313878823_The_importance_of_first_impressions_in_a_job_interview

emotions influence the hiring decision—it is not your company's role to employ people just because you like them or because they need a job, and the evaluation process ideally prevents that. It is never wise for an interviewer to get so wrapped up in a candidate's case that they lose objectivity.

26.4.2 HANDLING GUT FEELING AND INTUITION

◇ IMPORTANT Gut feeling and intuition are valuable—it is not usually wise to ignore them. However, making a *decision* based purely on gut feeling or intuition can allow bias to lead to poor outcomes. Unexplained gut feeling indicates there's either more signal to collect or something to discuss and understand better. A good interviewer understands *where* their intuition is coming from *at least well enough to explain it to others* or to highlight ways to evaluate whether the intuition is accurate.

An interviewer might say, "I feel like the candidate is inflating his past work and didn't really do what he said he did in the previous job." This is a judgement based on intuition, rather than fact. Without facts, you can't rule out bias or determine if the suspicion reveals a true problem on the part of the candidate. Instead, to fact-check the intuition, the interviewer can ask extremely specific questions about past projects: "You mention you designed and deployed the internal evaluation tool at AcmeCorp in Python. Which web framework and database did you use? Why? How did you deploy it?" Vague candidate answers to every question on work they said they've done likely indicates that the interviewer's intuition revealed a true negative signal, one that can be documented to others.

26.4.3 THE DANGER OF "CULTURE FIT"

> "Screening candidates on how they make you feel and whether they seem like someone you could be friends with is a mistake. It's poorly correlated with job performance and invites bias."
> — Ammon Bartram, co-founder, TripleByte[554]

If you search the term *culture fit*, you'll get a lot of headlines about how important it is to hire for culture and that it's "hard to define, but everyone knows when it is missing."[555] In reality, hiring for culture fit can lead to

---

554. https://triplebyte.com/blog/what-companies-mean-by-culture-fit
555. https://www.businessnewsdaily.com/6866-hiring-for-company-culture.html

unfair and biased hiring practices, as well as a company that's closed off to diversity of all kinds.

Culture fit is shorthand for the many vague assessments or unexamined feelings hiring teams sometimes use to determine whether a candidate "belongs" at a company. While in most cases the intentions behind these assessments are not sinister, testing for this kind of vague quality can devolve into a "friend test" or "likability test" where candidates are assessed not on potential to do the job but on similarity, kinship, or familiarity to the assessing employee.

⚠ DANGER Culture-fit assessments are enormous sources of bias, including affinity bias, where interviews and decision-makers favor candidates who are similar to them, and likability bias, where candidates who are pleasant to spend time with are viewed as being more competent than those who aren't. The "person I would enjoy hanging out with" and the "person best-equipped for a job" are not the same.

At one point, Stripe had a "Sunday test"[556] to identify candidates "who make others want to be around them,"[557] but ended up moving away from that test since it was commonly misinterpreted.[558]

If your goal is candidate-company fit, rather than looking for culture fit, you can assess for values alignment. A focus on values, instead of on culture, has a better chance of resulting in a diverse group of people who are motivated by the same things.

> "Shifting our focus from 'culture fit' to 'values fit' helps us hire people who share our goals, not necessarily our viewpoints or backgrounds."
> — Aubrey Blanche, Global Head of Diversity and Inclusion, Atlassian [559]

Having a defined set of values can help you interview and assess candidates in a fair and effective way to find those who will succeed at your company. For example, for companies that value people who focus on sup-

---

556. https://firstround.com/review/How-Stripe-built-one-of-Silicon-Valleys-best-engineering-teams/
557. https://gigaom.com/2012/04/28/6-secrets-for-building-a-super-team/
558. https://twitter.com/cupcait/status/579416472797118465
559. https://www.fastcompany.com/3060118/how-google-pinterest-and-others-use-internships-to-push-their-diversity-i

porting the company's mission, the hiring team can seek candidates who show excitement and passion about that mission.

Additionally, you can assess candidates not just for compatibility with your company values, but also for:

- Their cultural contribution[560] or culture add.[561] This refers to what new viewpoints and opinions a candidate might bring to your company.
- Their adaptability[562] to different cultures. Some research has indicated that this type of adaptability is more important than initial *fit*.[563]

26.4.4 ANCHORING WRITE-UPS IN EVIDENCE

The goal of the notes taken during the interview is to allow the reviewer to produce a final write-up that describes what happened, what conclusions the interviewer came to, and why. It's particularly important for interviewers to:

- Summarize what happened in the interview so that others can draw their own conclusions.
- Justify their decision with specific evidence based on what the candidate said or did during the interview and how it relates to the standards outlined in the rubric for the question.
- Explain why they did not choose other similar options. For example, if an interviewer is a "solid yes" on a candidate, why weren't they a "strong yes" or a "weak yes"? Forcing a clear justification relative to the alternatives makes the write-up much clearer and avoids fuzzy thinking that leads to bias.

Building rubrics[§31.1] and using them in interviews gives clarity and structure to these notes and prevents interviewers from veering off in unhelpful directions.

The Medium Engineering team detailed the various technical and nontechnical capabilities they interview for in a three-part guide[564] that provides specific rubrics for evaluating and grading each one.

---

560. https://www.linkedin.com/pulse/how-i-hire-its-all-cultural-contribution-fit-diego-rodriguez/
561. https://business.linkedin.com/talent-solutions/blog/diversity/2016/ban-the-term-culture-fit-and-other-great-diversity-tips-from-pandora
562. https://www.gsb.stanford.edu/insights/look-beyond-culture-fit-when-hiring
563. https://faculty.haas.berkeley.edu/srivastava/papers/Enculturation%20Trajectories.pdf
564. https://medium.engineering/engineering-interviews-grading-rubric-8b409bec021f

26.5 Coordinating Interviewers

It's best if every interviewer knows their exact role in the process. Are they asking a coding question? If so, is there a specific question or a category of questions from which they can draw? If they are asking another type of question, what is their focus?

Coordination among interviewers helps avoid asking the same technical questions multiple times, because repetition reduces the breadth of signal you're able to collect. (Having multiple people ask the same *behavioral* questions can be helpful and is rarely problematic.) Some applicant tracking systems, like Lever,[565] allow interviewers to attach public notes to a candidate's profile; or people can write down questions they asked and share them on whatever system the team uses.

◇ **CAUTION** Some companies have interviewers huddle between interviews to share directions to probe into, but this can be logistically challenging and can lead to bias. It's better not to use this method unless there is something *very specific* one interviewer believes another interviewer should probe.

The recruiter or hiring manager can also send an email out to the interviewers the day before the onsite interviews to outline the candidate's background, the role, and what each interviewer should assess. Such messages usually include notes on what the candidate seeks in their next role, what they like about your company or team, and anything that has resonated with them so far.

◇ **IMPORTANT** A big part of coordination is scheduling. Whether all interviews take place on the same day or over a few days may be candidate preference; you can check with them. Most candidates will not want to stay home from existing jobs over multiple days just to be available for three different half-hour calls, and they shouldn't be expected to. Moreover, it's wise to confirm interviewer schedules in advance and not to reschedule on applicants. Rescheduling gives the applicant a bad impression and has an outsized effect on them if they are currently employed, have family obligations, or are interviewing at multiple companies. Candidates are more likely to drop out if scheduling is messy.

---

565. http://hire.lever.co/

Basic coordination information, such as questions to be asked, can also be included in the calendar invites for the interviews; although to reduce bias and preserve candidate privacy, the reviewing team should limit what background information and personal details it shares in advance with interviewers.

27 Technical Interview Formats

27.1 *Selecting Interview Formats*

Technical interviews can be conducted in person or remotely, with one interviewer or a small group, synchronously or asynchronously, on a whiteboard, a laptop, or as a take-home test. Which **technical interview formats** will be most effective—and how those interviews should be conducted—depends on what signals the company finds most useful to gather. Each format collects different information, and each has pros and cons, pitfalls, and associated time and effort investment from both sides. When choosing a format, the company should consider whether it can be scaled and still conducted in a way that is fair to and useful for the candidates.

Deciding on formats can be a balancing act between time savings for the company and interviewers, quality of the signals that are truly predictive, and the need for a positive candidate experience.

Many processes will involve a combination of several formats for technical interviews:

- Phone screens or video call screens.
- Take-home tasks or assignment.
- One or more onsite visits with in-person meetings, one-on-one interviews, pair or panel interviews, or working sessions. Onsites can be technical or nontechnical, or both.
- Fully remote meetings.

Generally, formats move from screening (which help disqualify poor fits) to assessments (to qualify and measure candidate-company fit). Assessments include the technical or nontechnical. As a candidate advances through the interview process, the interview can ask more theoretical questions. Along the way, companies sell to candidates—but efforts to sell usually increase as a candidate moves through the pipeline, all the way to the onsite. Effort on both sides increases the further a candidate gets. But be wary of adding too much to the interview loop in the hopes of further defining the signal. There *is* a point of diminishing returns, and strong candidates are unlikely to stay through a never-ending process. If you aren't getting the signal you need, it's time to look carefully at each format you've chosen and figure out what's not working.

27.1.1 TABLE: ONSITE AND REMOTE FORMATS

	SYNCHRONOUS	**ASYNCHRONOUS**
Onsite	Onsite conversation, Whiteboarding, Onsite coding	Onsite task or project
Remote	Phone screens, Remote conversation, Remote coding	Take-home coding project, Portfolio or prior work sample

27.1.2 TABLE: TYPES OF INTERVIEWS BY FORMAT

FORMAT	**EFFORT AND SIGNAL**	**STRENGTHS**	**WEAKNESSES**
Qualification call (general)	Low	Orients candidate; Sells them on process	May lose good candidates who need more selling or personal touch up front
Phone screen (technical)	Low	Time-efficient on both sides for disqualifying a candidate, especially if interviewer is technical and trained	False negatives high if interviewer is not technical (HR or recruiter); May lose good candidates who need more selling or personal touch up front; Difficult to do well, i.e. minimize both false positives and false negatives
Remote conversation	Medium	Logistically easier; Less costly; Ideal for remote workers	Less warm and personal for candidate; Less signal for company on personality and team chemistry
Onsite conversation	Medium	Largest volume of signal; Good for assembling signal from many interviewers at once; If done well, effective and time-efficient on both sides	Need a properly trained interviewing team and processes; Logistical costs

FORMAT	EFFORT AND SIGNAL	STRENGTHS	WEAKNESSES
Onsite Whiteboard	Medium	Good for architectural questions; Can work for coding as well without requiring language-specific setup	Whiteboards are not representative of actual coding Whiteboard coding is controversial and disliked by many candidates
Remote coding (Coderpad style)	Medium	Much more representative of real programming than whiteboard coding Better signals on knowledge of a specific programming language	Fewer human cues make it more impersonal and stressful; Coding in a new environment can be awkward and stressful for some
Onsite coding or pair programming	Medium	Similar to Coderpad style, but can be more friendly or personal	Requires skill and preparation from the interviewers for consistency
Onsite task or project	High	Giving the candidate a little more time and a project can be highly representative of real work	Harder to structure and do well; Can be confusing or stressful for candidates
Take-home coding project	High	Much more representative of real programming than whiteboard coding; Optionally can pay candidate for their time	Demands a lot of time from candidate; Hard to scale and avoid cheating Biased against those without flexibility to do take-homes
Portfolio or prior work sample	Medium to high	Can be an excellent signal if it exists; Open source work can also show popularity and utility of the work	Most candidates do not have this

27.1.3 **FIGURE: INTERVIEW FORMAT USAGE**

Based on data from their experience with over 900 engineers, TripleByte found that interviewing practices and formats vary quite a bit across companies.

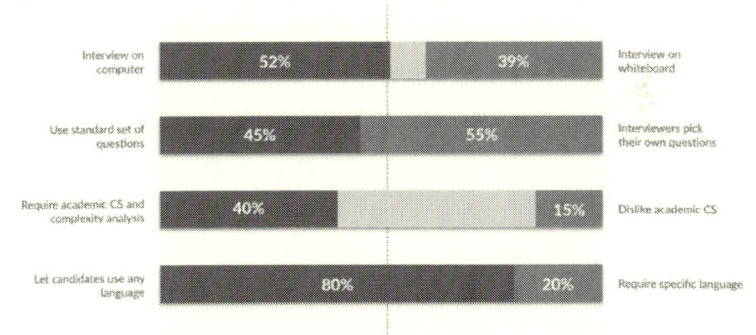

Interview on computer	52%	39%	Interview on whiteboard
Use standard set of questions	45%	55%	Interviewers pick their own questions
Require academic CS and complexity analysis	40%	15%	Dislike academic CS
Let candidates use any language	80%	20%	Require specific language

Source: TripleByte[566]

🏁 CONTROVERSY The "best" interview format for coding questions is a notoriously controversial topic. While many companies rely primarily on onsite, face-to-face coding interviews, a significant fraction of engineers consider "whiteboard coding" to be intimidating, stressful, and not predictive of job performance. On the other hand, alternatives like take-home tasks have drawbacks as well.

So how do you decide which style to use? Given the trade-offs, the answer may differ by company, by role, and sometimes even by candidate. For example, an internship-style arrangement might work for an entry-level candidate without a lot of work experience, while a laptop-based interview may help a more experienced engineer showcase their skills. Some companies combine methods (for instance, having a whiteboard interview as well as a laptop-based one). You might also offer candidates a choice of which assessment method they prefer, though that significantly increases the company's work to develop, maintain, and evaluate the different assessment methods in a fair way.

◇ IMPORTANT When choosing or evaluating formats, consider how each format relates to general hiring and interviewing principles.[§7]

---

566. https://triplebyte.com/blog/how-to-interview-engineers

According to Scott Woody, Dropbox used to do a lot of take-homes, because they found they got some of the strongest signal possible on a candidate's ability to solve problems in unique ways. But they had to start moving away from them because they couldn't contain the cheating.[567] If we apply this back to the principles, we see how it was easy (if disappointing) to make the decision to switch formats—it's not *fair* because some people are cheating, and it's not *effective* because you can't assess people's work properly or comparatively. The company had gone about their commitment to the format in the right way: they built up a robust process around take-homes, wrote and used detailed rubrics, conducted blind assessments to minimize bias, and despite all of this, encountered an unavoidable pitfall. They wisely pivoted.

In reality, no technique is perfect, and the bulk of ineffectiveness in the industry results from poor adherence to principles in both design and execution. A well-designed and properly conducted whiteboard interview is more effective than a sloppy laptop interview or a take-home exercise that frustrates a candidate. Select whatever format will cover the skills that correspond to the requirements of the job. This will protect efficiency, effectiveness, and the candidate experience. When in doubt, you may wish to revisit both the hiring principles (of candidate experience, accurate assessment, fairness, and efficiency) as well as the interviewing principles (of minimizing bias, being predictive of on-the-job work, avoiding questions that can be gamed, and being mindful of both your and your candidates' time).

27.2 *Technical Phone Screens*

A **technical phone screen** is an early conversation between a candidate and a current employee of a hiring company with technical ability. Most commonly, technical phone screens are conducted by engineers at the hiring company, but they may also be conducted by others, such as recruiters with deep technical knowledge. The content of a technical phone screen can range from a simple conversation to live coding.

---

567. Note that not all companies who rely on take-homes have reported struggling with cheating.

⚑ CONFUSION Note that for some candidates—particularly high-value candidates, referrals, and outbound candidates—interviewers may begin with a more general first conversation[§24] to get to know the candidate and gauge their interest. Depending on their experience, these candidates may skip technical phone screens altogether.

◇ IMPORTANT In general, technical phone screens are better for *disqualifying obviously poor candidates* than for qualifying them. Secondarily, they can help identify potential superstars whom interviewers will want to focus additional energy on courting.

It is easier and more important in a short, abbreviated phone screen to figure out that a candidate doesn't understand something like recursion and thus fails to qualify than to assess whether they have deep algorithmic ability, which is hard to measure quickly and reliably. Harder questions tend to make bad phone-screen questions because the phone format makes hard questions more difficult for candidates to succeed at, and because even strong candidates may miss any given interview question. Starting the process with harder questions also means you are exposing your question set to a larger pool of candidates, increasing the likelihood of leaks.[§26.3.1] Therefore, a phone screen process focused on sorting out bad fits will work better than one that tries to search only for stars.

> 💬 STORY "At Dropbox, we tried moving hard questions to the front on the theory that harder questions are a better filter and that we would save time downstream. Many fewer candidates made it through the initial screening process, reducing the number of onsites. Only the truly outstanding candidates made it through, and we filtered out a lot of the lower-skilled candidates. However, we also filtered out a large number of candidates who could have been good. On examination, we realized that if you gave a good candidate two hard questions, they would usually get at least one down well and struggle a bit on the other. These people would do well on a full interview panel, but if you happened to give them the wrong question in the the phone screen, you would reject them, which increased the rate of false negatives. We moved to a system where the phone screen is focused on filtering out obvious wrong fits while giving room for truly exceptional candidates to shine." —Scott Woody, former Director of Engineering, Dropbox

> **STORY** "At Triplebyte, we get to see how the same candidate does at different companies. And it's far more common than you might think for someone to be screened out top of funnel at one company and then go on to do really well at another company. This is fine, as long as the screening question that was used really is in an area that the company cares about. There is far more variance in candidate knowledge (even experienced, skilled candidate knowledge) than most hiring managers think. So, make sure if you ask a screening that requires knowledge of, say, time complexity, that you really do need people to understand that. Because there are productive, experienced, senior engineers who don't understand complexity analysis. And if you don't require web dev experience, make sure you don't ask a question that requires someone to understand fullstack dev." —Ammon Bartram, co-founder and CEO, Triplebyte

27.2.1 SKIPPING THE PHONE SCREEN

The phone screen is almost always necessary because online challenges, whether or not they are combined with resume screens, will not give you enough signal to move someone to an onsite. You can often skip the initial phone screens for candidates whose previous experiences make it clear that they would be minimally capable of performing in the onsite process (for example, that they possess baseline coding fluency and problem-solving skills). Having candidates share open-source work on GitHub can be a strong early sign of programming ability. Phone screens might also be skipped for people who are high-valued or are referrals. If the chance that someone would fail the phone screen is very low, and you have the resources to bring them onsite, it's wise to do so. The more stages you include in the process, the more likely some number of candidates will drop out.

Removing a step is a simple way to accelerate the pipeline and should not compromise signal if the same material is covered in later stages.

27.3 Onsite vs. Remote

Typically, the large part of the interview process happens onsite, but this is changing as more companies build remote teams or wish to accommodate candidates who are not local. You can use many interview formats either in person or remotely; this includes even live coding challenges.

A company's resources and the candidate's availability usually determine whether a particular part of the process will be conducted remotely or onsite.

Remote interviews have a few specific use cases:

- Typically (but by no means universally), remote interviews are concentrated earlier in the funnel and may include:
  - Online challenges and take-homes.
  - Phone screens, both general and technical.
  - Technical screening questions, questions where the candidate can code in the browser during a screen share, and light behavioral questions. Note that while you may encounter binary decision points or spikes in the signal during remote interviews, this is not a useful format for making more fine-grained decisions.

- You can conduct assessments of candidate portfolios or previous work remotely and asynchronously, but portfolio reviews can also be an onsite activity where the candidate takes the interviewer through a work sample.

- Remote post-onsite follow-up interviews can be used to clarify anything that came up during the onsite and to talk about next steps.

The hiring team will likely build into the pipeline some kind of remote assessment, from technical screens to post-onsite follow-ups, so it's important to understand the possible constraints as well as the benefits.

Confidence in what signal you're extracting will be weaker over the phone, so it may be preferable to ask questions with clearer signals, like questions with a right or wrong answer. It's also important to ensure that every candidate, to the extent possible, goes through the same loop when it comes to remote vs. onsite.

> STORY "The signal isn't weaker or stronger with remote interviews, it just manifests differently. If I talk to some people onsite and others remote, I'm going to perceive the phone signal to be weaker, because humans just have stronger attachment to in-person experiences and can gather signal from a variety of different cues in person." —Scott Woody, former Director of Engineering, Dropbox

🔥 CONFUSION If you're hiring for a remote position, should candidates still be brought in for an onsite? Onsite interviews are enormously important for selling candidates on the role, team, and company. If the position is remote or remote optional, have everyone go through the same process, because you're comparing people, not remote performance compared to onsite performance. If a candidate cannot come onsite because of family obligations, a current job, or other concerns,[568] put your best, most senior interviewers on that person.

27.4 Onsite Interviews

The **onsite interview** is a series of interviews held at the company's office for several hours to a full day. Onsites can be a crucial part of the interview experience for candidates and companies alike because they offer an extended opportunity for assessment on both sides. Onsites typically include pair interviews, pair programming, live coding, debugging, non-coding technical interviews, and nontechnical interviews.

🌀 CONTROVERSY Some companies have a multi-day process where the candidate comes back onsite several times. This can slow down your hiring process and lead to a bad candidate experience; but for early-stage startups or key roles, the opportunity to spend more time with the candidate may be worth the risk.

The pros of onsites are numerous—they provide the highest signal you can get. The human factor is important here: candidates get a real sense of the day-to-day output and environment of a company, and if you train your interviewers well, the onsite allows for a more conducive environment for comfortable communication. Onsites are very important for selling the job to candidates, who will get to experience the team firsthand, usually for the first time. Most candidates would prefer to interview in person, though in some cases it is essential to offer a remote option.

Some interviews provide much higher signal in person than they would over the phone. Technical non-coding formats like architectural interviews are nearly impossible to conduct when you don't have a shared

---

568. Don't ask too many questions to figure out why a candidate can't come onsite. It is illegal to ask questions in an interview scenario about health or family.

whiteboard to work from. Behavioral interviews are easier to assess when you can also read a person's body language and facial expressions.

⚠ DANGER   A risk of onsites is that they can be a source of bias; they require more evaluative efforts from interviewers than things like coding challenges do, and interviewers tend to feel more comfortable rendering verdicts based on false signal. For example, handwriting or communication style can color how an interviewer interprets code on a whiteboard. But few people are actually qualified to make such judgements. Interviewers might think, "This person was nervous at the whiteboard," and infer that the candidate is inexperienced or has a reason to be nervous. Such judgments are usually wrong and tend to be based on unconscious biases. Interviewers tend to uprank nervous-seeming candidates who look like them or have a similar background, while penalizing or downgrading candidates for nervousness when they are underrepresented or have a different background. It is crucial to train interviewers and use structured interviews, to keep candidate performance from being a function of who is conducting the interview or what mood they are in at the time.

27.4.1 STRUCTURING THE VISIT

⚠ CAUTION   Many believe coding-intense interviews provide the noisiest signal in onsite interviews. Ideally, an interview loop includes multiple sessions and multiple technical formats to avoid a situation where one bad interview tanks a candidate. In general, coding questions can also be the most tiring for candidates because they are being asked to solve new problems rather than talk about previous work. Discussing previous work gives you some of the best signal on a candidate's coding ability and their problem-solving skills. On the other hand, if you have too many questions or formats, you will wear candidates down. It's important to measure out the day, with easier, more straightforward interviews coming earlier. Coverage of other technical skills (such as deep diving into a prior project) and nontechnical interviews can come later in the day.

> 📖 STORY   "To get in more questions (better signal) without tiring the candidate, design the questions so that they flow together. For example, you might ask them to first build a simple API. Then add rate-limiting. Then maybe solve an algorithm problem that comes from efficiently rate-limiting across multiple machines. Then maybe add a

> frontend client. The thematic connection of the problems allows the candidate to stay focused on one codebase. This is not super common across the industry, but it's something that we've seen work really well for us." —Ammon Bartram, co-founder and CEO, Triplebyte

Lara Hogan provides a template[569] you can use to determine the list of signals you need to gather to make a hiring decision, and assign those signals to people in different interview slots. This is a great place to start planning out who will cover what for your onsite interviews. Marco Rogers adds even more detail to his post that includes an onsite interview schedule template,[570] notably including a second interviewer in each session and capping the total number of sessions at four.

Finally, having some kind of wrap-up at the end of the day with a hiring manager is an important part of giving the candidate some closure on the day and a chance to ask questions and hopefully meet their future manager. Additionally, given how important the manager-team member relationship is, this is an important part of building toward a successful close. You can also learn a lot about a candidate's perspective through the questions they ask, and while you will be giving them time during the other interviews to ask questions, they may have new questions and insights by the end of the day and may be feeling more comfortable.

27.4.2 TYPICAL ONE-ON-ONE INTERVIEW STRUCTURE

Technical one-on-one interviews often follow a simple form. This general overview illustrates how most in-person interviews are conducted:

Pre-interview prep. Most interviewers will require at least a few minutes before the interview to get into the right mindset, make sure they understand what questions to ask, and what the expectations for the candidate are. This need not take more than 15 minutes, but new interviewers may experience nervousness leading up to the interview throughout the day.

Greeting. Welcome the candidate and set them at ease—they may be experiencing high stress, information overload, or energy drain. A positive greeting gives them a chance to settle into the conversation and get used to the interviewer. Energy and enthusiasm are infectious; interview-

---

569. https://medium.com/making-meetup/onsite-interview-loop-template-da9a3cd87f20
570. https://firstround.com/review/my-lessons-from-interviewing-400-engineers-over-three-startups/

ers who bring genuine excitement to the interview can help a tired candidate show what they are capable of. Ask if they need to use a bathroom or would like something to drink. It's the human thing to do. Making them comfortable is not only the right thing to do, it will also make it easier for you to assess their actual capabilities.

Interviewer introduction. It's both helpful and just friendly for interviewers to let the candidates know who they are before diving into the details. It's awkward to talk to someone you know nothing about, and intros build some initial rapport while providing a chance to highlight one or two things the interviewer likes about the company.

⚠ DANGER Some interviewers might try to make conversation without realizing that it is against the law to ask certain questions in interview settings. Common illegal interview questions[571] include asking about marital status or age.

Introductory questions, usually short and easy. Most interviews start with an easier warmup question or questions, which could be a simpler version of a difficult question that will be asked later. The warmup allows the interviewer to adjust their approach based on whether things are going better or worse than expected. Some candidates won't realize the initial question is *not the hard part of the interview* and will over-solve or over-think it. Good interviewers help the candidate understand the flow of the interview so they can manage the time and nudge the candidate away from being unnecessarily thorough or careful in this phase.

You might start with a version of the question where a simple solution would work. For example, you may pose a coding question where the first version of the problem can be solved with storing everything in memory.

Follow-up questions, usually meatier. A gradual increase in difficulty ensures that candidates can be assessed on a spectrum of how far they were able to get, not whether they had a single "aha" moment or got stuck on something far too hard. The meatier follow-up question or questions should consume half or more of the overall interview time.

Using the example above, once the candidate understands the problem and has something working, you can introduce new requirements that up the challenge, like increasing the amount of data to a degree where it will no longer fit in memory.

---

571. https://ocs.yale.edu/get-prepared/illegal-interview-questions

Questions from the candidate. The final question-and-answer section allows candidates to learn more about the company and provides insight into what the candidate is concerned or excited about. It's important for interviewers to write these down for use in the closing process.

Tell them what will happen next. This is the time to clarify the next steps in the process, including the approximate timeline. Helping the candidate estimate when they will know if they're moving forward can help reduce stress, leading to a better candidate experience. For instance, for phone screens or after the last session in an onsite, it's important to let the candidate know that there will be a later follow-up and when they can expect to hear back. In between onsite interviews, the candidate should know when and where they can meet the next interviewer—whether they should wait in their current interview room or whether they will be escorted to another room.

⚠ DANGER It's important for the interviewer to refrain from sharing their assessment with the candidate during or immediately after the interview. Even when the interviewer feels certain of the outcome, the interview is just one data point in the process, and their opinion might change when they see the full set of feedback from colleagues or take some time to reflect. It's helpful to remember that the period during and immediately after an interview can be stressful for candidates, and that stress and adrenaline may cause them to be less likely to properly interpret (or handle) any feedback. Thus, an appropriately neutral but generally positive closing is to thank the candidate for their time and indicate that you enjoyed the discussion.

◇ IMPORTANT It is, however, equally important to deliver a response in a timely manner. If you take too long to give a candidate any feedback at all, they may read the silence as impolite disinterest on the part of the company or convince themselves they don't want the job anymore.

In the late stages of the process, candidates often ask about the actual solution to a coding problem they were presented with or whether there was a better approach than the one they took. Time permitting, answering neutral technical questions like this is fine and can lead to a more engaged technical discussion that gives the interviewer more signal—a candidate that is truly interested in better ways to solve a problem is usually a more thoughtful engineer.

27.4.3 PAIR INTERVIEW

In **pair interviewing**, two interviewers simultaneously work with and assess a single candidate. Typically, one interviewer leads the interview while the other observes. Microsoft's Developer Division[572] and Twitter, among others, use pair interviewing exclusively.

🔍 CONFUSION Some companies or teams use a form of pair interviewing to onboard new interviewers; this is called shadowing.

> *"Add another colleague into the mix as a second interviewer. I've found that it not only brings a higher fidelity and signal to the conversation, but also breaks down the flow and nature of the conversation. Sometimes a person will be talking to the candidate, and other times, they'll address their colleague. I find questions and answers bouncing between three points opens up the discussion and evaluation much more."*
> — Marco Rogers, veteran engineering manager[573]

Pair interviewing can yield more complete signal from an interview—if one interviewer notices something that the other interviewer doesn't, they can collaborate to assess what the outcome should be. They may help reduce bias, by bringing two perspectives to the same situation. This format can also help to root out bias on the candidate side.

> 💬 STORY "When pair interviewing with a male colleague, I've sometimes seen candidates only speak to or make eye contact with him. This is behavior that likely wouldn't have been seen were I interviewing solo—it would be super unlikely for a candidate to ignore the one person talking to them. Pair interviews can help to reveal if a candidate treats one member of the pair noticeably differently, which can be useful signal for how they might treat different teammates." —Ryn Daniels, Senior Software Engineer, HashiCorp

---

572. https://blog.usejournal.com/rethinking-how-we-interview-in-microsofts-developer-division-8f404cfd075a
573. https://firstround.com/review/my-lessons-from-interviewing-400-engineers-over-three-startups/

Pair interviewing also creates quality related feedback loops, since interviewers can share their thoughts with one another on how the interview was conducted. That said, pair interviewing effectively doubles the amount of interviewer time spent per candidate, and it is wise to evaluate whether it is worth that extra cost.

> *"Pair interviewing does add extra interviewer load, but interviewers seem to like it since it gives them increased confidence in their assessment and a mechanism for learning and feedback—a bit like paired programming."*
> — Jan Chong, Senior Director of Engineering, Twitter[574]

The likelihood of success in pair interviews may depend on the specific pairing. For example, having a pair made up of a manager and a more junior person can be problematic. Risk is lower if the junior person is shadowing the manager and therefore is not expected to question the candidate directly. But if they're meant to be partners in the interview, the junior person may feel intimidated by the manager and be unwilling to risk asking the wrong questions of the candidate. Structured interviewing and careful planning can mitigate this risk; each person in the pair can be assigned a tack to take, or an area to focus on, or specific questions.

A pair of developers who are of equal rank and similar disposition may work best; variant personality style causes greater risk. When a candidate is focusing hard on answering questions, having to switch between, say, a low-energy interviewer and a high-energy interviewer can be extremely difficult and tiring. This does not set the candidate up for success.

◇ IMPORTANT It might seem intimidating to a candidate when more than one interviewer walks into the room—you can mitigate this by letting the candidate know in advance that you will be conducting a pair interview.

27.4.4 PANEL INTERVIEWS AND PRESENTATIONS

A **panel interview** is one in which three or more interviewers simultaneously evaluate a candidate.[575] Typically, companies select interviewers to represent a variety of perspectives regarding the open position.

---

574. Interview with Ozzie Osman, 2019, San Francisco, CA.
575. A panel interview is not the same as an *interview panel*, which simply refers to the people who will be interviewing a given candidate.

Panel interviews have downsides for the candidate experience. Having to address multiple interviewers at once can feel like an interrogation; introverts in particular usually do better in one-on-one settings. One upside is that panel interviews give the candidate a chance to meet more of the team. But for most people, panel interviews are intimidating.

That said, there are a few possible benefits of this format for the company.

One company benefit is that in a very consensus-based hiring process, a panel interview makes it possible for more people to be involved. It may also be useful when multiple hiring managers are looking for different types of candidates or are trying to route a candidate to the right role or team. However, with everyone asking different questions, the likelihood that the interview will get deep enough for a strong signal is low.

Panel interviews can be beneficial for reducing bias, when answers can be gauged by multiple people of varying backgrounds. However, it's important not to misrepresent the diversity of your company or overburden underrepresented employees.

◇ CAUTION Although it may seem that panel interviews can give signal on how a candidate will work in a group, panels may not reflect the team the candidate would work with or may lack the dynamic of a collaborative team, particularly if the group feels artificially put together, or no one has specific questions to ask that they couldn't get signal on in another format. Inadequately trained panelists may give off a vibe that they do not want to be there, hurting the candidate experience and downgrading their perception of the company. It's hard enough for candidates to adapt between different types of people at the same time, especially in a situation that is already stressful. So if you decide to use this format, it helps to make sure each panelist has a clearly defined reason for being there.

In the end, most people just hate presenting in front of groups. Panel interviews often do not meet the candidate experience principle.

A similar, and often preferable, alternative is to have the candidate give a **presentation** to the team. One hiring manager[576] told us that a team he worked for tried presentations and ended up scrapping it because the signal they got was of so little value. One hire they made based on the person's presentation ability ended up not being a strong fit for the role;

---

576. Alex Allain, Dropbox

they had gotten signal on the wrong kind of communication ability, one that wasn't relevant to collaborative work. While engineers do sometimes present ideas to groups, like in design reviews, it's a relatively infrequent activity and usually less formal than a typical presentation.

On the other hand, presentations are fairly common for research or scientist positions, because the work requires conference presentations. Similarly, if the role you're hiring for requires similar work as a core component—product managers or a sales position—a presentation evaluation makes more sense.

27.5 *Whiteboard Interviews*

A **whiteboard interview** is a technical problem-solving assessment that takes place in real time and typically involves a candidate writing code and sometimes diagrams on a whiteboard while onsite.[577] A similar kind of interview can be done in person with pen and paper.

🗩 CONTROVERSY Whiteboard coding questions are controversial in the industry and their merits are hotly debated.[578] Whiteboard coding questions do not accurately mimic the environment that a candidate will usually work in—they have no access to a compiler, editor, or reference material as they normally would. They also bias toward candidates with fresh, detailed memory of a language or library and against developers who prefer a more iterative model of writing and testing code incrementally. Reacting to these potential flaws, Hiring Without Whiteboards[579] provides a popular, extensive, collaboratively sourced list of companies that don't use whiteboard coding.

◇ IMPORTANT Looking at whiteboarding more broadly, however, can dissolve what appear to be inherent constraints of the format. As more than one senior engineer put it to us: "No one is good at coding on a whiteboard."[580] Accepting that can be the start of something interesting. If

---

577. Some people take the concept literally and consider only interviews that involve writing code on a whiteboard to be whiteboard interviews. Others interpret the concept more broadly or metaphorically.
578. https://www.forbes.com/sites/vivekravisankar/2015/05/04/the-rise-and-looming-fall-of-the-engineering-whiteboard-interview/#1b53591f1c82
579. https://github.com/poteto/hiring-without-whiteboards
580. https://hackernoon.com/its-time-to-retire-the-whiteboard-interview-qyr32sd

hands-on coding tells you what an engineer knows and how they use their knowledge, whiteboarding interviews may better cover the *why*—why does the engineer make each choice? When conducted well, whiteboarding gives signal on an engineer's communication and collaborative abilities, as well as how they think through problems and theorize solutions.

> 🔖 STORY "The whiteboard is just the visualization mechanism and is useful in any talking interview. The whiteboard could be a laptop. Generally the whiteboard is just a way of drawing things. It's a visual mode of communication." —Scott Woody, former Director of Engineering, Dropbox

Physically writing a lot on a whiteboard can be unfamiliar or stressful for those who've not done it much. A helpful alternative is to offer a pencil and pad of paper to a candidate who is not comfortable on the whiteboard. This requires that the interviewer be able to sit next to them to review and discuss as they write.

27.6 Hands-on Coding Interviews

Hands-on coding interviews include all formats where a candidate uses a computer and not a whiteboard. They are often part of an onsite, but can also be conducted remotely.

In a hands-on coding interview, an interviewer will give the candidate a technical problem; the candidate will typically use a code editor to solve it. This provides signal on whether a person has done this kind of work before, the nature of their coding style and problem-solving style, and what practical set of skills they have. Because most programmers are more comfortable with writing code than completing a task on a whiteboard, hands-on interviews move along more quickly, allowing you to go deeper and get more volume of signal.

27.6.1 PROS AND CONS OF HANDS-ON CODING INTERVIEWS

Are hands-on coding interviews better than whiteboard interviews? It's complicated!

Some advantages of hands-on coding interviews include:

- Technical candidates are more familiar with the coding experience, which may be particularly relevant for candidates who rely heavily on the features of their IDE.
- Hands-on coding interviews are based on a more natural style of writing and debugging code incrementally, which allows the candidate to display confidence in their work.
- The candidate can use reference materials.
- The candidate can provide an exact transcript of the code at the end of the interview.
- Because hands-on interviews are live, they offer little room for cheating.

The primary downsides of this approach are:

- Not all candidates have laptops, so the company may need to provide them.
- Laptops may have hardware or software issues that delay the interview; whiteboards rarely do.
- Unless the company provides scaffolding, the candidate may need to write a bunch of boilerplate code to get started. If the company does provide scaffolding, it likely needs to do so for a large number of languages, and the logistics of getting the scaffolding to the candidate can present a hurdle. (One possible alternative is to have the candidate modify or debug an existing codebase, allowing the collection of additional signal on other skills relevant to software engineering like reading and working with new code.)
- The candidate may get caught up in such non-essential elements of the problem as making sure their code compiles or looking up the exact right library function, rather than focusing on solving the more fundamental aspects of the problem. While these are also skills required of an engineer, they're more basic than the translation of ideas to code, and detract from evaluating that.
- Most programmers do not perform their work in front of other people; the pressure of having someone watch them code can be enough to throw candidates off their game.

- It can be somewhat awkward for the interviewer to watch the candidate work without staring over their shoulder. While this can be mitigated by using an app like Coderpad,[581] the editing experience when using such an app will not be what the candidate is used to.

Those downsides notwithstanding, for the right kind of question, having people code on a laptop can offer a better candidate experience. Hands-on, synchronous work more closely mirrors a real working environment, with back-and-forth between the parties, and with no expectation that a candidate do something perfectly without feedback.

While online challenges screen for basic coding skills, synchronous, hands-on formats are closer to assessments, because they allow you to measure how a candidate reasons their way through problems. This results in better signal on a candidate's talent, not just their skill or knowledge base. Interviewers can course correct, and can increase the difficulty of the question or questions as the interview proceeds, depending on how the candidate is performing. Signal is also more accurate because candidates can't ask friends or look up answers.

Compared with online coding challenges, hands-on coding interviews are more expensive; they require an interviewer to be present in person, over the phone, or in a shared screen environment, as well as the cost of transporting the candidate to an onsite. They also require far more training and preparation from interviewers.

Compared with the whiteboard environment, where everyone is expected to fumble (or to hesitate or be more playful in how they use the whiteboard), candidates are expected to be more precise and efficient when working in a code editor. Some fumbling might be expected for people earlier in their career, who may perhaps be not as familiar with different coding environments or who haven't spent thousands of hours coding—especially when working with an interviewer looking over their shoulder. That doesn't mean a less senior person isn't right for the role you're hiring for. If the person can be trained on the job, how much they fumble in hands-on work doesn't matter as much; the interviewer's focus then becomes evaluating talent over skill.[582]

---

581. https://coderpad.io
582. http://www.onstartups.com/author/dharmesh-shah

Some companies opt to constrain candidates on language or environment, putting candidates in a place they may not be familiar with. Language requirements are normal, but environmental requirements are rarely standard unless you use a specific coding environment like iOS or Android. Barring role requirements, restricting language or environment is an artificial constraint that will give you poor signal on their ability and may cause you to lose a third to half of your candidates.

On the other hand, unconstrained choice on language and environment means interviewers must prepare more thoroughly and may receive more variable signal. Has a candidate made a smart language choice, like using a typed vs. untyped language? If they use a typed language, errors will be apparent; if they use an untyped language, the interviewer needs to know how to find the errors the candidate might make.

To remedy this, it's best to train interviewers to ask the candidate doing the coding to talk them through their work, rather than just watching the candidate deliver the code. "If anything, more talk, less code," as Scott Woody put it to us. This can be harder than it seems, especially when the interviewers are junior engineers who want to appear accomplished and impressive to candidates. It's very reasonable for an interviewer to say, "I haven't seen a solution like this before. Can you talk me through it?"

> 🅂 STORY "I tend to recommend that interviewers try to take an attitude of 'How would I interact with someone I was pairing with or mentoring?' This cuts down on seemingly adversarial attitudes that can make candidates nervous. It's hard to be at your best when it feels like someone is wanting or waiting for you to fail." —Ryn Daniels, Senior Software Engineer, HashiCorp

> 🅂 STORY "It's gauche to judge someone purely on language expertise. You can learn a language if you're a good engineer. That said, if they need to be an expert in Go, go ahead, force them to use Go in all their interviews. That's appropriate. What I find more often is an implicit expectation that you're an expert in whatever language you use. In reality, we're all searching the internet for help with our work. That's just more realistic." —Scott Woody, former Director of Engineering, Dropbox

In short, in the best case, hands-on coding can give you fine-grained, practical signal. What do they know, and how do they use that knowledge? As with other formats, building clear rubrics and communicating the signal you're trying to get from a hands-on interview can help avoid judgments based on work style or approach.

CANDIDATE We suggest Yangshun Tay's Tech Interview Handbook Cheatsheet,[583] especially when preparing for hands-on interviews—it includes how candidates can explain their work in a hands-on. There are also helpful reminders here for preparing for other types of interviews, like phone screens.

27.6.2 SOME HANDS-ON INTERVIEW FORMATS

A **live coding challenge** is an exercise or work sample that provides the company with content for assessment that mimics the work a candidate might do on the job. Within live coding challenges, there are two variations: a company may ask a candidate to work on a project on their own while onsite, or the candidate may be assessed in a **pair programming interview**, in which the candidate interacts directly with the existing team on a project.

Pair programming and live coding make the most sense when the role is for a coding-only position. With senior positions, which require a lot more than coding ability, these formats might be a waste of time—there are other ways to evaluate how someone thinks through code and approaches problems, and how they lead others.

The challenge is to design something close to what the candidate would be doing on the job; giving a puzzle on recursive algorithms when the role will not require that kind of work will not give you relevant signal. It also has to be possible to complete the challenge in a reasonable amount of time.

With pair programming and live coding, candidates can't cheat. The skills demonstrated are practical. The candidate may have told you that they know what a singleton pattern is, but can they write one or recognize one in code? Live work helps to track how the candidate applies their knowledge, which a candidate can help with by walking the interviewer through what they're doing in detail. This may be especially important for recent graduates.

---

583. https://yangshun.github.io/tech-interview-handbook/cheatsheet/

Live coding presents the same kinds of challenges as other hands-on formats—most engineers do not spend their time coding in front of others. The pressure and awkwardness of doing so can be challenging enough to throw off a candidate and give you false signal on their abilities. You'll see how quickly and efficiently the candidate produces work, but only to a point; the pressure of the live environment can hobble some engineers. Live work is a skill in and of itself. Dealing with that anxiety or not being affected by it measures something different from coding ability.

> **STORY** "An interview is as contrived as a blind date. When you meet someone by accident, glorious music plays and you get to see the real them. A lifetime movie is made. When you go on a blind date or a Bumble mixer, it's so predatory and awkward. Same thing with live coding. If you start failing, you're going to spiral out of control because of the stress. In real life, someone corrects you, a bug is filed, you go home, you come back the next day and you fix it. With the coding experience live, you make a mistake, EVERYONE knows it, and you can't reset all that well unless you're very controlled." —Aaron Saray, engineer

> **STORY** "I've seen companies with open-source efforts tackle a ticket with the applicant. It's interesting because it requires the interviewer to find a ticket before each interview that is appropriate, and if the project isn't sufficiently large, that's hard to do for multiple candidates; the ticket will always be different. But it gives two options: either they can pair on the open ticket or, if it's a senior candidate, they can review an existing PR and make adjustments." —Laurie Barth, Staff Engineer, Gatsby

Debugging interviews are exercises in which candidates are asked to find solutions to real-world bug problems in codebases. Debugging is a critical task for most engineering roles, and an interview of this type can give insight into how the candidate reasons and works with their tools. These interviews also test for how well a candidate can read others' code and make changes that respect existing designs.

Debugging may give a narrower slice of insight into the candidate than a take-home, which usually entails a mix of debugging and building.

The challenges of debugging interviews are mostly logistical. Debugging interviews require a lot of time on the part of the interviewers to develop the right question and build up scaffolding code in a language and environment with which the candidate is relatively familiar.

Note that some debugging interviews may be "great in theory, bad in practice." As many as a third or even half of your candidates just won't be able to solve the challenge. The more standardized language and development of iOS or Android environments make them a possible exception.

27.7 Take-homes

A **take-home assignment (take-home or takehome)** is a coding task given to technical candidates to complete on their own time. Candidates are typically given a day to several days to complete a take-home.

🚩 CONTROVERSY Take-homes are controversial. While there are many pros for the companies assigning them, they are less valuable in terms of the candidate experience. Nonetheless, they do have some advantages for candidates.

27.7.1 BENEFITS OF TAKE-HOMES

🧑 CANDIDATE Take-homes remove a lot of the stress associated with onsite challenges. Candidates get to use their own tools and work in the style they would if they were on the job. They can review and iterate on their work, take time away to think or rest, and rewrite. One senior engineer put it this way: "Most employees 'take home' their work if you think about it. You get work, you go away and think, you do it, you sleep, you come back and review it. That's how our jobs work."

For companies, take-homes have arguably the lowest false negative rate of any interview format—"the truest signal," as Scott Woody, former Director of Engineering at Dropbox, put it to Holloway. A few factors account for this:

- Take-homes give the candidate enough time to do the work in an environment that they're comfortable with, so you eliminate the noise of a whiteboard interview.

- It's very hard to hide weaknesses in coding ability in a take-home, and follow-up conversations can tell you almost everything you need to know about how a candidate thinks through problems.
- Follow-ups also allow you to weed out and correct for any negative signal or false signal—for example, if a candidate cheats, talking through their work will help you figure that out.

Follow-ups are an important part of the take-home evaluation; in this respect, take-homes are the first step of a larger conversation. A good take-home will mimic assignments the candidate might reasonably be asked to do on the job and will give you practical signal on their abilities, creativity, and style.

Here's how a sample assignment might progress. Let's say the take-home is something like "Build a simple web-based calculator app" or "Build an AI version of Tetris." When the candidate returns, you might read the code and interrogate it together, bringing the initial asynchronous assessment into a synchronous evaluation:

1. You ask the candidate to critique their work.
2. You may then ask them what they would do given another 20 hours; or say, "How would you invest 10 more hours on this?" Questions like "What feature would you remove?" and "What feature would you add?" will further refine your understanding of their work.
3. An additional useful question is, "What shortcuts did you take, and why did you think that was the right shortcut?"

27.7.2 DOWNSIDES OF TAKE-HOMES

◇ CAUTION The major downside of take-homes is the time commitment they require. Because the market is so competitive, asking a strong candidate to give up their weekend for a take-home can lead them to drop out of your process. Senior candidates may feel that being asked to do a take-home is a waste of their time. For these reasons, take-homes usually make sense further along in the funnel. They require a lot of engineering time and investment from interviewers and candidates, so they aren't ideal for screening. Some companies opt to pay candidates for the time they spend on these assignments, but this doesn't always make a difference. A senior manager at Dropbox told us that before the company pivoted from take-homes, 20% of candidates would simply not complete them. Less-competitive candidates were more likely to complete the assignment, because they didn't have competing offers. The pass-through rate was close to 10%. If you're asking candidates to invest 15 hours, and their chance of passing through is 10%, the value asymmetry is strong.

Despite the high signal achieved, interviewers, too, spend hours of their time designing take-homes, scaffolding in multiple languages, and reviewing code, and with such a low pass-through rate, this hardly pays out.

⚠ DANGER The other major con of take-homes is that they explicitly discriminate against people who have families or adverse financial situations, or who work more than one job. If these candidates are in the hiring pipeline at more than one company, they may receive multiple take-home assignments at once, making them impossible to complete, and this may cause the candidates to drop out of your process.

Take-homes also open up the possibility that a candidate may cheat by asking friends to help or collaborate. Additionally, with a take-home, you're asking candidates to work in a vacuum, which doesn't match to most work environments, where you're hopefully able to ask questions and get feedback as you progress.

◊ CAUTION Take-homes are difficult to timebox and thus difficult to assess fairly. If candidates have been given 48 hours to turn in an assignment, you might be comparing candidates who spent 40 hours with those who spent only 2.

One way to avoid this false signal is to pay people an hourly rate for the assignment; but candidates can lie, either saying they worked more hours so as to receive the pay or fewer hours because they want to look impressive.

There are situations in which the pros of take-homes outweigh the cons. Smaller companies may find it easier to assign take-homes than to expend the time and resource investment in a longer pipeline, where multiple interviews would be needed to get the same signal. Younger engineers trying to break into the industry may prefer take-homes because they provide a chance to demonstrate skills they haven't yet had a chance to prove on the market. If there's a candidate you haven't gotten clear signal from yet, adding a take-home to their pipeline will usually tell you one way or another whether the bet will pay off. Scott Woody, former Director of Engineering at Dropbox, told us that people who tend to shine on take-homes have nontraditional backgrounds: "They're hackers, or they never took CS in college, and they'd fail out of our normal process. But we can see they've been doing all this practical work on the side, so let's give them this practical thing and they're going to build something singular."

27.7.3 TAKE-HOME TIPS

Using a tool like Takehome.io[584] can help with timeboxing take-homes. It might seem like the option of timeboxing would help solve a lot of the cons of this format, but many engineers[585] hold the opinion that time limits introduce further artificiality that compromises what could otherwise be a clear signal. There are tradeoffs any way you approach it.

If you do choose to give take-homes, it's important to be clear with the candidate that the results will only be used for evaluation and not to produce work for the company. You might also provide an upper bound on the amount of time a candidate should spend on the take-home. When sending candidates the assignment, it's important to let them know *what it is* that you will be evaluating—the code? the creativity? the speed? This will help ensure that they don't waste time on something that won't translate as much to the assessment and the eventual job. You likely also will want to avoid noting things as nice-to-haves unless they are truly necessary for the assessment.

One idea worth noting to help make the candidate experience better is to replace the take-home with a project that is done in the office during the onsite. Such a project still requires a logistical burden, but has the benefit of feeling like a symmetric exchange of time, particularly if it replaces multiple interview questions. The goal is to mimic the benefits the take-home has for candidates—let them work alone.

🕮 **CANDIDATE** Understanding the reasons why a company might choose a take-home problem can help candidates prepare. This guide[586] from Jane Phillips has a host of practical suggestions for tackling take-home coding challenges, along with an FAQ on common scenarios, like needing more

---

584. https://takehome.io/
585. https://news.ycombinator.com/item?id=16364805
586. https://www.fullstackinterviewing.com/2018/02/02/the-ultimate-guide-to-kicking-ass-on-take-home-coding-challenges.html

time or what to do if you're not familiar with a language or framework in the take-home problem.

27.8 Prior Work Assessment

Some companies choose to ask candidates for past work samples rather than asking them to write code (though you can do both). The nice thing about this approach is that it allows you to see something that the candidate actually did in a real-world setting. However, it can be difficult for many candidates to provide this kind of work sample if they don't have an open-source presence, and evaluating these work samples may take more time and require a great deal of interviewer effort to evaluate. Prior work assessments can be:

- **Synchronous.** The candidate walks the interviewer through a completed project or portfolio.
- **Asynchronous.** The candidate sends work to the interviewer for them to review, and/or the interviewer reviews the candidate's open-source projects (likely on GitHub).
- **Both asynchronous and synchronous.** The interviewer looks at the sample without the candidate present, then meets with the candidate to discuss the work.

Looking at past work can show you the technologies with which a candidate is familiar and how they architect solutions. Past work that is open-source or a "passion project" demonstrates what the candidate is really interested in doing and allows them to shine. When not explicitly associated with a previous position, this kind of work also can show you where candidates made mistakes or curious choices and where they may have cut corners. As with discussing a take-home, looking at past work can offer illuminating discussion with the candidate: Why did they make those choices? What would they have done differently, given the time or hindsight?

Unfortunately, it's not always easy to tell exactly what work is the candidate's and what was done collaboratively or primarily by a colleague, or when they came into the project with their own contribution.[587] Candidates might share work that isn't relevant to the job requirements, and looking through work that has nothing to do with the job requirements may be a waste of time.

If interviewers do choose to dive into specific previous work, it's best to give the candidate advance warning and also a general direction of the kinds of topics you would like to cover. This allows the candidate time to refresh their memory of the work they choose to showcase. At the same time, building in extra time puts some pressure on the interviewer to actually dive deep to ensure the candidate is not just giving a rehearsed presentation.

28 Technical Interview Questions

Interview questions generally fit into three categories: coding questions, non-coding technical questions, and nontechnical questions.

Coding questions usually form the foundation of most technical interviews because all software engineers must be able to write code. Coding questions are also usually the easiest to administer and assess. But there are a variety of technical skills that cannot be evaluated with only a coding interview.

Coding questions are technical interview questions that require writing code, either on a whiteboard or in a hands-on format. **Non-coding questions** can be technical questions where coding is not involved, such as design or architectural questions, or generally nontechnical, like behavioral questions.

Many of the skills that you will need from senior engineering talent are most usefully assessed outside of a coding interview, including system design, technical strategy, relevant domain expertise, and nontechnical skills like leadership and mentorship.

---

587. Sometimes GitHub commits can help clarify this, but it's rarely fully reliable since people can and commit code from others, and some commits look large but are trivial (like formatting changes). If it's unclear, it's usually best to ask who wrote what, and confirm their familiarity with the code.

28.1 Coding Questions

Coding ability assessment is essential to the interview process. But there are many kinds of coding questions, and they have varying difficulty, style, and efficacy at measuring coding skills in ways that are representative of the challenges of the job.

It's generally important that your question bank cover both basic and more advanced coding. If you have only questions that are sufficiently easy that you feel any strong engineer should be able to answer (FizzBuzz,[588] for example), then you're not going to get enough signal on the candidate's problem-solving or ability to handle anything that is non-trivial. But if questions are mostly very hard, false negatives become common. Since coding questions can be noisy, you will typically want multiple interviewers and questions on your interview loop.

◊ CAUTION Focusing *exclusively* on coding in the interview process is generally unwise. Doing so provides a poor candidate experience as well, because candidates want to show what they've done and what they know, not just their ability to solve toy problems.[589]

28.1.1 KINDS OF CODING QUESTIONS

The spectrum of types of coding questions you can ask ranges from those that are heavily algorithm-focused (like a dynamic programming problem) to those that more closely resemble real-world scenarios. It's best to match the kind of coding questions you ask to the kind of work you expect candidates to do; this practice gives you more useful signal and is more engaging for the candidate. It is not wise to include coding questions that are either math problems in disguise (unless mathematical skill is a job requirement) or that feel arbitrary. Even strong candidates may struggle with problems that feel completely artificial.

The one caveat is that if you are hiring recent graduates, you can reasonably expect that they have taken algorithm classes in college; testing them against those types of questions will give you some signal of how much they were able to retain. However, if you're hiring for entry level roles and comparing people with CS degrees to bootcamp graduates or

---

588. https://www.tomdalling.com/blog/software-design/fizzbuzz-in-too-much-detail/
589. https://www.researchgate.net/publication/334448588_Hiring_is_Broken_What_Do_Developers_Say_About_Technical_Interviews

those who are self-taught, this approach will produce strongly biased results.

Almost all good coding questions will have a way to scale in difficulty so that every candidate can make at least some amount of progress. The wider the difficulty range of your question, the more you can distinguish great candidates from merely competent ones.

It's possible that any candidate you test has seen leaked questions[§26.3.1] from your prior interviews. But what you think could be an indicator could also be completely benign—no problem is going to be new to everyone, and there's almost always some chance that you will ask a question that someone has heard elsewhere. Making sure that the questions you ask reflect the skills required for the role will help you steer clear of generic, low-signal questions.

28.1.2 CHOOSING LANGUAGES

It's generally best to let the candidate choose the programming language that they use for coding questions, unless language expertise is critical to the role. Strong engineers are usually able to pick up new languages quickly. But some roles do demand deep expertise in complex languages. In either case, it's most effective to be clear with the candidate about their options and to encourage them to use the languages they are most comfortable with. If they choose a language that they think will impress you but that they do not use regularly, or if they choose one used by your company, they may underperform.

How demanding to be about language and library knowledge requires careful judgement. Unless it is a hands-on format, it's important to remember that the candidate answering coding questions doesn't have access to the resources they normally would. This means you can relax your expectations around language syntax and library functions. Whiteboard code will never compile, so don't treat it like it has to.

On the other hand, it's *not* OK if the candidate really doesn't know the language itself. Someone using curly braces and semicolons in Python indicates that they have very little familiarity with the language. Someone forgetting a semicolon in C++ is not a big deal. However, the most frequent issue is for a candidate to get distracted by trying to remember something specific that has no bearing on the result of the interview. It's usually fine to let a candidate make up library functions that are "close" to what the real library function is if their memory fails them—but equally, inventing "magical" library functions that solve too much of the problem is not a good indicator. In most cases, if someone would use a library in real life, it's wise to let them use it in an interview.[590]

28.1.3 WHEN ARE CODING QUESTIONS NECESSARY?

Some have questioned the necessity of intense coding interviews and suggest placing a greater focus on design questions, behavioral interviews, and other tests of knowledge.

On the one hand, coding questions in artificial environments under the pressure of an interviewer's watchful eye can make people perform poorly, making for ineffective coding assessments. On the other hand, coding questions are meant to screen for necessary technical skills. There are people who simply cannot write code or who have only studied computer science and never really practiced engineering in work environments. Looking at experience alone isn't always a good indicator of how the person will perform in the new role. A coding interview can help ensure that this person is able to do the work.

Another approach is to only ask relatively easy coding questions to verify that the candidate can code fluently, and then use other interview techniques to test other skills. Other resources like past work samples may be reasonable alternatives for measuring the person's likelihood of success in the role.

Strictly no-code interviews may make sense for certain senior roles, where communication and high-level problem solving are more central to success, and actual coding is more limited. For some junior positions, it may be easier to teach code than it is to teach good communication, so if you're planning on having the person learn a lot on the job, factors like problem-solving and collaboration skills might be more important. (There are training programs and coaches available to improve employees' coding abilities in these situations, if there are not enough available resources to mentor them in-house).

---

590. An exception is if part of the role in fact requires building or re-implementing such library functions. Another variation is to allow a candidate to use any library function, but afterwards, to ask if they know how that library function works. Strong, more senior engineers ideally have good intuition or deep familiarity with a platform's libraries, and this knowledge can be an extra, positive signal.

> **STORY** "The best no-code interviews I've seen involved diving into a candidate's resume and talking about past projects—reaching the edge of their knowledge on the topics and probing one step further. It allows them to show off what they know and gives an accurate picture of what they don't. It requires a very senior engineer to do it correctly, but it works beautifully." —Laurie Barth, Staff Engineer, Gatsby

> **STORY** "Dropbox has a pretty high bar for coding questions. It's not entirely clear if, from first principles, you ought to design a hiring system this way, but it's the system we understand and operate." —Alex Allain, Engineering Director, Dropbox

28.2 Non-coding Questions

Coding questions collect signal on a person's ability as a programmer. The non-coding questions collect the majority of the other technical signals that help determine if the candidate has the experience relevant to the role and job level.

It's best for more senior interviewers to ask non-coding questions and to spend time calibrating on how to evaluate the non-coding portion of interviews, because these interviews:

- Require higher-level skills that cannot be evaluated by more junior engineers who lack them.
- Require more judgment to assess a candidate's choices in a context that the candidate is not fully familiar with.
- Are simply more difficult to administer, as they are open-ended and require adapting follow-up questions to a wider range of circumstances than can come up in most coding interviews.

Non-coding interviews may also require more shadowing time to ramp up than coding questions, and they are often somewhat more company-specific, because companies assess and value non-coding technical skills differently.

These interviews break down into roughly three categories: those that assess what a candidate has done previously, those that assess specific non-coding technical and domain knowledge, and those that assess a candidate's ability to think through new problems or situations.

> 📖 STORY "If you use interviews for leveling, make sure that they give you enough information for that assessment. If a candidate whizzes through, but you assess them at a low level just because there wasn't enough challenge to peg them higher, this is a problem." —Laurie Barth, Staff Engineer, Gatsby

28.2.1 ASSESSING PREVIOUS TECHNICAL WORK

Interviews that assess previous technical work generally follow a rough progression:

1. The interviews start out with the big picture of a particular situation or project. This involves getting the facts and high-level context.
    i. How well does the candidate understand and describe the business context, the problem that was addressed, and any critical constraints their team was dealing with?
    ii. Does the candidate understand the big-picture system architecture and design?
    iii. Can they identify what part of the system they worked on, what their own personal contribution was, and what their role was in relation to the rest of the team?
2. Next, the candidate can pick some specific elements they personally worked on to go deep into. Within those areas, the interviewer can ask the candidate to dig into the details of the system, focusing on decisions they made and why they made those decisions.
    i. What would they do differently if they were working on this project now?
    ii. How would their decision have changed if some set of constraints had been different?

It's common for candidates to talk about a system that they used or interacted with but did not personally build. It is the interviewer's job to get the candidate to identify their own contribution to the system and then to go deep into the areas where they feel most comfortable assessing technical decisions. It is critical to understand the technical decisions that the candidate made, because the point of the interview is to assess their ability to design a system under real-world constraints.

As part of this, the interviewer can also seek the underlying reasons for decisions. The candidate will hopefully have a compelling reason for each choice, although that could be something pragmatic like "we had to move fast, and we had experience in this stack." Not every decision needs major deliberation, but as an interviewer, you will be looking to see if the candidate understands every decision they made.

Additionally, because no system design is perfect—and the interviewer may in fact disagree with the design—the interviewer can then ask the candidate what they learned and would do differently. A strong candidate will be able to demonstrate their ability to identify problems, recognize when things didn't go well, and iterate on a solution.

Finally, by asking the candidate how they would have changed their decision if some constraint had been different (for example, you have a month rather than a quarter to build the system), you get a chance to validate that they understand the decision well enough to adjust it in the face of new information.

◇ CAUTION All of these questions require that a trusted senior engineer exercise a tremendous amount of judgment and have the ability to pattern-match the challenges a candidate faced with their own experiences—which makes these probably the most difficult of all technical interviews to calibrate on.

28.2.2 ASSESSING TECHNICAL AND DOMAIN KNOWLEDGE

Nontechnical interviews may also focus on assessing specific elements of a candidate's technical knowledge. For example, you might ask them to explain a complex technical topic or ask questions about their knowledge within a particular domain. The former is similar to an assessment of past work, where you want to validate that the candidate understands the topic well by assessing underlying reasons for decisions. The latter is more about testing domain knowledge and can be used when filtering out candidates who lack fundamental knowledge in computer science or when specific domain expertise is relevant to a role.

28.2.3 DESIGN, PRODUCT, AND ARCHITECTURAL QUESTIONS

In the third form of this interview, the interviewer asks the candidate to demonstrate a non-coding technical skill during the interview, so as to give insight into how they think through challenges. These interviews can include all sorts of relevant problems, like:

- Designing a new system, architecture, or algorithm at a scope and domain appropriate to the role (sometimes called a System Design Interview[591]).
- Product thinking, such as handling ambiguous product specifications, prioritizing what to build, or evaluating trade-offs of implementing different features.

These interviews may be easier to calibrate than ones that evaluate a candidate's prior work because the problem-solving follows a more consistent flow, and you can write very clear rubrics.

⚠ CAUTION At the same time, beware of groupthink and rigidity in assessments. Senior engineers may be wedded to specific architectural patterns, for example, and they may dock those with a different perspective. But there is immense value in having someone come into your organization with fresh perspectives, especially at the senior level.

One skill that you will expect candidates to demonstrate is the ability to handle more open-ended problems, so it's wise to frame them accordingly, especially for more senior levels.

---

591. https://github.com/checkcheckzz/system-design-interview

28.2.4 TABLE: DESIGN, PRODUCT, AND ARCHITECTURAL QUESTIONS

PROMPT	EVALUATION
Imagine we've gone back in time and we're about to build Acme product again from scratch. We want to get to a prototype within four weeks. It doesn't have to be perfect, but it needs to have the key parts in place. Can you take five to ten minutes to flesh out for me how you'd approach this?	Has the candidate thought through the product and the key features ahead of time? Are they able to draw a sensible diagram of the major services they would need to have in place and the interfaces by which they might communicate? Are they able to arrive at a decent schema for the service? Extra points if they realize any of the complexities (for example, comments might require editing history to be stored).
One of the things about our service is that it pulls from APIs like Twitter and AngelList. They have API quotas that prevent us from pulling in all the data we want. Can you walk me through how we might design a system for prioritizing the most important calls?	Is the solution adaptable to future third-party services? Is the solution adaptable to ongoing changes in API rate limits/quotas? Do they have examples where they've worked backward from what the customer is going to care about into their solution?

28.3 *Technical Question Pitfalls*

28.3.1 MIND GAMES

⚠ DANGER There are some interview questions that are designed to see how the candidate reacts to the parameters of the question, like asking an impossible question, never giving enough guidance on what the question is really about for the candidate to succeed, or being incredibly silent or non-interactive during the interview. Anything that feels like it could even possibly be considered a mind game is bad territory to be in.

Not only is this a poor way to treat a candidate (and strong candidates with other options will rightly drop out if treated like this), but an interview must assess candidate-company fit *for both sides*. Candidates want and need to know how you work and communicate, and it's your job to demonstrate that to them.

> *"If you go into an interview with the intention of lording your knowledge over a candidate, showing them how smart you are, they can tell. And if you ask questions but don't really listen to the answers, it's all too obvious."*
>
> — Eric Ries, author of *The Lean Startup*[592]

28.3.2 SHIBBOLETH QUESTIONS

A **shibboleth question** is an interview question that seeks to quickly assess a candidate's general capabilities in an area by asking a question that the interviewer believes anyone in that area ought to know the answer to.

⚠ **DANGER** These questions are dangerous because not everyone will agree on what the common knowledge base in an area is, and asking for very specific knowledge will filter out qualified candidates. For example, not all software engineers will necessarily know dynamic programming.

These kinds of questions can be used by technical screeners and even recruiters if you have a high enough volume of candidates that you need some way to filter and also can't find another way to distinguish otherwise equally qualified candidates. But it's risky and does not create a good candidate experience, because it suggests you care more about factual knowledge than general ability, which rubs people the wrong way. It's also problematic for candidates from nontraditional backgrounds. Anything keyword-based, especially when assessed by a non-coder, is going to be biased against them.

28.3.3 BRAINTEASERS AND FERMI PROBLEMS

⚠ **CAUTION** Two other specific kinds of questions to watch out for are brainteasers[593] and Fermi problems.[594] These kinds of questions used to be popular,[595] but neither have been shown to correlate with job performance and may annoy many candidates or distract from more practical and relevant signals.

⚠ **DANGER** It's critical not to fall into the trap of trying to compete with the interviewee or to impress them for the sake of the interviewer's ego.

---

592. http://www.startuplessonslearned.com/2008/11/abcdefs-of-conducting-technical.html
593. https://www.quora.com/What-is-the-hardest-thing-about-hiring-programmers/answer/John-Byrd-2?ch=99&share=975c4ec0&srid=OYIQ
594. https://en.wikipedia.org/wiki/Fermi_problem
595. https://www.theatlantic.com/business/archive/2013/06/google-finally-admits-that-its-infamous-brainteasers-were-completely-useless-for-hiring/277053/

29 Nontechnical Interviewing

Because engineering does not take place in isolation, everyone you hire must be able to work well with other people. As your organization grows, and as individuals become more senior, the nontechnical aspects of the job become increasingly important.

There are several ways to evaluate nontechnical skills, including behavioral questions, situational questions, and role-playing. It is critical to anchor your assessment of nontechnical skills in your defined company values, so as to ensure you are hiring people with the skills that map to the expectations you will have for them once they join. Just Googling "icebreaker questions" or asking candidates to "tell me about your hobbies" will not produce results that will serve you well. It's important that nontechnical interviews be just as serious and structured as every other aspect of the interview process.

As discussed in Preparing Interviewers,[§26] it may make the most sense to have senior people conduct nontechnical interviews, which are typically harder to assess than straight coding interviews. Some managers recommend conducting all nontechnical interviews as pair interviews,[§27.4.3] including one senior person and one less senior person. This can help to reduce bias when assessing subjective answers and helps to train junior interviewers in a kind of active shadowing. (Recall that you may have to adjust for the possible pitfalls of having different-level pairs.)

While many companies wait to conduct the nontechnical interview until the onsite after technical screens and assessments, some managers opt to incorporate a kind of nontechnical screen earlier on.

> STORY "Incorporate the most important two or three behavioral questions into the prescreen, to give nontechnical skills equal weight to coding ability. Our current practice is that we have a 30-minute phone prescreen (or Zoom, face-to-face, whatever is lowest barrier for the candidate). Then we do back-to-back technical and behavioral-fit interviews, each an hour long." —Benjamin Reitzammer, freelance CTO

29.1 Types of Nontechnical Questions

29.1.1 BEHAVIORAL QUESTIONS

Behavioral questions assess nontechnical skills and values alignment by asking candidates about prior experiences and the way in which they handled specific situations. Many behavioral questions aim to extract specific positive or negative examples of the candidate's performance against the expectations of the organization.

> ⊚ STORY "To make this anchoring easier, it helped our team to spell out the company values with as specific as possible descriptions of how someone who exhibits the company values behaves or acts, such as: 'You openly communicate your thoughts, feelings, and concerns and contribute to an environment which allows this.' Of course this can also be done by formulating negative behaviors and actions that will not be tolerated. Based on these concrete descriptions, it's possible to derive situations in which they may arise and then formulate behavioral or situational questions based on these situations. For example, an organization that values feedback-seeking individuals might use the above description for their value of 'feedback-seeking.' A possible behavioral question then could be, 'Tell us about the last time you provided feedback to team members.'" —Benjamin Reitzammer, freelance CTO

Examples of behavioral questions:

- "Tell me about a time you had to deal with a difficult co-worker."
- "Tell me about a time you made a mistake. How did you handle it?"
- "Give me an example of a goal you didn't meet and how you handled it."
- "Tell me about a time a project you were responsible for was falling behind. What did you do?"
- "Tell me about a time you had to deliver bad news. How did you handle it?"
- "Tell me about a time you mentored someone." Possible follow-up questions include:
  - "What did you learn from it?"
  - "What would you do differently next time?"

- "What did you think worked particularly well?"
- "Give an example of a project where you had to convince your peers or boss to take an approach that you suggested, but they were hesitant to try."
- "Tell me about a conflict you had with a co-worker."
- "Have you ever taken guidance from someone more junior than yourself?"
- "Tell me about a time you had to take an unpopular position."
- "Name some improvements or experiments you made in your most recent position."
- "What was the most helpful feedback you received from a colleague or manager?"
- "Tell me about the last time you provided feedback to team members."
- "Tell me about a time you gave a compliment to a team member."
- "Tell me about a situation where a first solution wasn't the right one. How did you find out and how did you iterate on the solution to find the right one?"

CAUTION As with non-coding technical questions, assessing a candidate's performance in these situations is difficult and requires judgment and experience. There are several common patterns to watch for that can be a negative signal in these interviews:

- Some candidates will consistently blame others for bad results and not take ownership or acknowledge their own failures. This is generally a concerning pattern of behavior—a red flag.
- Candidates may avoid getting into specific details. This is often a sign that they're uncomfortable doing so and may indicate that they realize they mishandled a situation and that getting into detail would reflect poorly on them. They may also be nonspecific about what they personally did vs. what other people did, and this may reflect situations where the candidate contributed less than it appears.
- Candidates may use "I" rather than "we" when describing the work done by their team. This might be a sign that a candidate is not a team player. However, be careful in judging a candidate harshly for using the first person; they are in an interview to assess their performance, and they've likely been asked to focus on the results of their work. The choice of "I" vs. "we" may simply come down to speaking style. This is

a place to give some benefit of the doubt until you see a strong pattern backed by additional evidence beyond speaking style.

Finally, new interviewers will often be too trusting of the candidate's self-assessment about something in their past going well. Instead, interviewers can be digging deep to look for base facts as evidence and can draw their own conclusions about the candidate's work. It's a good idea to practice the art of the follow-up[596] to dig deeper into a candidate's answers.

Behavioral questions have the benefit of focusing on what a candidate actually did in a particular situation. But because there might be candidates who have never experienced the situation you describe, having a hypothetical version of the question can be a great idea.

29.1.2 SITUATIONAL QUESTIONS

Situational questions (or hypothetical questions) ask a candidate to explain how they would approach a specific challenge. The advantages of situational questions matched to job-relevant skills are that they allow an interviewer to evaluate candidates against a more objective rubric than behavioral interviews, and they challenge candidates to make choices in real time.

◊ IMPORTANT Well-designed situational questions avoid scenarios where it's relatively easy to identify what *should* be done but not so easy to take the appropriate action when presented with a difficult situation. For example, it's easy for someone to say that they would own up to a mistake; it's harder to actually do it. Instead, it's best to focus on situations where the hard part is identifying the core problem and/or devising a solution. Additionally, incorporating behavioral questions into the interview process will allow you to gauge how the candidate might actually behave.

You can often rephrase a behavioral question as a situational one through a slight change in wording. For example, "How would you deal with a colleague who doesn't deliver on their commitments?" is the situational form of the behavioral question, "Tell me about a time you worked with a colleague who didn't deliver on their commitments." This may make the two types of questions seem interchangeable, but some experts

---

596. https://hbr.org/2014/11/tactics-for-asking-good-follow-up-questions

have strong opinions[597] (often backed by data) on which form is more effective at evaluating candidates.

Ultimately, it matters less which you use (a mix is probably fine) and more that your questions are structured and your interviewers are calibrated to give consistent feedback. Adam Grant gives some specific details[598] on situational questions that can help interviewers overcome confirmation bias.

29.1.3 TOPGRADING

A **topgrading interview** is a type of behavioral interview in which the interviewer asks targeted questions about a candidate's experiences in all prior roles, proceeding chronologically through the candidate's career. If you make one of the questions about each prior role be the name of the candidate's boss, the company can confirm the candidate's description of their experiences through reference checking.

To learn more about topgrading, see "The Art of Interviewing 10x Engineers,"[599] a podcast discussion between Dan Portillo and Wade Foster; the "Topgrading Interview" section of Matt Mochary's *The Great CEO Within*[600]; and *Who: The A Method for Hiring*,[601] by Randy Street and Geoff Smart, who helped coin the term.

29.1.4 ROLE-PLAYING INTERVIEWS

Role-playing interviews ask candidates to act out specific challenging scenarios, such as interacting with a difficult co-worker. Role-playing interviews give the interviewer a chance to see how a candidate would realistically approach a particular situation.

Role-playing interviews require very well-defined scenarios so that the candidate's performance can be accurately evaluated. Even with a well-defined scenario, these interviews can be hard to evaluate because of the contextual nature of problem-solving and interpersonal interactions. For

---

597. https://www.inc.com/jessica-stillman/star-wharton-professor-adam-grant-says-this-popula.html
598. https://www.linkedin.com/pulse/20130610025112-69244073-will-smart-companies-interview-your-kids
599. https://soundcloud.com/greylock-partners/greymatter-podcast-the-art-of-interviewing-10x-engineers
600. https://docs.google.com/document/d/1ZJZbv4J6FZ8Dnb0JuMhJxTnwl-dwqx5xl0s65DE3wO8/edit#heading=h.w1yl31z0tqdz
601. https://www.amazon.com/Who-Method-Hiring-Geoff-Smart/dp/1400158389/

example, a candidate who relies on relationships and deep insight into other people may not perform well in a role-playing interview where they're asked to interact with someone they've never met.

29.2 Sample Nontechnical Questions

It's beyond the scope of this Guide to develop a bank of nontechnical questions, especially because these questions depend so heavily on your company's goals, values, and mission—not to mention the specific details of the role for which you're hiring. We've included a few categories of questions you can consider, however, and resources to help you dive deeper into which questions will work best for your needs. New Relic has an excellent post on evaluating potential managers[602] that covers their approach to designing nontechnical questions and their rubrics for evaluating them.

> **STORY** "You have to let the candidate surprise you. It makes the process of coming up with these questions easier, because you don't have to come up with all the possible answers. You can look at who are the super productive and thoughtful people on your team, the very valuable people on your team, seniors, lead people, and then ask something specific about them: 'What do they excel at?', 'In what situation did they do something really great?' Then try and turn that into a question. One example might be that 'a senior person stood up for someone else in a daily standup meeting.' Now come up with a related behavioral question. Identify situations where senior people really shone a positive light on the kind of behaviors you're looking at. On top of that, look at your company's values and build questions from there. 'You are the kind of person who values feedback.' Ok, now you know you can ask, 'What kind of feedback cycles do you have in your work? How do you give feedback?' Determine what you optimize for, and build questions from those behaviors." —Benjamin Retizammer, freelance CTO

---

602. https://blog.newrelic.com/technology/hiring-software-engineering-managers-interview/

29.2.1 TRAITS AND VALUES QUESTIONS

When thinking about values alignment, it is critical to know your company and team's values, and then use your nontechnical interview questions to assess how the candidate has previously demonstrated—or undermined—those values.

◇ **IMPORTANT** Remember, values alignment is not the same as culture fit. If someone has behaved unethically in the past or demonstrated a lack of integrity, that's a good reason not to hire them; if someone doesn't seem fun, that's not.

Values alignment can often be determined through behavioral or situational interviews that test for how a candidate makes decisions, passes judgments, or how they react to making mistakes. This is not about delivering "correct" answers—the point is to assess whether a candidate's values related to work style, communication, and mission align with the company's.

The most effective questions focus on sussing out a candidate's values and allow you to evaluate them based on how well they line up with company values:

- **If a company values humility/humbleness.** Does the candidate demonstrate ownership for their mistakes or have examples of taking feedback from others?
- **If a company values biasing for action.** Does the candidate have examples of making decisions in situations where the path forward was unclear?
- **If a company values depth of expertise.** Does the candidate have examples of going the extra mile to understand something?
- **If a company values working as a team.** Does the candidate have examples of supporting teammates through a difficult time or putting the team's goals ahead of their own?

29.2.2 TABLE: TRAITS AND VALUES QUESTIONS

PROMPT	EVALUATION
"Tell me about when you gave a compliment to a team member."	How the person feels about giving positive feedback. Do they think about the word *appreciation*, is it about positive feedback, or very technical things like, "I like your code."
"Imagine you join and everything here has gone wildly successful. Three years from now, what would you want to look back on and be proud of?"	Mission alignment and passion. Are they excited about the core mission? How much do they care about being a great manager and supporting their team? Do they only focus on their own accomplishments?
"Name some improvements you've made or experiments you've tried."	Self-awareness and what they view as improvement. Again, do they only focus on their own improvement and/or narrow improvements ("I made function X faster"), or do they have a broader view on the value of experimentation and process improvements?

29.2.3 AGENCY QUESTIONS

Another thing to screen for is agency—how much responsibility does the candidate feel comfortable or eager to take on when it comes to solving problems? This is especially important as the company gets bigger.

When assessing agency, it's important to ask both situational and behavioral questions. Not every candidate will have had the same opportunity to demonstrate agency in their careers, especially if they've been in unsupportive work environments—but they should be able to tell you what they would do in a hypothetical situation.

There are questions that can give you signal on how a candidate feels agency that don't require them to have had a leadership position. For example, a lot of people come to the manager to complain about something at the company. But what you want is someone who will come to you and say, "I saw this problem, and here's how I can make it better."

Foundry Group co-founder Jason Mendelson[603] screens for agency with the following question: "Can you share a moment from your career where you felt like you'd been slighted?" Everyone's got one.

Next, ask them what they did about it. Do they throw their boss under the bus, do they burn their peers or those below them? Do they go higher?

---

603. https://twitter.com/jasonmendelson?lang=en

> 🕮 STORY "I interviewed a salesperson who delivered a great answer to the agency question. He had a shared quota with a salesperson, and she went on maternity leave. So he went and asked the boss, 'Since she's on maternity leave, I'm not responsible for the whole quota, right?' And the boss said, 'No, you need to hit all of it.' And he's like, 'That's bullshit.' And so I asked him, 'What did you do?' And he said, 'I fucking hit the quota.'" —Andy Sparks, co-founder and CEO, Holloway

29.2.4 TABLE: AGENCY QUESTIONS

PROMPT	EVALUATION
"What got you interested in Acme Inc.?"	General alignment. This rarely totally weeds out a candidate, but sometimes raises red flags where the candidate is interested in totally different things than what the company is focused on. Superstar candidates will also have a chance here to distinguish themselves by the energy they answer with and will often have way more to offer here than average candidates.
"Imagine I was a new engineer joining your team at [their current/previous company], what are some key things you'd want me to know right away about the customers of that product and how it shapes the way it should be built?"	Curiosity, bias for understanding customer and product needs. Great engineers won't just leave it to the product team to figure this out; they'll actively be curious about what makes their customers tick and be able to communicate it to their team. Weaker candidates here will often just confuse you with a jumble of information about different market segments or platitude type statements. Star candidates help you right then and there to understand the key types of users of the product, what each one needs, and often one or two special details about their psychology that wouldn't be obvious.
"What's a recent fairly large project you worked on at your last company? Roughly when did the project start and finish? At the halfway point of that timeline, tell me a bit about how you were sizing the project up? What percent complete did you feel you were?"	Risk assessment and ability to tell if a project is really on track or not. Some candidates will only be able to tell you basic stuff here ("Well we finished half the stories in the SCRUM plan, so we must have half way, right?"). Strong candidates understand how to look back at their project plan, but they go much further. They could talk about things like: Is the customer scenario actual coming together? Are we able to show it to people and see it work for them? Are we running into new tech issues we couldn't foresee that we've proactively raised with affected parties like product? They might talk about how they front loaded the riskiest part, and they're able to qualitatively speak to how they're seeing it really behave now.

PROMPT	EVALUATION
Follow-up: "Towards the tail end of that project, what factors were you considering when thinking about whether it was time to ship?"	A standard answer would be something like "the stories are all implemented so we're done" or "all the tests passed." Stronger candidates certainly get those things, but they add in more nuance: Is the customer scenario or the key original objective really coming together? They thought about whether they should also add some other element, but realized they needed to just get it out there so they could get feedback. They had a solid plan for deployment and operations. They accounted for how future development experience would work for others (e.g. wiki is updated with how to pull the repo and setup dev boxes).

29.2.5 THE 5-MINUTE COMMUNICATION QUESTION

One of the most important signals to get from nontechnical interviews is how a candidate communicates. No matter what kind of role you're hiring for or at what level, communication is key. If an employee struggles to communicate an idea with their peers, boss, or junior engineers, they're going to be frustrated. They might blame everyone else for not understanding them, or even worse, be disappointed and begin to feel isolated. The vast majority of technical hires need to be able to collaborate and coordinate. To do that, not only do they have to be able to share ideas, thoughts, and challenges—they have to be able to do so quickly.

To assess a candidate's communication style, Kevin Morrill came up with a high-signal assignment:[604]

> *I want you to explain something to me. Pick any topic you want: a hobby you have, a book you've read, a project you worked on—anything. You'll have just five minutes to explain it. At the beginning of the five minutes you shouldn't assume anything about what I know, and at the end I should understand whatever is most important about this topic. During the five minutes, I might ask you some questions, and you can ask me questions. Take as much time as you want to think it through, and let me know when you want to start.*

There is a wide distribution of possible topics here. How to braid hair, how to install drip irrigation, the difference between precision and recall in search quality assessment, the basics of brewing beer, quantum

---

604. https://www.inc.com/thebuildnetwork/the-one-interview-question-you-should-ask.html

mechanics, the function of reduplication in John Milton's *Paradise Lost*, or training a dog to sit.

While what the candidate chooses to explain to you is definitely interesting, the signal you gather is from how they do it. First off, how much time did they take—if any—to come up with a topic and sketch out their five minutes before letting the interviewer know they were ready? Did they write themselves an outline? Did they set something up on their laptop or a whiteboard? Some of this is presentation style, but whatever they do (or don't do) before they start talking can tell you how much they value organization, planning, structure, and preparation. The bottom line: those who prepare always do better.

The candidate's delivery style can tell you about their empathy. Do they pause to check if you're keeping up, asking, "Does that make sense? Are you with me so far?" Are they trying hard to reach the audience where they are, by using analogies or posing questions? If you try to sidetrack them or throw them off a bit, do they say, "That's not what I meant" or "Perhaps I didn't explain that well," and try again? Of course, be careful not to play mind games. Some candidates won't feel comfortable pushing back on the interviewer.

Another thing to check for is whether the candidate sets themselves a timer. Some people don't need to because they did debate in high school or have a great internal clock, and others might not have heard the bit about a five-minute limit or choose to ignore it. If a candidate is neither of these, they should set themselves a clock.

🚩 CONTROVERSY   Some people who like to use this question are looking for whether the candidate sticks to the five-minute mark, docking them if they go over. Kevin Morrill, the author of this question, says the interviewer shouldn't stop them at five, so they can see how closely the candidate was listening or how much they overestimate their abilities to self-regulate. Others may be more forgiving of the time limit if a candidate seems excited by their subject or thinks the interviewer wants to hear more. A candidate is likely to expect the interviewer to cut them off when they're satisfied.

Candidates may stop before the five-minute mark; if they've communicated the most important things to you about their topic, they've done their job. The purpose of the five-minute communication question is to tell whether, if someone has a great idea about improving the product or speeding up a system, they can communicate it to you in less than five minutes.

Less strong candidates tend to:

- jump into a presentation without a plan for what they want to get across
- finish either way too fast (so that the interviewer didn't really learn much) or go way overtime (demonstrating a lack of planning)
- not ask questions to learn about the audience
- never check in to see if you're following an explanation
- make tons of assumptions about what you already know or understand.

Stronger candidates tend to:

- think a bit about what topic makes sense to tackle
- come up with an outline for what they want to cover
- ask you what you already know about the topic
- draw analogies to the things you already know
- check in with you: "Does this make sense to you?"
- use the whiteboard to express themselves
- get to something that's actually interesting about the topic
- give you back a summary of what was covered
- finish on time.

29.2.6 MANAGEMENT SKILLS

Whether someone will be a good manager or not is the subject of countless books, courses, and blog posts (and perhaps a future Holloway Guide!). In lieu of covering this in detail, we provide a few suggested questions to include for assessing management ability and suggest additional recommended reading.

29.2.7 TABLE: MANAGEMENT SKILLS QUESTIONS

PROMPT	EVALUATION
"Tell me about your management and leadership philosophy."	The basic answer here is something like "My job is to make the goals clear, and then get out of the way." Star candidates know not to be needlessly overbearing, but they have tons more to offer than that. "I work with my team to understand what talents they have and also what motivates them. When someone works on a project, I make sure I know their blind spots they don't understand, and I always have some mitigation to compensate (e.g. more frequent check-ins, training, get them a mentor, etc.) I make sure that my team gets feedback. I make sure the things that matter are in my team's control (e.g. great tools, monitoring/instrumentation so they can see what's going on)"
"Have you ever had to fire someone? What led up to it? What did you do when you realized things were off track?"	There are few "wrong" answers here, you're more looking for the depth of insight the person has accumulated here. Examples of what you might hope to get: Understanding where they could have given feedback sooner; Understanding where the employee wasn't getting a clear enough message on impact, and how they personally could have done better here; Understanding of how they'd improve hiring process; Understanding of how they'd improve their own feedback process; Understanding of how to go through a performance improvement process.
"In our initial conversation, we talked about the immediate needs of the team. Do you have any questions about that? Tell me how you would go after these challenges in the first 90 days?"	The answers to this question will depend heavily on the role—the degree of strategy and proactivity you're looking for will vary significantly if you're looking for a development manager or a VP of Engineering. But this person should demonstrate awareness of what is required of their level (or ask good clarifying questions to get there), and provide ideas and tactics accordingly.
"When a problem arises on the team, how do you decide at what point to step in and address it?"	Some candidates might not admit to any problems, or a tell a story about when their manager solved a problem for them and how they'd emulate that. Stronger candidates acknowledge that no team is without problems, and has an example of how they constructively resolved a conflict with respect and empathy.

29.3 *Further Reading on Nontechnical Interview Questions*

- First Rounds' 40 favorite interview questions[605]
- Workable's question bank[606]

- Devskiller's list of 45 behavioral questions[607]
- Big Interview's guide to behavioral interview questions[608]
- Hired's 30 behavioral interview questions[609]

30 Best Practices for Interviewers

30.1 *Staying Engaged*

⚠ CAUTION Interviewing is an active process that requires the interviewer to be completely engaged. This requires that interviewers not be on their phone or check email or Slack. If you take notes on a laptop, turning off notifications will prevent interruptions. Candidates can *tell* when the interviewer is distracted, and it makes their performance worse. Likewise, the interviewer's active engagement at all times will ensure they are collecting the clearest possible signal.

Being engaged with the candidate also ensures the interviewer feels like a human being to the candidate. An interviewer who sits silent and stone faced will intimidate the candidate, who will then underperform.

At the same time, effective interviewers will guard against giving the candidate unintended hints. This is a matter of some judgment, but it is likely that if a candidate is constantly pausing and looking at the interviewer, they're fishing. If it's clear they're focused on the problem at hand, small positive signs at points of breakthrough can reinforce progress.

---

605. https://firstround.com/review/40-favorite-interview-questions-from-some-of-the-sharpest-folks-we-know/
606. https://resources.workable.com/interview-questions/
607. https://devskiller.com/45-behavioral-questions-to-use-during-non-technical-interview-with-developers/
608. https://biginterview.com/blog/behavioral-interview-questions
609. https://hired.com/blog/candidates/30-behavioral-interview-questions-should-be-ready-to-answer/

30.2 Note-Taking During Interviews

It's essential for an interviewer to take some form of notes during an interview. These notes can be turned into a formal write-up, ideally as soon as possible after the interview itself. New interviewers should typically budget about the same length of time for their write-up as they spent on the interview, although with a great deal of practice and good in-interview note-taking, the time commitment will go down by half or more.

Good notes capture the questions that were asked and give a high-level description of what happened during the interview, including both candidate answers and any key moments in the discussion.

When interviews include coding questions, a complete report will capture the candidate's written code, to allow the hiring team to objectively evaluate the results and consistently calibrate the process. A complete and final write-up will include a high-level assessment of the code quality.

Some interviewers are able to capture more detailed quotes while the interview progresses. This makes reconstructing the interview and creating a good write-up easier and can be particularly useful for folks whose schedules preclude a full write-up immediately following the discussion. However, note that good interviewers will only take down this level of detail if they can simultaneously stay engaged with the candidate.

30.3 Keeping the Interview on Schedule

The first step to collecting signal is making sure the interview is moving along on schedule.

Timing in interviews is critical. If the candidate isn't moving quickly enough through the full range of questions, the interviewer may find it necessary to intervene. This may include asking the candidate to skip over less essential parts of the discussion so as to stay on time.

Interviewer boredom can be a clue that the interview is going off track in one of these ways:

- The candidate is stuck and needs a hint. One useful tactic is to set them at ease by explaining, "Even if you don't know the solution right away, I'd like to hear how you are thinking about the problem, so feel free to share your possible approaches as you work through it."

- The candidate is talking too much about something they have already made sufficiently clear. In this case, the interviewer may tell the candidate that since they definitely understand the topic, they can progress to the next question.
- The interview as a whole is off course and needs to be pivoted.

Near the end of the interview, you may have to choose between letting the candidate finish working through what they're on and leaving time for selling and any candidate follow-on questions. If the candidate's evaluation hinges on what they do in these last few minutes, it's best to give them that time; but you may still need to help them reach a good stopping point so that their mind doesn't stay in the question during subsequent interviews.

30.4 Seeking Clarity in Questions and Answers

> *"I'm not interviewing for the right answer to the questions I ask. Instead, I want to see how the candidate thinks on their feet and whether they can engage in collaborative problem solving with me. So I always frame interview questions as if we were solving a real-life problem, even if the rules are a little far-fetched."*
> — Eric Ries, author of *The Lean Startup*[610]

The best interview questions are short and clear. Short and clear questions ensure candidates answer the question you meant, not just those they've previously thought about and are primed to respond to.

Good interviewers use a balance of open and closed questions. Open (or "open-ended") questions, such as "How would you approach that challenge?", allow the candidate to determine the direction of the discussion and show how they handle ambiguity. Open questions do not have a yes, no, or otherwise simple answer. Closed questions have specific answers, such as "How many months did you spend on this project?" These questions are good for gathering basic facts or seeking clarification.

Interviewers may need to probe into ambiguous or obfuscated answers, which are often signs that the candidate either doesn't know the answer or is trying to hide something (perhaps avoiding an admission of

---

610. http://www.startuplessonslearned.com/2008/11/abcdefs-of-conducting-technical.html

fault, in a behavioral interview). Ambiguity requires specific or direct follow-up questions.

Sometimes a candidate may say something that just doesn't make sense given the context shared in the interview. For example, they may describe previous work experience in a way that sounds problematic to the interviewer, but the candidate doesn't acknowledge the problem. This sometimes happens because the candidate may not recognize that they've left out key context or details. This situation requires further questions, even leading ones,[611] to clarify whether the candidate behaved correctly but just failed to communicate clearly during the interview. Any time a possible exculpatory explanation exists, a good interviewer will pursue it to avoid later questions about whether their assessment was correct.

Eric Ries stresses, "No matter what question you're asking, make sure it has sufficient depth that you can ask a lot of follow-ups, but that it has a first iteration that's very simple." This gives you the opportunity to probe further into what the candidate may or may not know. Ries distinguishes between degrees of "not-knowingness" that give you additional signal:

- The candidate doesn't know, but can figure it out. Perhaps it's been some time and they can't recall all the details, but they have a strong intuition that leads them in the right direction.
- They don't know, but can deduce it given the key principles. If you fill the candidate in on the basic rules, can they reason from there? Would that change the way they approach the problem at hand?
- They don't understand the question. Ries notes that "Most questions require a surprising amount of context to answer. It doesn't do you any good to beat someone up by forcing them through terrain that's too far afield from their actual area of expertise." If it is their area of expertise, you know you've hit a point to consider in your evaluation. If it's not, it's best to move on—it's not fair or efficient to ask them to keep struggling through at that point.

---

611. https://www.thoughtco.com/leading-question-persuasion-1691103

30.5 Hinting and Helping Candidates Shine

A key part of extracting signal is making sure the candidate is able to put their best foot forward. An interviewer's job entails setting up the candidate to shine—but it's up to the candidate to actually shine. While the interviewer/interviewee relationship has an inherent adversarial component, if it's clear that the interviewer is trying to set the candidate up for success, it can de-stress the process. Strategies might include outlining the flow of the interview before it begins, making it clear what the interviewer is looking for, and clarifying how the candidate can best provide answers. Giving appropriate guidance and hints can help get the candidate unstuck.

Much like the process of scaling the question, good hints are metered out carefully, starting with more general hints and gradually getting more specific. An interviewer who solves the problem for the candidate definitely doesn't intend to hire them, so hints that answer for the candidate aren't appropriate unless it's clear they are not a fit. It's also important to time hints properly—not too early, before the candidate has time to think; and not too late, when the interview runs overtime. This timing will vary by question (some questions take longer to answer than others), but if a candidate is clearly stuck for more than a few minutes, it's usually time to get them unstuck. Also note that letting a candidate flounder for too long restricts what information you can gather as an interviewer. A candidate stuck for 45 minutes on a single aspect of a question might have performed brilliantly on the rest of the question, but for you to discover that, you'd have to give an appropriate hint so that they can move along.

Hints can take multiple forms:

- Nudging a candidate toward or away from a particular approach that they mentioned. This is especially important early in the question, so that the candidate doesn't work on a mis-scoped problem. In this scenario, you might say something like, "Don't worry about how this would work when stored on disk; you can focus on solving this in memory."
- Giving the candidate general hints toward a solution. You might say, for example, "You mentioned binary trees; you might want to explore that direction further." When they're running out of time, these kinds

of hints help a candidate get unstuck from a bad path that you believe they would eventually discard anyway.
- Giving the candidate general feedback on the solution. This might sound like the following: "I think you may have a bug" or "It seems like there are cases this solution doesn't handle." These hints give the candidate a chance to discover the gaps independently and also allow the interviewer to assess the candidate's ability to reason about their solution.
- Giving the candidate specific feedback or direction. You might say, "What happens if you pass the argument 8 to this function?" These kind of hints are certainly strong, and might indicate some concern that the candidate isn't able to track down the problem in question, but they give the interviewer a chance to validate that if a bug does turn up in a work setting, the candidate will be able to find it. These hints usually won't invalidate a coding interview because this mimics the way most people run their code to find issues in real-life situations.
- Telling the candidate exactly why something is wrong and asking them to address it. "If your solution were to handle multiple connections simultaneously, it would have race conditions. How could you fix this?" This kind of hint can either be part of making a question harder, like if the initial problem statement didn't include these constraints, or can be a sign that the candidate missed something critical to the problem. This kind of hint is a last attempt to see how the candidate handles the problem. Is their response, "Oh, of course, that was silly of me," followed by an immediate explanation of how to fix it, or do they seem confused by why that is an issue in the first place? If they follow up with the former, you're back on track.

For the sake of candidate experience, if at all possible, you'd like the candidate to get to a satisfying stopping point by the end of the interview. Being half-finished with a problem will carry over and negatively impact the rest of their day. Given that coding questions are particularly noisy, it's most helpful to make the signal you get from each one be as independent as possible. If the interview has gone south, and it's clear the candidate cannot recover, the next goal will be to lead them to that satisfying conclusion using whatever hints are needed, or even by explaining the problem directly.

30.6 Collecting Candidate Feedback

Not every company collects feedback on the interviewers and process from candidates who have gone through an interview loop. But doing so can be very helpful in determining pitfalls in your process, especially when it comes to the candidate experience. The key to collecting candidate feedback is to do so only if you have the intention of using it to improve your process. (See Diversity and Inclusion in Tech[§9] for more.)

You might send something like a "candidate experience survey" to each candidate directly after their interview process, regardless of whether they received or accepted an offer. A second alternative is to send surveys out in batches once a quarter or at some other interval.

The survey might ask a combination of qualitative and quantitative questions. Quantitative questions ask candidates to rank the experience or a subset of the experience on a scale of 1–10 or to rank how likely they would be to interview at the company again, on a 1–5 scale. Qualitative questions might include:

1. "How was your experience?"
2. "Would you recommend this experience to someone else?"
3. "Was there anything your recruiter or hiring manager could have done better?"
4. "Anything else, positive or negative, you'd like to share?"

If your company has a recruiting function, you may wish to ask some targeted recruiting questions.

◇ CAUTION It's critical to keep candidate feedback anonymous.

31 Evaluating Interviews

When interviewers know what to expect from interview questions—what makes an answer "poor," "fair," "good," or "excellent"—they are less likely to let noise and bias slip into their evaluations. Rubrics are systems that make it easier for interviewers to provide and discuss feedback on candidates, because everyone will be working from the same set of expectations.

A **rubric** is a set of guidance, usually written, for evaluating candidate's answers to interview questions. Included in this guidance may be examples of answers at different quality levels, or prompts to help the interviewer perform their assessment. Rubrics may also provide interviewers with a series of questions to use, typically of increasing difficulty.

In a structured interview, rubrics are essential to keep interviewers on track and ensure an effective and fair process. Even with a rubric, it can be tricky to specify *exactly* what a good or bad performance looks like—there's always variation in each individual and room for human judgment or interpretation. You might think of rubrics as a starting point to help foster fair and productive interviews and evaluations.

There are many ways to write technical and nontechnical rubrics, and every company has their own method.

31.1 Building Rubrics

Teams design rubrics differently. Rubrics can be perfunctory, with just a list of questions to ask and simple pass/fail boxes to check, or they can be detailed, including briefs on why each question is being asked, descriptions of what different levels of success are for each question, and/or what would be expected of different candidate levels for each question. The more detailed the rubric, the more fair and systematic the process—but the greater the challenge of designing and maintaining it.

Rubrics do not remove the need for flexibility in any given interview. They help you to score a candidate's progress through a question, and can even allow you to be more flexible by preparing you to pivot when something unexpected comes up.

> STORY "All good questions have variable depth. Like, there's a point halfway through the question where it's clear the person's not going to get through it. So you might have a 20-minute version of a 60-minute question. That can go the other way, 'This person is going through this so fast, let's make it harder.' It's like a rip cord, where 15 minutes in I know whether I can pivot to the shorter version or longer, or end it, or add the next layer of the onion. It's about preparing to offer extensible difficulty, variable difficulty." —Scott Woody, former Director of Engineering, Dropbox

> **🔊 STORY** "One way to increase the reach of a question bank is to structure the rubric to call out what answers you would expect at what candidate level. This can help minimize bias (everyone knows what 'senior' means for this), and, where it makes sense, reduces the need to have different question sets for different levels." —Ryn Daniels, Senior Software Engineer, HashiCorp

31.1.1 A SAMPLE TECHNICAL QUESTION RUBRIC

Question: Write a program that prints out the elements of a binary tree in order.

What we are looking for in this question:

- The candidate asks appropriate clarifying questions, such as what data type is stored in the tree and what the output format should be.
- The candidate is able to independently write the initial version of the program without significant interviewer intervention or coaching.
- There are either no bugs, or the candidate is able to find and fix all of their bugs in a proactive, independent fashion (that is, the interviewer does not have to point out that there is a bug or give them a test case).
- The candidate uses all language features in an appropriate way—it's OK if they make syntax errors or don't know the names of library functions.
- The candidate is able to describe the Big O notation performance of their program accurately, and they do not use unnecessary memory or do inefficient operations such as visiting a node multiple times.
- **An excellent performance:** Requires hitting all of the above bullets, and will typically result in a "solid yes" for the candidate.
- **A good performance:** Requires at least four of the five bullets—typically, someone can get a "good" rating as long as the issues are largely in making up-front assumptions rather than having significant bugs or logic errors. A good performance will typically result in a "weak yes" for the candidate. The simplicity of this question means that somewhat shaky performance can also result in a "weak no."
- **A fair performance:** The answer fails on multiple topics, such as having multiple bugs and also not being able to describe the Big O performance. A fair performance on a question this easy should result in a "solid no" for the candidate.

- **A poor performance:** The candidate cannot complete the problem, even with significant hinting.

◇ IMPORTANT   Note that in many technical questions, the rubric will get more technically specific about exactly what kinds of answers are or are not OK for each level. This question happens to be a simple one, so it doesn't demonstrate much detail.

31.1.2 EVALUATING CODING QUESTIONS

When writing rubrics for coding questions, keep in mind that there is a great deal more to assessment than whether or not the candidate solved the problem. Interviewers might want to evaluate the following, for example: Was the code well written? Did the candidate reason through the problem well? Did they do a good job of evaluating their own code's correctness? Were they able to answer follow-up questions?

However, some things are not appropriate to include in the evaluation of a coding interview.

◇ CAUTION   Interviewers should ignore anything that is an artificial result of the environment. If the candidate is writing whiteboard code, this includes the candidate's handwriting and whether the code was visually messy. Viewing variable naming and duplicated code leniently is also wise. If you have concerns, you can ask the candidate about the choices they made; it's likely they were just avoiding rewriting code or writing long names.

It's not appropriate to penalize a candidate harshly just because they have a bug! It's very hard to write correct code, especially in the context of an interview. You will most likely want to see a strong thought process and an ability to translate ideas to code and model the flow of execution of a program, but mistakes will inevitably happen. You can expect that candidates should find bugs when given hints or a test case, though. If someone simply cannot execute their own code objectively, or if they cannot find a bug even when it's been pointed out to them, that indicates a serious issue.

31.1.3 A SAMPLE NONTECHNICAL QUESTION RUBRIC

Question: Tell me about a conflict with a co-worker and how you resolved it.

What we are looking for in this question:

- Do they identify a real conflict?
- Can they explain the co-worker's perspective? (Bonus points if they had to do work to discover that perspective.)
- Can they explain what the root cause of the disagreement was and what the "right" answer to the conflict should be from a third party's perspective?
- Did they resolve the conflict in a constructive, low-drama way? (Alternative, bad options: avoiding facing up to the conflict; escalating prematurely; playing politics to get what they want.)
- Was the solution they reached actually a good solution to the problem from the perspective of a neutral observer?

When asking this question, if you do not hear some of the elements the rubric is looking for, you should ask follow-up questions to touch on those areas. For example, ask how their co-worker saw the situation if they don't explain it directly on their own.

- **An excellent performance:** This requires covering all of these points, or a demonstration that the candidates *could* have touched on them, without prompting, or with only light/moderate prompting (for example, a raised eyebrow, a questioning look, or a subtle follow-up question designed to nudge the candidate and see if the answer was top of mind).
- **A good performance:** Touches on all of the elements of the answers, but might have required heavy prompting in one area (for example, directly asking what the co-worker's opinion/viewpoint was, or having to dig deep yourself to understand the root cause).
- **A fair performance:** Similar to a "good" performance, but with more prompting needed and generally lower-quality answers, giving the interviewer lower confidence in the response (for example, if the candidate cannot give specifics or they remain vague even after prompting).

- **A poor performance:** The candidate plays politics, resolves the question in their favor without accounting for the wider interest, or simply can't give an example of having dealt with conflict.

◇ IMPORTANT People have varying definitions of what a "conflict" is, so you may consider adjusting the phrasing of this question if you feel you're not getting the right signal. Ryn Daniels recommends asking the candidate, "Tell me about a time you disagreed with a colleague on a decision" or "Tell me about a time when you changed your mind." Each of these questions can reveal the same things: how the candidate interacts with others, and whether and to what degree the candidate is self-reflective and flexible in the face of new knowledge.

> 💬 STORY On nontechnical interviews, the rubrics tend to be less directly referenced because they're likely to cover individual questions, of which there are many (whereas there tends to be one big technical question), so the write-ups might tend to anchor more on a meta-rubric of the general types of things you're looking for and highlight specific questions where the interviewer did poorly. —Alex Allain, Engineering Director, Dropbox

31.2 Collecting Interviewer Feedback

31.2.1 INTERVIEWER WRITE-UPS

Ideally, interviewers will record their feedback on the candidate as soon as possible. The fresher the interview is in the interviewer's mind, the more complete and objective it is likely to be. Additionally, since next steps rely on this information, waiting a while to record your feedback can slow down decision-making.

The write-up justifies the decision with concrete evidence based on the rubric, by identifying which parts of the rubric were or weren't met. A sample write-up based on the technical question above might look like this, for a performance evaluation of "fair":

The candidate struggled with this problem overall, earning no more than a "fair" on the rubric and a "no hire" on the interview. Mapping how they did to the rubric:

1. The candidate asked appropriate clarifying questions ("What kind of data is stored in the tree?", "Do you care about performance?"); they assumed the output would be printing to stdout—the interview was off to a good start.
2. The candidate struggled to write a correct version of the program; their initial attempt only printed the left and right branches of the tree one level deep.
3. The candidate struggled to identify their bugs when they walked through the program themself; for example, they failed to recognize that they didn't handle the empty tree correctly and had to be prompted to handle multiple levels deep. With significant, repeated hinting (including giving a concrete example case) the candidate eventually did fix their issues.
4. The candidate wrote reasonably idiomatic language.
5. The candidate couldn't properly describe the Big O of their solution (they claimed it was O(1) instead of O(n)).

⚠ DANGER It's important that no interviewer be exposed to other interviewers' feedback before they have submitted their own. Seeing other feedback can bias an interviewer, which can diminish the quality and fairness of decisions. This is especially true if someone more junior is exposed to the opinion or feedback of someone more senior. Check to see if your ATS (if you're using one) can help hide other interviewer's feedback as it gets submitted.[612]

The level of detail required in interview feedback can vary from company to company, depending on how that feedback will be used. For example, feedback used as notes to help an interviewer remember key points to

---

612. Lever is one ATS we are aware of that supports this.[613]
613. https://help.lever.co/hc/en-us/articles/204503195-How-can-I-hide-interview-feedback-

discuss during a debrief session may be less detailed than feedback that will be shared with and used by an independent hiring committee.

That said, the more comprehensive the feedback, the less room for relying on memory that might fade (even over the course of a few hours or days) or "gut" instinct (that may be prone to bias). And the hiring team may want to revisit that feedback further in the future—for example, when deciding whether to reconsider a candidate or to analyze the hiring decision. Providing a structured form for interviewers to provide feedback makes this easier. Many tools[§39] can help enforce timely and structured submission of feedback.

31.2.2 FURTHER READING ON INTERVIEW FEEDBACK

- "How to write great interview feedback"[614] (Josh Sassoon)

31.2.3 COMPONENTS OF GREAT FEEDBACK

> This section was written by Kevin Morrill.

Comprehensive feedback will do the following:

- **Paint a narrative.** An interviewer's feedback ideally will clearly convey what they talked about with the candidate. What questions did the interviewer ask, and how did the candidate answer them? Are there code snippets that can be included in the feedback? This helps the team draw conclusions from the collective set of interviews. One of the best ways to make a narrative clear is to quote the candidate, instead of jumping straight into your own interpretation.

- **Tie positive and negative aspects to core competencies.** Anything that went well or poorly in the interview will ultimately relate back to the competencies, skills, and traits you are interviewing for. At the very least, it's helpful for the interviewer to connect observations outside core competencies to a predicted situation on the job.

- **Make a predictive statement about on-the-job performance.** Why will a particular behavior the candidate demonstrated matter on the job?

---

614. https://medium.com/thumbtack-design/how-to-write-interview-feedback-28d49be8f975

- **Be written down.** All the data collection in the world is useless unless you write it down and have it available for the debrief session and hiring manager or committee.
- **Convey a clear decision.** Interviewers hopefully will walk away from the interview with a clear sense of whether the candidate is a fit. If they're not convinced, that's a default "no hire"—there is no such thing as a neutral opinion. The spectrum of "hires" extends from "strong no" to "strong yes." For a "strong yes," you will feel like you need to chase them to the parking lot and get them on board immediately, and you would be worried if they joined a competitor. Below that, but still not in the "no hire" range, you may feel like they will raise the average level of performance on the team. Some companies allow the interviewer to specify how confident they are of their rating.
- **Convey secondary signals.** For instance, maybe the candidate performed well in a technical interview, but was somewhat rude. It's useful to disentangle those two signals.
- **Identify gaps.** Comparing across interviewers' feedback, the team can also figure out where there are areas or open questions that need follow-up (either via another interview or through conversations with the hiring manager or recruiter).
- **Support an audit.** if you ever make a hiring mistake and have to fire someone, one of the first postmortem activities is to evaluate the interview loop and figure out what happened. If you have great notes, you can learn and improve the process.

31.2.4 WRITTEN FEEDBACK EXAMPLE

Here's an example of an interviewer's effective written feedback:

- Recommendation: HIRE
- Pros: High intelligence (keen awareness of concretes, able to employ abstractions), results oriented, good communication, aptitude for organizing code effectively.
- Cons: Questionable organization and time management skills.
- Details:
  Matt worked out to be a very impressive candidate. I am convinced he would do very well with the kinds of problems we solve and immediately drive value to our customers.

I started by talking with Matt about evolving our architecture to support data on locations coming from multiple sources and then making a verdict on what the actual location is based on all of that data (rather than our "first-in wins" model). He probed on the problem of when conflicts arise, doing the math to realize that even a 1% conflict rate is about 2,300 results to manually review. He assessed that this is too much human work and that an algorithmic approach is in order. I like that he carried through the math and actually thought about it at a concrete level. Weaker candidates just take the problem as given and plow forward assuming it must be a problem worth solving.

He talked about technology choice by saying "Do you want to stay Postgres?" I clarified that we're on MySQL and said he had the power to change technology but needed to have a good reason to do it. He talked through what that would mean and immediately gravitated to indexing needs as being key. For key/value-oriented storage, it would be harder to efficiently query on things like last_updated, as you'd only have one key to work with. At one point in his thought process he said aloud, "My intuition says..." and proceeded to explain his thinking. I took this as a very good sign, since Courtland brought up that he charged forward on a weak answer to interest rate impact, even though he probably didn't know what he was talking about. This kind of verbal queue says to me that when he's working in his comfort zone, he documents his assumptions and critically evaluates them.

At one point I foolishly said that he should probably just ignore the overwritten data; I didn't mean to trick him, but in retrospect this worked out to be a good example of challenging a manager when they're wrong. He made a good case for how you could use changes in the data from the same source to tell you the accuracy of a location. This was also another good example of him thinking intelligently on the fly. Love that he could take something abstract, like whether to save data, and pull it down to concrete about a specific startup's migration to make the decision.

We then talked through what the guts of his black-box "Rules Engine" would be. I've actually been thinking a fair amount about this, having coached Bryan Chang on his dev design. He proceeded to lay out a design while thinking on his feet; it was far better than my own thought process that benefited from far more time and knowledge about our challenges. Right out of the gate with no prompting/leading he said, "If statements would be stupid" you want "rules and authority rank." He came up with a system where we could pass around references-to-function that embodied the rules. Each function could return either a final answer or a weighted answer. I had never thought about using weighting, which is a pretty cool thought.

To close out, I asked him the five-minute communication question. He seemed to get right away what things he should be preparing for. He said aloud, "Let me make sure I can encapsulate key points." He asked if I knew anything about Shakespeare (for some reason many candidates that are worse communicators don't take the liberty to ask, and this shows in their work as they tend to be very black box and harder to work with). He wrote an outline before he started. He then proceeded to give an impassioned explanation of Shakespeare's use of verse. The big red flag is that he went over by at least 50% in time and didn't seem phased by this despite all his careful preparation. In some cases I've seen this be a predictor of poor organization that carries through into delayed projects on the job.

31.2.5 LEAKING CANDIDATE INFORMATION INTERNALLY

⚠ DANGER Be careful discussing candidates on a public forum like Slack. Even if the audience is limited, if one person makes the wrong comment, Slack discussions can easily spiral in unhelpful, inappropriate, or unfair directions. Without care, interactions like this could even become the basis for a lawsuit.

By contrast, a senior employee can create a clearly organized, in-person debrief that avoids these challenges. However, remote teams may treat Slack discussions as the equivalent of in-person debriefs. If this is the case, you can train interviewers on appropriate conduct in this forum, and managers can make sure they steer the conversation if it becomes unhelpful.

While the interview process includes the whole interviewing team—and good decisions here require transparency—there is no reason to reveal information about candidate performance beyond the decision-making audience. It is important to make sure candidates do not accidentally see their own interview feedback or discussions about them, if they do eventually join the team.

32 Legal Considerations for Interviewers

Some parts of the hiring process are dictated by law. Laws differ depending on the size of your company and the jurisdiction in which you operate. For example, California prohibits companies from asking candidates about their salary history,[615] but most states still allow such questions.[616] Giving legal advice is outside the scope of this work, but you can read more about the types of things you can and cannot do in an interview process below.

Many legal restrictions relate to questions that companies cannot ask candidates during the interview process. Generally speaking, companies are prohibited from asking candidates about the following topics, either directly or indirectly:

- age
- citizenship
- criminal convictions
- disability
- family and marital status
- gender and gender identity
- national origin
- medical history
- race and ethnicity
- religion
- salary and benefits history
- sexual orientation
- whether the candidate has ever filed a worker's compensation claim.

In addition, companies are prohibited from collecting and using genetic information in making employment decisions.[617]

⚠ DANGER Some interviewers might try to make conversation without realizing that what they're asking is illegal. Be wary of questions that do not explicitly refer to these issues but nonetheless drive at the same information. For example: When did you graduate from college? (age); How many

---

615. https://californiaemploymentlaw.foxrothschild.com/2017/12/articles/advice-counseling/questions-california-job-interviewers-need-to-avoid-in-2018/
616. https://www.washingtonpost.com/business/2019/08/15/more-states-are-banning-questions-about-salary-history-job-interviews-what-say-if-youre-asked-about-it-anyways/
617. https://www.genome.gov/about-genomics/policy-issues/Genetic-Discrimination

sick days did you take this year? (medical history); Do you live alone? (family and marital status); Where does your husband work? (family and marital status, gender and gender identity, sexual orientation). Even indirectly posed questions like these are discriminatory and illegal.

Companies are permitted to seek voluntary demographic data from applicants as long as a particular candidate's data is not shared with any employees who can affect whether that candidate receives an offer.[618] Moreover, many companies[619] are required to report annually the number of their employees by sex, race/ethnicity, and job category to the federal government.[621]

---

618. https://www.eeoc.gov/federal/upload/2017-approved-Applicant-Form.pdf
619. These requirements apply to all companies with over 100 employees, and certain other companies that have government contracts, as per EEOC regulations.[620]
620. https://www.eeoc.gov/employers/reporting.cfm
621. https://www.jdsupra.com/legalnews/eeoc-releases-instructions-for-39592/

PART VI: AFTER THE INTERVIEWS

33 Checking References

In hiring, **references** are a candidate's former colleagues or supervisors who can speak to the candidate's skills or past job performance. Candidates usually directly identify a set of references for the company to contact; but for referral candidates there also exists an implicit assumption that the individual who referred them will act as a reference.

If you are a hiring manager, you know that feeling of uncertainty: A candidate may seem incredibly promising, perhaps even passed a technical interview with flying colors. But no one on the team has worked with them before. What will they really be like to work with? What will make them successful? In what situations have they performed well or poorly in the past?

References allow the hiring team to collect the information needed to bolster confidence about the hiring decision. Checking references is an essential part of hiring well and wisely. Unfortunately, prospective employers often conduct reference checks informally, rather than as an established part of the hiring process. When rushed or performed poorly, reference checks can produce misleading or unfair results. But there is an effective way to give reference-checking the attention it deserves.

⚠ CAUTION It's not usually a good idea—or thoughtful—to ask for references until someone is fairly far into the hiring process.[622,623] Checking references when you're unlikely to hire someone is a waste of both the social capital of the candidate (who is asking a favor of the reference). and the time of everyone else involved.

---

622. https://twitter.com/alinelernerLLC/status/1170144889180323840
623. https://twitter.com/alinelernerLLC/status/1171168468458065920

⚠ DANGER Always obtain a candidate's prior consent before reaching out to anyone at their current employer. Most candidates are job hunt without their current employer's knowledge, and attempting to get a reference from a current employer could put the candidate in a very tough position or even get them fired.

33.0.1 THE PURPOSE OF REFERENCES

When making important hiring decisions, companies of all types look for the most telling and predictive signals possible, and that includes the opinions of people who know the candidate's work well. This signal is just as important for junior hires as it is for senior hires.

> 📖 STORY "Many people treat references as just a filter or a way to potentially screen out candidates they may otherwise have hired. But references can be both a positive or negative signal. I once had a candidate who did OK on his interviews—no red flags, but definitely would not have been hired solely based on interview performance. I happened to closely know one of his professors, so I reached out and received a really glowing reference. I trusted that reference more than the interview feedback, so we hired that candidate and he went on to do really well." —Ozzie Osman, lead author of this Guide; co-founder, Monarch Money

💬 CONTROVERSY Informal polls of people who have made many hires reveal that when properly considered, signals based on extensive past work experience are far more reliable than what can be obtained during a few hours or days of interview processes. But prevailing opinions about references differ wildly,[624,625] and the available research also isn't conclusive.[626,627] One aspect of references that nearly everyone agrees on is that they are another point in the interview process where bias and noise can influence the outcome. For hiring teams, it helps to be aware of the challenges and to aim to make reference checks as structured as possible.

---

624. https://www.ere.net/whats-wrong-with-reference-checks-part-1/
625. https://www.skillsurvey.com/debunking-reference-checking-myths/
626. http://maamodt.asp.radford.edu/Research%20-%2010/2006-Feb-References.pdf
627. https://psycnet.apa.org/record/2010-19935-005

Most commonly, references serve four purposes:

- To identify "red flags" serious enough to make the team decide not to move forward with a candidate. Mark Suster refers to this as seeking any "disconfirming evidence"[628] that the hiring team might have missed in the interview process.
- To identify the strongest or best-fitting candidate when the hiring team has multiple candidates who are otherwise equally qualified. (This is a lucky situation for the hiring manager!)
- To gather more information on how to make the candidate successful in their new position. Hiring managers often overlook this purpose of references, but the resulting ideas can be especially valuable to manager and new hire alike.
- To help in closing the candidate. This too is an oft-overlooked use of the reference call. Often, references will speak to candidates about how the call went, and a positive call can play in your favor: "I just got off the phone with Sonia—that role sounds really awesome!"

Candidate back references may provide the hiring team with confidence in a candidate early in the funnel. This is typically someone known to the team who strongly vouches for the candidate's skill or fit for the role. Although this is a less common use of references, in some situations, it can convert a candidate who looks like an unlikely fit on paper (such as a graduate student or a person coming from another industry) into a more promising one who is worth advancing further in the funnel.

◇ IMPORTANT As with any new meeting, it's wise to treat every reference call as a potentially long-term relationship. For hiring teams, this means respecting and building trust with references just as you would with candidates. References can become part of your network: If the reference has common interests or related skills, this is a chance to get to know them and give them more information about your company and what excites you.

CANDIDATE Respecting and building trust with references also applies to candidates; this helps maintain lasting relationships that are not transaction-based alone.

---

628. https://bothsidesofthetable.com/how-to-make-better-reference-calls-d493a12714f0

33.0.2 ASKING FOR REFERENCES

In *Who: The A Method for Hiring*,[629] the authors recommend that the hiring manager conduct four references and other team members conduct an additional three, for a total of seven. Two to four is more typical, however. Conducting only one will naturally provide a skewed perspective.

Almost any candidate who's not fresh out of school will be able to give two or three professional references. (Note that when recruiting from colleges and universities, candidate references may be professors rather than former colleagues or bosses.) If a candidate is hesitant about giving references, it may be a sign that either they are not really interested in the job, or they have had trouble building relationships they can now draw upon.

While it's tempting (and logistically easier) to ask candidates for references from previous managers, hiring teams will get a more complete picture by taking the time to talk to former colleagues. *Harvard Business Review* reported the results of a study[630] that found that former managers are more likely to focus on whether a former employee met deadlines, was proactive, and was organized and efficient, while former colleagues provided insights into whether candidates were helpful, collaborative, and listened well.

CANDIDATE Candidates applying for jobs feel the stress of reference checks as well. You've done great (you hope) on an interview, and the hiring manager calls and asks you for references. Does that indicate how far you are in the process? Who should you pick as a reference? What questions will the hiring manager ask the references, and what will they say about you?

- As a candidate, when you ask an old colleague or manager to be a reference, you're asking for a favor. Usually it is gladly given, but the best references are often busy people. If you're excited about a job and think you have a serious chance of getting it, tell the reference so that they know their investment of time will make a difference.
- On the other hand, occasionally companies will stall for time with a candidate they're not likely to hire by asking for references. Conversely, they may ask too early in the process, before they're certain the candidate is a serious contender. If you're afraid this is the case, it's

---

629. https://www.amazon.com/Who-Geoff-Smart/dp/0345504194
630. https://hbr.org/2017/08/references-should-come-from-a-candidates-coworkers-not-just-their-boss

reasonable to ask your hiring manager or recruiter to tell you how far along you are in the process so that you can give your references a realistic idea of when they might receive a call.
- If you're applying for many positions, it's also thoughtful to wait until you can narrow down the set of options so a reference doesn't have to have more than a couple calls.

33.1 Talking to References

Hiring teams usually conduct reference checks over the phone. A few larger companies have in-house recruiters send forms or emailed questions, but these are usually impersonal and may be less effective for the hiring team than one-on-one conversations. References have a hard time quantifying or evaluating others' skills using checkbox-style and similar form answers that can make it feel like an answer might (intentionally or unintentionally) hurt the candidate. A conversation between industry colleagues is more comfortable and can allow helpful nuances and details to emerge. Usually a candidate can make reference introductions to the hiring team, so setting up a call will likely be the easy part.

Although it's not universal practice, the best person to do reference checks is most likely the person making the hiring decision. It's even better if that person is also the candidate's future manager.

⚠ CAUTION At larger companies, references are often done by HR staff or recruiters, but they may not capture certain valuable information if they don't know the exact needs of the role. Because HR staff and recruiters often are juggling multiple pipelines, they may be more likely to forget details gleaned from the reference process by the candidate's first day on the job.

Good preparation for checking references includes taking a little time to research the reference's background; this provides information to help put anything they say into context. Make sure you understand what their relationship to the candidate is or was. Plan what you want to discuss. What areas of the candidate's experience can this reference speak to? About what are they credible?

The hiring team doesn't need a fully prepared, rigid script, but will benefit from having a clear agenda and approach in mind, rather than calling off the cuff. Assuming the best of the reference will produce the most forthright conversation. Most people prefer to be honest, yet it's helpful to expect that many references won't want to speak ill of the candidate or hurt their chances of getting a job.

33.1.1 DURING THE CALL

General guidelines to follow are to say hello, explain who you are, confirm they're ready to talk, and thank the person for their time. Be friendly to set them at ease. Confirm how long they are available to talk—a hurried or interrupted reference call will be unproductive.

A reference call might look like this:

- **Establishing trust.** (3-5 minutes) Ask if they'd like a very short background on you and your company and why you're talking to the candidate. Be brief. Imagine you're in their shoes. What would you want to know? Give them enough information on yourself that they can get a sense of who they are talking to. (Are you a founder? Manager? Technical? Business? What domain have you worked in during your career?) To build trust and rapport, discuss any other common interests or areas of overlap.
- **Establishing mutual purpose.** (2-3 minutes) Remind them that the goal of the call is to measure fit between the candidate and the role, based on the experience the reference has had working with the candidate in the past. Ask if that sounds good, and pause and listen for anything they might want to tell you up front.
- **Asking questions.** (20+ minutes) Ask questions that you've planned, but follow up on things the reference says that may lead to useful insights.

◇ CAUTION Throughout the discussion, be careful to listen exactly to *what* the reference says, and not confuse it with *how* they say it. You don't know the reference, so it can be easy to be thrown off by communication style.

◇ IMPORTANT Take notes. You'll want them later.

33.2 Designing Reference Questions

First-time hiring managers usually know or are told that they need to check references and may eagerly solicit or set up the calls. But at some point the reality of the challenge becomes apparent: How exactly do you get helpful and reliable guidance about one person you don't know, from someone you know even less? And even more challenging, how do you do it in a short window of time, like a 30-minute call? Surely any reference who is a friend of the candidate will just say positive things anyway—how do you know if you can trust this person's judgment? Worse, you may have heard that legal considerations make most references largely perfunctory and a waste of time,[631] so why spend the time in the first place?

When preparing your questions for a reference call, it's often best to sequence from basic, factual questions to more high-level and subjective questions. This way, you can let the reference ease into the discussion with answers to simple questions, that are closed—that is, have one possible answer. In other words, ask about job title and technology stack before you ask about communication skills.

- Start by asking a little about the reference themselves, how well they know the candidate, and how long they worked together and in what context.
- What was the role of the candidate at the time the two worked together? Did one report to the other? Were they on the same team? How did the team fit into the larger organization?
- Did the candidate's role, responsibilities, or title change over the course of their working together?

---

631. https://www.linkedin.com/pulse/reference-checks-legal-lawyer-talks-fact-vs-fiction-turkewitz/

Then the questions can be a little more advanced:

- Ask anything you need to know about the product the candidate focused on, or the nature of the work, such as the tech stack (if you didn't ask that at the outset) or the key challenges of the team at the time.
- What was the candidate known for being good at on the team?

Ask EQ[632]-related questions, covering at least the following:

- Communication skills and style, including any specific needs or aspects that would be good for a future manager to know.
- What others on the team thought of the candidate.

Ask about fit:

- Any kinds of work the reference thinks the candidate is a great fit for.
- Any kinds of work the reference thinks the candidate is a less than ideal fit for.
- Any other things they can add or suggest to make the candidate successful.

For all these questions, be specific, but open-ended. Listen carefully, take notes, and follow up on details.

33.2.1 REFERENCE QUESTION PITFALLS

⚠ DANGER Some key pitfalls include:

- Phrasing questions in a way that encourages the reference to take a bluntly negative position, or makes them feel they're being critical of the candidate. This will cause most references to shut down.
- Asking for overly precise or numeric rankings of skills. This is a good way to get a subjective, inflated answer. Instead, focus on comparisons with the team the candidate worked with, or on clear but qualitative characteristics.
- Asking vague questions where answers will give little signal.
- Asking closed questions or feeding answers to the reference. Give them space to suggest or provide detail.

---

632. https://en.wikipedia.org/wiki/Emotional_intelligence

- Being biased by your own opinion of the candidate, good or bad. Confirmation bias means hearing only what confirms what you already think. Listen attentively. Ask neutral questions that elicit real answers. Ask for clarification wherever you're unsure what the reference meant.
- Rushing the call. Be mindful of time, but without enough depth and context, you'll get no useful information.

33.2.2 INEFFECTIVE REFERENCE QUESTIONS

- *"What can you tell me about Anne's work?"*
  This question is way too general and will result in equally general answers. Only specific questions that yield specific answers will be helpful in the hiring process.
- *"So what was it like working with Anne?"*
  Again, this is too general a question.
- *"How would you rate Anne's ability in algorithms on a scale of 1 to 10?"*
  Very few references provided by a candidate will give a low number on a quantitative rating. In addition, no matter how precisely you phrase the question, one person's 7 is another person's 9. Without knowing the reference really well, the answer is almost always useless.
- *"Does Anne know Python and JavaScript?"*
  This is a low-signal question because "know" is far too vague—it can mean anything from an expert to someone who studied languages in college. The best way to learn the answer to this is to test for it.
- *"We notice she was really strong at Python and database management. Did you notice that too?"*
  This gives the reference little room except to agree or disagree, and feeds them your own bias toward the candidate's skills.
- *"What would you say are Anne's greatest weaknesses?"*
  This rarely elicits candid information; most people are not willing to answer that question about a colleague to a stranger.

33.2.3 EFFECTIVE REFERENCE QUESTIONS

- *"Can you tell me how long you were at Zenith and what your role was there?"*
  The answers can provide essential understanding of what the reference knows about the work environment they shared with the candidate.

- "Can you explain Anne's role at the time you worked together? How closely and for how long did you work together?"

    Follow-up: "How big was the team? And how did the team fit into the overall organization?"

    The answers signal how accurate the reference's take on the candidate will be.

- "What was one of the more valuable pieces of work Anne did while on your team? Can you give me an example?"

    Follow-up: Ask for details and have them walk you through Anne's notable accomplishment.

- "Anne worked for three years on your team at Zenith Labs. How did her role evolve during that time?"

    If the candidate grew in responsibility, this is a positive sign you'll want to know more about.

    Follow-up: If the answer is no, it's worth noting and asking if the reference can say why. This could be related to the candidate, but could also have been due to organizational or structural factors.

- "Can you talk a little about her communication skills? How did they compare to others on the team?"

    It's much easier to discuss how someone compares with others on the team than to assign numeric rankings or make judgements of "good" or "poor" skills. From there, you can start to dig deeper into specific skills and projects that person worked on.

- "One skill that's very important to us is database administration. Anne tells us she has experience in that. Can you tell me about her work in that area?"

    Follow-up: "Who else did database administration on your team? How did their work compare?"

- "You and Anne rebuilt the entire Widget Deconstruction mechanism over a period of about a year, correct? What parts of that did each of you do, and why?"

- "You say her team was eight engineers. Usually there are specific people on a team who are highly respected or known as the go-to person for certain problems or questions. Were there any areas where Anne was that go-to person who was most experienced or most skilled?"

    Follow-up: "Can you give examples?"

    Follow-up: "How did her skill in Python compare to the others on the team?"

- "Would you say Anne is most suited to a highly technical individual contributor role? Or do you think she would be ready for and enjoy filling a tech lead position on a small team?"

  Particularly if you know the reference is close with the candidate, questions that focus on how the candidate can be helped to succeed and what makes them happy may encourage candidness
- "We noticed during interviews that Anne is unusually quiet and at times hesitated to convey her ideas. We weren't sure if this was her style day-to-day, or just interview nervousness. Can you say anything about how she communicates with a team? How about one-and-one?"
- "What sort of team and working style would be ideal for Anne to be successful and excited about her work?"

  Follow-up: "Are there any types of work or teams you think would be a less than ideal fit?"
- "If you were hiring, are there roles for which you would hire Anne again? What kinds of roles?"

  The kinds of roles the reference recommends can reveal a lot about Anne's strengths and preferences.

33.3 Soliciting Back-Channel References

In addition to talking with the references a candidate has listed, hiring teams may also solicit **back-channel references (or back references)**—that is, people the candidate has worked with but not listed as references. Hiring teams often source back-channel references without the candidate's knowledge by checking the candidate's LinkedIn connections or consulting with others who may know them.

Some consider back-channel references to be more reliable than candidate-sourced references, as a back-channel reference will likely have some association with the hiring team and so be more inclined toward greater fairness and honesty. Hiring teams use back-channel references far more commonly for senior hires. And in some industries and geographic areas (like Silicon Valley), the social graph among senior candidates, executives, investors, and former colleagues is dense enough that hiring teams almost certainly will use them.

The best approach for soliciting back-channel references is usually different from what is used for candidate-supplied references. In the case of the back-channel reference, usually the person on the team who best knows the reference will reach out, in any format that feels suitable. A short email might say something like:

Subject: Feedback on Anne Jackson?

Charlie, we've been making a few hires here at Acme Megatronomatics and we're considering Anne as a candidate for Senior Forward Deployed Widget Architect. We've enjoyed getting to know her and are considering making her an offer.

Is there anything you can share about her suitability for this role? Would you have time for a call? I'm free today after 3 p.m. and tomorrow after 2 p.m. If that's not possible, anything you can share by email is also helpful.

Thank you in advance!

Best, Barbara

◇ CAUTION When soliciting back-channel references, it's important to be mindful of a candidate's privacy and trust. . This can entail informing candidates ahead of conducting back-channel references so that they are not surprised when they hear you've been asking about them and so you don't put their current employment at risk. Advance notification might look like this: "In addition to the references you gave us, we may contact other people we know who may know you. Is there anyone that you wouldn't want to be aware that we're considering working together?" You can also mention the person you're talking to by name ("I'm catching up with Charlie this week—do you mind if I ask her about your time working together?"), but in that case, you need to be mindful of the *reference's* privacy, since she may not want you to tell the candidate you two talked.

33.4 *Interpreting Reference Feedback*

When interpreting reference feedback, consider where the person is coming from. If the reference trusts you, they are more likely to give you candid feedback. If they are closer to the candidate, they may not want to risk any negative feedback being attributed to them, or they may feel the relationship colors their ability to provide objective feedback.

In general, references will be more positive than negative. Some recommend mentally compensating[633] by discounting positive comments by 30% and amplifying negative comments by 30%. While this is an arbitrary number, it does highlight the importance of perspective. You can take outrageously positive or negative comments with a grain or two of salt.

Next, think about the context in which the candidate and reference knew each other. How closely did the reference and the candidate work together? How equipped is the reference to judge the candidate's work? For instance, "I've managed over a dozen engineers and Anne is the strongest I've had on my team by far," is a lot more compelling than, "Anne has been great to work with, but that was my first job out of school and I've only been here a few months."

You also may consider whether the reference's criteria for assessment is consistent with your own. For instance, traits that lead a candidate to success (or hold them back) at a large company may differ significantly from traits that lead to success at a much smaller company.

◇ IMPORTANT The limited nature of reference checking makes it more subject to possible noise and bias than interviews. You may have spoken to the reference on a bad day. People grow and change—would you give *yourself* a glowing reference for every job you've held, and would those references all be reflective of the type of work you can do now?

Find out how veteran recruiter Jose Guardado learned the hard way about the power of a (slightly) negative reference comment in "How Reference Checks Can Go Wrong: Managing subjectivity in reference feedback,"[634] up on the Holloway blog.

As with any part of the hiring process, references aren't a perfect source of information. Ultimately, a negative reference for a candidate should definitely give you pause, but if you believe in the candidate based on other data points, it doesn't need to completely disqualify them. You can always follow up with the candidate to see if you can figure out if anything has changed since the time they knew the reference.

---

633. https://www.linkedin.com/pulse/20131002155905-456201-3-essential-steps-to-doing-a-thorough-reference-check/

634. https://www.holloway.com/s/trh-jose-guardado-reference-checking

34 Making a Decision

Anyone who's run interview processes for enough candidates will be able to recall instances in which a smart manager made a bad call. Whether it's hiring or passing, there's no way to know whether this decision is the right one for the long run, but somehow a decision has to be made. It's worth recognizing that no matter how careful and structured your hiring process is, it can never involve 100% certainty, because it is a human process and we are neither mind-readers nor oracles. But the more thoughtful you are about how decisions are made and what factors to consider, the more confident you can be.

📄 **CANDIDATE** Knowing how a company you're interviewing with makes hiring decisions will help you have a sense of your timeline with that company, and make the (often stressful) process less opaque. For instance, Google tends to take longer to extend an offer, since offers require both hiring committee and senior leader approval. When interviewing with a company, you can ask your recruiter or interviewer how that company makes hiring decisions and why.

How a company makes hiring decisions is usually related to the company's decision-making philosophy in general. Netflix has a culture that values trust, freedom, and "diffuse accountability,"[635] and thus allows teams (and managers) to make their own hiring decisions. Google, on the other hand, believes that well-designed committees can make better decisions than giving a manager unilateral power. This philosophy usually extends beyond hiring to promotions and even technical and product decisions. Because hiring philosophy and strategy may be aligned with how a company or team runs day-to-day, it's often a good idea (and fair) to share with the candidate how this decision will be made—it helps set them up for success and gives them important insight into the company.

34.1 Decision-Making Archetypes

> "Before you make an offer to someone, think about whether you'd like to have 10 times as many people like them in your company."
> — Patrick Collison, co-founder and CEO, Stripe[636]

---

635. https://jobs.netflix.com/culture

Part VI: After the Interviews

No two companies make hiring decisions in exactly the same way. Nor should they. Companies tend to design their decision-making processes in a way that reflects both their goals and their philosophy on recruiting.

At many smaller startups, the decision-making process tends to be relatively informal. As a company grows and management layers start to form, there is a risk that hiring quality can deteriorate. Hiring managers, faced with an urgency to build out their team, may be less selective about who they extend an offer to, racking up diversity debt in the process. Hiring managers may also be less aware of the company's culture or do not participate in it fully, which can lead to cultural dilution. This is why understanding how hiring decisions are related to company philosophies and are part of maintaining company values is essential—the risks for losing those things over time is great. At the same time, as a company grows, strategies have to change. It wouldn't make sense for a company of 100 to involve every employee in a hiring decision, even if that was the practice when the company was 8 people.

We've put together a list of (somewhat fictitious) company archetypes to help illustrate how different goals, philosophies, and company values can impact how hiring decisions are made.

34.1.1 CONSENSUSCO (SMALL COMPANY)

ConsensusCo is a startup that believes in decision-making by consensus. Tyranny is the enemy—everyone should be involved and have a say. ConsensusCo might have a culture that is conflict-averse and prone to groupthink, leading them to "default to no" when hiring. Or it might have a culture that values healthy debate and disagreement a little too much. Any interviewer or team member can veto the candidate. Overall, ConsensusCo tends to be slow and conservative when hiring, and might hire engineers who are similar in personality and skill set to its current team. But, when someone is hired, the team is fully invested in the newcomer's success.

CANDIDATE Candidates who interview with ConsensusCo should expect to meet a large part or the entirety of the team.

---

636. https://twitter.com/patrickc/status/1068236758616174592

34.1.2 AGILECO (SMALL COMPANY)

At AgileCo, everyone might get a say, but the hiring manager (often the founder) makes the ultimate decision about who gets hired. In some extreme circumstances, AgileCo might not tell its employees what position a candidate is interviewing for or allow interviewers to share their feedback with each other (especially if the candidate is a potential executive). In theory, AgileCo holds a "hire slow, fire fast" mentality. In practice, this means many people in the company privately will talk about hires who weren't right or weren't qualified. That said, the team understands that speed is important and that some risks might need to be taken, and most of the time believes management is taking reasonable risks.

34.1.3 COMMITTEECO (MEDIUM TO LARGE COMPANY)

CommitteeCo believes that "false positives," or bad hires, should be avoided at all costs. CommitteeCo is highly scientific about its hiring practices and has collected significant academic research and in-house people analytics that show that interviewers and hiring managers are often prone to cognitive biases and poor decision-making. At CommitteeCo, a candidate's application must go through a highly calibrated, impartial hiring committee and multiple senior reviews before an offer can be extended. This slows down the hiring process, but CommitteeCo believes it can quantitatively prove that this process is superior. Since CommitteeCo is hiring for company fit over team fit, it views software engineers in a somewhat commoditized fashion and expects to be able to easily move them between teams and managers. In fact, many new engineers at CommitteeCo don't find out their actual team assignment until after joining.

CommitteeCo is a highly desirable employer and uses its selective employment process as a marketing point. That said, hiring managers there are secretly frustrated, and in fact, the more senior they get, the more likely hiring managers are to try to subvert parts of the process. Candidates interviewing at CommitteeCo are also frustrated, but often a lot less secretly.

34.1.4 ACCOUNTABILITYCO (LARGE COMPANY)

AccountabilityCo values individual responsibility, trust, and decentralized decision-making. Hiring managers are empowered to make their own decisions and can make them quickly. This results in more flexibility, and a team at AccountabilityCo can hire a candidate with some rough edges if they are a good fit for the team. AccountabilityCo is liberal about firing. An engineer that ends up not being a fit can expect to quickly be out of a job (perhaps with a severance package). A manager that makes poor hiring decisions can expect the same.

AccountabilityCo is very critical about introducing any steps that might undermine managers' autonomy. With this increase in decision-making freedom comes a cost—hiring managers "own" a lot of the recruiting process and, in addition to making a final decision, have to dedicate large chunks of time to everything from crafting roles to sourcing candidates.

34.1.5 PRAGMATICCO (LARGE COMPANY)

Often, AgileCo's grow up to be PragmaticCo's. PragmaticCo straddles the spectrum between AccountabilityCo and CommitteeCo. PragmaticCo is generally anti-process, but understands that *some* process can be good. The company believes that it must have some amount of checks and balances and oversight on hiring decisions, but finds pragmatic ways of doing so (for instance, requiring a senior executive to review any hiring decision).

The process at PragmaticCo might be very fluid and evolve as the company faces different growing pains. For instance, as the company expands, it might realize that it's no longer working well to have a senior exec review hiring decisions, as the gap between executive responsibilities and the day-to-day needs of teams grows. They experiment with other methods, like having a "bar raiser" on every interview loop.

34.1.6 FIGURE: EXAMPLE DECISION-MAKING ARCHETYPES

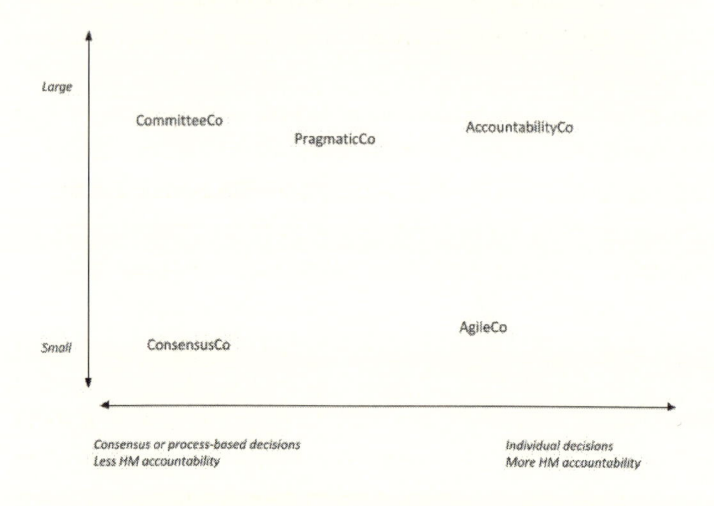

A scatter plot with vertical axis ranging from "Small" to "Large" and horizontal axis from "Consensus or process-based decisions / Less HM accountability" to "Individual decisions / More HM accountability". Plotted points: CommitteeCo (upper left), PragmaticCo (upper middle), AccountabilityCo (upper right), ConsensusCo (lower left), AgileCo (lower right).

Source: Holloway

34.2 Decision-Making Techniques

While any of the above archetypes can be highly successful, each has pitfalls, and the way a company makes hiring decisions can impact the candidate experience and the type of people that get hired. The techniques employed to make hiring decisions are often driven by an underlying philosophy about who should be empowered to make decisions and how those decision-makers should be held accountable.

As you're building your process, you might use these techniques:

34.2.1 DEBRIEF SESSIONS

In a recruiting **debrief session (or huddle)**, interviewers, recruiters, and the hiring manager meet to discuss all the feedback from a candidate's interview process and discuss the candidate's performance. In advance of the session, the hiring manager should circulate interviewers' written feedback for the entire group to review. The discussion in the debrief session itself is led by a moderator, often the hiring manager.

As this Guide uses the terms, debrief sessions differ from postmortem meetings in that debrief sessions are about assessing candidates' performance while postmortem meetings are about assessing the recruiting and hiring process for a role.

At many companies, the moderator is the hiring manager, but not always. For example, at some companies, an impartial moderator is assigned to avoid any authority bias[637] that might affect more junior interviewers (Dropbox used this technique in the past). Others start with the most junior team members to try to avoid biasing them with the opinions of more senior members.

In a debrief, every interviewer should have an answer to the question: "Should we hire this person?"[638] Healthy debate should be encouraged to avoid groupthink[639] (to see examples of this in action, you can read about the Asch conformity tests[640]). By the end of the meeting, it should be clear whether to reject the candidate, move them forward, or if additional information might be required.

A good debrief session can serve multiple purposes:

- **Assemble and combine feedback.** By collecting and discussing all the feedback, the hiring manager can create a clearer view of how the candidate performed. It's good to probe for "patterns in the noise." For instance, maybe multiple interviewers detected a (positive or negative) personality trait in the candidate, but didn't detect it with enough confidence to weigh it heavily. Or maybe the candidate was rude or condescending to interviewers (or recruiters) of a particular gender, age, or perceived status. There might be an area that wasn't thoroughly tested and requires further information.
- **Discuss uncertainties and disagreements.** A healthy debate can help surface where perceptions differ and help elicit how interviewers really feel about a candidate. The goal is not to come to universal agreement, but to be welcoming of opinions and explicit about uncertainties and about where people disagree, and why.

---

637. https://en.wikipedia.org/wiki/Authority_bias
638. https://www.fastcompany.com/3064073/this-crucial-step-is-missing-from-your-hiring-process
639. https://en.wikipedia.org/wiki/Groupthink
640. https://en.wikipedia.org/wiki/Asch_conformity_experiments

- **Calibrate and learn.** Group discussions can help interviewers learn from each other and better calibrate how they interview and evaluate candidates. It's often a good practice to tell everyone that a secondary goal of every debrief session is to help each other improve at *future* interviewing and hiring decisions.
- **Build teamwork on decisions.** The verbal discussion can help every interviewer feel heard and bought into the final decision. It helps reinforce the fact that recruiting is a team effort. If the previous three goals are handled well, it can make the whole team more confident that hiring decisions are being made well and with the right inputs.

34.2.2 SENIOR LEVEL (OR EXECUTIVE) REVIEWS

At many large companies, before a hiring manager can extend an offer, a more senior leader of the company must review a candidate's feedback packet and sign off on the offer. The assumption is that senior leaders will have a broader view of what the organization needs, be better-calibrated, and be more impartial toward the immediate hiring pressures the team is facing. At some companies, the senior review might just be the hiring manager's own manager. At other companies, it might be someone higher up the chain of command or even from another team. For instance, Google co-founder Larry Page signed off on all offers[641] until this became impractical.

34.2.3 HIRING COMMITTEES

In technical recruiting and hiring, a **hiring committee** is a group of employees who did not participate in a candidate's interview loop and are tasked with deciding whether to extend an offer based on the interviewer's feedback and the candidate profile.[642] The members of a hiring committee are often from a range of job levels, which can make the decision process feel less hierarchical than requiring senior approval and may produce better decisions.

> **CONFUSION** Hiring committees don't fit this description in all industries. In academia, for instance, the members of the hiring committee conduct interviews but may not have final say on extending offers.

---

641. https://www.quora.com/What-does-it-mean-when-Larry-Page-signs-off-on-every-hire-Does-he-really-learn-about-every-new-hire
642. https://www.quora.com/What-happens-during-a-Google-hiring-committee-meeting

Google, a strong proponent of hiring committees,[643] points to research[644] suggesting that a diverse group of employees reviewing offers might result in better, less-biased decision-making.

⚑ CONTROVERSY The effectiveness of hiring committees isn't without controversy, so it's good to understand the trade-offs.[645]

There are different types of hiring committees. The ones employed by Google are composed of impartial "peers and managers" from different teams. At Facebook or Dropbox, the hiring committee might be composed of directors or other senior leaders.

Since hiring committees, by design, introduce decision-makers who don't interact directly with the candidate, there are a couple of prerequisites to making them successful. First, interviewers should be well-calibrated[§26.2] and must write very clear and consistent feedback[§31.2] (this is good practice, regardless of whether you're using hiring committees). Second, hiring committee members should have enough context on the role to enable them to make the proper assessments. Given all this, even companies that use hiring committees in general sometimes break out of that model for roles that are highly specialized.

⚑ CONTROVERSY It's rumored that Google once had a hiring committee review anonymized versions of their own interview packets, and the committee rejected themselves.[646]

34.2.4 BAR RAISERS

There can be lighter-touch approaches to introduce a decision-maker from outside the immediate team into the mix. For instance, at Amazon, every interview loop must contain a special interviewer known as a "bar raiser." Bar raisers are interviewers who hail from outside the team with the immediate hiring need—to ensure that they are as objective as possible. They receive special interview training and calibration so that they are more effective at assessing things like values alignment. They also hold veto power over hiring any candidate and may often moderate the

---

643. https://rework.withgoogle.com/guides/hiring-hire-by-committe/steps/introduction/
644. https://journals.aom.org/doi/10.5465/255866
645. https://www.quora.com/ls-it-better-for-interviewers-to-make-hiring-decisions-or-for-a-hiring-committee-to-make-a-decision-by-reading-written-feedback
646. https://twitter.com/skamille/status/984203945034895362?lang=en

interview debrief.[647] Coinbase also uses[648] the bar-raiser method. Microsoft uses a similar system, known as the "As Appropriate"[649] interview. As Appropriate interviewers are senior leaders who conduct a candidate's final interview and work with the hiring manager to make a final decision.

> "Considering how little we have centralized, we use the bar-raiser group as a type of glue across organizations. We select bar raisers from the pool of experienced folk at Amazon, not just those who can interview well, but more importantly—those who deeply understand our leadership principles. As bar raisers, we then try to hire people who can understand and act on our principles."
>
> — David Anderson, General Manager, Amazon[650]

34.3 Choosing a Decision-Making Strategy

No matter the strategy your company employs, it should align with your hiring goals and your company values. To that end, the following questions will be helpful to discuss among your team:

34.3.1 CONSENSUS OR ACCOUNTABILITY?

It's worth considering the trade-offs between the different methods of decision-making.[651] These should be consistent with your company's culture, and some cultures are inherently more consensus-driven than others.

Requiring consensus will probably mean more selective hiring, since doubt from any interviewer can mean rejecting the candidate. This may be even more important for candidates for a leadership role. On the other hand, allowing some discretion for the hiring manager might be useful in certain cases. After all, the entire process is noisy and a judgment call

---

647. https://firstround.com/review/Mechanize-Your-Hiring-Process-to-Make-Better-Decisions/
648. https://blog.coinbase.com/bar-raisers-at-coinbase-if-youre-not-a-hell-yes-you-re-a-no-68145c6fbe60
649. https://www.quora.com/What-is-the-Microsoft-hiring-process-like-and-what-really-happens-behind-the-scenes-after-an-interview
650. https://www.linkedin.com/pulse/how-interview-amazon-leadership-david-anderson/
651. https://kengcrawford.files.wordpress.com/2012/04/crucial-conversations-ch9-move-to-action.pdf

might be needed. Or, in some cases, the hiring manager may want to augment the team with skills or traits that the current team is undervaluing. Assessing candidate-company fit or candidate-team fit requires an objective sense of the team's strengths and weaknesses—it's hard for teams to reflect on what they lack.[652]

Most of the decision-making techniques described above prevent managers from making unilateral hiring decisions. But when managers can't freely choose who will join their team, they may feel it is because the company doesn't trust them to make their own hiring decisions, and feel less empowered on all fronts. As we mentioned earlier, Netflix's culture of "diffused accountability" allows managers (and teams) to make hiring decisions independent from the rest of the company and without a lot of structured process. The company strives to have managers who feel like they "own the hiring decision every step of the way."[653] Imposing any friction or external decision-making could undermine their sense of accountability.

⚠ CAUTION However, managers can be reluctant to take ideas from the team for the wrong reasons, often because they are tasked by *their* managers to focus on short-term outcomes.[654] In hiring, this can be particularly problematic when individual decision-makers or hiring managers override disagreement among the team related to interpersonal or values-related concerns—for example, underrepresented interviewers being ignored by hiring managers when they raise concerns about a candidate's attitude or views. If anyone on the team is worried that bringing someone on will affect their safety or ability to thrive at the company, the decision-maker needs to listen.

It's important that the team agrees on who is responsible for making a decision and understands the hiring structures in place. Even if the hiring manager (or committee) is right about the candidate's skills and potential, the candidate will still have to rely on the rest of the team to succeed, especially in the critical first few months.

---

652. http://www.startuplessonslearned.com/2008/12/assessing-fit-wit-wisdom-of-crowds.html
653. https://business.linkedin.com/talent-solutions/blog/hiring-managers/2017/how-netflix-recruiter-and-hiring-manager-relationship
654. https://psnews.com.au/2019/04/22/outputting-input-why-managers-ignore-their-employees-ideas/

34.3.2 HIRING FOR TEAM OR COMPANY?

One way to think about this is whether you prefer hiring for each team or hiring for the company overall. If every team can make local decisions, it can be hard to ensure consistency in hiring, especially at larger companies. This can impact a company's ability to move engineers internally and even allow cultural silos to form. Many companies with team-based decision-making also are also quick to let employees go if they are no longer a fit for the team they were hired for.

On the other hand, using techniques like hiring committees, which introduce decision-makers who won't work closely with the candidate or team, will result in decisions that weigh the candidate's fit for the company as a whole.

34.3.3 HOW IMPORTANT IS SPEED?

One of the core principles[§7] is to keep the recruiting process as fast as possible, while balancing speed with the principles of effectiveness and fairness. Efficiency is extremely important for the candidate experience, especially when a candidate is anxiously waiting on the final offer decision and may also be hearing back from other competitors.

But speed must be balanced with the principles of effectiveness and fairness. Having one person responsible for a decision will certainly be fast—but with only one person's perspective, will it be fair? Is there enough confidence in that person's decision that the candidate will thrive at the company and be in it for the long term?

A more structured process designed to emphasize effectiveness and fairness will usually lead to longer decision times. Companies with multiple layers of approval, typically large companies, are notorious for taking a significant amount of time to make a final decision. In Facebook's early days, the company tried to work against this trend by having hiring committees meet on a daily basis for fifteen minutes to ensure faster turnaround times. There is always a tension and a balance to be found between these principles, and the more experience a company has in hiring, the more likely they are to figure out strategies that can meet that balance.

34.4 Decision-Making Tips and Pitfalls

Now you're set up to navigate the final decision about whether to make a candidate an offer. You have developed a philosophy and strategy around hiring, decided what you're looking for ahead of time, designed and administered structured interviews, and agreed on who should be making the final decision. And sometimes, the decision can be straightforward. But often, things are not so clear cut—after all, you're working with limited (and noisy) information.

Here are some tips for making the final call:

- **Stick to your hiring criteria as best you can.** Did the candidate actually demonstrate the skills required for the role? How did they perform against a calibrated rubric? Take into account all the positions you had on strategic issues, such as how strong of a fit[§5.4] you need for this role. Putting all of that together, is this someone who will be successful once hired?
- **Look for patterns as you put all the feedback together.** Sometimes, a behavior that might seem minor in one interview could be a red (or green) flag if it shows up as a common theme. For instance, did the candidate exhibit a bit of arrogance across all interviews? A single interviewer may have interpreted this quality as confidence, but if it shows up several times, it might be something else. It's worth noting that interview debriefs can help surface these patterns more readily, but absent them, the decision-maker (hiring manager or hiring committee) will need to look deeply at the feedback and possibly follow up with interviewers. Reference checks[§33] are also a good way to surface or dig into potential patterns.
- ⚠ DANGER **Be conscious of what pressures you are subjected to and how they might bias you.** Your personal disposition (risk tolerance) and your situation (hiring urgency) may push you to commit different types of hiring errors. The decision-making techniques we discussed above can help mitigate these errors, but it's still worth being aware of how these pressures might manifest themselves:
  - If you are a hiring manager with an urgent need to fill a role, you might be prone to overlook a candidate's weaknesses out of desperation.
  - If you are risk averse, you might find excuses to reject any candidate just to play it safe.

- If you are hiring based on consensus, you might hire for lack of weakness over presence of strength.

◇ IMPORTANT If you find that you're frequently struggling to decide on candidates, that could be a sign that your interview process is not well designed. Make sure you have defined[§16] what you're looking for concretely and communicated that to (or designed it with) the team. Ensure that your interviews actually test for those things, and that you have calibrated rubrics[§31] to help you evaluate candidates. Be aware of the cognitive biases[§10.1] that can impact people's judgements, and check that comprehensive feedback is being independently gathered, written, and relayed to decision-makers.

This whole process leads to a weighty decision that will have a significant role in the course of someone's life. It can feel overwhelming to anyone. One way to lower the stress of this high-stakes decision is to realize that everyone wants the same thing—to find the right fit. While the candidate may be really excited about your company, they might be excited about a *company they have in their head* and not the *actual company you work for* with the day-to-day challenges and requirements of its engineers. If the job requirements are beyond their skills, that day-to-day experience will be awful for them as well as the company. Coming to an objective conclusion about a candidate is to everyone's advantage.

34.5 Rejections

If the decision is to reject a candidate, the right thing to do is to deliver that decision with grace, respect, and speed. At this point, candidates have probably invested a large amount of time and effort in your recruiting process. Whether they receive an offer or rejection may have emotional and material repercussions, impacting their self-esteem as well as their career.

◇ CAUTION How you handle this interaction will also affect your future recruiting prospects. Bitter candidates may not apply again, even if the right role comes along in the future. They may also speak poorly of your company to their friends and colleagues, or on forums like Glassdoor, Blind, or Reddit, thereby deterring other potential candidates and affecting your brand. You might feel like you'd rather spend time on active candidates rather than rejected ones, but consider this an investment in your company's brand and in upholding your company's values—as well as your personal reputation. Indeed, as is so often true, doing the right thing is good for business.

- **Deliver the decision promptly.** The longer you wait, the more pent up emotions the candidate might develop. If your decision-making process might take some time, you should set expectations for the candidate about when they should expect to hear back from you. If you're still deliberating, reach out and give the candidate an update. If you have already decided but are stalling because you are dreading letting the candidate down, realize that the longer you wait the worse it will feel for both you and the candidate. If the candidate is reaching out to ask you for an update about your decision, you probably haven't managed this properly.
- **Be considerate.** Dismissing a candidate by firing off a generic email, quick text, or voicemail might feel quick and painless to you but will make a candidate feel disrespected. More direct communication is better. A personal email is better than a generic note, but a call is often best, if feasible. Getting on a call to break the news shows courtesy, even if the conversation might feel uncomfortable for you. On Twitter, Jennifer Kim offers some great advice[655] about what language to use. (Of course, if it's taking a lot of back and forth and several days to schedule a call with a candidate just to deliver a rejection, this is inefficient and even unfair for both sides.)
- **Hold yourself accountable.** By making a decision reasonably quickly and delivering it in a considerate, direct way, you are respecting your position by owning the relationship and the decision with the candidate. You're making an important decision in someone's life, and neglecting a rejected candidate—or, worse, ghosting them[656]—means you're not doing your job.

---

655. https://twitter.com/jenistyping/status/1107742365198905344
656. https://www.thebalancecareers.com/ghosting-job-candidates-can-destroy-your-reputation-4173212

◇ IMPORTANT If you're doing this well, candidates walk away from your process wishing they could still work with you, even after being rejected. A tangible sign of this is if candidates who you have rejected later refer other candidates to your company.

34.5.1 SHOULD YOU GIVE FEEDBACK TO REJECTED CANDIDATES?

🗨 CONTROVERSY Many companies don't give rejected candidates any specific feedback, citing legal risk, lack of time, and angry candidates[657] as the primary reasons. This can be frustrating for candidates, who, upon asking for more specific feedback, are told that the company has a policy against doing so. But many managers who try offering feedback learn that candidates often react negatively when given concrete reasons for rejection, and eventually move[658] to a "no feedback" policy.

While there are costs and risks associated with giving feedback, it can be helpful and can generate goodwill with candidates. If you'd like to give feedback to candidates, make sure you understand how to avoid the legal risks.[§32] Only offer feedback if you can phrase it in a way that's both specific and constructive. TripleByte offers more advice[659] on when and how to offer feedback. There may still be a subset of candidates that react negatively. But, if you believe in the value of feedback, don't let a few negative instances trick you into generating bureaucratic scar tissue[660] (that is, superficial reactions to one or a small set of negative events).

As a final note for the hiring manager: in addition to candidate goodwill, having a norm of providing feedback to candidates can, as a side effect, force you to be more rigorous about your decision-making. If you find yourself constantly resistant to giving feedback to candidates, it might be a sign of a broader failure in your process. Ask yourself:

- Is your decision-making structured enough? Do you have a clear method of assessing and evaluating candidates that will allow you to objectively determine when and why they aren't a fit?

---

657. https://www.quora.com/When-Google-or-Facebook-rejects-a-candidate-why-don%E2%8 0%99t-they-give-him-her-a-simple-explanation-for-the-rejection-to-help-the-candidate-wo rk-on-the-gaps-in-their-knowledge/answer/Gayle-Laakmann-McDowell
658. https://www.quora.com/Why-are-hiring-managers-and-recruiters-so-reluctant-to-give-feedb ack-to-unsuccessful-candidates/answer/Xavier-Amatriain
659. https://triplebyte.com/blog/rejection-feedback
660. https://m.signalvnoise.com/dont-scar-on-the-first-cut/

- Are you failing to build enough trust with candidates earlier in the process? A relationship of trust with candidates should make it easier for you to offer (and for them to accept) constructive feedback.
- Are you rejecting out of default, laziness, or busyness without having reasons you can articulate and communicate?
- Are you rejecting candidates for reasons that could have been easily determined earlier in your recruiting process? Often, you might hesitate to give a candidate feedback if they are missing an obvious requirement for the job, and informing them of that reason would expose that you just wasted your and their time by not realizing that sooner.

35 Extending an Offer

Many hiring managers and recruiters aim to have their offer acceptance rate be 70% or higher. You have hopefully built up enough trust and rapport with a candidate by now that you have some idea of what their answer will be—but how you go about extending the offer can be the difference between a *yes!* and a *no, thanks*.

35.1 Timing Your Offer Delivery

> This section was written by Jose Guardado.

Once the candidate clears evaluation, and you've identified the title, level, and compensation for your offer, you are ready to deliver it. But is the candidate ready to cut off all other interviews and accept your offer? It's important to know your candidate's timing preferences and constraints, specifically around competing offers. Coming in too early can hurt your chances, and coming in too late may preclude your ability to even compete.

◇ IMPORTANT Timing alone doesn't usually win offers, but it can definitely lose them. A well-timed offer gives your company a chance to compete. It won't guarantee success, but it can eliminate a guaranteed failure. Companies spend a lot of time and focus on the evaluation and assessment of talent, and once a candidate is determined to be a good fit, they rush to extend an offer. But they may or may not understand their candidate's schedule or their own odds of success.

Jeff Markowitz, partner at Greylock, uses this method:[661] ask the candidate on a scale of 1 to 10, 10 being an absolute "yes," how ready they are to accept the offer. If the answer is anything but 10, you know you have more work to do, and this is your opportunity to address concerns directly. Many managers won't extend an offer if they do not have certainty it will be accepted.

An alternative to this timing technique that many hiring managers and recruiters use is the "quick offer": making a decision and extending an offer to the candidate really quickly after the interviewing process (typically within 1–2 days, but sometimes even on the same day as the final interview). This can communicate confidence and capitalize on momentum, but if the candidate isn't ready to accept right away, that excitement can wane.

A middle ground is to quickly let the candidate know that you are *preparing* to extend an offer, and that way keep the momentum going, but tell them you want to work with them to better understand their state of mind and propensity to accept so you can extend the right offer.

35.2 *Offer Deadlines*

🚩 CONTROVERSY When you extend an offer, should it have a deadline or an expiration date? There are differing schools of thought on using timing as a forcing function. Some believe a strict deadline creates urgency and improves the odds of acceptance. And, generally, the longer the elapsed time since an offer has been extended, the less likely it is to be accepted; time can kill excitement.

An **exploding offer** is an offer that expires if not accepted within a tight timeframe. Anecdotally, an offer is considered exploding if it allows the candidate less than a week to respond,[662] but the timeframe may be as

---

661. https://techcrunch.com/2015/02/06/how-to-make-an-executive-offer-and-succeed/
662. https://angel.co/blog/how-to-deal-with-exploding-offers

short as one or two days,[663] or the offer may even require an immediate response.[664]

⚠ CAUTION   Deadlines can sometimes work, but arbitrary deadlines like those in exploding offers can be counterproductive.[666] They might force a candidate into a premature decision (premature rejections or acceptances are both bad). The pressure of deadlines can make the candidate feel anxious, or give them the impression that the company is behaving unfairly,[667] and other companies you are competing with might use this to undermine you. Avoid aggressive deadlines and unnecessary pressure around timing.

That said, you might need an answer within a certain timeframe. For instance, you may have limited headcount and need to know whether you should keep trying to hire (or extend other offers), or you may need to fill a role by a certain start date. If you have these types of practical necessities, using deadlines can make sense—you should explain these reasons to your candidate so that the deadline doesn't feel arbitrary. It's completely fine to say something like: "We think you're a perfect fit for us, but we do have to fill this position and we do have other candidates in the pipeline, so we'd love an answer by next Monday. In the meantime, I'm happy to make myself and my team available to answer any questions to help you with your decision."

⚠ CAUTION   Some candidates might try to take advantage of open-ended offers by stringing you along, consuming you and your team's bandwidth even if they aren't serious about joining your company. They could be indecisive, they could be shopping around for offers, or they could be just using your offer as leverage against another company's offer. If you've been running your process properly, have a good understanding of the candidate's situation, and are timing your offer delivery well, there's not much more you can do to persuade them to make a decision. Candidates who aren't serious shouldn't receive an offer yet—or maybe at all.

---

663. https://news.ycombinator.com/item?id=8286586
664. Zorc, Sasa, and Ilia Tsetlin. "Deadlines, Offer Timing, and the Search for Alternatives."[665] *Operations Research*, p. 4.
665. https://papers.ssrn.com/sol3/papers.cfm?abstract_id=2739675
666. https://pdfs.semanticscholar.org/f493/64e6b7575743008ed40e7add7afe82e3a36a.pdf
667. https://www.crawfordthomas.com/2016/04/01/exploding-offer-hurts-recruiting/

There are a few other approaches we've seen work successfully to create a sense of urgency *without* arbitrary pressure. The first is to use a candidate-determined deadline. Ask the candidate how much time they think they need to reach a decision, and, if it's reasonable, use that as the deadline. Another is to have a deadline, but agree mutually on when the deadline starts. For instance, tell your candidate that offers are a very precious thing for your company, and so they come with a one-week deadline, but let them choose when the clock starts ticking.

An additional technique is to offer an incentive (such as a sign-on bonus) to candidates who accept an offer within a certain timeframe. Remember to make sure incentives are structured, however—if you're delivering sign-on bonuses arbitrarily or only to those candidates who appear to be fielding other offers, or whom you see as more competitive, a lot of bias can creep in.

35.3 *How to Extend an Offer*

After all the effort both your team and the candidate have put into the process, letting a candidate know they are formally getting an offer is a fun and celebratory occasion—second only to having the candidate accept that offer, then join and thrive at your company! We recommend you deliver the news in person if possible, or over the phone if necessary.

A common question, at this point, is who should deliver the offer, which can be unclear, especially if a hiring manager and recruiter have been partnering together on the process. Ideally, the hiring manager delivers the good news in person or over the phone. After all, they will be the one the candidate is likely working with and will be best equipped to build the candidate's excitement about joining the team.

Here are a few things to do when delivering the offer:

- **Clearly state that you're extending an offer.** A lot of times, you might start by saying things like "the team really enjoyed meeting you" and "thank you for sitting down with us." But keep in mind that common niceties like these are the same things you say to begin letting a candidate down politely. Don't bury the lede[668] or be anticlimactic!

---

668. https://en.wiktionary.org/wiki/bury_the_lede

Keep it simple and straightforward: "We're thrilled to offer you a position of Software Engineer at Acme Technologies."
- **Convey your excitement about the prospect of them joining.** If you need to pump yourself up, remind yourself of all the effort you've both put in so far, and think about how fulfilling it will be for you and how impactful it will be for your company if the candidate joins and succeeds. (If you're having trouble doing this, it could be a sign you didn't make the right decision, but it could also be coming from nerves that the candidate will say no.)
- **Give them specific, positive feedback from the process.** You want the candidate to feel uniquely appreciated. Make it personal. You want them to think "these people really get me," and not "these people designed a recruiting process that happened to spit out a decision to hire me."
- **Build on the excitement.** Translate your own excitement into the concrete reasons why you'll be thrilled to see them in the position. Tell them about real challenges the team has been facing, why they are the person who can help meet them, and what they'd get to work on as soon as they join.
- **Ask them how they are feeling.** Even if a candidate is clearly expressing some amount of happiness, dig deeper to try and get a sense of how close they are to accepting the offer and what questions they might still have. You can remind them of considerations they brought up earlier in the process and offer information that can help them or access to your team to answer further questions. For example, you could say something like, "I know when we talked earlier you had some questions about our product roadmap, so our Product Manager would love to hop on a call with you later this week to talk through that in more detail."
- **Be aware of other decision-makers.** For many couples, decisions are made together, or by a whole family. Changes in employment and livelihood can bring up strong emotions that cut to the heart of a family's security and stability.

If you are a startup trying to close a candidate, you must understand how the family is evaluating risk and whether the spouse may be taking a lead role in determining that risk. Without being pushy or obnoxious, you can offer to help talk to the spouse. This can be particularly helpful and appropriate if the family has questions about complex things like equity, logistics and costs of moving from one city to another, and work-life balance at the company.

- **Check in on competing offers.** Do they have other offers yet? Do they expect to receive other offers, and if so, when? It's wise to get a sense whether getting more offers is essential to them, or are they willing to make a decision primarily based on this offer.
- **Provide a confidant for the candidate.** If you haven't already, make sure there is someone the candidate can talk to privately. There might be issues that a candidate is uncomfortable discussing with their future potential manager or teammates. These can include potential cultural conflicts, reporting structure issues, confidential information around health benefits, or even compensation. Often, the recruiter plays the role of confidant, though it could be a member of HR or a manager of a different team.
- **Go the extra mile.** There are a few other ways you can add some extra care when you extend an offer. For instance, at some companies, the entire team will be on the call to break the news and show excitement (though after breaking the news, usually the team will step out so the hiring manager can have a more intimate discussion with the candidate). Other techniques include sending the candidate a gift basket with company swag.
- **Answer compensation questions.** Explain to the candidate that you'll be following up with a written offer letter, which will detail the candidate's compensation and benefits package. If you know the candidate's expectations, and feel like your offer will meet them, you could walk through compensation now.
- **Follow up.** You want to stay top-of-mind, and be aware of any changes in the candidate's status or thinking (for instance, new offers they get, or evolving decision-making criteria). After extending the offer, maintain regular contact. You don't want to be pushy, but strong lulls in communication are your enemy here. Try to aim for a touchpoint every 2–3 days. It might seem like a lot, but you don't want to be caught surprised by the news of them signing another offer. Simple emails or short calls will do to stay top-of-mind.

◇ CAUTION For a lot of companies, as soon as the offer is formalized, they may feel a shift in power dynamics. While throughout the process it may have felt to them like they held more cards than the candidate, once an offer has been extended, suddenly the candidate has more power. If you feel this strongly at this stage, the way you run your process needs work. It could be that you aren't doing a good job getting the candidate excited about joining earlier in the process, that you aren't invested in the realities of the technical hiring market, or that you have not focused on the candidate's perspective throughout the process. If you've made the entire process a two-sided evaluation, there's little in the way of a "power inversion," even if technically you are waiting on the candidate's decision.

35.3.1 OFFER LETTERS

An **offer letter** is a formal, written document inviting a candidate to join a company and outlining key details about the terms of that employment. A typical offer letter includes the candidate's job title; who they will be reporting to (name and/or position); compensation information (base salary, equity, bonus if offered, et cetera); a summary of their benefits; the start date; and how long the offer is valid for. A company may wait to send an offer letter until the company and the candidate are already close to agreeing on the offer's terms.

It's standard practice to send a formal offer letter via email. It's a good idea to use a template for this, and some recruiting tools can help automatically generate these letters. It's also a good idea to make sure that all offer letters are reviewed by a few pairs of eyes before they go out—this isn't the time for a typo (especially on compensation or title).

Also check with your legal counsel to confirm you're presenting all the necessary details properly (an offer letter is not a legal contract[669] but it should be consistent with the ultimate employment contract). In general an offer letter should include the following:

- A greeting
- Description and title
- Reporting information, including full-time or part-time status
- Start date
- Compensation (salary and stock/equity details, if applicable)
- Any conditions such as background checks
- Benefits and eligibility, including:
    - Insurance coverage

---

669. https://www.lawtrades.com/blog-post/offer-letter-vs-employment-contract/

- 401(k) plan
- Paid time off
- Flexible spending accounts
- Educational assistance
- Flexible work hours
- Work from home options

- An acceptance deadline, if applicable
- Acknowledgement of offer and confirmation of acceptance

Most ATS tools support creating and sending offer letters, and here are some templates or other resources that can help generate them:

- Paperwell[670]
- Clerky[671]
- Carta[672]
- Avodocs[673]
- Indeed[674]

35.4 Explaining Equity

Earlier we explained how providing equity compensation[§18] can be a great way to incentivize and reward potential and existing employees, especially for startups. But understanding the value and purpose of equity can be really difficult and often intimidating to candidates and the managers tasked with explaining equity to them. It's worth dedicating special attention to equity when communicating an offer.

Make sure the candidate is sold on the *future* of your business. If you're an early-stage startup, it is not possible to know how much a share of the company will be worth or how long it will take for ownership to become valuable. The candidate needs to believe in the future of the company for an equity package to be enticing; hopefully, they believe the company will be more likely to succeed when they join the team. And hopefully, you have been working on this throughout the process, but if the candidate

---

670. https://github.com/Paperwell/Startup-Employee-Offer-Letter
671. https://www.clerky.com/hiring
672. https://carta.com/blog/a-better-offer-letter/
673. https://business.axdraft.com/en/business
674. https://www.indeed.com/hire/c/info/job-offer-letter-format

still has concerns at this stage, you, your team, or even your investors can help make sure they believe in your company.

Next, help them understand the basics of equity compensation. You can refer to the Holloway Guide to Equity Compensation[675] as needed.

Work through what the equity you are offering could be worth in different scenarios. One technique we've found that works well is to have a spreadsheet that you can use with candidates to play these scenarios. How is the value of their equity determined now? How many shares are they getting, and how many shares are outstanding? What is the vesting schedule and, in the case of stock options, what is the exercise price and window? How much might all the equity be worth if the company ends up going public or getting acquired at different valuations? This can help them understand, concretely, what the equity you are offering could be worth.

Equity calculators like Front[676] and Salary or Equity[677] can be used to help walk a candidate through the equity portion of their offer.

35.5 Negotiation

Once you've made an offer, you should be prepared with a strategy for negotiations and an understanding of how much—if anything—you are willing to negotiate.

35.5.1 SHOULD COMPANIES NEGOTIATE?

⚠ DANGER You want to avoid *zero-sum negotiating* with a candidate, where each party feels they need to "win" a negotiation. How much you pay someone or what role and title they have should closely reflect their likely value to the company rather than their willingness and ability to negotiate. These types of negotiations, especially if they vary depending on candidate behavior, create a risk of pay inequity and unfairness for everyone. Research shows[678] that the pay gap that disadvantages women and underrepresented people is due in part to how negotiations are handled, the

---

675. https://www.holloway.com/g/equity-compensation
676. https://comp.data.frontapp.com/
677. https://salaryorequity.com/
678. https://sloanreview.mit.edu/article/getting-the-short-end-of-the-stick-racial-bias-in-salary-negotiations/

behaviors expected of underrepresented candidates in negotiations, and the pressures they often face throughout the hiring process.

◇ CAUTION Your intention when negotiating might be to try and make things work for the candidate because you value them. But negotiations can send implicit signals that can lead to distrust. By negotiating, are you implying that you don't actually know how to value the candidate? Or that you do, but are trying to underpay them? Both of those signals can be dangerous in the relationship between a future employee and the company.

🗨 CONTROVERSY Liz Davidson argues[679] that refusing to negotiate salaries is one of the best ways to close the pay gap. If your company has decided not to negotiate salaries, make that clear to the candidate early. Some companies, like Reddit[680] and Clover,[681] have tried a clear "no salary negotiation" rule—this can be a relief for some candidates who would otherwise be stressed about finding the balance between negotiating too hard or not hard enough. But you have to really commit to it. A no-negotiation policy can also be discriminatory if you're not careful. If you tell candidates that you don't negotiate, but then allow for exceptions with candidates who are outspoken enough to negotiate anyway, the end result could also be that you end up paying unfairly.[682]

Some companies allow some room for candidates to negotiate, but will increase the compensation of candidates who don't negotiate to the same level as those who do after offer acceptance.

---

679. https://www.forbes.com/sites/financialfinesse/2018/04/11/a-powerful-way-to-close-the-pay-gap-dont-negotiate-salaries/#37e08a9d2209
680. https://www.businessinsider.com/reddit-doesnt-negotiate-salaries-ellen-pao-2015-6
681. https://twitter.com/polotek/status/1178121398763474944
682. https://twitter.com/MeganSpeir/status/1178113864237322240

35.5.2 HOW SHOULD COMPANIES NEGOTIATE?

A common refrain among companies is that they have to allow negotiations because negotiating offers is so pervasive in the industry. Some of these companies even lower the offers they extend by some margin to account for that negotiation (this is sometimes known as "low-balling"). We don't think "everyone's doing it" is a good argument when it comes to practices that can lead to unfair outcomes. Instead, consider the following:

- As a company, do your research, survey the market, and really understand the market for compensation. Have an opinion on what's fair, and a way to map roles to compensation,[§18.3] and make sure that your hiring process is mapping people to the right roles and the right levels.[§17]
- Be as transparent as you can with candidates about your compensation philosophy. A good rule is: are there any pieces of information this candidate might discover in the future that would cause them to feel unfairly treated, bitter, or resentful? The industry is trending toward more transparency around pay,[683] and the cost of paying all of your employees fairly is miniscule compared to the trust you can lose if you don't.
- Be thoughtful about when and how you first discuss compensation,[§18.6] and make sure you understand the candidate's needs and preferences.
- Use equity as a lever when possible, especially for startups. Explain the value of equity[§35.4] clearly. As discussed in our section on compensation,[§18] you might allow candidates to trade between equity and cash, depending on their needs.
- It's normal to have practical needs around income and compensation, but mostly, people just want to be compensated fairly. You and a candidate working together to find creative ways of making things work will feel very different than an adversarial negotiation.

⚠ CAUTION Although you want nonconfrontational negotiations, also be wary of judging candidates for negotiating hard. Judgements like "They're being too aggressive," are often themselves applied with bias.

---

683. https://business.linkedin.com/talent-solutions/blog/trends-and-research/2019/why-these-3-companies-are-sharing-how-much-their-employees-make

Studies have shown this influences the gender and Black-white pay gaps.[684,685]

If you've done all of the above, and you have a concern about how a candidate conducts themselves in a negotiation, it's best to get feedback from others present in the room. Does this indicate something about their personality, their values, or their priorities that you missed earlier, or are they simply being reasonable but firm negotiators? Ultimately, even if you are fair, transparent, and disciplined about your compensation, you will still find situations where there is a gap between what you offer and what the candidate is willing to accept (or what another company is offering them). Try to understand whether there is a problem with your compensation framework, whether a competing offer is off the mark, or whether you're looking at a candidate with a unique situation. If it's the latter, be aware of the cost of bending the rules for exceptional cases.[§18.5] Is this candidate truly exceptional and worth bending the rules for, or are you simply bending them because they are a good negotiator? Are there other creative ways you can find that can fulfill the candidate's needs, without jeopardizing the integrity of your compensation structure?

If you're caught in a situation with a candidate who has (what you believe to be) a disproportionately high competing offer, be careful about how you proceed. These battles are tough to win. If you attempt to match the competing offer and end up winning the candidate, you might end up doing more damage to the fairness and integrity of your incentive system—is this employee now being paid a lot more than his colleagues at the same level? You may want to ask why they think the competing company feels like they need to compensate candidates so disproportionately, but be careful about undermining their other offer. Don't be petty. (Perhaps the candidate believes your offer to be disproportionately low.) If the candidate is considering a high competing offer, you can ask them how important compensation is to them (even if you've discussed it already), with the goal of figuring out if there are other areas where adjustments that matter to them could be made instead. If you don't have the funds to offer a higher salary, are there benefits that could be afforded them, or a higher percentage of equity with an adjusted vesting schedule?

---

684. https://www.newyorker.com/science/maria-konnikova/lean-out-the-dangers-for-women-who-negotiate
685. https://sloanreview.mit.edu/article/getting-the-short-end-of-the-stick-racial-bias-in-salary-negotiations/

35.5.3 THE CANDIDATE'S PERSPECTIVE ON NEGOTIATIONS

🎓 CANDIDATE Before accepting any job offer, you'll want to negotiate firmly and fairly.[686] You're planning to devote a lot of your time and sanity to any full-time role; help yourself make sure that this is what you want.[687,688]

It's perfectly natural to be anxious[690] about negotiations, whether you're going through this process for the first time or the tenth. There is a lot at stake, and it can be uncomfortable and stressful to ask for things you need or want. Many people think[691] negotiating could get the job offer revoked, so they'll accept their offer with little or no discussion. But remember that negotiations are the first experience you'll have of working with your new team. If you're nervous, it can help to remind yourself why it's important to have these conversations:

- Negotiations ask you to focus on what you actually want. What is important to you—personal growth, career growth, impact, recognition, cash, ownership, teamwork? Not being clear with yourself on what your priorities really are is a recipe for dissatisfaction later.
- If you aren't satisfied with the terms of your offer, accepting it without discussion can be tough not just for you but for your new company and colleagues as well. No one wants to take on a hire who's going to walk away in just a few months when something better comes along. For everyone's sake, take your time now to consider what you want—and then ask for it.[692]
- The negotiation process itself can teach you a lot about a company and your future manager. Talking about a tough subject like an offer is a great way to see how you'll work with someone down the road.

---

686. http://cefne.com/en/harvard-method-negotiation
687. https://hbr.org/2016/12/think-strategically-about-your-career-development
688. This section has been adapted from the Holloway Guide to Equity Compensation.[689]
689. http://www.holloway.com/g/equity-compensation
690. https://www.pon.harvard.edu/daily/negotiation-skills-daily/the-impact-of-anxiety-and-emotions-on-negotiations-how-to-avoid-misjudgment-in-negotiation-scenarios/
691. https://www.forbes.com/sites/tanyatarr/2017/12/31/here-are-five-negotiation-myths-we-can-leave-behind-in-2017/#250ff99b15f9engaging
692. https://www.earnest.com/decision-making/articles/negotiating-job-offers-science-asking-want

A Guide like this can't give you personalized advice on what a reasonable offer is, as that depends greatly on your skills and experience, the marketplace of candidates, what other offers you have, what the company can pay, what other candidates the company has found, and the company's needs. Negotiations are full of pitfalls and unconscious bias, and they work differently company to company. All candidates should take the time to understand their worth and the specific value they can add to a company, so that they are fully prepared to negotiate for a better offer if need be.

- **Do you have the right expectations?** Have a good understanding of what you want and need (in cash and/or equity, as well as benefits), based on your personal situation and on market rates. You can use tools like Glassdoor[693] to research typical compensation for your role or company (though of course, companies can have very different compensation philosophies).
- Having offers from other companies can also help you understand market rates and provide negotiation leverage, if needed. Candidates with competing offers[694] almost always have more leverage and get better offers. If you don't have any other offers, Levels.fyi[695] is a great tool for understanding industry standards. You can also get this information from mentors and peers from your industry.
- **What's the company policy?** Find out the company's policy on compensation and negotiations, by asking them directly and double-checking by doing research. First, decide whether you agree with those policies. Are they fair? Are they thoughtful? Do they change your perception of the company? If they do negotiate, the usual advice on negotiations applies. If they don't, at least you'll have certainty that you're not being taken advantage of.
- **Is this a startup?** Salaries at startups are often a bit below (or a lot below) what you'd get at an established company, since early on, cash is at a premium. For very early-stage startups, risk is higher, offers can be highly variable, and variation among companies will be greater, particularly when it comes to equity.

---

693. https://www.glassdoor.com/Salaries/index.htm
694. https://www.shrm.org/resourcesandtools/hr-topics/employee-relations/pages/using-a-job-offer-as-leverage-is-no-longer-a-big-no-no.aspx
695. https://www.levels.fyi

- The dominant factors determining equity[696] are what funding stage[697] a company is at and the role you'll play at the company. If no funding has been raised, a higher percentage of equity to cash may be required. Once significant funding of an A round is in place, most people will take typical or moderately discounted salaries. Startups with seed funding lie somewhere in between.
- Many companies will give some leeway during negotiations, letting you indicate whether you prefer higher salary[698] or higher equity.[699]
- **Am I being treated fairly?** Hopefully, the company is working hard to ensure that all candidates are given equal treatment[700] in the hiring process, but inequalities may persist.[701] Workplace disparities[702] in pay and opportunity span race and gender, with research focusing on inequality in the U.S. workplace,[703] the technology industry,[704] and executive leadership[705] and its well-documented lack of diversity.[706] In negotiation itself, gender bias[707] is an issue, where women are often made to feel that they shouldn't ask for what they deserve. According to research at MIT Sloan,[708] there are a number of discriminatory practices in negotiations that have contributed to the Black-white pay gap. If you believe you are being unfairly discriminated against in an offer negotiation, *Time* offers a number of options[709] for recourse.

---

696. https://www.holloway.com/g/equity-compensation/sections/typical-employee-equity-levels
697. https://www.holloway.com/g/equity-compensation/sections/stages-of-a-startup
698. https://hired.com/blog/candidates/salary-vs-equity-how-decide-whats-right/
699. https://www.investopedia.com/articles/personal-finance/041515/equity-vs-salary-what-you-need-know.asp
700. https://rework.withgoogle.com/guides/pay-equity/steps/introduction/
701. https://iwpr.org/publications/gender-wage-gap-2017-race-ethnicity/
702. https://digitalcommons.ilr.cornell.edu/cgi/viewcontent.cgi?article=2208&context=articles
703. http://www.pewresearch.org/fact-tank/2016/07/01/racial-gender-wage-gaps-persist-in-u-s-despite-some-progress/
704. https://www.eeoc.gov/eeoc/statistics/reports/hightech/
705. https://aflcio.org/paywatch/company-pay-ratios
706. http://fortune.com/2017/06/09/white-men-senior-executives-fortune-500-companies-diversity-data/
707. https://www.newyorker.com/science/maria-konnikova/lean-out-the-dangers-for-women-who-negotiate
708. https://sloanreview.mit.edu/article/getting-the-short-end-of-the-stick-racial-bias-in-salary-negotiations/
709. https://time.com/5561226/paid-less-man-negotiation/

Harvard Business Review has a useful set of negotiation tips[710] for candidates.

> Our Guide to Equity Compensation[711] has additional coverage of negotiation for companies and candidates.

35.6 Closing

You don't have to feel powerless after you've made an offer as you're waiting for a response. In addition to maintaining contact with the candidate, there are several things the company can do while the candidate is deciding.

35.6.1 MAKING THE TEAM AVAILABLE

Once a candidate is close to the finish line, you need to pull in all the resources you can. You should by now have an understanding of what might be holding the candidate back from making a decision. What questions remain unanswered for them? What doubts do they have? Facilitate discussions with your team, if a candidate:

- **Has questions about the role.** Have them talk to peers in similar roles.
- **Is curious about culture.** While we've discussed the dangers of "culture fit" from the company perspective, it's more than likely that a candidate will want to feel like they will be empowered and accepted at a company. If they're uncertain or just curious about the culture at a company, can they spend more time with the team? Maybe join a team lunch, dinner, or even a meeting?
- **Is worried about other practical considerations.** If they have concerns around the commute, moving, finding daycare, et cetera, offer to help think things through. Connect them with other teammates who have been through a similar experience. For instance, if they are concerned about a move, connect them with a teammate who recently made that move; if they're worried about finding and affording daycare or schools in a new location or working childcare into the demands of

---

710. https://hbr.org/2014/04/15-rules-for-negotiating-a-job-offer
711. https://www.holloway.com/g/equity-compensation/

the position, connect with someone who can offer help—note that at a larger company, this person might be in human resources.

- **Is unsure about the company's prospects.** Have them talk to someone on the business side, or, for startups, the founder or one of the investors. This has the simultaneous effect of showing them that you value them enough to pull in busy, senior people.
- **Is worried about compensation.** Help them work through the math. This can be especially useful for candidates who are relocating to an area with different costs of living. They might be worried about expenses, but once they break down the numbers, they might realize that things are not as scary as they seem. Alternatively, your candidate might be teaching you something about the practicality of your offer. Listen closely to their concerns, and you might revisit the offer. If their concern is around equity, help explain the equity part of their offer to them, and send them a link to our free Guide to Equity Compensation.[712]

Of course, this all takes a tremendous amount of effort from you and your team, and it should. No matter what you do, you will sometimes lose candidates and it might feel like that time was wasted. But if a candidate joins the team without getting all their questions answered, they can end up leaving quickly, which is an even bigger risk than having people drop out of the process later. If a candidate is genuinely qualified and seriously excited about your company but needs some assurances or guidance, you should pull out all the stops.

35.6.2 PREPARING FOR COMPETING OFFERS AND COUNTEROFFERS

A candidate may be fielding offers from other companies.

⚠ **DANGER** One way some companies make their offer appear more attractive is undermining a candidate's competing offers (or current job). Bad-mouthing other opportunities might work with some candidates, but usually comes across as petty, or worse. It's better to ask a candidate questions that get them thinking than to directly undermine a competitor. When possible, repeat back to them things they had mentioned in the past. For instance, if you're a startup going up against a larger company, you can ask them something like: "When we talked earlier in the process,

---

712. http://holloway.com/g/equity-compensation

you had mentioned that you care most about learning opportunities and personal impact. How does that factor into your current decision-making?" In addition to sounding a lot more authentic and a lot less rude than direct attempts to influence their thinking, you may discover pieces of their decision-making that you didn't know about before.

> **STORY** "Once, I was trying to hire a new grad for a startup, but the candidate was leaning toward joining Microsoft because the offer had higher cash compensation. Upon digging into the candidate's situation, it became clear that his heart was really with the startup. But, he was about to graduate, wanted to fly his father from Europe to attend his graduation, and didn't have the cash to afford it. We offered to cover the cost of his father's trip, and the candidate signed." —Zack Isaacson, Partner, Sweat Equity Ventures

STARTUP Trying to compete with big, established companies as a startup is challenging for a number of reasons, especially when it comes to compensation packages. TripleByte offers a few suggestions[713] for unique aspects that startups can offer, which may come in handy if you're trying to close with a candidate who is interviewing or currently works at Google-scale companies.

Once your offer has been made, even after the candidate has verbally accepted it, you can expect further competition from their existing employer or other companies, who will scramble, sometimes desperately, to counteroffer—that is, to give them an even better offer now that they know the candidate has options.

IMPORTANT To guard against a counteroffer from their existing employer, it's important that you strengthen your candidate's resolve *before* they accept your offer by preparing them for the counteroffer. Explain that most employees who stay at a company because of a counteroffer end up leaving[714] in a few months anyway; the underlying issues rarely disappear. Do they really want to be at a company that only gives them what they want when they're on the brink of leaving?

---

713. https://triplebyte.com/blog/convincing-engineers-to-join-your-team
714. https://www.phaidoninternational.com/careeradvice/why-you-should-never-accept-a-counter-offer-715030102955935

Similar advice applies for counteroffers from other prospective employers. Remind them why they chose your company, and explain that if a company only reveals a really good offer after they've lost a candidate, that probably speaks to their overall culture and attitude and how much they value the candidate.

35.6.3 OFFER ACCEPTANCE

CANDIDATE Once you decide to accept an offer, be sure to respond quickly and in writing. The Balance Careers provides detail[715] on what to include and a few sample templates.

Having a candidate accept an offer should be a cause for celebration, both for you and for the candidate. For you and your team, it's a culmination of countless hours expended on finding, evaluating, and convincing a candidate to join you. It's worth taking a moment to celebrate and reflect. Many managers send team-wide celebratory emails announcing an offer acceptance.

CAUTION However, it's a common mistake to assume that once a candidate has accepted an offer verbally or by signing a document, your work is done. In reality, the period *after* accepting can be critical. A lot of candidates can experience acceptance remorse.

Acceptance remorse is a sense of regret that candidates may experience after agreeing to join a company. For some candidates who experience acceptance remorse, it may not set in until they actually start working.[716] For others, it can start as soon as they've said yes.[717]

Not all candidates will experience acceptance remorse, of course, and you have some control over whether it happens. Unnecessarily rushing a candidate into responding to an offer is a good way to have them feel some amount of regret or trepidation, as is refusing to be transparent about things like compensation. From this point on, the best way you can help the candidate avoid acceptance remorse is by expressing your excitement, answering questions, and keeping up momentum—but in a chill way.

---

715. https://www.thebalancecareers.com/job-offer-acceptance-letter-2062550
716. https://www.csmonitor.com/2007/0806/p13s02-wmgn.html
717. https://workology.com/what-is-candidate-acceptance-remorse/

First, find a way to celebrate their acceptance. Your immediate reaction to them accepting your offer should be really positive. Some companies encourage a candidate who has verbally accepted an offer to come in and sign the offer letter in person, in the presence of (the obviously ecstatic) team. You can have teammates reach out to them and express their excitement about them joining. It can also be fun to invite them to a team lunch, dinner, or activity.

Maintain regular contact until they start their new job. Don't drop off the face of the planet between the offer acceptance and start date.

Make sure to put the new employee in touch with someone at HR (or whomever handles paperwork and logistical questions). Especially if there is a relocation involved, help your new employee with these challenges by introducing them to the people they need to talk to, without them having to ask.

Give them updates about the team. Tell them about the exciting upcoming challenges and projects your team is facing, why you believe that they are going to be able to help the team meet those challenges, and the work they will be ramping up on when they start. Make it as real and visceral as possible.

Keep some balance, of course, since they want a chance to unwind in between jobs, and you don't want to overwhelm them or stress them out. But some people may be so excited that they ask you for advice on how to prepare. Do you have books you and the team all love that you can recommend, or perhaps internal manuals to help them ramp up? Both fun and practical options can work here. Having something in mind to offer them can help the new employee feel engaged with the company even before their first official day, while still getting to relax before it all begins.

APPENDICES

36 Appendix A: Decision-Making

Before going into the specifics of why people take certain jobs and how to build a value proposition for your company, it's useful to have a basic understanding of a few models of decision-making.

The first idea to understand is that people are not always strictly rational. As much as this affects you when making hiring decisions,[718] it also affects job-seekers. You might unfairly reject a candidate who doesn't "feel right," but it's a legitimate part of the recruiting process to try to appeal to both the hearts *and* minds of candidates.

If you'd like a more formal basis for the psychology of decision-making, the book *Thinking Fast and Slow*[719] by Nobel Prize-winning psychologist Daniel Kahneman breaks our thinking processes down into two "systems." System 1 operates fast and automatically using heuristics and emotions, but is prone to mistakes and biases. System 2, on the other hand, is slower—it is more deliberate, rational, and requires conscious effort. But System 2 is also prone to behaving irrationally. For instance, System 2 is really good at crafting "after-the-fact" stories to justify System 1's conclusions (this is known as confabulating,[720] and there have been interesting scientific experiments[721] to demonstrate its startling power).

There are other similar models that psychologists have written about—for instance, Jonathan Haidt uses the analogy of the conscious mind as a rider on top of an elephant, which represents the unconscious mind in the book *The Happiness Hypothesis*.[722] But for the purposes of this Guide and of understanding decision-making, we recommend, at the very

---

718. https://docs.google.com/document/d/1oa9ANOdrkKd834YEs3XNxh_D_WhtDZaH2UQtoFHJSGc/edit?ts=5dbfc99e&pli=1#bookmark=id.13qzunr
719. https://www.amazon.com/Thinking-Fast-Slow-Daniel-Kahneman/dp/0374533555
720. https://en.wikipedia.org/wiki/Confabulation
721. http://www.powerofstories.com/our-brains-constantly-confabulate-stories-which-builds-a-meaningful-narrative-for-our-life
722. https://www.amazon.com/Happiness-Hypothesis-Finding-Modern-Ancient/dp/0465028020

least, reading a summary of *Thinking Fast and Slow*[723] to familiarize yourself with the two-system model and understand the different biases that we are all prone to.

Next, it's important to be aware that there are certain patterns of behavior that can influence us in irrational ways. A great read on this topic is the book *Influence*,[724] by Robert Cialdini, in which he discusses six different principles of persuasion: reciprocity, scarcity, authority, consistency, liking, and consensus (summarized here[725]). Cialdini gives examples of how each of these principles can be "weaponized" to influence others' decision-making. When hiring, you should definitely *not* use these principles as weapons to manipulate— because it's unethical, and furthermore, even if you do succeed at tricking someone into joining a company that's not a good fit for them, the result will be detrimental to both parties. But, you can use these principles to reinforce your value proposition to candidates (and perhaps more importantly, avoid making mistakes that cause these principles to work against you).

Joining a company is a high-stakes decision, both materially and emotionally. So for most people, it will involve gut-level Systems 1 instinctual thinking as well as deliberate (sometimes agonizing) Systems 2 considerations. This means that not only are people's needs complex, specific, and situational, it's also not easy to fully understand them (even for the candidate). But when recruiting, you still need to try, even if that sometimes means helping candidates develop clarity about what they really want while also educating them about your opportunities and what your company can offer. It will be difficult, but your recruiting process should speak to both the rational and the irrational reasons people change jobs or join companies. Sometimes, when you're talking to candidates, you'll feel their System 1 and System 2 tugging at each other (their rational mind wants to join one company, but their gut or heart is leaning elsewhere). And you should be aware that, even with the best intentions, candidates won't always communicate the truth[726] about what they want.

---

723. https://erikreads.files.wordpress.com/2014/04/thinking-fast-and-slow-book-summary.pdf
724. https://www.amazon.com/Influence-Psychology-Persuasion-Business-Essentials-ebook/dp/B002BD2UUC
725. https://www.influenceatwork.com/principles-of-persuasion/
726. https://docs.google.com/document/d/10a9ANOdrkKd834YEs3XNxh_D_WhtDZaH2UQtoFHJSGc/edit?ts=5dbfc99e&pli=1#bookmark=id.3jtnz0s

As a final, often-overlooked note on how people make big decisions: they rarely make them in a vacuum. Often, the decisions they make will be shaped by those around them. Younger candidates may face pressure or expectations from their parents (for instance, to join a large, well-known company). Candidates with families will (we hope!) consult with their partner, especially if a new job will affect their work-life balance or income or require a move. And any candidate may be influenced by their friends or mentors, which can be a particularly potent force if those friends or mentors work at the company they're considering joining.

37 Appendix B: Communicating Your Brand

> This section is available in the digital edition at Holloway.com.

38 Appendix C: D&I Reading List

> This section is available in the digital edition at Holloway.com.

39 Appendix D: Tools and Products

> This section is available in the digital edition at Holloway.com.

ABOUT THE CONTRIBUTORS

Osman (Ozzie) Osman is co-founder and head of engineering at Monarch Money. He has built products and engineering teams at companies including Quora and Google. Ozzie has also started two companies that have been acquired, and advised dozens of other startups. He is the lead author of the Holloway Guide to Technical Recruiting and Hiring.

Aditya Agarwal is a Partner-in-Residence at South Park Commons—a collective of technologists, tinkerers, and entrepreneurs who have come together to freely learn, explore new ideas, and help each other launch their next venture. Prior to SPC, Aditya was the CTO and VP of Engineering at Dropbox; he came to Dropbox via the acquisition of Cove, a company that he co-founded. Prior to Cove, Aditya was one of Facebook's first engineers. He is also an active investor and advisor to Silicon Valley startups.

Alex Allain is a Director of Engineering at Dropbox, author of Jumping into C++, and the creator of cprogramming.com, a resource on C and C++ established in 1996 and used by millions to learn to program.

Jose Guardado is the founder of Alpha Talent. In previous roles, he worked as a Talent Partner at Y Combinator and Andreessen Horowitz. Before that, he led recruiting at multiple Silicon Valley startups.

Jennifer Kim is a startup advisor, formerly Head of People at Lever, and founder of Inclusion At Work, a diversity and inclusion resource.

Aline Lerner is the co-founder and CEO of interviewing.io, an anonymous technical interviewing platform where companies like Facebook, Uber, and Dropbox have hired great software engineers. Before that, she wrote code, ran hiring at Udacity, and wrote a lot about hiring on the internet. Her work on the subject has appeared in dozens of publications, including Forbes, the Wall Street Journal, Business Insider, and Fast Company.

Joshua Levy is co-founder of Holloway, a digital publishing startup. He has authored and edited long-form, online works in business and engineering, including the Holloway Guide to Equity Compensation, that have reached over a million readers. Josh has built software and led technical teams in Silicon Valley for 15 years at BloomReach, Cuil, Viv Labs (sold to Samsung), and SRI (on the technology that led to Siri). His interests include typography and design, knowledge and collaboration systems, AI, web search, cloud infrastructure, and open source.

Viraj Mody is an engineering leader, currently scaling the team at Convoy. Prior to Convoy, Viraj was an engineering leader at Dropbox for 5+ years, initially in San Fransisco and later in Seattle, where he helped establish Dropbox's largest engineering outpost. Viraj joined Dropbox by way of Audiogalaxy, his music streaming startup. Viraj is an alum of the University of Texas at Austin.

Kevin Morrill has hired over 70 engineers and conducted over 1,000 interviews. He's hired at startups like Mattermark, Referly and HelloSign as well as big companies like Microsoft. He consulted with companies like Le Tote, NexTravel, Asseta and more for technical hiring.

Jason Wong is a leadership coach and fractional VP of Engineering with almost two decades of experience in building and scaling web applications across a range of industries from academia to online media and e-commerce. Formerly a Senior Director at Etsy, he currently works with leaders and companies to improve their engineering management practices and establish inclusive cultures.

Scott Woody has been obsessed with recruiting since early 2011, when he started a company building out Applicant Tracking Systems. He sold that company to Dropbox in 2013 and eventually moved into managing the Subscription Growth team at Dropbox. He grew his team from three to 50 over the course of four years, interviewing hundreds of candidates, debriefing hundreds more, and interfacing with all aspects of the Dropbox recruiting process.

About Holloway

Holloway publishes nonfiction reference works that help readers level up their careers, on topics ranging from tools and technology to teamwork and entrepreneurship. Holloway's book-length resources are published on a digital web platform where readers can easily discover what they need, and authors and editors make ongoing improvements.

Holloway seeks exceptional authors who can help people navigate the challenges of modern work. If you're a writer with a manuscript or idea, please get in touch at *hello@holloway.com*.

Made in the USA
Las Vegas, NV
17 May 2022